THE NEW STRATEGIC MANAGEMENT

Organization, Competition, and Competence

THE NEW STRATEGIC MANAGEMENT

Organization, Competition, and Competence

RON SANCHEZ

IMD—International Institute for Management Development
Lausanne, Switzerland

AIMÉ HEENE

University of Ghent
Ghent, Belgium

Acquisitions Editor *Susan Elbe*
Editorial Assistant *Jessica Bartelt*
Marketing Manager *Charity Robey*
Managing Editor *Lari Bishop*
Associate Production Manager *Kelly Tavares*
Production Editor *Sarah Wolfman-Robichaud*
Illustration Editor *Benjamin Reece*
Cover Design *Jennifer Fisher*

This book was set in Times by Leyh Publishing LLC and printed by R.R. Donnelly & Sons. The cover was printed by Lehigh Press.

This book is printed on acid-free paper.∞

ISBN: 0-471-89953-4

Printed in the United States of America

10 9 8 7 6 5 4 3 2 1

This volume is dedicated to everyone interested in meeting the challenge of effectively leading organizations in today's increasingly complex, challenging, and competitive environments.

BRIEF CONTENTS

PART VI *GLOBAL STRATEGY*

PART VII *STRATEGIC LEADERSHIP AND STEWARDSHIP*

CASES

TABLE OF CONTENTS

PREFACE

WHY ANOTHER TEXTBOOK ON STRATEGIC MANAGEMENT?

The field of strategic management is relatively young—perhaps thirty or so years old—but during its relatively brief history, it has become an essential element of management practice and education around the world. Given the central importance of the strategic perspective in managing contemporary organizational and competitive issues, it is no surprise that the field of strategic management has attracted a host of textbooks. Further, given the inherently multidisciplinary nature of the organizational and competitive issues addressed from the strategic perspective, it is no surprise that the many available textbooks on strategic management offer a wide diversity of perspectives on strategic issues. Today, a number of strategic management textbooks individually offer what are essentially marketing, organizational behavioral, financial, or economic perspectives on strategic issues facing organizations.

What has been lacking, however, is a strategic management textbook that overtly tries to integrate the many relevant perspectives into a coherent framework for understanding strategic issues in all their multidimensional complexity—without allowing a single disciplinary perspective to dominate the representation and analysis of strategic issues. What this textbook aspires to offer is an integrative, multidisciplinary, and coherent framework for defining and addressing strategic management issues.

Another notable aspect of current strategic management textbooks is their considerable length. Recent editions of several strategic management textbooks exceed one thousand pages in length. In effect, many strategic management textbooks now try to address almost every conceivable aspect of managing an organization. In their efforts to be comprehensive in addressing management issues, however, such textbooks inevitably raise the question, "What is strategic about strategic management?" If strategic management is concerned with all aspects of managing, then there is no real distinction made by the term strategic and the boundaries between what is strategic—and therefore should occupy the attention of strategic managers—and what is not strategic becomes hopelessly blurred.

This textbook goes against the current trend towards ever widening the scope of management issues addressed under the heading of strategic management. What this textbook offers instead is the view that only certain concerns are the essential responsibility of top managers and thus must be attended to by top managers in their role as strategic managers. That limited set of strategic concerns therefore should occupy strategic managers' attention, and the many other issues facing organizations that lie outside this set of strategic concerns should be considered operational issues to be delegated to operational managers in an organization. By defining the essential concerns of strategic managers, this textbook defines the boundaries that separate strategic from operational concerns in organizations.

This focus on the essential aspects of strategic management also brings an important benefit to teachers of strategic management. By reducing considerably the scope of what are regarded as strategic issues in this textbook, teachers should find time in a full strategy course to amplify and expand on those topics that they want to emphasize in their teaching or that their students find especially intriguing.

A related aspect of this textbook is the inclusion of several mini-cases to be used along with a limited number of full-length cases. Full-length cases have the advantage of offering students the opportunity to analyze a detailed description of a situation and, through their analysis, to try to discern the essential strategic issues in a situation and to identify the strategic options available to managers. In the process of analyzing cases, however, much time is often spent simply reading lengthy cases that often—quite intentionally—include much information that is extraneous to the strategic issues broached in the case. The valuable time spent in reading long cases—especially for the increasing number of non-native English speakers now studying in management programs around the world—often detracts from the pedagogical purpose of a case, which is to improve the ability of students to grasp and apply key strategic management concepts.

The mini-cases in this textbook reduce an important type of business situation down to its essential features, and challenge students to consider how the strategic management concepts introduced in the textbook can be applied to identify and analyze the strategic issues in the business situation described in each mini-case. This focus is sharpened by posing a few key questions at the end of each mini-case. In effect, the mini-cases help students to use their valuable time in deepening their understanding of key strategic management concepts, rather than spending scarce study time just to read through a lengthy case. This feature of the textbook should be especially relevant to students in executive MBA programs, whose study time is usually under pressure and who are already aware that strategic issues are invariably embedded in complex organizational and competitive situations.

WHAT IS THE "COMPETENCE PERSPECTIVE" USED IN THIS TEXTBOOK?

The competence perspective used in this framework is the result of a decade of theory development in the 1990s by an international network of strategic management researchers and practitioners. The stimulus for this development effort is the belief that to be relevant to contemporary organizations and competitive environments, strategic management theory and practice must become more *dynamic, systemic, cognitive,* and *holistic.* These desired improvements in strategy theory are often referred to as the "four cornerstones" of the competence approach to strategic management.

The *dynamic* cornerstone in the competence approach to strategic management holds that strategy theory and practice must recognize the inherently dynamic nature of market preferences and the technologies available to serve market preferences. Market preferences today are evolving rapidly around the globe, sometimes at an apparently increasing rate. The technologies available to organizations as means for serving market preferences are also changing, making possible new kinds of products, processes, and forms of organizational coordination. In contrast to some traditional strategy theories premised on economic notions of competitive equilibria, the competence approach presumes that the "natural" state of markets and technologies is disequilibrium. Thus, the competence approach takes seriously the challenge of helping strategic managers understand how to create competitive advantages under conditions of competitive disequilibrium and continual organizational change.

The *systemic* cornerstone of competence theory holds that organizations are goal-directed human systems, and as such have certain system properties, system requirements, and systemic ways of behaving that strategic managers must understand and manage. In their organizations, strategic managers have the essential role of *system designers*, and their fundamental responsibility is therefore the design and implementation of a successful strategic logic for their organization as an open system for value creation and distribution. Strategic managers must learn to manage the continuous flows of critical resources into and out of their organizations, as well as assuring their effective use within an organization. Strategic managers must also understand how to identify and access the many firm-addressable resources that increasingly lie outside the boundaries of their organization, but that may be available to use in the organization's value-creation processes.

The *cognitive* cornerstone of the competence approach holds that in today's complex and dynamic competitive world, the task of defining and implementing a viable strategic logic is an intellectual challenge of the first order. No individual manager, nor even a team of top managers, can hope to solve all essential aspects of the "dynamic situational puzzle" that an organization faces. Strategic managers must learn how to involve and fully use the collective intelligence of all participants in their organization's value creation processes in order to define and implement a successful strategic logic for sustainable value creation. Moreover, in fulfilling their responsibilities to lead their organization in defining its strategic logic, strategic managers must rise to the unique intellectual challenge of strategic management—i.e., learning to manage their own cognitive processes. Strategic managers must be the most active learners in learning organizations. They must be open to change and provide intellectual leadership in processes for identifying changing market opportunities and designing effective strategic responses.

The *holistic* cornerstone in the competence approach holds that competition occurs not just in markets for products, but also in markets for resources as organizations vie to attract and retain the best possible inputs to their value creation processes. Thus, strategic management must be concerned not just with creating value through success in product markets, but also with distributing value to all providers of the resources that enable an organization to sustain successful value creation processes. As more and more product-market competition becomes knowledge-based and as knowledge workers become recognized as the key strategic assets of an organization, the expectations of the people whose intelligence and efforts make organizations successful are also changing. Employees, suppliers, and other providers of critical resources today are evaluating organizations as a means for achieving their own personal goals, and strategic managers must help their organizations attract the best resource providers by continuously offering the best prospects for goal fulfillment by all stakeholders.

AN INVITATION

We hope that the textbook we have put together here will offer an appealing, innovative, practical, and effective approach to teaching, studying, and practicing strategic management in a contemporary context. This first edition of this textbook is intended to be only the beginning of a process which scholars, practitioners, and students of strategic managers around the world are invited to participate in improving. We welcome communication from everyone interested in contributing to the further development and improvement of the competence approach to strategic management and of this textbook.

Ron Sanchez
IMD—International Institute for Management Development
Lausanne, Switzerland

Aimé Heene
University of Ghent
Ghent, Belgium

ABOUT THE AUTHORS

RON SANCHEZ

Ron Sanchez is Professor of Strategy and Technology Management at IMD—International Institute for Management Development, Lausanne, Switzerland. He was previously on the faculties of University of Illinois (Champaign-Urbana), University of Western Australia, and Copenhagen Business School, where he will again be Visiting Professor of Management in 2003–2004. He has also taught in many countries of the world, including Argentina, China, India, Finland, France, Germany, Morocco, Sweden, and the United Kingdom. Professor Sanchez has degrees from MIT (Massachusetts Institute of Technology) in psychology, comparative literature, architecture, and engineering, as well as a Ph.D. in Technology Strategy. He also received an MBA (with Honors) from Saint Mary's College of California. Before becoming a management professor, he worked as a design engineer, as a technical and market development representative for a major trade association, and as founder and manager of a firm specializing in organizing joint product development projects between American and Japanese companies.

Professor Sanchez has published widely on the competence-based approach to strategic management, including several books and numerous journal articles. His related research and writing interests include strategic flexibility, modular product and process architectures, knowledge management, and options theory.

AIMÉ HEENE

Prof. dr. Aimé Heene holds a Ph.D. in educational sciences and an MBA from Ghent University (Belgium). He is an associate professor at Ghent University and at Antwerp University Management School. At Ghent University he is the head of the Department of Management and Organization. Prof. Heene teaches strategic management for private and for public organizations and currently focuses his research on competence-based management in social profit organizations. He has been the vice-president of the Dutch-Flemish Academy for Management, a founding member and secretary of the Flemish Strategy Society, and a member of the advisory board of the European Foundation for Business Qualification.

Prof. Heene has published three books in the Dutch language on strategic management and has served as a co-editor of several English-language volumes on competence-based strategy theory. Prof. Heene is a member of the editorial board of several journals. Since 1992, he has co-chaired six international conferences and workshops on competence-based strategic management.

PART I

ORGANIZATION AND STRATEGIC MANAGEMENT

CHAPTER 1

ORGANIZATIONS, STRATEGIC MANAGEMENT, AND ORGANIZATIONAL COMPETENCE

INTRODUCTION

This book presents a competence-based framework for the strategic management of organizations. In this chapter, we explain some of the fundamental concepts on which the competence approach to strategic management is based.

First we consider what we mean by *organizations,* and we describe some basic properties of organizations that greatly influence the objectives and methods of strategic management. We then consider what it means to *manage* an organization and what the objectives of *strategic management* processes are within an organization. Finally, we discuss what *organizational competence* means, and we consider the essential strategic management processes for *building, maintaining, and leveraging* competence.

1.1 ORGANIZATIONS AS SYSTEMS FOR VALUE CREATION AND DISTRIBUTION

The Concept of Organization

Organizations are collections of people who interact with each other in specific, usually repeated ways over some period of time. To attract people to its activities and thereby to assure its continued existence, an organization must bring some form of benefit—whether psychological, social, cultural, professional, or economic—to the people who participate in its activities. In this book, we refer to the creation of benefits for participants in organized activities as the process of **value creation.** We also use the term **value distribution** to refer to the ways that the value an organized activity creates is allocated among the participants in the activity.

To create and receive value through participation in an organization, each participant depends to some extent on the activities of one or more other participants in the organization's processes for creating and distributing value. Thus, an **organization** is *a system of interdependent actors who collectively share some goals for creating and realizing value through their interactions.* (See Highlight Box 1.1 for further discussion of what we mean by a *system.*)

In the following chapters, we consider how organizations as systems differ in the kinds of value they create for their participants, in the ways that people interact in processes for creating value in a given organization, and in the ways that value may be distributed to each participant in an organization's activities. Because the competence-based framework for strategic management presented in this book focuses on the processes of value creation and value distribution that all viable organizations must sustain, the concepts discussed in the following chapters can be applied in strategically managing all organizations. Thus, the competence-based framework that we present here is relevant not just in the strategic management of for-profit firms, but also in the strategic management of not-for-profit organizations, public agencies, and social and cultural organizations.

HIGHLIGHT BOX 1.1

What is a *system?*

A *system* is a collection of *interacting elements,* which means that the "state" or condition of one system element affects and may be affected by the state or condition of one or more other system elements. In organizations as systems, system elements may include individuals, groups, or other organizations. The interactions between organizational system elements include flows of resources that each person or group within the organization provides or receives. Organizational system elements are *interdependent* when they depend on resource flows from other system elements to perform their individual activities within the organization as a system.

In the diagram, for example, "M" may be a manager who depends on flows of several kinds of resources to perform her or his activities as manager. M may depend on funds provided by the finance department (composed of people or groups A, B, and C), on market information provided by sales manager X (who receives information from organizations in distribution channel Y), and on policies and objectives agreed with senior managers N. In return, M may be expected to provide flows of revenues to the finance department, newly developed products to the sales staff and distribution channel, and various performance results to senior management.

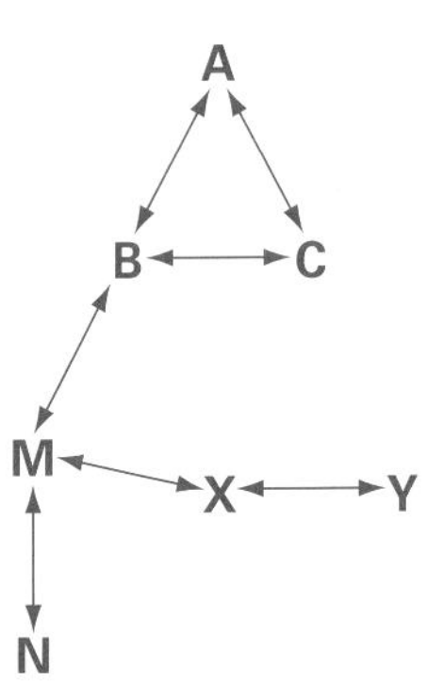

A **system** is a collection of interacting, interdependent elements.

1.2 MANAGEMENT AS A PROCESS OF COORDINATING

The Concept of Management

Management is the term we use to denote the processes through which an organization tries to maintain and improve its ability to create and distribute value by coordinating the interactions of participants in the activities of the organization as a system. The activities that managers try to coordinate may include both the internal interactions among the organization's own participants and the external interactions of an organization's participants with other people and organizations.

Management processes involved in coordinating value creation and distribution include such activities as the following:

- *Gathering and interpreting data* about the organization's environment and about its own internal condition
- *Making decisions* to take specific actions to maintain current approaches to creating value
- *Implementing actions* through directives, policies, resource allocations, and other means
- Distributing rewards and sanctions to participants in the actions undertaken by the organization

In later chapters, we examine these essential management coordination activities in greater detail.[1]

[1] Gathering and interpreting data are discussed in Chapters 4, 7, 9, and 10. Decision making and implementing actions through directives, policies, resource allocations, and other means is discussed in Chapters 7 and 10. Distribution of rewards and sanctions is considered in Chapter 7.

1.3 STRATEGIC MANAGEMENT: DEFINING AND ACHIEVING ORGANIZATIONAL GOALS FOR VALUE CREATION AND DISTRIBUTION FOR ALL STAKEHOLDERS

The Concept of Strategic Management

The term **strategic management** refers to management processes that are concerned with two major tasks:

1. *Defining* the organization's goals for value creation and distribution
2. *Designing* the way the organization will be composed, structured, and coordinated in pursuing its goals for value creation and distribution

An organization is composed of resources. As we will discuss in greater detail later, the term **resources** refers to any tangible or intangible assets and any human skills and capabilities that are useful and available to an organization in pursuing its goals for value creation and distribution.

To be successful in defining an organization's *goals* for value creation and distribution, strategic managers must be able to articulate goals for the organization that, if achieved, will create and distribute value to *all providers of the essential resources* needed to sustain the activities of the organization. We use the term **stakeholders** to refer to individuals or other organizations that provide essential resources to an organization and that therefore have an interest or "stake" in receiving some form of value from the organization in return for the resources they provide.

Organizations depend not just on their own resources to carry out their activities, but also on at least some resources that are owned or controlled by other people or organizations. For example, an organization may have its own employees, offices, factories, and equipment, but each of these elements of the organization also relies on a variety of inputs from suppliers (materials, equipment, expert advice), distributors (maintaining inventories, providing market information), customers (purchases, feedback on products), governments (permission to operate, provision of infrastructure), financial institutions (loans), shareholders (investment funds), and other essential resource providers. Thus, to maintain flows of all the resources needed by an organization to support its value creation and distribution activities, strategic managers must manage the organization as an *open system* of resource flows from and to a number of stakeholders. Strategic managers of an organization must therefore be able to define goals that include the creation and distribution of value not just for its own members, but for all people and organizations that provide essential resources to the organization's activities.

The second task of strategic management involves gathering and deploying the resources the organization will need to be effective in achieving its goals. To do so requires that strategic managers must answer the following questions:

- What resources will the organization use to create value?
- How will value-creation tasks be allocated among individuals and groups?
- Which activities internal and external to the organization will be monitored, and how?
- How will information be gathered and distributed?
- How will decisions be made?
- How will the performance of individuals and groups in creating value be determined, and how will they be rewarded in distributing value?[2]

[2] The different kinds of resources an organization can use to create value are discussed in Chapter 7. How value-creation tasks may be allocated to individuals and groups, how information will be gathered and distributed, and how decisions will be made are all discussed further in Chapter 7. What activities internal and external to the organization should be monitored, and how, is discussed in Chapter 9. How the performance of individuals and groups in creating value should be determined and rewarded is discussed in Chapter 7.

In defining the goals of their organization and in gathering and deploying resources to achieve those goals, strategic managers are in effect responsible for designing their organization to be *an effective goal-seeking open system.* Figure 1.1 summarizes (i) the essential *system elements* and (ii) the key *interactions* among system elements that strategic managers must coordinate in designing an organization as goal-seeking open system.

At the core of a system design for an organization is the organization's **Strategic Logic,** which we define as *an organization's operative rationale for achieving its goals through coordinated deployments of resources.* In other words, the Strategic Logic represents the shared ideas of the people in the organization about the nature of the organization's goals for creating value, the resources needed to achieve those goals, the ways resources will be coordinated in pursuing those goals, and how value created by the organization will be distributed to all the stakeholders that provide resources to the organization. In effect, the Strategic Logic expresses the essential *system elements and interactions* that people in the organization believe will enable the organization to achieve its goals for value creation and distribution. In Chapter 3, we present a more formal model of the system elements and interactions that must be included in the Strategic Logic of an organization.

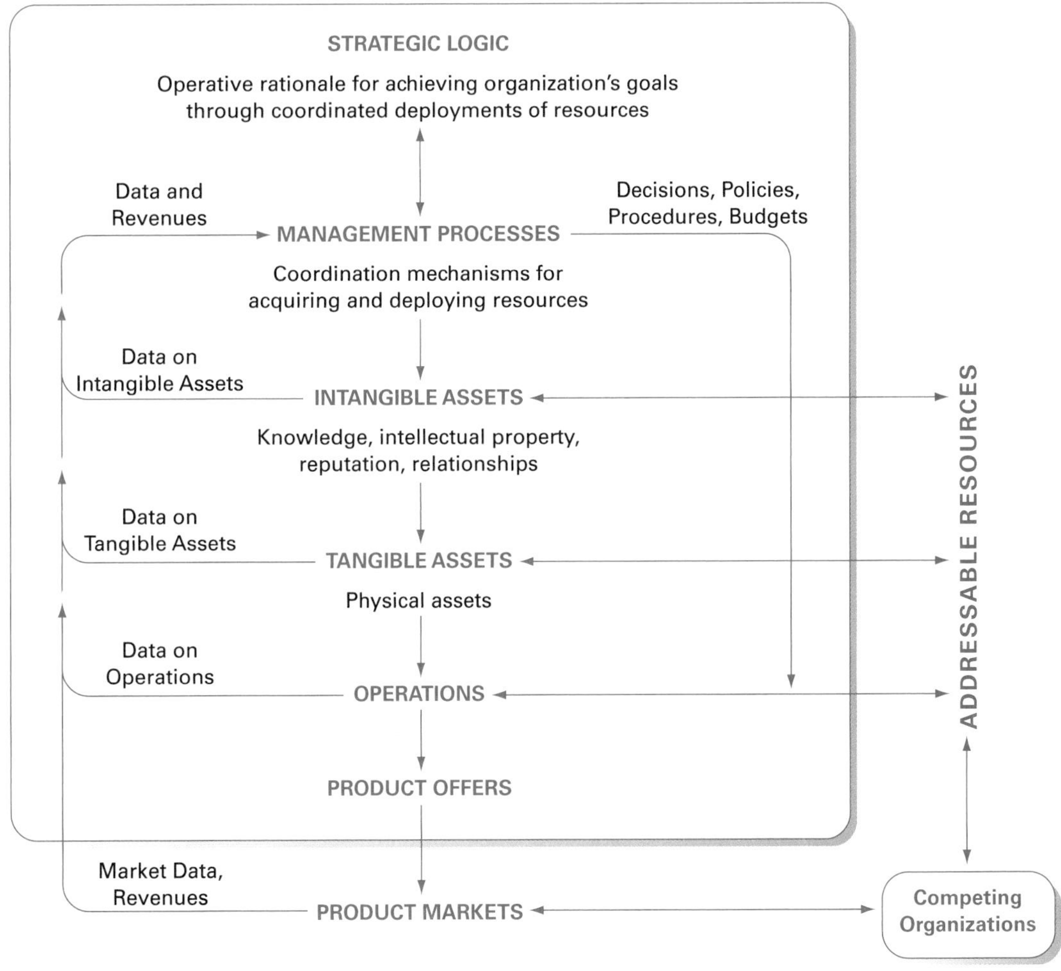

FIGURE 1.1 Model of an Organization as a Goal-Seeking Open System

To translate a Strategic Logic for achieving goals into action, strategic managers must also design an organization's *management processes,* which include all the processes an organization uses to gather and deploy the resources used in its activities. Thus, management processes include the following activities:

- Gathering data on the organization's environment and its own internal activities
- Interpreting the data the organization gathers
- Making decisions to acquire, access, or retire specific resources and to continue, discontinue, or modify certain activities for using those resources
- Setting policies, procedures, plans, budgets, and other means for initiating and coordinating desired activities
- Defining performance objectives and measures for activities, and distributing rewards to the providers of resources for carrying out those activities

Through its management processes, an organization seeks to acquire or access both the *intangible resources* (like knowledge, brands, and goodwill) and *tangible resources* (like equipment, buildings, and land) required to sustain its value-creating activities. As Figure 1.1 indicates, an organization may use its own current resources in its activities, but it must often acquire new or *addressable resources* provided by external resource providers, outside the boundary of the organization. Because other organizations may also want to acquire or access similar addressable resources, however, strategic managers must be able to design their organization as a system for creating and distributing value that will be successful in *competing for the essential resources* the organization needs to continue its value-creating activities. To attract the best employees, suppliers, locations, and other essential resources to its activities, an organization must be able to create and distribute value that is more attractive to the providers of those resources than the value offered by other organizations.

The *operations* of an organization include all its activities that use resources to create and distribute value. At the "core" of an organization's operations are its activities of product creation, product realization, and stakeholder development. We refer to these activities as the *Core Processes* of an organization; they are discussed further in Chapter 8. The output of an organization's operations is its *product offers.* An organization also competes against other organizations in attracting customers to its product offers in the *product markets* each organization chooses to compete in.

As Figure 1.1 also indicates, the design of an organization as an open system will usually include certain kinds of *feedback* from the organization's environment, such as flows of *revenues* from providing its product offers and various kinds of *data* about its position in its product markets. Other forms of feedback usually include data intended to monitor the condition of the organization's own internal resources and activities.

In the competence-based approach to strategic management, competition is seen as occurring between organizations that have different Strategic Logics and system designs for attracting and using resources to create and distribute value. Strategic managers contribute to an organization's competitive processes through their dual role as articulators of the organization's Strategic Logic and as designers of the organization as an open system capable of attracting and deploying the resources needed to carry out its Strategic Logic and achieve its goals. In some cases, strategic managers may try to adopt or "imitate" the design of an organization that is currently successful in pursuing similar kinds of goals. In other cases, strategic managers may try to create new or modified organizational designs that would be more effective than existing designs in achieving a given set of goals. In following chapters, we develop a framework for articulating an organization's strategic goals and for designing an organization as an open system capable of achieving those goals.

1.4 MANAGING STRATEGICALLY TO BUILD, MAINTAIN, AND LEVERAGE ORGANIZATIONAL COMPETENCE

The Concept of Competence

In the competence-based framework, the objective of strategic management is the creation of an organization that is *competent* in creating and distributing value to all providers of resources essential to maintain the activities of the organization. In this regard, we adopt the following definition of organizational competence:

> **Organizational competence** is the ability of an organization to sustain coordinated deployments of resources in ways that help the organization to achieve its goals.

This concept of organizational competence establishes three important conditions that the system design for a competent organization must meet. First, to be regarded as competent, an organization's activities must be effectively *coordinated* through its management processes in pursuit of its goals. Second, the organization's deployments of resources must have a clear *intention* of achieving organizational goals by creating and distributing value in specific ways. Third, the organization's management processes must be based on an articulated *rationale* (i.e., a Strategic Logic) as to how carrying out its coordinated deployments of resources will help the organization to achieve its goals. If an organization's activities are not coordinated in ways that contribute effectively to achieving its goals, or if its activities lack the intention to achieve its goals, or if the organization's activities lack purposeful rationale for achieving its goals, then any attainment of its goals that an organization happens to achieve may reasonably be regarded as a matter of luck, not as the result of its organizational competence.

Creating a competent organization requires a Strategic Logic and system design capable of sustaining simultaneous processes of building, maintaining, and leveraging organizational competences (see Figure 1.2).

Competence building is any process by which an organization creates or accesses qualitatively new kinds of resources (including new assets or new capabilities) or develops new abilities to coordinate and deploy new or existing resources in ways that help the organization achieve its goals for value creation and distribution. For example, developing, producing, and marketing new kinds of products often constitutes competence building, because doing so usually requires using qualitatively new kinds of assets and capabilities.

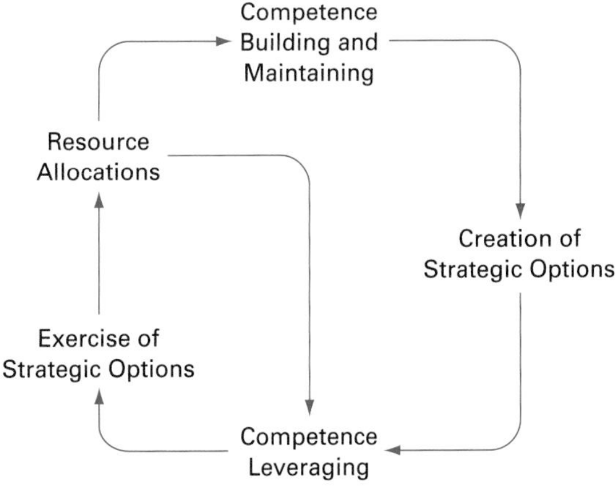

FIGURE 1.2 Competence Building, Maintaining, and Leveraging

Building new organizational competence creates, in effect, new *strategic options* for future action in pursuit of the organization's goals. Developing a new technological capability and a new distribution channel, for example, may create a new competence that gives an organization new options to offer new kinds of products to new customer groups.

In a dynamic competitive environment, an organization must engage in **competence maintenance** to continually adapt and improve its coordinated deployments of resources in order to maintain its options for taking actions in pursuit of its goals. Thus, along with its activities for building new competences, an organization must also sustain activities for maintaining the competences that it previously created.

Competence leveraging is the use of an organization's existing competences to create and distribute value in ways that do not require qualitative changes in the resources the organization uses or in the ways it coordinates its resources. Competence leveraging may be carried out using currently available resources or may involve quantitative increases in the same kinds of resources the organization already uses. For example, increasing production of current products by hiring more employees and extending the hours of operation of an existing factory operation is a form of competence leveraging.

Competence leveraging, in effect, is *the exercise of one or more of an organization's current strategic options* created by prior competence building activities. Leveraging competences and exercising strategic options for action generates flows of resources, including financial resources such as revenues from sales of products.

As suggested in Figure 1.2, the resources generated by competence leveraging must be allocated both to building new competences and to further competence leveraging. Thus, to sustain its processes of value creation, an organization's Strategic Logic and system design must include management processes that direct resources to simultaneous competence building and leveraging activities.

The competence-based strategic management view that an organization creates value through simultaneous processes for competence building and leveraging corresponds closely to contemporary finance theory's approach to determining the value of firms. As indicated in Figure 1.3, contemporary finance theory holds that the market value of a firm is determined by its cash flows from current operations and its opportunities or "real options" to create new cash flows in the future. Similarly, the competence-based view of organizations recognizes that the value-creating processes of an organization include both competence leveraging activities that generate current cash flows and activities for building new competences that create new strategic options to generate future cash flows.

In several chapters of this book, we explore a number of central issues facing strategic managers in defining a viable Strategic Logic and in designing organizations as open systems that are effective in both leveraging current competences and building new competences for the future.

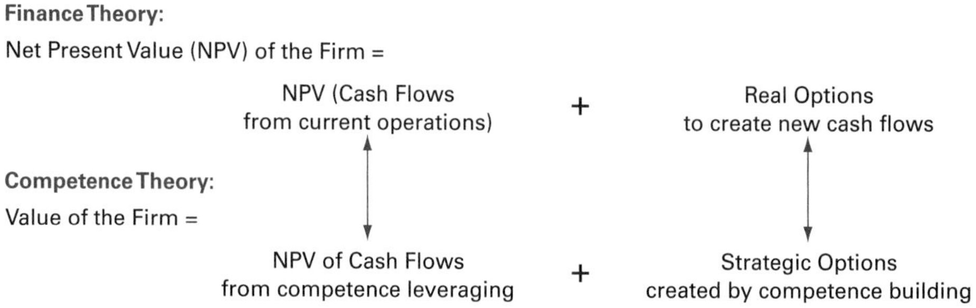

Finance Theory:

Net Present Value (NPV) of the Firm =

NPV (Cash Flows from current operations) + Real Options to create new cash flows

↕ ↕

Competence Theory:

Value of the Firm =

NPV of Cash Flows from competence leveraging + Strategic Options created by competence building

FIGURE 1.3 Correspondence of Competence Theory and Finance Theory in Describing How Firms Create Value

KEY TERMS AND CONCEPTS

value creation The creation of benefits for participants in organized activities.

value distribution The ways that the value an organized activity creates is allocated among the participants in the activity.

organization A system of interdependent actors who collectively share some goals for creating and realizing value through their interactions.

management The processes through which an organization tries to maintain its ability to create and distribute value by coordinating the interactions of the participants in its activities.

strategic management The management process that defines an organization's goals for value creation and distribution and designs the way the organization will be composed, structured, and coordinated in pursuing those goals.

resources Any assets or capabilities that are available to an organization to use in pursuing its goals for value creation and distribution.

stakeholders Providers of resources essential to an organization's processes for creating value and who therefore have a legitimate interest or "stake" in receiving value in return from the organization's processes for distributing value.

Strategic Logic An organization's operative rationale for sustaining coordinated deployments of resources in ways that will help the organization achieve its goals.

organizational competence The ability of an organization to sustain coordinated deployments of resources in ways that help the organization achieve its goals.

competence building Any process by which an organization uses qualitatively new kinds of resources or new abilities to coordinate resources in ways that help the organization achieve its goals for value creation and distribution.

competence maintenance The process of continually adapting and improving an organization's coordinated deployments of resources in order to maintain their effectiveness in achieving the goals of the organization for value creation and distribution.

competence leveraging Any process by which an organization seeks to achieve its goals for value creation and distribution by using resources and coordination abilities that are qualitatively similar to the resources and coordination abilities the organization already possesses.

REVIEW QUESTIONS

1 What are the essential characteristics of an organization required to attract and retain participants in its activities?

2. What are some of the key management processes involved in coordinating the activities of an organization?

3. What are the two fundamental tasks of strategic management?

4. What three conditions must be met to consider an organization competent?

5. What processes of an organization create new strategic options for action by the organization?

6. What processes exercise an organization's current strategic options for action?

PART II

PERSPECTIVES ON ECONOMIC ORGANIZATION AND STRATEGIC MANAGEMENT

CHAPTER 2

ECONOMIC ORGANIZATION: THEORIES OF MARKETS, FIRMS, AND THEIR INTERACTIONS

INTRODUCTION

As we discussed in the previous chapter, strategic managers' two fundamental roles are (i) defining the goals for an organization, and (ii) designing the way the organization will be composed, structured, and coordinated in pursuing those goals. In performing these fundamental roles, strategic managers must lead the organization in defining a Strategic Logic that provides the essential rationale for how the organization will achieve its goals through coordinated deployments of resources. The Strategic Logic is the core of the design of an organization as a goal-seeking open system engaged in sustainable processes of value creation and value distribution. Thus, in creating and carrying out a Strategic Logic, strategic managers engage in the activity of *economic organizing.*

In this chapter, we investigate some essential perspectives on economic organizing that strategic managers must understand and be able to use in creating a viable Strategic Logic for managing the resources and processes in an organization. We first discuss the central concept of *economic exchange* and how exchange can create value for exchangers of resources. We then consider two alternative ways of organizing economic exchange. We first consider the use of *markets* as an institutional framework for coordinating exchanges of resources, and we identify *efficiency* benefits that may be realized from coordinating exchanges of resources through markets. We then consider the use of *hierarchical coordination* of resource exchange within an *organization,* and we discuss several perspectives on why coordinating exchanges of resources through organizations may create economic benefits that may be difficult to achieve through market exchanges. Finally, we summarize the key economic concerns that strategic managers must keep in mind when deciding whether to use markets or hierarchical coordination in managing the resource exchanges that organizations must sustain to function successfully as open systems for the creation and distribution of value.

2.1 ECONOMIC EXCHANGE

Economic exchange is the trading of one resource for another.

Economic exchange is the trading of anything of value for anything else of value. Economic exchange thus includes both the traditional bartering of goods for goods, as well as the more contemporary use of money to *mediate* the exchange of goods—i.e., the trading of goods and services for money and money for goods and services.

To sustain value-creation processes, organizations require many kinds of resources. An organization obtains needed resources by exchanging resources it currently has for those resources it does not currently have or that it needs more of. The resources that people or other organizations may trade with an organization include not just specific goods and services, but their time, energy, skills, loyalty, ideas, knowledge, and learning capacity.

Exchanges of resources may be coordinated through markets or within organizations.

Exchange of resources may take place across the boundaries of an organization as an open system, as when a firm purchases materials or services from a supplier, licenses a technology from another firm, or contracts for access to a distribution channel. Exchange of resources may also take place internally, within the boundaries of an organization as an open system. Employees (including managers) exchange their efforts to help the organization create value for some share of the economic value the organization creates, as well as for intangible benefits like opportunities to perform interesting work, to improve skills through learning on the job, to work in pleasant surroundings, and so on.

Exchanges of resources across the boundaries of an organization generally occur through market transactions, while exchanges of resources within an organization's boundaries are normally hierarchically coordinated by managers. We next consider the nature, benefits, and potential limitations of both market and hierarchical coordination approaches to organizing exchanges of resources.

2.2 MARKETS AS MECHANISMS FOR EXCHANGING RESOURCES

In economic theory, a **market** refers to *a process and associated set of norms for exchanging resources,* not a specific place where exchange takes place. A market process is one in which transactions are conducted "at arm's length." In market exchanges, buyers and sellers make no commitments to each other beyond the terms specified in the exchange transaction itself. In **market transactions,** terms of exchange are typically confined to a description of the good or service to be provided, delivery terms (if any), and the price and payment terms. In effect, the relationship between buyer and seller is wholly contained within the terms of the exchange transaction and does not continue beyond the conclusion of the exchange. (If a warranty or maintenance and repair services are agreed upon as part of the exchange, in effect the exchange continues until the terms of the warranty or service have been met.)

Markets may offer cost efficiency in exchanging resources.

Under certain conditions, market transactions may be the most efficient way to organize exchanges of resources. Those conditions are defined by the basic assumptions in classical economics about the way that buyers and sellers behave in market transactions and about the way that markets function. We next consider those assumptions, and the reasons why market transactions can lead to efficient exchanges of resources when actual market conditions conform to those assumptions. We also consider several ways in which the conditions under which exchanges sometimes must take place may not be consistent with the assumptions about markets in classical economics, resulting in inefficient markets or **market failures.**

Goods, Information, Prices, and Efficiency

In classical economic theory, markets are the optimally efficient process for coordinating the supply of and demand for goods (or for coordinating the exchange of resources, as we would say using competence vocabulary). Market exchanges are optimally efficient under the following assumed conditions:

- Buyers and sellers are *utility maximizers.* Buyers will seek out the lowest price available for the goods they want to obtain, and sellers will try to obtain the highest price they can for the goods they have to offer. Exchange will take place only when the price at which a seller is ready to sell a product matches the price that a buyer is willing to pay.
- The goods that are offered by sellers can be *observed or described* adequately, so that a buyer has sufficient understanding of the good he or she would receive

to determine its utility and to make a decision whether to proceed with a transaction to acquire the good.

- Markets achieve the coordination of supply and demand through the *price mechanism.* Prices of all goods on offer are assumed to be known by all buyers, and prices that buyers are willing to pay for goods are assumed to be known by potential sellers. In economic terms, buyers and sellers are assumed to have *perfect and complete information* about prices of goods available in the market. Having full information about prices of goods, buyers will only buy at the lowest price available in the market, and only when the utility they will derive from use of a good exceeds the market price of the good. Sellers, in turn, will allocate their available resources to producing goods that would bring them the greatest surplus of price over costs available in the market.

Market efficiency depends on perfect and complete price information.

When these assumed conditions actually exist, markets will lead to efficient allocation and exchange of resources. Sellers will allocate their resources to producing goods that will bring them the greatest possible return on their efforts. In economic terms, sellers will act to maximize *producer surplus* (the excess of the market price of a good over the costs of resources consumed in producing the good), given the prevailing market prices for goods and resources. Buyers in turn will exchange their (financial) resources only for goods that offer the greatest *consumer surplus* (the excess of the utility derived by the buyer from the use of a good over the price paid by the buyer for the good).

If sellers did not know the market prices for goods they could provide, they might allocate their resources to the production of goods that would not bring them the greatest surplus of price over costs, that is, to a suboptimal value-creation activity. Analogously, if buyers did not know the lowest prices available in the market for goods, they might use their resources to buy goods that demand a higher price but that offer a lower level of utility than might actually be available in the market. Thus, the perfect and complete price information assumed to be available to buyers and sellers in markets makes possible the efficient allocation of resources by producers/sellers and makes the utility-maximizing possibilities for buying goods known to buyers/consumers, thus creating value for both buyers and sellers.

When Markets Work and When They Fail

Markets can lead to efficient allocations and exchanges of resources when the assumed conditions discussed above actually exist, or at least approximately so. When efficient market conditions do exist, strategic managers can take advantage of markets in two important ways. Prevailing prices in various product and resource markets help strategic managers discover which product offers the organization is capable of providing profitably. In essence, product market prices help managers identify the product opportunities on which they could most profitably focus the organization's resources for creating and realizing value. Similarly, prices in resource markets help managers decide which combinations of resources would offer the most cost-effective way of creating and realizing various products the organization could provide. Thus, the price information available in efficient markets for products and resources helps managers identify and evaluate promising opportunities for value creation.

In a number of situations, however, the conditions necessary for efficient markets may not exist:

Conditions under which markets may be inefficient or fail

- *Incomplete or imperfect price information.* Accurate and complete price information on all available goods and resources in a market may not be available to buyers and sellers. Sellers with incorrect or incomplete price information may allocate their resources to the production of goods that will have lower value in the market than other goods they are able to produce. Buyers may purchase goods at high prices because they are simply unaware that lower prices are available, or they may not purchase some goods or resources at all because they are not aware that they are available. The more imperfect or incomplete the price information available to buyers and sellers, they more likely they are to make inefficient allocations of resources in production and purchase decisions. Lack of full price information therefore tends to result in suboptimal value creation by producers and suboptimal value obtained by buyers as they engage in exchanges of resources.

- *Inadequate assurance about products.* The opportunity for buyers to observe goods may be limited, and descriptions of goods available from sellers may not be reliable enough or otherwise adequate to induce potential buyers to make a purchase. Potential buyers may have concerns about the quality of the goods they would receive, and adequate guarantees about quality or serviceability of a good may not be available from sellers. In a market in which the norm of *caveat emptor* ("buyer beware") prevails, buyers may refrain from purchasing goods that actually would bring them a surplus of utility over price, because they cannot verify to their satisfaction the true nature of the good. On the other hand, some buyers may decide to take a chance on purchasing a good, only to learn after purchasing that the good is defective and does not provide the hoped-for utility. Sellers who cannot adequately explain the nature and quality of the goods or resources they have to offer may fail to attract buyers, and their potential for creating value will not be realized.
- *Incommensurable goods.* Buyers and sellers may not be able to compare prices of goods, because the goods on offer in a market differ in some significant respects. Markets function most efficiently for goods that are *commodities*—goods that are identical and interchangeable in all essential respects and thus enable potential buyers to directly compare prices from different sellers. When goods are *differentiated,* however, and offer different "bundles" of utility (or "benefits" in marketing terminology), potential buyers may not be able to directly compare prices and may have difficulty imagining the way in which the benefits offered by one good would compare to the benefits offered by another good.
- *Innovative goods* (those not previously available in a market) may pose a special challenge to potential buyers. Buyers who have difficulty imagining how they would use and derive value from an innovative good may refrain from buying a good that would actually deliver significant value to them once they become familiar with the good and learn how to use it effectively. For example, some people today who could afford to purchase a personal computer have not done so because they are afraid they cannot understand how to use it, even though with a few simple lessons they could derive considerable benefit from using e-mail or other functions of the computer.

When situations with incomplete or imperfect information exist, potential producers/sellers may allocate resources to producing products other than those that would actually maximize value for buyers, and buyers may purchase products other than those that would actually be value maximizing for them. The result is resource allocations and exchanges that are not optimally efficient. However, an even more severe consequence may occur. Markets may actually *fail;* that is, exchanges do not take place at all. Potential sellers do not allocate resources to producing goods they fear they cannot sell, and potential buyers do not purchase goods they fear they will not understand or be able to use.

In such situations, other approaches to organizing exchanges of resources may be required to overcome the potential inefficiencies or failures of market transactions. We therefore next consider a number of reasons why it may be more beneficial to carry out certain kinds of resource exchanges within organizations rather than through market transactions.

2.3 ORGANIZATIONS AS FRAMEWORKS FOR EXCHANGING RESOURCES

Exchanges of resources may also be hierarchically coordinated within organizations.

In the economic theory of the firm, organizations exist to provide hierarchical coordination of certain resource exchanges needed to sustain value-creation processes. **Hierarchical coordination** means that managers use the authority vested in the management hierarchy of the organization to arrange internal exchanges of resources within the organization that cannot be arranged satisfactorily through market transactions. Managerially coordinated exchanges of resources may be preferable to market-mediated exchanges when markets for certain kinds of resources are inefficient or when markets simply do not exist for certain resources (i.e., *market failure* occurs in the supply of a given resource).

We now consider a number of resource exchange situations in which it may be advantageous or necessary for managers to coordinate resource exchanges hierarchically within organizations. Each of these situations has been studied by an economist or management thinker who helped us understand how organizations can improve the exchange of resources—and thus improve value-creation processes—in ways that markets often cannot.

Adam Smith and the Gains from Specialization of Labor[1]

Specialization of labor improves efficiency of resources.

To induce people or organizations to contribute their resources of time, energy, knowledge, and intelligence to an organization's value-creation processes, an organization must offer something valuable in return. In effect, to come into existence and to remain in existence, organizations must help individuals or other organizations to achieve a level of goal attainment that they could not otherwise achieve. An organization must therefore create benefits for its providers of resources that exceed the benefits they could achieve through their own efforts.

The early English economist Adam Smith argued that creation of benefits beyond those that individuals could achieve on their own is only possible when a complex task is divided into smaller tasks that are executed and controlled by a single individual. Such "division of labor" makes it possible for each person to specialize in performing a single task, and the resulting **specialization of labor** brings two important benefits. First, specialized individual workers do not waste time switching from performing one kind of task to another—a common feature of the craft approach to production in which one worker performs all tasks involved in producing a good. Moreover, specialization of labor can lead to a deepening of a worker's expertise and skill in performing a given task, and such learning effects can collectively improve the efficiency with which an organization performs its overall work. Achieving greater efficiency through specialization of labor, however, requires effective managerial coordination of tasks that have been divided and allocated to the various members of an organization.

Exchanges of specialized resources (specialized skills and labor) are likely to occur under the hierarchical coordination of an organization rather than through market transactions

[1] Smith, A. (1812). *An Inquiry into the Nature and Causes of the Wealth of Nations.* London: Ward, Lock & Co., Warwick House.

for several reasons. From a technological perspective, the technical decomposition of a complex task into a set of complementary specialized tasks needs to be coordinated. This coordination may require knowledge of production processes that one or a few organizations may possess, but that may not be widely available in a market at large. From an operational perspective, to achieve an efficient, balanced flow in an overall production process, the appropriate level of output from each specialized task must be determined and realized. Coordinating the right output levels from many specialized tasks may be easier or more feasible through a management hierarchy than through market transactions, especially if demand levels for the finished good fluctuate. From a financial perspective, hierarchical coordination may be less risky than relying on market transactions with many individual suppliers, whose individual output is necessary to the overall production process, but who are each free to switch to the production of another good or to demand a higher price for his or her output.

Frederick Taylor and Scientific Management[2]

Scientific management means understanding the "science" of a task and providing incentives for improvement.

In the late 1800s and early 1900s, an American engineer named Frederick Taylor observed that the specialized tasks assigned to workers in factories were often performed inefficiently as a result of what he considered faulty "initiative and incentive management systems." Taylor argued that inefficiency resulted because factory owners did not offer workers any incentives for increasing productivity. Indeed, workers were typically averse to improving productivity, because an increase in the output of each employee often resulted not in the expansion of a firm's output and sales, but rather in laying off at least some of the workers in order to hold output constant. Management's lack of interest in expanding output made it necessary for each worker to "soldier" (work more slowly than he or she could) in order to protect his or her job. In addition, the craft-based approach to organizing work at the time did not encourage active investigation of alternative or innovative ways of performing tasks that could improve efficiency.

Moreover, motivational issues aside, Taylor argued that a factory worker performing a single specialized task would be unlikely to fully understand the "science" in the overall task being performed in the factory, and thus would not be able to understand clearly the specific ways in which his or her specialized task contributes to the overall work of the factory. Because individual employees did not understand the ways in which they could contribute to the overall performance of a factory, productivity improvements were unlikely to be identified and achieved even if individual workers were motivated to improve their performance.

To remedy the endemic low productivity of workers in factories, Taylor proposed a systematic approach to redesigning productive work based on what he called the "Principles of Scientific Management."[3] Taylor's **scientific management** approach rests on four principles. First, it is the duty of the management to develop a "science" or deep technical understanding of each work process and task to be performed. Second, employees should be carefully selected and trained in the current scientific understanding of their process and task. Third, management should work with each employee on an individual basis to assure that he or she can perform an assigned task according to the principles of the science underlying that task. In effect, management should observe the performance of each employee and help each employee learn how to do a task in the best possible way. Fourth, organized work should be clearly divided between workers and the managers. The

[2] Taylor, F. W. (1967). *The Principles of Scientific Management.* New York.

[3] Ibid.

role of observing and coaching should be performed by managers, while workers should be executors of the tasks defined by managers.

Taylor also argued that each worker's success in achieving superior performance should be rewarded. Higher wages, shorter working hours, and better working conditions should be awarded to workers when they are able to improve efficiency and productivity.

Taylor's principles of scientific management suggest several reasons why it may be more advantageous for managers to coordinate resource exchanges (e.g., the exchange of labor and skill for employee compensation and benefits) within an organization rather than through market transactions. Managers can only build up their understanding of how specialized tasks can best be performed through close study of individual tasks carried out within a well-coordinated overall process design. Opportunities for close study of a stable set of complementary specialized tasks may be difficult to arrange through market transactions. Further, managers should directly monitor the work performed by each worker to be sure that it conforms to the science that underlies the task. Such monitoring of task performance may also be difficult to arrange in market transactions.

Central to Taylor's notion of scientific management is the idea that an organization will be more effective than markets in coordinating exchanges of resources when its managers have expertise in the science underlying specialized tasks, when they understand the critical interactions between tasks that have to be managed to improve the performance of an overall production system, and when they share the value created through productivity gains with the workers who learned to improve their performance. In essence, Frederick Taylor proposed that when managers develop the right knowledge, management processes, and incentive systems, an organization can outperform market transactions in allocating and coordinating human and technical resources in the production of goods.

Henry Fayol and Administrative Management[4]

After studying several kinds of organizations, an early French management thinker, Henry Fayol, concluded that organizations carry out six basic kinds of functions or operations:

- Technical operations (production, manufacturing, transportation)
- Commercial operations (selling, buying, exchanging)
- Financial operations (searching for and managing capital)
- Security operations (protection of material and personnel)
- Accountancy operations (bookkeeping, preparing financial statements)
- Administrative operations (coordination of the other five operations)

The first five operations were commonly recognized and attended to by managers of organizations in the early 1900s. In proposing the sixth function of "administrative operations," however, Henry Fayol was drawing managers' attention to the need to coordinate and integrate the other five functions in the overall processes of an organization.

Fayol defined the administrative function as consisting of five operations (Fayol's original French terms are given in parenthesis):

Administration is one of the basic functions in an economic organization.

- Policy making and planning (prévoir)
- Organizing (organiser)
- Giving instructions (commander)

[4] Fayol, H. (1916). Administration Industrielle et Générale: Prévoyance, Organisation, Commandement, Coordination et Controle. Paris: Bulletin de la Société de l'Industrie Minérale; Urwick, L. (1956). *The Golden Book of Management.* London: Newman Neame Limited.

- Coordinating (coordonner)
- Controlling (controller)

Fayol argued that all these capabilities are needed to execute the sixth operation of administration, but that these capabilities could be taught and learned. In effect, Fayol argued that managing was a capability that could be developed and improved within an organization, and that doing so would lead to improvements in the performance of the other five functions of the organization.

Fayol's ideas, like those of Frederick Taylor, suggest that organizations whose managers develop administrative skills may provide "administrative guidance" or coordination for resource exchanges that can improve the efficiency of an organization's productive operations. When managers possess these skills, their hierarchical coordination of resource exchanges within an organization can be more efficient than coordination purely through market transactions. In effect, both Fayol and Taylor proposed early versions of a "competence-based theory of the firm" by arguing that firms exist because they develop competences that result in more efficient coordination of resource exchanges than can be achieved through market transactions.

Alchian and Demsetz: Team-Based Production[5]

The economists Alchian and Demsetz argued that when "resources are owned and allocated by such nongovernmental organizations as firms, households, and markets," cooperation among resource owners can increase productivity in exchanging, allocating, and using resources. They also noted, however, that an organization typically does not own all its required resource inputs and thus cannot coordinate all its resource exchanges using "power, fiat, and disciplinary action."

Team production is an important form of economic organizing.

Alchian and Demsetz focused on the analysis of employment relationships in organizations and interpreted them as contracts for the exchange of resources between employee and employer. This contractual interpretation of the employer-employee relationship helped to clarify limits on the use of authority-based directives and disciplinary power in coordinating resource exchanges in organizations. Like Frederick Taylor, Alchian and Demsetz argued that the joint use of input resources provided by different parties will be optimized when "it facilitates the payment of rewards in accord with productivity."[6] Therefore, organizations that develop better ways of "metering productivity and metering rewards"—i.e., monitoring productivity and allocating rewards according to that productivity—may achieve superior performance in coordinating resources. Metering effectively may be difficult and pose specific challenges to managers, however, as illustrated in the example of team production.

Alchian and Demsetz defined *team production* as a productive process in which several types of resources are used and in which the product is the result of interactions between the resources involved. In other words, the product of team production is not simply the sum of separable outputs of each cooperating resource. The intermingling of several resources in team production creates an organization problem. The inputs from individual team members are not easy to observe and measure. As a result, it may be costly and challenging to devise ways of precisely monitoring individual performance (productivity) and effectively relating productivity to rewards for individuals. This monitoring problem may lead to low employee motivation to improve productivity and even the

[5] Alchian, A. A., & Demsetz, H. (1972). Production, Information Costs, and Economic Organisation. The American Economic Review, LXII(5), 777–795.

[6] Ibid., 778.

possibility that some team members will "shirk" and become "free riders" on the efforts of other team members.

Alchian and Demsetz proposed that organizations can try to overcome this problem of team production by providing specialized monitors who observe the performance of individual team members. The monitor is responsible for devising the most cost-effective way of measuring the output performance of each team member, estimating the marginal productivity of each member, and apportioning rewards to team members according to their individual contributions to productivity of the team. Based on his or her analysis of a team's production process, the monitor is empowered to give instructions to the team on how to improve performance, and to replace team members who are suspected of shirking. The performance of the monitor is then evaluated on the basis of improvements made in the performance of the team he or she monitors.

What Alchian and Demsetz essentially propose is that organizations may do a better job of coordinating resource exchanges than markets when their managers have skills in monitoring and improving the performance of team-based production. In effect, Alchian and Demsetz compare the managed organization to a privately owned market in which managers can search for combinations of resources and ways of coordinating resources that improve the productivity of the resources available to an organization.

Transaction Costs Analysis: Managing the Risks of Exchange[7]

Hierarchically coordinating resource exchanges within an organization can reduce the risks of opportunistic behavior.

In his well-known paper on the nature of the firm, Ronald Coase argued that organizations exist because they offer a better way of managing risks that are inherent in certain market transactions for resources.[8] Coase argued, in effect, that the existence of firms suggests that hierarchical coordination of certain kinds of resource exchanges within organizations results in lower costs than bearing the risks of using markets for coordinating those exchanges. Coase's ideas were extended by economist Oliver Williamson, who developed the "transactions costs" framework for explaining why certain economic exchanges are coordinated within organizations rather than through markets.[9]

In the transactions cost perspective, the central issue is the risk of "opportunistic behavior" by a buyer or seller in a market transaction when it is not possible or practical to write an enforceable "complete contract" to govern the transaction. Suppose an "economic organizer" wants to organize a productive activity that requires a specific kind of resource as an input. If the economic organizer makes a market contract with a resource provider for the supply of that resource, but situations arise in the future that are not anticipated in the contract or that cannot be managed through effective enforcement of the contract, the provider of the resource could "hold up" the economic organizer and demand an exorbitant price for the required resource. If comparable resources are not readily available in the market, the economic organizer may have no choice but to pay the price demanded by the resource provider. In effect, using market transactions to arrange access to specific resources may lead to high costs when the risk of opportunistic behavior by resource providers cannot be managed through the contracting process.

[7] Coase, R. H. (1937). The nature of the firm. *Economica,* 386–405; Hodgson, G. M. (1993). Transaction Costs and The Evolution of the Firm. In C. Pitelis (Ed.), *Transaction Costs, Markets and Hierarchies.* Oxford: Basil Blackwell Ltd.; Madhok, A. (1996). The Organization of Economic Activity: Transaction Costs, Firm Capabilities, and the Nature of Governance. *Organization Science,* 7(5), 577–590; Maher, M. (1997). Transaction cost economics and contractual relations. *Cambridge Journal of Economics,* 21, 147–170.

[8] Coase, R. H. (1937). The nature of the firm. *Economica,* 386–405.

[9] Williamson, O. (1975). *Markets and Hierarchies: Analysis and Antitrust Implications.* Glencoe: The Free Press.

In the transactions cost perspective, organizations will internalize resources (i.e., to take ownership of resources) and hierarchically coordinate the internal exchange of resources when the risks of opportunistic behavior by market transactors are perceived by economic organizers as too great. In this sense, coordination of resource exchanges within organizations may offer a better way of managing the risks of certain resource exchanges than use of market transactions. In general, the more frequently a resource exchange is likely to be needed, the more the exchange involves a specific kind of resource that is not widely available in a market, and the more uncertain the future situations in which a resource will be used, the greater the likelihood that exchanges for the resource will be more efficiently coordinated hierarchically within an organization rather than through market transactions.

Agency Theory: The Separation of Ownership and Control[10]

Prior to the 1970s, little attention was paid to the motivations that could affect managers in their decision-making processes. In fact, a common assumption was that the same person was both owner and manager of a firm. Financial economists Jensen and Meckling recognized that in many organizations the owner (principal) and the manager (agent) were different people and that this "separation of ownership and control" in the modern organization leads to a divergence of interests. In other words, the agent who as manager has day-to-day control of the firm may not always act in the best interest of the principal who actually owns the firm.

The separation of ownership and control requires aligning incentives for principals and agents.

Jensen and Meckling proposed that in an organization where the manager is also 100 percent owner, the owner-manager can maximize his or her utility through a combination of investing some current resources in the firm to generate future economic returns and spending remaining current resources on perquisites (big offices, luxurious office furniture, company cars and jets, "working" vacations, etc.). If some part "x" of the ownership of the firm is sold to an external party, however, the claim of the manager-owner on future returns in the firm falls to $1 - x$. However, a similar reduction is unlikely for the perquisites that the manager enjoys. While costs for perquisites are borne jointly by all owners of the firm, perquisites are consumed solely by managers. Thus, one consequence of the separation of ownership control is that managers may tend to spend money on perquisites that benefit themselves, but bring no benefit to the firm and its owners.

To prevent excessive spending on perquisites by managers, owners must establish processes for monitoring managers, but these processes incur *monitoring costs.* Nevertheless, it is unlikely that what are in effect absentee owners can fully monitor managers, thereby leaving room for managers to engage in some level of discretionary spending on nonproductive perquisites (creating a *residual loss,* in the terminology of principal-agent theory). The challenge to owners of a firm is to devise compensation schemes for managers that will achieve an effective **alignment of interests** between owners and managers of a firm, and thereby reduce the costs of monitoring and the residual loss from employing managers.

The principal-agent perspective on economic organizations suggests that the efficiency of resource allocations within an organization depends on the extent to which managers are

[10] Jensen, M. C., & Meckling, W. (1976). Theory of the Firm: Managerial Behavior, Agency Costs and Ownership Structure. *Journal of Financial Economics,* 305–360; Meggison, W. L. (1997). *Corporate Finance Theory. Reading,* MA: Addison-Wesley.

motivated to use the organization's resources in value-creation activities rather than in consuming organizational resources in various perquisites. Thus, top-level managers who have an organization's interests foremost in mind will understand the need to align their own compensation and other incentives with value-creation goals that will directly benefit their organization.

2.4 THE COMPETENCE PERSPECTIVE ON ECONOMIC ORGANIZING

The competence perspective addresses important dynamic, systemic, holistic, and cognitive concerns in economic organizing.

The foregoing economic theories contribute in important ways to our understanding of the benefits to be derived through economic organizing and of the roles that managers play in realizing those benefits. They explain some potential cost advantages of using efficient markets to coordinate exchanges of some resources, but they also suggest a number of ways in which hierarchical coordination of resource exchanges within organizations may enhance their value-creation potential. When deciding how best to organize the resource exchanges needed to sustain value-creation processes, strategic managers must assess the relative advantages and potential limitations of using markets *versus* hierarchical coordination within an organization.

Fundamental as they are to our thinking about how to organize value-creation processes, however, the economic theories we discussed here do not address all the concerns that strategic managers must consider when deciding how to organize value-creation processes. Some important aspects of economic organizing not adequately addressed in economic theory, but that strategic managers must deal with nevertheless, include the following:

- *Dynamics of economic organizing.* The preceding economic theories pay little attention to the dynamics that must be managed in processes for exchanging resources. They offer little or no insight, for example, into the dynamics of competition and cooperation among firms as they compete in resource markets while often working together to create new resources (e.g., collaboration in creating new technologies). Nor do these theories offer insights that can help manage the interactions between managers and employees as they look for ways to work together to achieve the organization's goals. In effect, the objectives to be pursued in managing resource exchanges are often made clear by economic theories, but the theories are generally silent on appropriate ways to manage resource exchanges to achieve those objectives.
- *Systemic aspects of economic organizing.* Economic theories have generally not been concerned with the challenge of integrating managerial decisions to be effective in addressing the multiple resource interdependencies that exist in organizations as open systems. Indeed, in much economic theory, management decision making is often represented as focused on a single issue that can be analyzed and decided in isolation from other issues affecting an organization. Strategic managers, however, must achieve systemic coordination of resource flows within an organization as an open system, and that task requires recognizing that management decisions typically involve a number of resources and simultaneously affect a number of resource providers.
- *Holistic nature of organizations.* Some economic theories stipulate that the purpose of all economic organizations is profit maximization or "maximizing economic rents." Different organizations may have different objectives, however, and all organizations must serve adequately the interests of all providers of essential resources in an organization's value-creation processes. Thus the concept of firm performance that strategic managers must serve is a more holistic one than the simple profit maximization objective assumed in much economic theory.

- *Cognitive processes in organizations.* Economic theories often assume that decision makers have perfect and complete information and "unbounded rationality." In other words, much economic theory assumes that managers have available and can correctly interpret all relevant information about a problem and can reason their way to a perfectly rational solution or decision. As we discuss several places in this text, however, strategic managers must often make decisions on the basis of limited and possibly unreliable information. Moreover, strategic managers, like all real human beings, are subject to "bounded rationality"—they can only process a certain amount of information and must often make decisions on the basis of incomplete information.

We next consider briefly two foundational concepts in the competence approach to strategic management that we will develop further in this text. These concepts are intended to help strategic managers understand a number of the key concerns that they will face in managing organizations, but that are not adequately addressed in current economic theories about economic organizing.

Economic Organizations as Open Systems Embedded in Markets

Economic organizations function as open systems embedded in larger systems.

Competence-based strategic management characterizes economic **organizations as open systems** that are embedded in larger systems (markets), which are in turn embedded in still larger systems (industries, national economies, and the global economy). Economic organizations sustain their value-creation activities by carrying out resource exchanges and other interactions with their environment—essentially through markets for outputs (products) and markets for inputs (resources). In product markets, economic organizations offer products and services to customers, and by offering products that create utility in excess of their cost, organizations create value for their customers. In resource markets, economic organizations acquire resources and capabilities from resource providers, and in return distribute value to them in many forms (payments, salaries, taxes, etc.).

Economic organizations also interact with external parties in two basic ways. They often *compete* with other organizations—for customers in markets for outputs and for the best resources in markets for inputs. However, economic organizations also *cooperate* in many ways, and may often simultaneously compete in some markets while cooperating in other markets. Many markets and industries are characterized by an increasing incidence of "hybrid" forms of interactions between economic organizations that compete and cooperate simultaneously. These hybrid forms of interaction are sometimes called *coopetition.*

Successful Economic Organizing as a "Virtuous Circle" of Value Creation and Distribution

In the competence perspective, economic organizations function through systemic processes that, when designed and managed under appropriate Strategic Logics, create a "virtuous circle" of value creation and distribution, as suggested in Figure 2.1. Several key processes must be managed well to create a virtuous circle of sustained value creation and distribution.

- Managers of an economic organization must discover opportunities for creating value in product markets. Managers must recognize needs and preferences of customers that are either unserved or that their organization can serve better than other organizations in a market. Managers must lead their organization in defining the product offers it will bring to market. Product offers must then be created (designed and developed) and realized (produced, shipped, serviced, and supported).

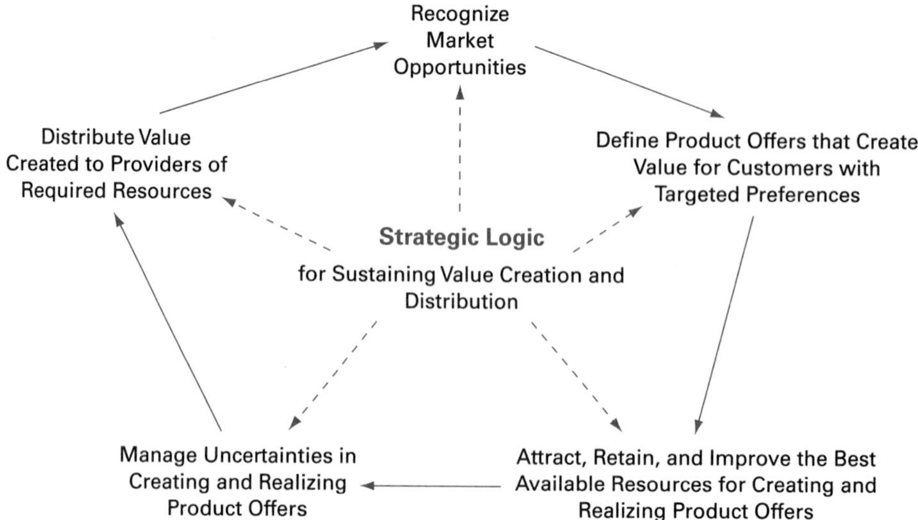

FIGURE 2.1 "Virtuous Circle" of Value Creation and Distribution in Economic Organizing

- Managers must succeed in attracting the best available resources to an organization's processes for creating and realizing product offers, and must find ways to improve the capabilities of available resources in creating and realizing product offers.
- Managers must lead an organization in anticipating and coping with a range of uncertainties that must be resolved in sustaining its value-creation and capability-building processes.
- Managers must devise effective ways to distribute the economic value created by an organization to the providers of resources used in the organization's value-creation processes. In this process, managers must be able to mediate the multiple interests of a potentially large number of stakeholders.

Designing Organizations for Sustainable Wealth Creation and Wealth Distribution

As suggested by the virtuous circle of Figure 2.1, processes for wealth creation and wealth distribution within an organization are systemically interdependent. The more value an economic organization is capable of creating, the more value it can—and must—distribute to its resource providers. The more value an organization can distribute to resource providers, the better the quality and the greater the quantity of resources the organization can attract to its value-creation processes, and the greater the value the organization can create. Designing mutually reinforcing, sustainable value-creation and value-distribution processes is thus essential for successful economic organizing. Strategic managers must find ways to give direction to and coordinate the systemic interplay between value-creation and value-distribution processes in ways that enable an organization to both build and leverage its competences.

KEY TERMS AND CONCEPTS

economic exchange The trading of anything of value for anything else of value.

market transactions A process and associated set of norms for exchanging resources.

market failure A failure of a process for exchanging certain kinds of resources to emerge and function.

hierarchical coordination Exchanges of resources carried out under the authority of a management hierarchy within the boundaries of an organization.

specialization of labor The division of work into specific processes in which individuals focus on performing one kind of task.

scientific management An approach to managing in which work is analyzed and tasks are studied scientifically, workers are trained to perform specific tasks, managers support workers in developing better skills for performing their tasks, and incentives are created for improving performance of a task.

alignment of interests The creation of incentives that induce managers and other employees of a firm to act in the best interests of the firm.

organization as an open system An organization viewed as a system in which resources flow into and out of the organization.

REVIEW QUESTIONS

1. What are the two basic contexts in which resources are exchanged?
2. What are the advantages of economic exchanges coordinated through markets?
3. What requirements must be met before markets function efficiently?
4. What advantages does specialization of labor bring to productive processes?
5. What task must managers perform well when working with specialization of labor?
6. What are the basic functions of an administrative process?
7. What are "shirking" and "free riding" in teamwork?
8. What is opportunistic behavior, and how can it be managed in economic organizing?
9. What are the most important ideas about the task of managing economic organizations that the competence perspective adds to prior economic theories of organizing?

CHAPTER 3

STRATEGIC MANAGEMENT: IMPROVING ORGANIZATIONAL CAPABILITIES FOR VALUE CREATION AND DISTRIBUTION

INTRODUCTION

In Chapter 2, we reviewed some fundamental theories about economic organizing. In this chapter, we examine a number of important perspectives on managing economic organizations that have been influential in shaping the field of strategic management over several decades. We also explain how the competence-based approach to strategic management draws on, integrates, and extends many of these perspectives in developing a new set of principles and practices for improving an organization's processes of value creation and distribution. These principles of competence-based strategic management, which we develop in the remaining chapters of this book, provide essential concepts for strategic managers to use in defining and implementing an organization's Strategic Logic for value creation and distribution.

As we shall see, the competence-based approach to strategic management is founded on a theoretical framework with four primary concerns, sometimes referred to as the "four cornerstones" of competence theory.

First, competence-based strategic management takes seriously the *dynamics* of both the organization's external environment and its internal processes for building and leveraging competences that enable it to respond effectively to its changing environment.

Second, competence-based strategic management sees organizations as *systems* of interacting resources and actors, and therefore pays close attention, both theoretically and in practice, to the challenge of designing organizations as systems capable of managing complexity, change, and uncertainty in both the external and internal environments of an organization.

Third, given the significant intellectual challenge inherent in creating and maintaining dynamically adaptive organizations, competence-based strategic management recognizes the essential role of managerial *cognition* in imagining, designing, and implementing effective organizational processes for value creation and distribution.

Fourth, competence-based strategic management adopts a *holistic* perspective on managing economic organizations. This perspective holds that strategic managers must design and manage processes of value creation and distribution that are effective in serving the interests of all providers of essential resources to an organization (i.e., the interests of all an organization's *stakeholders*). Moreover, the diverse interests of an organization's various stakeholders must be clearly represented in and served by the goals that strategic managers set for their organization.

As we shall see in the chapters to follow, the theories and perspectives that we discuss below have contributed in important ways to the competence-based approach to managing these four fundamental concerns.

3.1 PRIOR THEORIES AND PERSPECTIVES ON STRATEGIC MANAGEMENT

Theoretical Bases

Ideas about the management of organizations that we would consider today as "strategic" in their perspective—that is, management ideas that are concerned with more than purely operational issues in organizations—have emerged from several influential individuals and schools of thought over the past 50 years. Competence-based strategic management incorporates a broad range of insightful ideas advanced by various strategic management researchers and practitioners in the past as well as recently. Importantly, the competence-based approach seeks to integrate these diverse ideas into a single coherent framework for strategically managing organizations. The objective of this integration is to create a better theoretical and practical framework for understanding the processes of value creation and distribution in organizations—and how strategic managers can improve these processes in their organizations.

In this section, we review a number of key ideas developed in prior theories of strategic management, and we identify their contribution to the competence-based approach to strategic management. These key ideas in the development of strategic management theory and practice are summarized in Figure 3.1.

The General Management and Business Policy Perspective[1]

During the period of strong growth of the world economy in the 1950s and 1960s, managers in many organizations faced a number of challenges in managing increasingly large

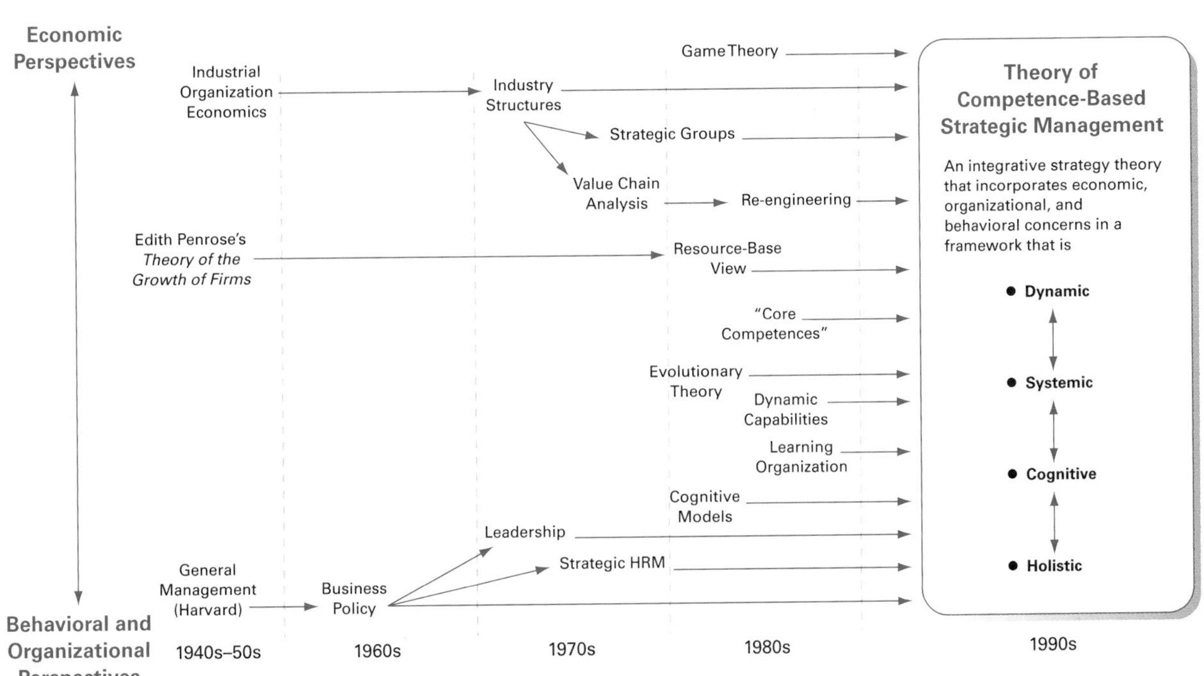

FIGURE 3.1 Evolution of Major Theoretical Perspectives in Strategic Management

[1] Grant, R. M. (1998). *Contemporary Strategy Analysis: Concepts, Techniques, Applications.* Oxford: Blackwell Publishers Ltd, 16–17.

and complex business organizations. The many practical challenges inherent in managing rapidly growing and globalizing organizations during this period attracted the attention of a number of management researchers who developed a set of ideas that we refer to today as the general management and business policy perspective. The basic objective of this perspective was to help managers develop better ways of making decisions and maintain coordination in increasingly large and complex organizations.

Researchers within the general management and business policy perspective, such as Kenneth Andrews, Alfred Chandler, and Igor Ansoff, sought to improve managers' ability to maintain direction and coordination in large organizations by investigating key decision-making processes.[2] Strategy was defined essentially as a *process* that can be decomposed into several sequential subprocesses, including the following:

- Identification and analysis of opportunities and threats
- Formulation of strategic plans to respond to selected opportunities or threats
- Implementation of strategic plans
- Design of systems for controlling implementation processes

In the general management tradition, strategic managers focus on defining policies.

In this view of the strategy process, a rather strong distinction is made between the long-term and short-term concerns and objectives of an organization, and between the roles of two kinds of managers in each of these time frames. Strategic managers should focus on defining and implementing *policies* that guide the organization into its long-term future, while operational managers should focus on applying those policies in dealing with the near-term concerns and objectives of the organization. In essence, the general management and business policy perspective holds that the successful organization will be one in which the long-term policies developed by strategic managers are implemented as a coherent set of current operational practices throughout the organization. Thus, many of the ideas developed within the general management and business policy perspective focus on developing policies that are effective in improving an organization's internal coherence and cohesiveness.

What the competence-based perspective shares in common with the general management and business policy tradition is a strong concern for creating coherence and building cohesiveness within organizations. Competence-based strategic management also recognizes that there are identifiable subprocesses within the overall strategy process, but to a larger extent than the general management and business policy tradition, it views these processes as systemically interrelated. Rather than seeing these subprocesses as sequential and thus neatly separable in time, the competence-based perspective treats strategy subprocesses as inherently interrelated and closely linked in time. In effect, in competent organizations that function effectively as adaptive open systems in dynamic environments, strategy formulation and strategy implementation processes will be highly interactive and will co-evolve simultaneously.

Industrial Organization Economics: The Structure-Conduct-Performance Paradigm

Industrial organization is a branch of economics that developed in the late 1950s and onwards to study the "structure" of various industries and the effects of a given industry structure on the competitive behavior and profitability of firms in that industry. Within this

[2] Andrews, K. (1971). *The Concept of Corporate Strategy.* Homewood, IL: Dow Jones-Irwin; Chandler, A. D. J. (1962). *Strategy and Structure: Chapters in the History of the American Industrial Enterprise.* Cambridge, MA: MIT Press; Ansoff, H. I. (1965). *Corporate Strategy: an Analytical Approach to Business Policy for Growth and Expansion.* New York: McGraw-Hill; Henderson, B. D. (1989). The Origin of Strategy. *Harvard Business Review,* November-December: 139–143.

perspective, the most important feature of industry structure is the degree of *concentration* of the industry—that is, the percentage of production capacity and resulting market share controlled by the top few firms.

The industrial organization perspective studies the structure of industries.

Economic research in this field has given rise to what is commonly called the structure-conduct-performance (SCP) paradigm in strategic management. The SCP paradigm holds that the structure of an industry determines the conduct of firms in the industry (*conduct* is the industrial organization term for a firm's strategy) and their resulting financial performance. In essence, the SCP paradigm argues that the strategies that managers devise for an individual firm are not likely to be significant determinants of their firm's performance. Rather, the relative size of the firm's asset base (i.e., its share of total production capacity) within its industry will primarily determine a firm's profitability. In effect, the larger the relative size of a firm's asset base within its industry—or in other words, the greater the share of industry assets concentrated in the firm—the better its relative performance will be.

Industrial organization economics has influenced the development of strategic management theory in several ways. Most fundamentally, it introduced the notion that the performance of a firm may depend more on the size of the asset base that a firm previously put in place, and less on a firm's current strategy. In addition, the industrial organization perspective is the foundation for Michael Porter's "five competitive forces" model for analyzing industry structures. In this model, a firm's profitability is also influenced by its size relative to its industry rivals, suppliers, and customers. (Porter's five competitive forces model is discussed in Chapter 9.)

Further investigations by strategic management researchers in the 1980s resulted in an important extension to the concept of industry structures. This research established that in many industries the strategy and performance of firms is not likely to be strictly determined by the relative size of a given firm's asset base within its industry. Rather, firms are likely to pursue various kinds of strategies within an industry, and an industry may include several clusters of firms pursuing essentially similar strategies. These clusters of firms pursuing similar strategies are called **strategic groups.**[3] Research into strategic groups shows that the relative performance of firms within an industry depends both on the strategic group a firm belongs to and on the relative size of the asset base of the firm within its strategic group.

Competence-based strategic management draws on the industrial organization perspective by recognizing that the relative size of a firm's asset base can strongly affect firm performance in certain kinds of industries, but that this is a "special case" applicable only to certain kinds of industries. The relationship between the size of a firm's asset base and its financial performance is likely to be especially important, for example, in industries in which significant economies of scale may be obtained by building large-scale production capacity, as in a commodity-processing industry such as alumina ore mining or petroleum refining. However, while the focus of industrial organization theory is the physical or *tangible* asset base of a firm, in many industries the critical assets for achieving superior performance are *intangible* assets—like knowledge, brands, and supplier and customer relationships. Thus, the competence perspective also pays close attention to the *intangible asset structure* of an industry—for example, the relative depth and breadth of a firm's knowledge base or the extent of brand loyalty that a firm enjoys.

In addition, industrial organization theory only tries to explain the impact of *existing* industry structures on firm performance, while the competence perspective is vitally concerned with how industry structures of both tangible and intangible assets come into existence, how they are maintained, and how they may strengthen or erode in the future. Thus,

[3] Daems, H. and H. Thomas, Eds. (1994). *Strategic Groups, Strategic Moves and Performance.* Oxford: Elsevier Science.

the competence perspective takes a more comprehensive and dynamic view of industry structures than does industrial organization economics.

Moreover, the competence perspective further extends the notion of strategic groups by grouping firms within an industry on the basis of their competence building and leveraging activities. As we discuss further in Chapter 5, competence-based strategic management identifies clusters of firms within an industry that have similar or diverging patterns of competence building and leveraging over time. This approach to grouping firms within an industry helps to identify not only firms that are currently competitors (those with similar competence leveraging activities), but also firms that will become competitors in the future (firms with converging competence building activities) and firms that will remain competitors only for a limited period of time (firms with diverging competence building activities).

Porter's Value Chain Model and Generic Strategies

Michael Porter's model of the value chain is one of the best-known and widely applied models of a firm's value-creation processes (see Figure 3.2). It describes the firm as a set of sequential activities that use the assets of a firm to produce, market, deliver, and support a firm's product offers. The value chain model contributes several ideas to competence-based management theory.

First, the value chain model identifies several kinds of value-creating activities that firms perform, and it distinguishes between (i) the primary activities through which value is created and (ii) the support activities that are needed to successfully perform a firm's primary activities. Second, the value chain model recognizes that activities performed in one stage of the value chain model affect later activities in the value chain, and therefore that the value created by a value chain depends on the effective coordination of all concerned activities. In effect, the value chain suggests that the different activities in a firm's value-creation processes are systemically interrelated. Thus, the value chain model

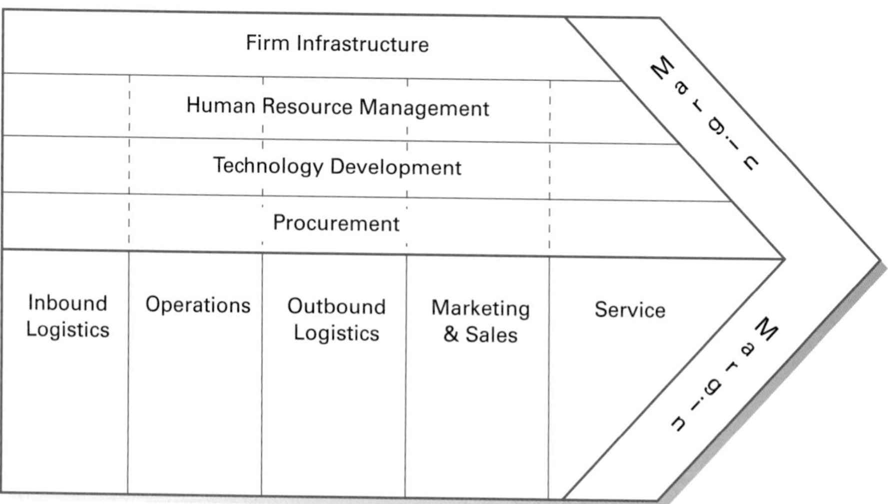

FIGURE 3.2 Porter's Model of the Value Chain

Source: Porter, Michael E. (1998). *Competitive Advantage: Creating and Sustaining Superior Performance.* New York: Free Press.

implicitly represents value creation as a system property—a notion that is explicitly adopted as a foundational concept in competence-based strategic management theory.

The Porter framework contains three basic or "generic" strategies.

Porter also proposed that firms use their value chains to pursue one of three **generic strategies:** a cost leadership strategy, a differentiation strategy, and a focus strategy.

The **cost leadership strategy** aims at minimizing the costs of the products and services a firm brings to the marketplace. Manufacturing firms pursuing a cost leadership strategy follow policies of purchasing materials in large volumes to get low costs of inputs, mass producing a limited range of products, marketing nonbranded or privately branded goods or services (to avoid advertising costs), making extensive use of automation to maximize economies of scale, locating any manual production in low-wage areas of the world, and aggressive pricing to build and maintain market share. Discount retailers such as Aldi (Europe) and Trader Joe's (United States) apply similar cost-reduction policies in structuring and managing their value chains of purchasing, distribution, and retailing activities.

A **differentiation strategy** aims at maximizing the perceived value of a firm's product offers. In contrast to the cost-leadership strategy, the differentiation strategy does not place primary emphasis on minimizing the cost structure of a firm's value chain, but rather on putting together a value chain capable of creating well-differentiated products with high perceived value for certain kinds of customers. The economic rationale behind the differentiation strategy is that certain customers will be willing to pay a premium price for a well-differentiated product, and that the premium price will profitably compensate the firm for the costs of developing and producing differentiated products. Manufacturing firms pursuing a differentiation strategy typically adopt policies of continually updating and extending their product range, marketing branded goods supported by significant investments in advertising and brand building, and providing high service and support levels. Retailers such as Nordstrom's department stores in the United States pursue a differentiation advantage by offering superior quality goods sold in upscale retailing environments and supported by high levels of customer service.

In a **focus strategy,** a firm focuses on a limited set of customers, and through either a cost leadership or a differentiation strategy or a combination of both, it tries to gain a competitive advantage over other firms pursuing either cost leadership or differentiation strategies on a broader industry-wide basis. For example, specialized hospitals, such as those that provide only plastic surgery or pediatric medical services, follow a focus strategy and often enjoy a competitive advantage over general hospitals in attracting the customers they are focused on serving.

In explaining his three generic strategies, Porter warned firms not to try to pursue a mix of generic strategies. Porter especially criticized attempts to mix cost leadership and differentiation strategies, which he argued usually results in a firm becoming "stuck in the middle"—creating high-priced but inadequately differentiated products that offer too little value to customers.

The competence perspective takes a view of competitive strategies that is different in one important respect from the three generic strategies advanced by Porter. While recognizing that pure cost leadership or differentiation strategies may occasionally be successful under some special market conditions, the competence perspective holds that to be successful in most product markets today, firms must offer well-differentiated products at competitive prices. Competence-based strategic management therefore assumes that the challenge most strategic managers face is developing an organization's ability to create well-differentiated products—and bringing those products to market profitably while selling at competitive prices. Thus, instead of counseling strategic managers to make a clear choice between cost leadership and differentiation strategies, the competence perspective focuses managers' attention on identifying and developing new approaches to product creation and realization that can meet the challenge of effectively combining cost leadership and product differentiation. (For example, Chapter 8 discusses the use of modularity in designing, developing, and producing products that are well-differentiated and that can be sold profitably at competitive prices.)

Strategic Marketing

The strategic marketing approach looks at the output side of competition.

The strategic marketing perspective, represented by authors such as Aaker,[4] Day,[5] and Levitt,[6] proposes an external, market-oriented approach to strategy that focuses the attention of the strategic managers on the "output side" of competition—in effect, on a firm's intended customers. Within this perspective, identifying and responding to customer needs and preferences is regarded as the central issue in strategy. Strategic managers should therefore be proactive with respect to markets. They should not only respond to changes in the market, but also try to influence the evolution of markets. Strategic managers should therefore ensure that the content of their firm's management information systems and control systems is sharply focused on tracking and analyzing market trends. Strategic planning, typically based on annually revised market forecasts, should therefore be complemented with strategic decision making based on real-time market data and analyses.

The competence perspective shares strategic marketing's essentially entrepreneurial approach to strategy making—an approach that takes the necessity of creating value for targeted customers as its starting point and allows for new initiatives and "emergent strategies" in response to changes in customer preferences. Strategic management should therefore not be exclusively focused on defining and committing to a single strategy for a firm in its markets, but should be capable of imagining and developing multiple market strategies, pursued either simultaneously or successively in responding to multiple and evolving market preferences. Because strategies can only be implemented successfully if they are internally consistent and coherent, however, strategic managers must also devise organizational structures and processes for coordinating effectively the potentially broad range of operations needed to support the various strategies a firm undertakes or might undertake in its markets. Thus, competence-based strategy also emphasizes the importance of developing management processes through which strategic managers are able to coordinate a firm's distinctive system of resources and capabilities in continuous processes of product creation and realization.

The Resource-Base View

Building on early writings by Selznick[7] and Penrose[8] and further work in the 1980s by Wernerfelt,[9] the resource-base view (RBV) essentially argues that any form of sustainable competitive advantage that a firm may develop results from the unique resource endowments of the firm. This view of the importance of a firm's resources is reflected in the value-resources-imitability-organization (VRIO) framework popularized by Barney,[10]

[4] Aaker, D. A. (1992). *Developing Business Strategies.* New York: John Wiley & Sons, Inc.

[5] Day, G. S. (1984). *Strategic Market Planning: The Pursuit of Competitive Advantage.* St. Paul, MN: West Publishing Company.

[6] Levitt, T. A. (1960). Marketing Myopia. *Harvard Business Review,* July–August: 45.

[7] Selznick, P. (1957). *Leadership in Administration.* Evanston, IL: Row, Peterson.

[8] Penrose, E. T. (1959). *The Theory of the Growth of the Firm.* Oxford: Basil Blackwell.

[9] Wernerfelt, B. (1984). A Resource-Based View of the Firm. *Strategic Management Journal,* 5, 171–180.

[10] Barney, J. B. (1997). *Gaining and Sustaining Competitive Advantage.* Reading, MA: Addison-Wesley, 145–162.

which proposes that an analysis of a firm's internal strengths and weaknesses should address four questions about the nature and use of a firm's resources:

1. The question of *value:* Do a firm's resources enable the firm to respond to environmental opportunities and threats?
2. The question of *rareness:* How many competing firms already possess such valuable resources?
3. The question of *imitability:* Do firms that lack a valuable resource face a cost disadvantage in obtaining it compared to firms that already possess it?
4. The question of *organization:* Is a firm organized to exploit the full competitive potential of its resources?

The resource-base view tries to understand the kinds of resources that are strategically important.

The key concepts in the RBV framework about what makes resources sources of a sustainable competitive advantage are summarized in a model developed by Peteraf. In this model, four properties of resources are necessary in creating a sustainable competitive advantage and thereby enabling a firm to earn above-average profits.[11] First of all, the resources a firm uses must be *heterogeneous.* In other words, the resources that a firm acquires and develops for its value-creation processes must be distinctive and different from the resources used by or available to other firms. Second, the heterogeneous resources that make a firm successful must originate in *imperfect factor markets,* which means that a competing firm either cannot acquire the distinctive resources that a successful firm possesses or must pay such a high price for such resources that it cannot subsequently earn an economic profit. Third, the distinctive resources that make a firm successful must be *imperfectly imitable and substitutable,* so that competing firms cannot imitate the successful firm's resources or substitute other resources in their value-creation processes. Fourth, the distinctive resources of the successful firm must be subject to *imperfect mobility,* so that the key resources of the successful firm cannot easily leave the firm and thus will remain inside the firm.

Grant, another leading researcher within the RBV, made an important distinction between a firm's *resources* and its *capabilities.*[12] Grant characterizes resources as inputs to a production process, but notes that only some resources in a firm are actually inputs to a productive process. In order to produce anything, resources must be coordinated, and a capability is what results when a firm can coordinate its resources effectively in performing some task or activity. In Grant's important extension of the RBV, resources are essential to the creation of a firm's capabilities, but a firm's capabilities are the source of any sustainable competitive advantage a firm achieves in its markets.

The competence-based perspective shares with the RBV an understanding that an organization's resources are *necessary* ingredients of competitive success. Therefore managers must pay close attention to an organization's processes for acquiring and developing unique, hard-to-imitate, and useful resources for its value-creation processes. However, the competence perspective also shares with economics the understanding that the *exchange value* (or market value) of a resource, which the RBV strongly emphasizes in its analyses, is not identical with its *value in use.* The real value of a resource to an organization comes from the uses to which a resource can be applied within an organization and the way the use of a resource is coordinated with uses of other resources. In effect, the strategic value of a resource is determined by the way a resource is embedded

[11] Mollona, E. (1998). Resource Accumulation Systems, Corporate Competence Evolution and Emergent Strategic Behaviour: A Feedback Approach. Working paper, London Business School, University of London, 5.

[12] Grant, R. M. (1991). The Resource-Based Theory of Competitive Advantage: Implications for Strategy Formulation. *California Management Review,* 33(3), 114–135.

and used within a *system of resources and activities* in an organization. Thus, the competence perspective holds that no analysis of resources alone would be sufficient to explain any competitive advantage that a firm may have. Only a full analysis of an organization's resources *and* the way they are deployed and coordinated with other resources can explain competitive advantage.

Further, the competence perspective also differs from the RBV by recognizing that a resource need not be contained within a firm to contribute to the creation of competitive advantage. Both *firm-addressable resources* (resources outside the firm that a firm can access when needed) and *firm-specific resources* (resources inside the firm) can be sources of competitive advantage if they are deployed and coordinated more effectively by a firm than by other firms in its industry. Thus, even ordinary resources readily available in the marketplace can contribute to the creation of competitive advantage if a firm's managers can devise better strategies than their competitors for deploying and coordinating those resources. For this reason, Grant's distinction between resources and capabilities is critical to understanding the role of resources in creating competitive advantage. Only through management's capabilities in deploying and coordinating resources can resources—whether unique to a firm or commonly available in a market—contribute to a firm's competitive advantage.

Evolutionary Economic and Dynamic Capabilities Perspectives

The resource-base view of the firm introduced into strategic thinking a conceptualization of firms as heterogeneous accumulations of resources and capabilities. About the same time, Nelson and Winter introduced an evolutionary economic perspective with a similar focus on a firm's distinctive capabilities.[13] Drawing analogies from evolutionary theory in biology, this perspective compares organizational routines in a firm to genes in an organism, and it explains the survival of a firm in a changing competitive environment in terms of genetic variation, selection, and retention. As an organization's environment changes, the genetic makeup of the organization (i.e., the endowment of routines it can use in responding to its environment) must vary. The competitive environment then "selects" which organizations will survive and which will not. Those organizations with routines that are capable of responding effectively to the competitive challenges of their environment are then "retained," or allowed to survive at least until the next wave of environmental change.

The dynamic capabilities perspective studies the path dependency of an organization's capabilities.

Subsequently, Teece, Pisano, and Shuen developed a dynamic perspective on organizational capabilities, suggesting that sustaining an organization's ability to create value in environments with significant change depends on the current capabilities of its internal technological, organizational, and managerial processes.[14] Sustaining value creation depends on a organization's ability to identify new opportunities and to organize effective and efficient processes to respond to these opportunities. The dynamic capabilities framework further argues that creating a competitive advantage requires distinctive ways of coordinating resources and capabilities. How a firm tries to coordinate those resources will be shaped both by the firm's current resource base and by the evolutionary path the firm has followed up to the current moment. In effect, the capabilities a firm has and can develop in the future are always **path dependent**—largely determined by prior evolutions in its capabilities—and cannot be changed quickly. Thus, a firm's capabilities are dynamic, but the kinds of new capabilities a firm can build and the rate at which the firm can build new capabilities are

[13] Nelson, R. and S. Winter. (1982). *An Evolutionary Theory of Economic Change.* Cambridge, MA: Harvard University Press.

[14] Teece, D. J., G. Pisano, et al. (1997). Dynamic Capabilities and Strategic Management. *Strategic Management Journal,* 18(7), 509–533.

constrained by its current capabilities, which are the result of its evolutionary path. Within the dynamic capabilities perspective, competitive advantage results when one firm develops current capabilities that are highly effective in responding to its environment, but other firms are unable to quickly replicate those capabilities.

The competence perspective shares with the evolutionary and dynamic capabilities perspectives an appreciation of the central role of organizational routines in using resources and creating capabilities, and it also agrees that a firm's survival will depend on its ability to use its routines and capabilities to pursue opportunities or to counter threats in its environment. At the heart of this view is the requirement that strategic managers must be able to synchronize a firm's internal dynamics of capability development and use with the dynamics of its external environment. In this sense, these perspectives—and one could argue, *all* perspectives on strategy—are essentially *contingency theories,* because they hold that achieving competitive success is contingent on achieving the best possible alignment or "fit" of the capabilities of an organization with the demands of its environment.

What the competence perspective adds to the evolutionary and dynamic capabilities perspectives is recognition of the fundamental role of managers' own cognitive processes in determining the path dependency of organizational capability development. In the competence perspective, the ideas and beliefs of strategic managers may create an organizational "mindset" that constrains the ability of a firm to identify and develop new capabilities, or they may act as a stimulus to the organization to actively pursue new capabilities. Thus, while the evolutionary and dynamic capabilities perspectives say little about the potential for managers to influence the path dependency of their organizations, the competence perspective holds that the "corporate imagination" of managers may be able to lead an organization's capability building processes in new directions and to accelerate its processes for building new capabilities. In essence, the competence perspective treats managerial cognitive processes as critically important in overcoming the constraints of path dependency and in choosing the best path for developing new capabilities.

Mintzberg's Theory of Emergent Strategies

Mintzberg argued that organizations have both deliberate and emergent strategies.

In his theory of emergent strategy, Mintzberg focuses on the processes through which organizations devise strategies and asks the question, "How do strategies form in organizations?"[15] Mintzberg's extensive research on the strategy process suggests that different types of strategies will result or "emerge" from different types of underlying processes. Further, Mintzberg also argues that whatever the type of strategy an organization adopts, its *intended strategy* (the strategy it planned) will always be different in important respects from its *realized strategy* (the strategy it actually implemented). When one compares the intended and realized strategies of an organization, it then becomes possible to distinguish between **deliberate strategies** (strategies that are implemented as intended) and **emergent strategies** (strategies that are implemented in the absence of an intended strategy or instead of an intended strategy).

Of course, pure forms of deliberate or emergent strategies rarely occur in practice. In most cases, the strategy that a firm follows will be a mix of "deliberateness" and "emergence." The various types of strategies actually followed in an organization will depend on the mix of deliberateness *versus* emergence in its actions. Mintzberg characterized the possible types of strategy as planned, entrepreneurial, ideological, umbrella, process, unconnected, consensus, or imposed strategy, in descending order of their deliberateness and ascending order of their emergence.

[15] Mintzberg, H. (1994). *The Rise and Fall of Strategic Planning.* New York: Prentice Hall; Mintzberg, H. and J. A. Waters. (1985). Of Strategies, Deliberate and Emergent. *Strategic Management Journal,* 6, 257–272.

Competence-based strategic management theory recognizes that different kinds of organizations use different kinds of strategy-making processes that lead to different kinds of strategies. It also shares Mintzberg's view that part of an organization's strategy is likely to be—and indeed even needs to be—emergent, because all managers (like all humans) have bounded rationality and thus face limits on their ability to represent, analyze, and plan responses to a complex and dynamic environment. Thus, some part of an organization's strategy—perhaps even the major part—will necessarily be more emergent than planned. At the same time, the competence perspective also recognizes that even an emergent strategy requires the use of some existing resources and capabilities, and acquiring resources and developing capabilities takes time and therefore requires at least some planning. Thus, in the competence perspective, planning and emergence are not seen as opposites, but rather as systemically interrelated processes. In dynamic environments, an organization's processes for building and leveraging competences must include *planning for emergence.* Strategic managers must plan today to acquire the resources, develop the capabilities, and put in place management processes that will support a range of emergent strategies that their organization may pursue in the future.

Game Theory

Game theory studies incentives for cooperation and competition among individuals.

The strategy a firm pursues cannot be decided without taking into account the current strategies and likely future strategies of competitors. A firm's strategy must be determined at least in part by the need to respond to competitors' strategies, and it will in turn influence the strategies that competitors pursue. Understanding and influencing interactions among competitors is therefore one of the central challenges in strategy theory.

Game theory is the branch of economics that analyzes incentives for competition and cooperation between interacting parties and ways in which each party may seek to optimize achievement of its goals through its interactions with another party. A game theoretic analysis can reveal how optimal attainment of goals can depend on achieving a balance between each individual's self-interest and the common interests of all interacting parties. When all parties in "repeated games" devise ways of interacting that enable each party to realize the greatest possible benefit on an ongoing basis, the parties are said to converge to a stable "Nash equilibrium" in which each party will voluntarily continue their established pattern of interaction.

Competence theory shares with game theory the recognition that interacting parties are usually better off when they can balance competition and cooperation, at least in the context of repeated games. This insight lies at the core of the competence view of organizations as systems for both value creation and value distribution. In contrast to Porter's five competitive forces model (discussed in Chapter 9) in which industry competitors, suppliers, and customers compete to maximize their own individual benefit in their interactions, the competence perspective argues that the participants in value-creation processes are likely to be better off individually and collectively if they cooperate to improve the capability of their processes for creating value. In essence, while the Porter model represents interactions between the parties in an industry as a **zero-sum game** in which one party can only gain at the expense of another party, the competence perspective argues that value-creation processes can be **positive-sum games** in which cooperative behavior can lead to better outcomes for all participants.

The task of strategic managers is therefore not just to define optimal objectives for the value-creation processes of their organization. They must also effectively *distribute* the value that the organization may create to all providers of resources to the organization's value-creation processes. Only by offering attractive prospects for goal attainment to all essential resource providers can an organization attract the best possible resources to its value-creation activities, and only through effective value distribution can an organization create a positive-sum game environment that invites cooperative behavior from the participants in its value-creation processes. Thus, a central challenge to strategic managers in the competence perspective is imagining and implementing Strategic Logics for positive-sum value-creation and value-distribution processes that are more effective at creating value on a sustained basis than the value-creation and value-distribution schemes of their competitors.

Core Competence Perspective

Prahalad and Hamel's notion of core competence

In a series of influential articles in the late 1980s and early 1990s, Prahalad and Hamel introduced a notion of the "core competence" of an organization. They describe a core competence as "... the collective learning in the organization, especially [about] how to coordinate diverse production skills and integrate multiple streams of technology."[16] In the Prahalad and Hamel view, companies can use their core competences to create value on an ongoing basis to bring to market a variety of products that address changing market needs and preferences.

The competence perspective developed in this book shares Prahalad and Hamel's focus on an organization's ability to coordinate its various skills effectively and to maintain high levels of organizational learning. The competence perspective differs from Prahalad and Hamel's approach, however, in its avoidance of the notion that an organization can actually have a "core competence." In the competence perspective, the competence of an organization results from the effective deployment and coordination of a *system* of interrelated, interdependent resources and capabilities. In an organization as a system of interacting resources and capabilities, it is unlikely that any single resource or capability or even a limited set of resources and capabilities can neatly be identified as the "core" of the organization's competence. Competence is rather seen as a *system property* of an organization that is not neatly decomposable into "core" and "noncore" elements. All resources and capabilities of an organization must be aligned and balanced in order to create competence, and in this sense none can actually be said to be more "core" than others.

Nevertheless, it is certainly true that an organization may develop specific capabilities that may bring important benefits to a firm's product offers and thus enhance its value-creation processes. Philips' capabilities in high-quality manufacturing or Sony's capabilities in miniaturizing product designs are examples of important capabilities that clearly enhance both firms' product offers, but neither of these capabilities can be neatly separated from the many other capabilities of these firms and called the "core" of their respective competences.

Strategic Flexibility and Strategic Options Perspectives

Strategic flexibility depends on both resource flexibility and coordination flexibility.

An important perspective developed in the 1990s is that strategic managers should improve the **strategic flexibility** of their organization to respond to the diverse demands that may result from the complexity, uncertainty, and change in the organization's environment.[17] In this perspective, a firm's strategic flexibility to respond to change can be understood as depending jointly on (i) the intrinsic *resource flexibility* of the resources and capabilities available to the firm, and (ii) the *coordination flexibility* of managers in redefining strategies for the use of the resources available to the firm and in reconfiguring

[16] Hamel, G. and C. K. Prahalad. (1993). Strategy As Stretch and Leverage. *Harvard Business Review*, March–April: 75–84.

[17] Sanchez, R. and J. T. Mahoney. (1996). Modularity, Flexibility, and Knowledge Management in Product and Organization Design. *Strategic Management Journal*, 17(Winter Special Issue), 63–76.

and redeploying appropriate "resource chains" in support of these strategies.[18] Strategic flexibility is created when the resource and coordination flexibilities that an organization develops give it identifiable **strategic options** to pursue alternative courses of action in its environment (i.e., alternative value-creation processes). In dynamic and complex environments with significant levels of uncertainty, the ability of a firm to respond to a range of possible opportunities or threats will be determined by the set of strategic options for action it previously created for itself.

The concept of strategic flexibility is an integral part of the competence view of strategic management. Given the human cognitive limitations of managers and their resulting inability to fully analyze and reliably predict all future changes in the environment of a firm, developing a range of strategic options for action is the only feasible approach to managing the irreducible uncertainties and ambiguities of a dynamic environment. Of course, the cognitive challenge to strategic managers in this process is imagining the *range of possible futures* a firm may face, and then defining and developing the most appropriate set of strategic options for taking action in those futures. A further challenge is putting in place management processes that can quickly redirect a firm's current activities to new courses of action as the environment of the firm evolves.

3.2 THE COMPETENCE-BASED APPROACH TO STRATEGIC MANAGEMENT

Fundamental concepts of competence-based theory

As noted in Section 3.1, the competence-based approach to strategic management incorporates and benefits from a number of important ideas developed in prior theories and perspectives on strategic management. In this section, we discuss some further essential elements in the competence-based approach. This discussion provides further explanations of the ways in which the competence perspective devises strategies that can be effective in responding to the dynamic, systemic, cognitive, and holistic nature of organizations and their environments.

Perceiving Opportunities for Value Creation

The beginning of the strategic management process is the perception by a firm's managers that opportunities exist to create value by bringing to market product offers that can serve the needs and preferences of potential customers. The perception of value-creating opportunities by managers has both external and internal dimensions. The external dimension depends on managers' perceptions of customer needs and preferences that a firm could serve by creating and realizing product offers. The internal dimension depends on managers' ability to imagine ways of attracting the resources and developing the capabilities needed to create and realize appropriate product offers. In evaluating these internal and external dimensions of opportunities for value creation, managers must perform two basic decision making processes: a process that determines the choice set of value-creation opportunities thought to be available to the organization (a process one might call the "marketing imagination" of the firm), and a process of choosing the most attractive opportunities (among those judged feasible) within the choice set.

Developing Sustainable Processes for Value Creation

The market opportunities selected by managers from the choice set thought to be available to a firm must then be developed. Developing opportunities for value creation requires three Core Processes through which a firm both builds and leverages its competences:

[18] Sanchez, Ron. (1993). Strategic Flexibility, Firm Organization, and Managerial Work in Dynamic Markets: A Strategic Options Perspective, *Advances in Strategic Management,* 9, 251–291; Sanchez, Ron. (1995). Strategic Flexibility in Product Competition. *Strategic Management Journal,* 16 (Summer special issue), 135–159.

- The *creation* of product offers (which includes service products)
- The *realization* of product offers, which includes all the processes involved in bringing developed products and services to targeted markets
- The *distribution of the value created* through successful product offers to the various providers of resources to the organization (i.e., its stakeholders) in order to sustain the organization's processes of product creation and realization

Competence building creates strategic options; competence leveraging exercises strategic options.

Carrying out these processes successfully and in a sustainable way requires building a "virtuous circle" of mutually reinforcing, positive-sum competence building and leveraging processes (see Figure 1.2 in Chapter 1). *Competence building* occurs when firms acquire or develop and learn how to use new and qualitatively different resources, capabilities, and ways of coordinating that determine the range of product offers it can create and realize. A firm's prior and ongoing competence building therefore determines the scope of its strategic options and thus its strategic flexibility to respond to opportunities and threats in its environment.

Competence leveraging occurs when a firm brings product offers to markets in ways that do not involve qualitative changes in the resources, capabilities, or modes of coordination used by the firm. In competence leveraging, a firm "exercises" and puts into action one or more of the strategic options created by its competence building.

Creating and realizing successful product offers depends fundamentally on the abilities of a firm's managers to imagine, evaluate, select, and undertake competence building and leveraging activities that will enable the firm to create and realize its intended product offerings. When managers are able to build and leverage appropriate competences, a firm can establish desirable market positions through its successful product offers. To maintain its market positions, strategic managers must also be able to imagine and put in place processes for distributing created value in appropriate kinds and amounts to the providers of resources. In this process, the market positions, competitive advantages, and value distribution policies that a firm establishes determine its ability to attract financial resources, loyal customers, and the best possible human resources and suppliers to its value-creation processes. Attracting superior resources then helps the organization build and leverage even better competences, which then leads to even better product offers, market positions, competitive advantages, and so on.

Aligning Value-Creation Processes with Competitive Environments

Designing strategies for sustained value creation

Creating successful and sustainable value-creation processes, market positions, and competitive advantages depends on achieving effective alignment of a firm's competence building and leveraging processes with its competitive environment. Although competitive environments can vary widely in their particular features, competitive environments can be fundamentally distinguished as being of four basic types, depending on the nature, speed, and uncertainty of change in a given environment: stable, evolving, dynamic, or transforming environments.

Stable environments are characterized by the lack of significant change in market needs, customer preferences, available or applied technologies, distribution channels, product offers, and competitors. The primary focus of strategic managers in stable environments will generally be achieving maximum cost efficiency in their firm's current competence leveraging activities.

Evolving environments are characterized by clear patterns of change in market needs, customer preferences, available or applied technologies, distribution channels, product offers, or competitors. The changes in an evolving environment are largely predictable and pose relatively little uncertainty for strategic decision makers. The main challenge for strategic managers in an evolving environment is developing the new capabilities, market positions, and other sources of competitive advantage needed to ensure a firm's smooth transition from current to future conditions in the environment.

Dynamic environments are characterized by rapid changes in market needs, customer preferences, available or applied technologies, distribution channels, product offers, or competitors, any or all of which confront strategic managers with high levels of irreducible uncertainty. This uncertainty may affect not just the future environment of an organization, but also its present environment. In highly dynamic environments, even current market needs and customer preferences may be unclear, technologies may be developing rapidly and creating significant technological uncertainties, and new competitors may be entering and existing competitors exiting at high or unpredictable rates. The main challenge for strategic managers in a dynamic environment is therefore identifying and creating a range of strategic options that improve the flexibility of the firm to adapt to a variety of alternative futures.

Transforming environments are characterized by radical, fundamental changes not just in the important elements of the environment, but also in the relationships among environmental elements as well. This kind of change "breaks the rules" of the current competitive game and creates a new set of competitive or cooperative relationships among organizations in an industry. Transforming changes can include, for example, the emergence of totally new marketing approaches or distribution channels, the evolution of new market segments, or the introduction of radically new product concepts that deliver unprecedented value to market at prices not thought possible earlier. The substantial uncertainty and surprise in transformative environments are likely to require that strategic managers substantially reorient the goals of the organization, reconstruct the organization's resource base and management processes, and do so within a limited window of opportunity.

Strategic Managers As Designers of Organizations As Systems for Value Creation

Organizations as systems, and strategic managers as system designers

Competence-based strategic management theory represents organizations as open systems of resources and resource flows that are deployed and coordinated in processes for value creation. In advancing this view of organizations, it is essential to remember that systems are cognitive constructs. In effect, a system is only recognized when an observer understands that certain entities are interacting and have at least some degree of interdependence. In other words, an observer must be able to detect that what goes on in one entity affects another entity, which may lead to changes in yet another entity, which may eventually lead to further changes in the first entity, and so on.

System design is the cognitive process of intentionally selecting the entities (resources) that will comprise the elements of an organization as a system and of defining the interactions that will take place between the selected system elements. System designers must also recognize and establish interactions that take place across the "boundary" of the organization as a system—that is, interactions between elements that are inside the system and elements that are in the environment outside the system. Strategic managers as system designers must also be able to design organizations that are adaptive systems, also called "living systems."[19] To be an adaptive system, an organization must be capable of generating the "requisite variety"[20] of actions needed to respond effectively to the complex, changing, and often unpredictable conditions in its environment.

[19] de Geus, A. (1997). *The Living Company: Growth, Learning and Longevity in Business.* London: Nicholas Brealey Publishing.

[20] Ashby, W. R. (1956). *An Introduction to Cybernetics.* London: Chapman and Hall.

To guide strategic managers in their work as system designers, competence-based strategic management defines a number of system design principles that managers should apply in designing organizations as adaptive and largely self-managing systems. (These system design principles are introduced throughout the remainder of this book.) To maintain the ability of an organization to function as an adaptive system, strategic managers must make sure that the organization is capable of executing the best mix of deliberate and emergent strategies. Making sure that these system design principles are constantly being honored in the design and functioning of an organization is the best way to ensure this capability. A clear focus on continuously honoring these system design principles for adaptive systems allows strategic managers to carry out their tasks on a truly strategic level and helps them to avoid falling into the trap of trying to "micro-manage" an organization to success.[21]

Competition As a Contest Between Managers' Cognitive Processes

As explained in Chapter 1, the competence-based perspective uses the term *Strategic Logic* to refer to the goals that an organization sets for itself and to the activities through which the organization believes it can best achieve its goals. Strategic managers of an organization are ultimately responsible for defining and communicating the Strategic Logic of an organization.

To carry out this responsibility, strategic managers must identify the set of goals that the organization could feasibly pursue, and they must then choose which of those goals the organization will actually pursue. To choose which goals an organization will pursue, strategic managers must decide which processes for value creation the organization could feasibly undertake—its choice set of *strategic options*—and which would offer the organization its best chances for success in its chosen product markets. Strategic managers must also determine the kinds of resources needed to undertake those value-creation processes, how the required kinds of resources can be attracted to or induced to cooperate with the organization in its value-creation processes, and how those resources can be coordinated most effectively.

Moreover, for the greatest chance of success, the Strategic Logic of an organization must be clearly understood and fully supported by all participants in the organization's value-creation processes. To induce essential resource providers to participate in and fully support an organization's Strategic Logic for value-creation processes, strategic managers must devise a plan for value distribution that provides an attractive level of goal attainment for all essential resource providers. Thus, strategic managers must understand what forms of value—financial rewards, attractive work conditions, job security, career development opportunities, recognition received for work performed, pride in belonging to the organization, etc.—can provide adequate goal attainment for each essential resource provider. Strategic managers must then devise processes for distributing an appropriate form and adequate share of the value that the organization creates to all providers of essential resources. Strategic managers must also communicate clearly both the organization's goals for value creation and its plan for value distribution to all essential resource providers.

The central role of managerial cognition in competition

To devise a viable Strategic Logic, strategic managers must contend with both the actual and possible actions of competitors in an organization's external environment and reconcile the often conflicting interests of the diverse resource providers that participate in its internal processes. Moreover, both external and internal environments of organizations are typically subject to high levels of complexity, change, and uncertainty. The task of defining and putting into action a successful Strategic Logic for value creation and distribution is often a

[21] Mollona, E. (1998). Resource Accumulation Systems, Corporate Competence Evolution and Emergent Strategic Behaviour. A Feedback Approach. Working paper, London Business School, University of London.

challenge. The inherent limitations of the imperfect information available to managers and the bounded rationality of the human mind mean that no manager can ever perfectly solve an organization's dynamic "situational puzzle"[22] and devise a truly "optimal" Strategic Logic. Within these limitations, strategic managers must strive to devise a better Strategic Logic for their own organization than the Strategic Logics devised by strategic managers in competing organizations. In this sense, the competence-based perspective views competition between organizations as essentially a *contest between the cognitive processes of strategic managers* in competing organizations to devise superior Strategic Logics that can become the basis for sustained success in achieving the goals of their respective organizations.

Strategy As "Stretch and Leverage"

To lead an organization in achieving its goals on a sustained basis, strategic managers must define and develop both a Strategic Logic that is effective in creating value in the organization's current product and resource markets, and Strategic Logics that will be effective in creating value in the organization's future product and resource markets. Thus, within the competence perspective, strategic managers must lead an organization not just in leveraging its current competences, but also in building new competences for the future.

This need for strategic managers to lead their organizations in both competence building and competence leveraging is what Hamel and Prahalad have in mind when they describe strategy as consisting of both "stretch and leverage."[23] Leading an organization to stretch beyond its current competences requires that strategic managers be able to envision new kinds of Strategic Logics for value creation and distribution. New Strategic Logics may involve innovative management processes for coordinating resources, as well as new kinds of resources that could enable new kinds of value-creation processes. In this sense, leading processes for competence building for the future is the essence of the "strategic vision" that strategic managers must contribute to their organizations.

[22] Bogaert, I., R. Martens, et al. (1994). Strategy As a Situational Puzzle: The Fit of Components. In G. Hamel and A. Heene (Eds.), *Competence-Based Competition.* Chichester, England: John Wiley & Sons Ltd., 57–74.

[23] Hamel, G. and C. K. Prahalad. (1993). Strategy As Stretch and Leverage. *Harvard Business Review,* March–April: 75–84.

KEY TERMS AND CONCEPTS

strategic groups Clusters of firms pursuing similar strategies within an industry.

generic strategies Michael Porter's view of three basic kinds of strategies—cost leadership, differentiation, or focus—that organizations should select and pursue.

cost leadership strategy A generic strategy based on minimizing the costs of products and services a firm brings to market.

differentiation strategy A generic strategy that tries to maximize the perceived value of a firm's products and services.

focus strategy A generic strategy in which a firm focuses on a limited set of customers and fine-tunes its products and services to serve the needs of those customers.

path dependency The notion that a firm's future capability development will be constrained to follow a trajectory that is largely determined by its past capability development.

deliberate strategy A strategy that has been implemented as intended.

emergent strategy A strategy that has been implemented in the absence of or instead of a deliberate strategy.

zero-sum game A competitive interaction in which one party can only gain at the expense of another party.

positive-sum game A cooperative interaction in which both parties can gain.

strategic flexibility The set of strategic options that an organization has created for itself.

strategic options The courses of action that an organization can feasibly undertake now or in the future.

REVIEW QUESTIONS

1. What concerns of managers were the focus of the general management and business policy perspective?
2. What are the main implications of the structure-conduct-performance paradigm for strategic management?
3. What are the main implications of the resource-based view for strategic management?
4. What insights do the evolutionary economic and dynamic capabilities perspectives offer for strategic management?
5. How does Mintzberg's view of firm strategies differ from earlier views?
6. What is the relevance of the strategic flexibility perspective for managers' cognitive processes?
7. What are the defining characteristics of the competence-based perspective of strategic management?

PART III

THE COMPETENCE-BASED APPROACH TO STRATEGIC MANAGEMENT

CHAPTER 4

DESIGNING AND MANAGING ORGANIZATIONS AS OPEN SYSTEMS FOR VALUE CREATION

INTRODUCTION

In the previous chapter, we reviewed a number of ideas that made important contributions to the evolution of thinking about strategic management. We also discussed a number of ways in which the competence-based perspective on strategic management introduces and integrates some further dynamic, systemic, cognitive, and holistic concepts about strategic management. The major sources of dynamics in an organization's environment are discussed further in Chapter 9, the cognitive challenges of strategic management are explored in Chapter 10, and holistic dimensions are addressed in Chapters 7 and 15. In the present chapter, we investigate some fundamental aspects of the nature and behavior of organizations as *open systems.*

We first discuss the *embeddedness and co-evolution* of organizations in larger systems—in product and resource markets, strategic groups, industries, economies, and society. We then consider the essential challenge of strategic management—managing the building and leveraging of competences by organizations as open systems for value creation and distribution. We then consider some of the critical *system properties* of organizations that both enable and constrain the ability of an organization to build and leverage competences. We then consider how the systemic nature of organizations requires strategic managers not just to define the *content* of an organization's current goals for value creation and distribution, but also to define, develop, and support the *processes* through which the organization's competences to create value will be built, leveraged, maintained, and defended. Each of these aspects of organizations requires close attention from strategic managers if their organization is to function effectively as a system for sustainable value creation and distribution.

4.1 ORGANIZATIONS AS SYSTEMS EMBEDDED IN AND CO-EVOLVING WITH LARGER SYSTEMS

A *system* is said to exist when a collection of entities (people, things, ideas) interact in ways that create interdependencies between the entities. As we will discuss more fully here, the competence perspective characterizes an organization as a system of resources (human resources, tangible resources, intangible resources) that interact and become interdependent in a variety of ways, the most important of which are determined by the organization's management processes, as suggested in Figure 4.1 (which is a simplified version of Figure 1.1 in Chapter 1). Inherent in this concept of an organization as a system of interacting resources is the notion of a *boundary* that separates those resources that are part of the organization from those that are not, as indicated in Figure 4.1.

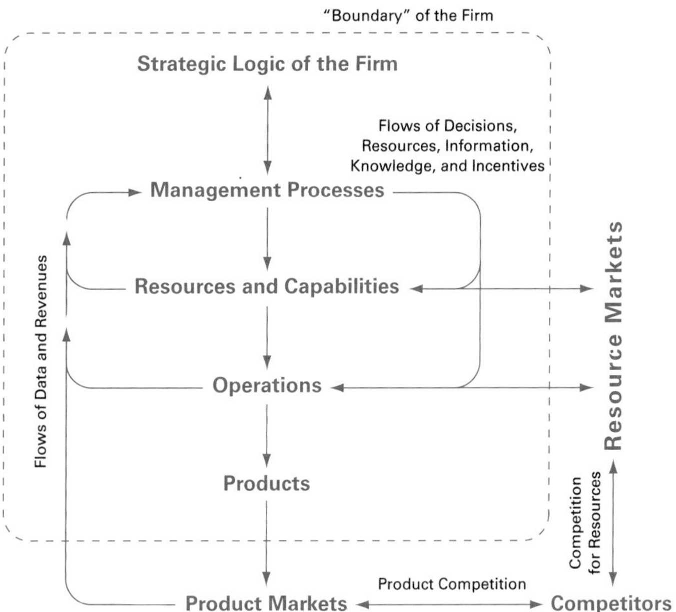

FIGURE 4.1 View of the Firm as an Open System

However, the competence perspective also views an organization as an *open system* of resource stocks and flows. This means that an organization will have important interactions across its boundaries, interactions between the resources within an organization and the resources in the environment of the organization. As shown in Figure 4.1, an organization provides products and services to its product markets, and resources (sales revenues) and market data (but possibly also more intangible resources like reputation and customer loyalty) flow from product markets into an organization. Similarly, resources flow between an organization and its resource markets (potential employees, suppliers, technologies, financial resources, energy). Organizations as open systems therefore depend for their survival on exchanges of resources with both product markets and resource markets in their environment. The dependency of an organization on resource exchanges with its environment in effect *embeds* an organization in its environment. Changes in the environment of an organization therefore often induce changes within an organization itself as a system, and changes within an organization may also lead to changes in the environment of an organization. In this sense, organizations tend to *co-evolve* with their environments.

The embedding and co-evolution of an organization with its environment occurs on several levels. An organization as an open system is embedded most directly in its product and resource markets, but it is also embedded in strategic groups within its industry, in its industry more broadly, in its national and regional economies, in the global economy, and in its society. Let us briefly consider some of the important ways in which an organization as an open system interacts with each of these levels of its environment.

An organization is embedded in its product and resource markets, strategic group, industry, and economy.

Product Markets and Resource Markets

All organizations must produce products or services that will be considered valuable by potential customers in the marketplace. If the products and services offered by an organization are perceived as sufficiently attractive by potential customers, they will exchange their resources for the organization's products or services. As we shall see in Chapter 6 when we discuss the Business Concept of an organization, these resources that customers may provide usually include revenues from sales of products, but may also include the time, energy, and feelings of loyalty that customers are willing to expend in the process of acquiring and using an organization's products and services.

To create and realize products and services for its targeted product markets, an organization must attract appropriate productive resources. Employees with specific skills and suppliers with capabilities to provide specific kinds of materials, components, and services must be attracted to the organization's product creation and realization processes. The organization may also have to attract information resources to identify its best opportunities for creating new products, as well as financial resources to fund its investments in developing products and production capacity. It may also need to secure licenses, permits, and forms of financial or legal support from local, regional, or national governments.

Strategic Groups

Strategic groups exist in both product and resource markets.

When an organization creates products and services and brings them to market, it is likely to find that it must compete against other organizations pursuing similar strategies—that is, other organizations trying to attract the same customers with the same or similar kinds of products. Because the strategies and resulting competitive interactions of these organizations will often influence them to adopt similar ways of transforming resources into products and services, such directly competing organizations constitute a *strategic group.* Thus, an organization is also embedded in the competitive system formed by the directly competing organizations in its strategic group.

The term *strategic groups* in strategic management has traditionally been used to refer to groups of organizations that compete directly against each other in product markets. However, the competence view of organizations as open systems of resource stocks and flows makes it clear that the concept of strategic groups can also be extended to firms that compete directly against each other in resource markets as well. Thus, within the competence perspective, a useful distinction can be made between *product-market strategic groups* and *resource-market strategic groups.* Through their competitive interactions with other organizations in both product and resource markets, organizations become embedded in and co-evolve with both kinds of strategic groups.

Industries

An *industry* can be defined broadly as the set of organizations that offer products or services intended to serve essentially the same kind of customer need in the same or closely similar ways. For example, people and organizations have a basic need to communicate. That need is served by several industries, each of which uses its own kinds of technology and other resources to serve that need. The need for real-time voice and data communication is served by the telecommunications industry. The need for communication through documents is served by the document-delivery industry, which includes both government agencies like the U.S. Postal Service and private firms like Federal Express. The need for face-to-face communication is served by the airline industry and other industries based on different kinds of transportation technologies.

Each of these industries competes against the others by providing *substitute products*—alternative ways of satisfying the basic need for communication. Firms within each industry also compete against each other, and may form several strategic groups as certain firms seek to offer similar products or obtain similar kinds of resources. At the same time, firms within an industry are also likely to *cooperate* with each other in important ways.

They may collaborate in developing precompetitive technologies, in agreeing on industry standards, in communicating the benefits of their industry's products to consumers, and in lobbying governments for regulations or laws that are favorable to their industry. The various interactions through which firms compete and cooperate within an industry and between industries embed individual firms directly in their own industry, but also in a larger system of competing industries. We will consider these and other aspects of the embeddedness of organizations in industries in Chapter 9.

National, Regional, and Global Economies

Organizations are also embedded in and co-evolve with national, regional, and global economies. Changes in the macroeconomic environment of an organization precipitate important impacts on both aggregate demand levels and on the demand and price levels for specific kinds of products and resources. (These impacts and their sources are explored more fully in Chapter 9.) To the extent that changes in macroeconomic conditions affect the products an organization may try to bring to market and the resources it may try to use to bring its products to market, organizations are also embedded in national, regional, and global economic systems.

Society

Because the actions of organizations in product and resource markets affect and are affected by human beings outside an organization in a variety of ways, organizations are also inextricably embedded in *social systems*. Further, because organizations are themselves composed of people as well as other assets, organizations are inherently social in their composition. For these reasons, organizations cannot realistically be regarded as purely economic entities. Rather, the social impacts of the decisions and actions of organizations—both on their own people and on other people outside an organization—must also be a concern of strategic managers.

Decisions of strategic managers can significantly affect the economic security and thus the psychological well being of all the participants in an organization's own value-creation processes—employees, suppliers, and customers. Although many people must contribute to any organization's value-creation processes, strategic managers bear the ultimate responsibility for the ability of their organization to succeed at creating value in the marketplaces they choose to compete in. If an organization is not successful in creating value, it will not have value (in the form of financial compensation, but also in the form of opportunities for satisfying work and career development) to distribute to the people who provide their skills and resources to its value-creation processes. (We explore the distribution of value to resource providers more fully in Chapter 7.)

The failure of an organization to be able to create value will ultimately lead to the failure and collapse of the organization itself. Organizational failures may often lead to loss of income, retirement benefits, and other kinds of financial losses for employees and suppliers, as well as disruptions of personal and family lives when employees have to look for new jobs and perhaps have to relocate to other areas to find employment opportunities. Strategic managers bear ultimate responsibility for the economic well being of an organization's stakeholders, as well as for working conditions and the physical safety of employees in their organizations.

Decisions of strategic managers can also affect the external environment of the organization in many ways. If an organization sells products with defective designs or manufacture, unsuspecting customers who use the organization's defective products may suffer injury or death. If an organization's processes or products cause pollution or otherwise degrade the physical environment, its activities may indirectly harm many people who live in the area affected by the organization's processes or products. Strategic managers therefore bear the ultimate responsibility for the impact of their organization on its environment. We will revisit these aspects of strategic management in Chapter 14, when we discuss the leadership and stewardship role of strategic managers in maintaining ethical conduct.

4.2 MANAGING COMPETENCE BUILDING AND LEVERAGING IN ORGANIZATIONS AS OPEN SYSTEMS FOR VALUE CREATION AND DISTRIBUTION

A central challenge to strategic managers is to successfully manage processes for both building and leveraging an organization's competences that enable it to create and distribute value on a sustainable basis. By any measure, this task is likely to be complex and demanding, especially in large organizations.

As suggested by the view of an organization's competence building and leveraging processes shown in Figure 4.2, strategic managers must oversee many different kinds of interactions across the organization's boundaries with its resource markets and product markets. Strategic managers must ensure that the organization accesses the best possible resources as inputs to its value-creation processes and targets the right product markets for the outputs of its value-creation processes. They must distribute the value created in product markets in the right forms and amounts to all providers of resources essential to sustaining the organization's value-creation processes.

Moreover, as suggested in Figure 4.2, strategic managers must determine the right strategic balance between competence building and leveraging processes. Typically, much of the value created by an organization in its interactions with product markets must be allocated to maintaining the organization's current value-creation processes. Employees must be compensated, suppliers paid, customers supported, and both tangible (machines, buildings) and intangible (relationships, brands) assets maintained. However, some part of the value created today by leveraging an organization's current competences must be invested in building new competences that will enable the organization to create value in the future. Deciding how much of the value currently being created by an organization should be

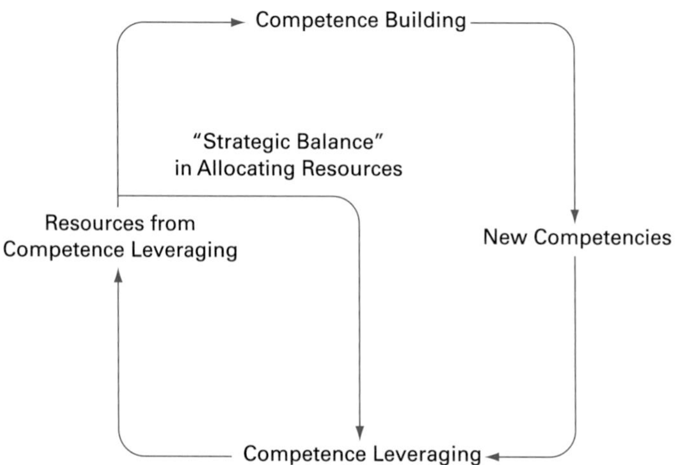

FIGURE 4.2 Achieving Strategic Balance in a Firm's Competence Building and Competence Leveraging Activities

invested in competence building to create new strategic options for the future, and in what forms, is a central responsibility of strategic managers. Only by allocating the right relative amounts of value created to competence building and competence leveraging can strategic managers create a sustainable "virtuous circle" of competence building and leveraging.

4.3 SYSTEM PROPERTIES OF ORGANIZATIONS AS OPEN SYSTEMS

The competence approach to strategic management emphasizes the importance of understanding some fundamental *system properties* of organizations that greatly affect the ways that organizations can and must be managed. As an open system of resource stocks and flows, an organization must continually replenish the stocks of the tangible and intangible resources it uses in its current value-creation activities of competence leveraging.[1] To build new competences, however, an organization must change some of the kinds of resources it uses, as well as possibly changing the way it tries to coordinate its resources. When strategic managers decide to make strategic changes in the way the organization creates value, they must understand certain system properties of an organization that become especially important when an organization tries to build new competences.

To understand the system properties of an organization that affect its ability to build and leverage competences, we first examine more closely each of the *system elements* in our model of an organization as an open system, as shown in Figure 4.1. We then consider how strategic managers' perceptions of **strategic gaps** in the system elements of their organization lead them to seek changes in the organization's resource stocks and flows. We then consider the ways in which two kinds of **control loops** may affect strategic managers' perceptions of and responses to strategic gaps in an organization's system elements. Finally, we consider the impacts of **causal ambiguity** and **dynamic response times** on the ability of an organization's strategic managers to effect strategic change in an organization's system elements.

System Elements and Their Interrelationships

As suggested in Figure 4.1, the system elements of an organization include its Strategic Logic, management processes, intangible resources, tangible resources, operations, and product offers. Each of these system elements has specific kinds of interactions with other system elements, as suggested by the arrows that indicate flows between the system elements. To understand the properties of an organization as a system, we first need to investigate more fully each of these system elements and their critical interactions.

An organization's Strategic Logic is its *operative rationale for achieving its goals through specific processes for value creation and value distribution.* Thus, an organization's Strategic Logic determines both the product markets the organization will undertake to serve now and in the future, as well as the nature of the other system elements the organization will use in serving its targeted markets:

- The *product offer(s)* the organization will bring to its targeted product markets
- The *operations* through which the organization will bring its product offers to its targeted product markets
- The *tangible resources* that will be used in its operations

[1] Dierickx, I. and K. Cool. (1989). Asset Stock Accumulation and Sustainability of Competitive Advantage. *Management Science,* 35,(12), 1504–1513.

- The *intangible resources* that will be used with the tangible resources
- The *management processes* that will be used to coordinate the intangible and intangible resources

A Strategic Logic consists of a Business Concept, Organization Concept, and Core Processes.

To identify clearly its targeted product market and the way it will create value for the targeted market, an organization's Strategic Logic must have an adequately defined Business Concept, Organization Concept, and Core Processes. The Business Concept defines the market segments the organization will try to serve, the product offers it will bring to its markets, and the key activities it must perform in bringing its product offers to its targeted market segments. The Organization Concept defines the resources the organization will need to use to carry out its Business Concept, the organization design it will adopt for coordinating its resources, and the controls and incentives it will put in place to monitor and motivate its resources. The Core Processes define the product creation, product realization, stakeholder development, and any transformative processes the organization must undertake in carrying out its Business Concept. (We will explore in detail these three essential aspects of a Strategic Logic in Chapters 6, 7, and 8, respectively.) Once defined by strategic managers, these three essential aspects of an organization's Strategic Logic will determine the specific kinds of system elements the organization will need in order to create value for its targeted market segment.

Management processes include gathering and interpreting data.

An organization's *management processes* include the essential processes for putting the organization's Strategic Logic into action through the creation and coordination of its other system elements. (Key aspects of management processes are investigated more fully in Chapter 7 when we discuss the Organization Concept.) Management processes must identify the intangible and tangible resources that will be needed in the organization's intended value-creation processes, attract those resources to the organization's value-creation processes (either as internalized resources or as firm-accessible resources that remain outside the organization), and coordinate the use of those resources in value-creation processes. Management processes therefore include the following aspects:

- Processes through which managers and other employees *gather data* on the organization's product markets, its resource markets, the larger industry and economic environment, and its other system elements
- Processes for *interpreting data* in assessing the condition of the organization's external environment and internal system elements
- Processes for *making decisions, setting policies,*[2] *and defining standard procedures*[3] for coordinating resources, as well as *allocating budgets* for gathering, using, replenishing, retiring, and replacing resources

An organization's *intangible resources* include the information, knowledge, and intellectual property rights internalized within or accessible to the organization, as well as the

[2] *Policies* are rules or guidelines that express the *limits* or *boundaries* within which action should be taken. Policies often provide rules or guidelines for making decisions that involve trade-offs for resolving conflicts among specific objectives. For example, a policy may stipulate that "Inventories of standard products shall not exceed quantities equal to three months' sales or fall below quantities equal to one month's sales." Policies may also address ethical issues that may arise in an organization's value-creation processes. For example, a firm may adopt a policy of prohibiting its salespeople from making disparaging statements about competitors or their products.

[3] Procedures specify the *step-by-step sequence of actions* to be followed in a specific situation or to achieve a given objective. They express *how* objectives will be achieved within the limits set by policy. They ensure that resources are committed to achieve goals, and they provide a process design against which progress can be measured. They may also be referred to as standard processes or "best practices" or given other names by various organizations. See also Quinn, J. B. (1995). Strategies for Change. In H. Mintzberg, J. B. Quinn, et al. (Eds.), *The Strategy Process* (European Edition). London: Prentice Hall.

relationships, reputation, customer loyalty, and brands it has developed. Intangible resources largely determine the ability of an organization to use its tangible resources effectively in its value-creation processes.

An organization's *tangible resources* include any land, buildings, machines, money, and other physical or financial assets available to the organization for use in its value-creation processes.

An organization's *operations* include any activities the organization performs in creating its product offers and bringing them to its targeted markets. Operations in this sense therefore include both *product creation* (the definition, design, and development of new products) and *product realization* (the production, distribution, and support of products). Key aspects of operations are discussed more fully in Chapter 8 on Core Processes.

The outputs of the operations in an organization's value-creation processes are the *product offers* it presents to its targeted markets. As we will discuss in detail in Chapter 6 on the Business Concept, a product offer is a fundamental marketing concept that includes customer perceptions of both the value and the cost of becoming a customer. Product offers therefore include not just the hardware, software, or service product *per se* of an organization, but also the services it provides to customers in support of its product, the image value of its products, and the personal interaction of people in the organization with its customers. The product offer also has four components of costs perceived by customers: financial, time, energy, and psychic costs. Strategic managers have responsibility for defining the four value dimensions and the four cost dimensions of a firm's product offer, and they must ensure that the organization's operations are in fact delivering the intended product offers of the organization to its targeted customers.

Strategic Gaps As Drivers of Strategic Change

Within an organization as a system, *strategic change* occurs when an organization changes its Strategic Logic and the management processes or the kinds of resources it uses to carry out its Strategic Logic. Undergoing strategic change essentially involves building new competences to bring new kinds of product offers to markets or to adopt new ways of creating and realizing current or future product offers. Such changes are motivated by the perceptions of strategic managers that strategic gaps exist between the current resources and capabilities of the organization as a system for value creation and the resources and capabilities the organization will have to have in order to achieve its goals. In effect, *strategic gaps* are perceptions by strategic managers of differences between the *current state* and the *desired state* of the system elements in the organization as a value-creation system.

The perception of strategic gaps within an organization is greatly influenced by the flows of data that its strategic managers receive and by the interpretive frameworks through which they look for meaningful information in the data they receive. (We explore managers' cognitive processes for interpreting data in Chapter 10.) The ability of strategic managers to perceive strategic gaps will depend in important measure on the data that strategic managers have available to them. As we will discuss next, the data available to strategic managers will largely depend on the kinds of *control loops* used by an organization to gather data about its environment and internal condition.

> The perception of strategic gaps in system elements drives managerial decision making and resource allocations.

Perception of Strategic Gaps Through Lower-Order vs. Higher-Order Control Loops

The data that drive strategic managers' perceptions of the need to change an organization's stocks and flows of resources are gathered through various kinds of feedback channels through which managers try to monitor the condition of the organization's system elements

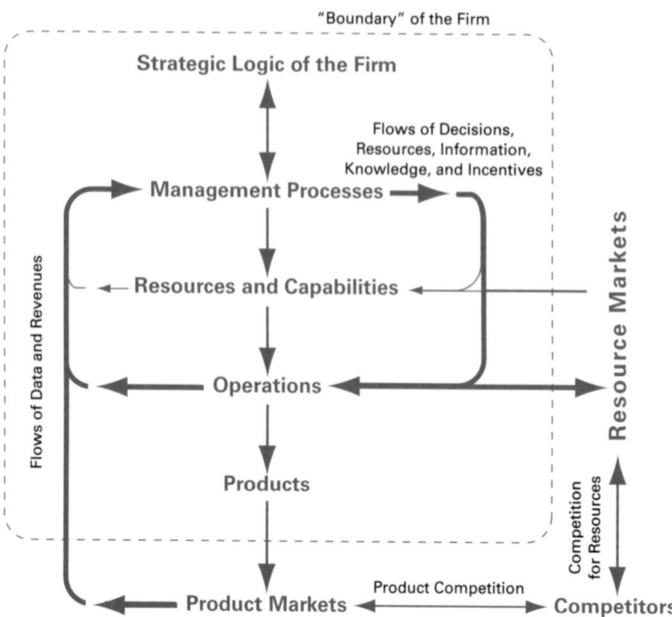

FIGURE 4.3(a) "Lower-Order" Control Loops in the Firm as an Open System

and its environment. In the competence perspective, the various feedback channels that managers use to gather data about an organization's systems elements and its environment are called *control loops.* An organization's control loops may be of two basic types: lower-order control loops or higher-order control loops. Strategic managers' perceptions of strategic gaps depend greatly on the extent to which managers rely on each kind of control loop to provide them with data.

Lower-order control loops gather data on an organization's system elements in the lower part of the model of an organization as an open system, as shown in Figure 4.3(a). Thus, lower-order control loops gather data on an organization's tangible assets (e.g., book or market value of land, buildings, machines, and inventories), its current operations (capacity utilization rates, labor productivity), and its current product markets (sales revenues, market share). In general, the standard financial accounting systems and operations management systems used by organizations typically gather data on these lower system elements. Lower-order control loops therefore usually generate "hard," numerically quantified data.

Higher-order control loops gather data on system elements in the upper part of the model of an organization as an open system, as shown in Figure 4.3(b). Higher-order control loops try to gather data on an organization's intangible assets (e.g., its knowledge assets, reputation, and relationships), its management processes, and its Strategic Logic. Clear ways of measuring these higher-level system elements, however, are often lacking. Higher-order control loops therefore typically generate "softer," more qualitative data that often rely on quite subjective judgments of observers. For instance, "soft," qualitative judgments are typically used to assess the adequacy of an organization's knowledge assets or its management processes for using its knowledge and other resources.

Both management researchers and managers in some organizations today are working on developing better frameworks for measuring higher-level system elements such as intangible assets and management processes. In the 1990s, for example, Volvo created the position of chief knowledge officer, a position that includes the task of developing metrics for evaluating that organization's knowledge assets. Most organizations today lack nonsubjective

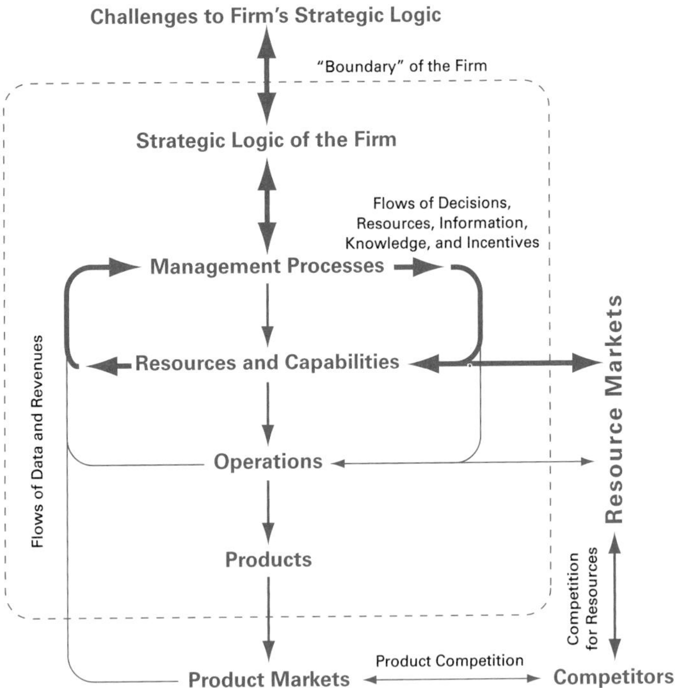

FIGURE 4.3(b) "Higher-Order" Control Loops in the Firm as an Open System

approaches to evaluating these higher-level system elements, however, and as a result many organizations have no systematic processes for monitoring the condition of these system elements. In such organizations, evaluations of higher-order system elements are generally not undertaken regularly or lead to sketchy assessments, at best.

Managers often tend to manage what they measure.

An old adage says that "We manage what we measure." The reason behind this tendency to manage what we measure may be that managers are basically paid to make a situation better than it would be if it were not managed. Managers tend to focus on managing those aspects of a situation that can be measured, because such measures are usually the most convincing way to demonstrate improvement in the situation they are responsible for managing. In any event, many managers focus on managing aspects of their situations for which ostensibly precise, "hard," quantified data are available. Quantifiable data are generally most readily obtained about an organization's current tangible assets, products, operations, and markets—its lower system elements. Data flows from lower system elements are normally useful in maintaining the efficiency of an organization's current competence leveraging activities.

Data flows from lower system elements, however, are not good indicators of a need for competence building processes for improving higher-order system elements. Deterioration in the condition of a higher system element (like loss of a reputation for quality) may take some time to cause observable deterioration in the performance of a lower system element (like declining market share). Thus it may take too long for deterioration in a higher system element to be discovered using data gathered through a lower-order control loop. For example, by the time that managers begin to suspect that a deterioration in current market share is the result of poor product performance that is in turn due to inadequate knowledge about a key technology in the organization's product, it may be too late to try to develop the new knowledge needed to improve the product and recapture lost market share. Thus, strategic managers' perceptions of strategic gaps in higher system elements need to be driven by higher-order control loops, even if the "data" generated by those loops are more qualitative and judgmental in nature. We revisit the challenge of discovering strategic gaps using "soft" data about higher system elements when we discuss managerial cognitive processes in Chapter 10.

Causal Ambiguity in Organizations As Systems

A causally ambiguous situation is one in which clear, definite cause-and-effect relationships have not been discovered. Because discovering cause-and-effect relationships between events relies on having accurate and reliable data about occurrences, situations about which precise data are not available often remain stubbornly causally ambiguous. Causal ambiguity may make it impossible for managers to know how to maintain control over a situation or to improve it, because they lack adequate understanding of the actual "causes" of an observed "effect," or of the means by which a future desired end could be achieved.

As suggested by the upward-pointing arrow on the left side of Figure 4.1, because data becomes less precise and reliable as one moves upward from lower to higher system elements, causal ambiguity about system elements increases as one moves upward in the model of the organization as a system. In essence, it is likely to be more feasible to discover clear cause-and-effect relationships in an organization's lower system elements than in its higher system elements. For example, there is likely to be less ambiguity about what needs to be done to maintain high efficiency in current manufacturing operations than about what needs to be done to achieve high effectiveness in an organization's management processes.

Causal ambiguity is a constant aspect of strategic decision making.

In spite of the high levels of causal ambiguity they will face, strategic managers must make decisions about ways to improve an organization's higher system elements—its Strategic Logic, management processes, and intangible resources. Thus, a key cognitive challenge to strategic managers is to devise ways of thinking through and arriving at conclusions about the causally ambiguous higher system elements in their organizations. (We will revisit this challenge in Chapter 10.)

Dynamic Response Times in Organizations As Systems

As the upward-pointing arrow at the left in Figure 4.1 also suggests, the dynamic response time required to change system elements increases as one moves upward from lower to higher system elements. In essence, this pattern of increasing dynamic response times suggests that an organization can change its mix of products more readily than it can change the way it operates, may change its operations (the way it uses its tangible assets) more readily than its base of tangible assets, may change its tangible assets more readily than its intangible assets (like knowledge and capabilities), and may change its intangible assets more readily than its management processes and Strategic Logic.

It takes longer to change the ideas an organization uses than the things it uses.

One consequence of this tendency to increasing dynamic response times is that an organization is likely to take a longer time—perhaps a much longer time—to change the *ideas* it uses than to change the *things* it uses. This observation implies that in dynamic environments that challenge organizations to find new ways to create and distribute value, the "bottleneck" in the ability of an organization to change may well be the mindset of top managers who are reluctant to give up old ideas about strategies and managing and to imagine new kinds of Strategic Logics and new approaches to management processes. Strategic managers therefore face the unique cognitive challenge of clearly recognizing their own fixed notions and deep assumptions and the resulting limits that they thereby impose on the ability of their organization to evolve with its changing environment.

4.4 COMPETENCE PROCESSES IN ORGANIZATIONS AS SYSTEMS

The competence perspective holds that to survive in a competitive environment, an organization must function effectively as a sustainable system for value creation and distribution. This imperative in turn requires that strategic managers create and maintain effectively functioning *processes* for value creation and distribution within their organization. Thus, strategic managers must attend not just to defining the content of an organization's goals for value-creation processes—defining its products and marketing strategies—but also to defining, developing, and supporting the full range of processes through which value will be created and distributed by the organization. Therefore, strategic managers must clearly define, design, and implement an organization's fundamental processes of competence building and competence leveraging, as well as attending to processes for competence maintenance and competence defense.

Competence Building and Leveraging

Strategic managers have ultimate responsibility for defining and successfully implementing the Strategic Logic of their organization. Carrying out this responsibility requires building and then leveraging organizational competences—a responsibility that imposes a range of significant demands on strategic managers.

Strategic managers are responsible for discovering and adequately defining the market opportunities that could be served effectively by the resources and capabilities their organization has or could develop. They must evaluate discovered market opportunities and define product offers that could be successful in serving those opportunities. They must then select those market opportunities and product offers that offer the greatest potential for value creation by the organization. They must identify the resources needed to create and realize product offers that can be successful in serving the targeted market opportunities, and they must define value distribution plans that are capable of attracting the resources needed by the organization's value-creation processes. They must also define and design management processes that will be effective in coordinating resources to create distinctive organizational capabilities in serving its targeted market opportunities.

Of course, strategic managers cannot perform all of these activities themselves. Rather, strategic managers must focus on defining and designing organizational processes for carrying out these activities, identifying and obtaining the best resources for these processes, providing the resources needed to support the processes, defining appropriate measures for monitoring the performance of individuals and groups carrying out the processes, and defining and delivering incentives that will motivate high performance by all participants in every process.

Competence Maintenance and Defense

Competence maintenance refers to processes that are intended to assure the ongoing availability—at the appropriate time and in the appropriate form—of resources and capabilities required by an organization's competence leveraging activities. Competence maintenance is often a strategically important process, because the performance or availability of some assets may decrease as a natural consequence of competence leveraging activities. For example, factory equipment will wear with use and must undergo regular processes of maintenance and repair to produce reliable products and thereby to maintain competence leveraging. Organizational processes of many types may also tend over time to become loose or slack in execution—and therefore to need continuous monitoring and periodic reinforcing to maintain even a stable level of performance. Thus, strategic managers are also responsible for maintaining the ability of an organization to fully leverage its current competences by defining and designing appropriate competence maintenance processes.

Competence defense refers to the processes for protecting an organization's assets, capabilities, and coordination activities against threats of actions by direct competitors or other organizations that could disrupt an organization's competence building or leveraging activities. For example, competitors may try to recruit key employees who play vital roles in an organization's processes, or may try to steal or otherwise obtain an organization's proprietary information or technology. Some individuals or organizations may also simply try to destroy an organization's resources or capabilities. A growing array of attacks on information systems by computer hackers is a fact of life for many organizations. Attacks by terrorist organizations or other criminals on an organization's people and other resources are also, lamentably, a significant threat in many parts of the world today. In the face of such threats, strategic managers bear ultimate moral responsibility for protecting the people and resources in their organizations, as well as ultimate business responsibility for defending the competence building and leveraging processes of their organizations from such threats.[4]

[4] Rotem, Z. and R. Amit. (1997). Strategic Defense and Competence-Based Competition. In A. Heene and R. Sanchez, *Competence-Based Strategic Management*. Chichester: John Wiley & Sons: 169–191.

KEY TERMS AND CONCEPTS

strategic gap The perception of a difference between the current state of a system element and the desired state of a system element.

control loops Feedback flows of data about an organization's product markets, product offers, operations, and tangible and intangible assets.

causal ambiguity A condition in which it is difficult to establish clear cause-and-effect relationships.

dynamic response time The time that it takes to change a system element of an organization.

REVIEW QUESTIONS

1. What does it mean to say that an organization as a system is *embedded* in one or more larger systems?
2. How is an organization related to other firms in its industry that are part of its strategic group?
3. What is the *strategic balance* that strategic managers must achieve in allocating an organization's resources?
4. What are likely to be the consequences if strategic managers rely on lower-order control loops to perceive strategic gaps in their organization's system elements?
5. Why does it take longer for an organization to change the ideas it uses than the things it uses?

CHAPTER 5

THE STRATEGIC LOGIC OF AN ORGANIZATION

INTRODUCTION

We previously discussed the nature of organizations as goal-seeking human systems that create value by offering products to markets and that distribute value earned in markets to the providers of the resources that sustain the organization's value-creation processes. We also reviewed a number of important economic theories about the organization of value-creating activities, as well as strategic management theories about how the value-creation processes of organizations can be made more efficient and effective. In this chapter we extend these foundational ideas by exploring the concept of an organization's **Strategic Logic**—the operative rationale of an organization for achieving its goals through value creation and distribution.

Defining and implementing the Strategic Logic of an organization is the most fundamental responsibility of the organization's strategic managers. As suggested in Figure 5.1, a Strategic Logic consists of three interrelated components:

- A **Business Concept** that identifies the intended customers of the organization and the product offers and key activities that the organization will use to create value for those customers.
- An **Organization Concept** that defines the resources the organization will use in its value-creating activities, the organization design for coordinating its activities, the controls it will use to monitor its value-creating activities, and the incentives—or plan for value distribution—that the organization will offer to attract and motivate resource providers in its value-creating processes.
- The **Core Processes** of product creation, product realization, stakeholder development, and organizational transformation through which an organization tries to create and distribute value on a sustainable basis.

Defining and implementing a viable Strategic Logic for value creation and distribution is an intellectually demanding task. It continually challenges strategic managers to be insightful in their understanding of markets for both products and resources and creative in imagining better ways of attracting both customers and resource providers to the organization's value-creation and value-distribution processes.

In following chapters we examine the three components of a Strategic Logic in detail. To set the stage for this more detailed discussion, however, in this chapter we summarize the essential features of an organization's Business Concept, Organization Concept, and Core Processes.

5.1 THE BUSINESS CONCEPT

The Business Concept is the "demand side" of an organization's Strategic Logic. It identifies the market for the products and services the organization intends to serve through its

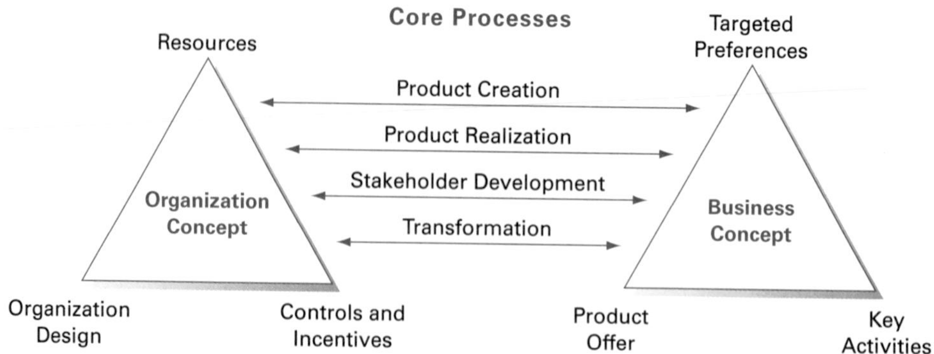

FIGURE 5.1 The Three Components of a Strategic Logic

value-creation processes, the kind of product and services it will offer, and the key activities in which it must excel in order to be successful.

To compete effectively in markets for products and services, an organization must be able to offer products and services that are perceived as having superior appeal by at least some people who then decide to become customers for the organization's products or services. The Business Concept rests upon the fundamental marketing notions that every potential customer will have *preferences* for certain kinds of goods and services, and that in order to persuade people to buy its products or services, an organization must discover and serve well the specific preferences of people who might become customers. Groups of people who share similar preferences for a given kind of product or service are known as *market segments.* No organization can hope to "be all things to all people," and so each organization must choose which preferences in a market it will try to serve, and which it will not. A Business Concept is therefore founded on a strategic organizational decision to undertake to serve certain identified preferences shared by the people who make up a targeted market segment.

To serve the preferences of people in a targeted market segment, an organization must create a *product offer* that has superior appeal to people in that market segment. The appeal of a product offer depends on the characteristics of the product itself (whether hardware or a service), plus the supporting services, image, and personal interactions that accompany the product, as well as the financial, time, energy, and psychic costs that people associate with the product. The Business Concept therefore also includes the design of a product offer that managers believe will be effective in appealing to the identified preferences of the targeted market segment.

The third component of an organization's Business Concept is the set of *key activities* at which an organization must excel to be successful in communicating and delivering its product offer to targeted market segments. These key activities are usually seen as *critical success factors* in implementing a Strategic Logic, and are usually monitored as *key performance indicators* of the organization.

The Business Concept defines an organization's theory of value creation.

The three components of a Business Concept essentially define the way an organization proposes to create value by competing in markets for products and services—by excelling at specific activities that are critical in delivering a specific kind of product offer to people with specific preferences. The other elements in an organization's Strategic Logic—the Organization Concept and Core Processes—must then be designed to enable the organization to sustain superior, consistent execution of its defined Business Concept.

5.2 THE ORGANIZATION CONCEPT

An Organization Concept defines how an organization will carry out its Business Concept.

To enable an organization to carry out its Business Concept, managers must devise an effective approach to organizing and coordinating the organization's value-creating activities. A basic task of managers is therefore to identify the *resources* an organization will need to carry out its chosen Business Concept effectively. Resources are any assets that are available and useful to an organization in its value-creating activities. Resources include tangible assets like land, buildings, machines, and equipment; intangible assets like knowledge, capabilities, reputation, brands, and relationships; and human assets, especially employees. Resources may be firm-specific (that is, owned or otherwise tightly controlled by an organization) or firm-addressable (not owned or controlled by an organization, but available to be used if and when needed).

Managers must also create an *organization design* for coordinating the organization's use of its resources in value-creating activities. In designing an organization, managers must determine *task allocations* (who will *do* what), the *distribution of authority* (who will *decide* what), and *information flows* (who will *know* what).

To provide feedback to both managers and employees about how well various tasks in the organization are being performed, managers must also establish controls—which essentially consist of various measures of performance—to monitor value-creating activities. In addition, managers must also define an organization's incentives in the form of rewards for good performance and sanctions for poor performance.

5.3 CORE PROCESSES

All the activities of an organization can be grouped in one of four Core Processes.

An organization's Business Concept and Organization Concept determine the kinds of value-creation and distribution activities the organization will undertake and how it will try to perform them. Of course, an organization may undertake many different kinds of activities in its efforts to create and distribute value, but in the Strategic Logic of an organization, all these activities may be grouped into four fundamental categories of activities, which we will call the Core Processes of an organization.

The first Core Process is *product creation*. Every organization must offer a product (whether hardware or service) in exchange for which it will receive resources (including financial resources) that enable the organization to continue. Some organizations may undertake development projects in an effort to create innovative product concepts and original designs, while other organizations may elect to offer rather ordinary or commonplace products. In either case, whether through creativity or imitation, an organization explicitly or implicitly decides and creates the product or products that the organization will offer to markets.

After an organization's product creation process generates the design of a product, the organization must then produce the product, deliver it to customers, and support the product in various ways, often including providing maintenance and repair services. We use the term *product realization* to refer to all the activities that an organization undertakes to make, deliver, service, and support its product offers. Like product creation, product realization is a core process that all organizations must sustain in order to survive.

To create and realize product offers, an organization must attract and use many different kinds of resources. Some of those resources may need to be adapted or specialized in various ways to work well in creating and realizing the organization's product offers. Thus, an organization must develop relationships with providers of many kinds of resources and must often work with those resource providers to develop specialized capabilities suited to the organization's products and targeted market segments. By investing in developing capabilities that help a firm create and realize its products, resource providers acquire a legitimate interest or expectation that an organization will distribute to them some of the value they help to create. In effect, by developing resources and capabilities that are especially beneficial to a specific organization, resource providers become stakeholders in the organization. We therefore refer to an organization's core process of attracting and developing resources as *stakeholder development.*

From time to time, an organization may undergo a profound change in the way it makes sense of its environment, defines its best opportunities for creating value, organizes its value-creation processes, distributes value to its resource providers, and undertakes other fundamental aspects of organizational life. For example, in recent decades movements such as total quality management (TQM), business process reengineering (BPR), environmental sustainability, and social responsibility have profoundly changed management thinking and precipitated upheavals in the way organizations work. We refer to these periodic deep changes in the way an organization thinks and works as *transformative processes.* Though they may occur only from time to time, transformative processes are a core process that all organizations must undergo periodically as the environment changes.

5.4 STRATEGIC LOGIC AS THE "DRIVER" OF COMPETENCE BUILDING AND LEVERAGING IN ORGANIZATIONS AND INDUSTRIES

Every organization is unique, if only because each organization involves different individuals, each of whom is unique in many ways. Therefore we can expect that each organization will have at least some characteristic differences in its goals for and approaches to value creation and distribution. Nevertheless, organizations often exhibit certain patterns of sensemaking and behavior that suggest that their individual Strategic Logics have important elements in common. In strategic management theory and research, the concepts of *cognitive maps, dominant logics,* and *strategic groups* suggest ways in which different organizations composed of different people may nevertheless begin to share common cognitive elements in their Strategic Logics.

Some strategic management researchers have discovered that managers of organizations competing in a given industry may share a common "cognitive map" that defines not only the participants in an industry, but also their respective competitive positions and roles.[1] In other words, in at least some industries, many managers do not believe that competition is wholly unfettered and unpredictable; rather, they expect that they and their competitors will interact in ways that are consistent with past patterns of competition and thus are largely predictable. Prahalad and Bettis introduced the term *dominant logic* to refer to a consistent way of creating value for customers that has been adopted by the most successful competitors in a product market.[2] In addition, the term *strategic groups* refers

[1] See J. Porac, H. Thomas, and C. Baden-Fuller. (1989). Competitive Groups as Cognitive Communities: The Case of the Scottish Knitwear Manufacturers. *Journal of Management Studies,* 26, 397–416. See also R. Reger and A. Huff. (1993). Strategic Groups: A Cognitive Perspective. *Strategic Management Journal,* 14, 103–123.

[2] Prahalad, C. K., and R. Bettis. (1986). The Dominant Logic: A New Linkage Between Diversity and Performance. *Strategic Management Journal,* 7, 485–501.

to organizations that adopt similar approaches to creating value for similar sets of customers in a product market.

In creating a Strategic Logic for their organization, managers may emulate some approaches and practices already in use in a given product market, especially the approaches and practices of currently successful organizations. Nevertheless, the Strategic Logic adopted by an organization will always be unique in at least some aspects of its approach to creating value for customers and distributing value to resource providers. Thus, each organization's Strategic Logic will shape in distinctive ways the kinds of competences it tries to build, the ways it tries to build those competences, and the ways it tries to leverage its current competences.

The concept of **competence groups** can be used to identify the similarities and the differences in the competence building and leveraging activities of organizations.[3] As indicated in Figure 5.2, organizations in *stable* competence groups share similar competence building and leveraging activities, suggesting that their Strategic Logics and competitive activities have much in common. Other organizations that currently engage in similar competence leveraging activities, but that exhibit important differences in the new competences they are building, can be categorized as constituting a *diverging* competence group, suggesting important differences in the longer-term goals in their Strategic Logics and in the future competitive activities of those organizations. Organizations currently engaged in different competence leveraging activities but nonetheless building similar competences for the future are identified as being in *converging* competence groups. Firms that have neither similar competence leveraging nor similar competence building activities are not competitors in product markets (although they may be competitors in resource markets) and do not form a competence group.

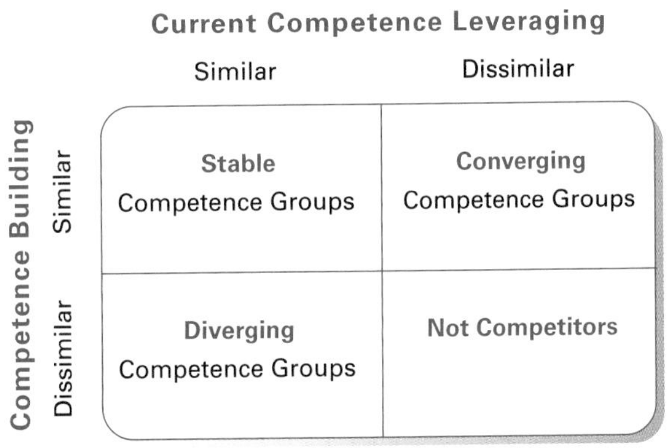

Competence Building \ Current Competence Leveraging	Similar	Dissimilar
Similar	**Stable** Competence Groups	**Converging** Competence Groups
Dissimilar	**Diverging** Competence Groups	**Not Competitors**

FIGURE 5.2 Competence Groups

[3] Gorman, P., H. Thomas, and R. Sanchez. (1996). Industry Dynamics in Competence-Based Competition. In R. Sanchez, A. Heene, and H. Thomas (Eds.), *Dynamics of Competence-Based Competition*. Oxford: Elsevier Pergamon: 85–99.

KEY TERMS AND CONCEPTS

Strategic Logic An organization's operative rationale for achieving its goals through its processes of value creation and distribution.

Business Concept The definition of the intended customers of an organization, of the product offers it will create for those customers, and of the key activities through which the organization's product offers will be brought to its intended customers.

Organization Concept The definition of the resources, organization design, and controls and incentives through which an organization intends to carry out its Business Concept.

Core Processes The processes of product creation, product realization, and stakeholder development through which an organization creates and distributes value, plus periodic transformative processes that fundamentally change the way an organization works.

competence groups Groupings of firms by their current competence leveraging and building activities to identify which firms are competitors now and which will be competitors in the future.

REVIEW QUESTIONS

1. What are the essential components of a Strategic Logic?
2. What are the implications of identifying a firm as a member of a converging competence group?
3. What are the implications of identifying a firm as a member of a diverging competence group?

PART IV

BUSINESS UNIT STRATEGY

CHAPTER 6

THE BUSINESS CONCEPT: WHO WILL BE SERVED, WITH WHAT, AND HOW?

INTRODUCTION

The previous chapter described an organization's Strategic Logic as consisting of a Business Concept, and Organization Concept, and Core Processes. In this chapter we examine in detail the three elements that make up a Business Concept.

In his classic book Defining the Business, Derek Abell explained that the most fundamental task of the strategic managers of an organization is to determine[1]

- *Who* will be served by our organization (i.e., who will our customers be)?
- *What* will we offer our customers (i.e., what will our products be)?
- *How* will we create and provide our products to our customers?

As suggested in Figure 6.1, no organization can hope to serve well all the potential customers for a good or service. Strategic managers must set boundaries on the groups of customers their organization will try to serve. Similarly, no organization can provide all the goods and services any group of customers might need. Strategic managers must therefore also determine the kinds of products an organization will create and offer to targeted customers. In addition, strategic managers must make important choices about how the organization will provide its selected products to its targeted customers—the technologies it will apply, the distribution channels it will use, the way its products will be serviced and its customers supported, and so on. Only when these questions have been answered and a good "fit" of customers, products, and means identified can there be a clear sense of the way an organization will try to create value through its activities.

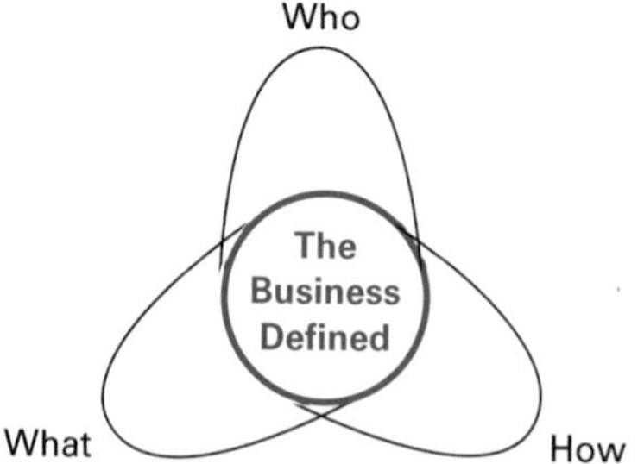

FIGURE 6.1 Defining the Business by Who, What, and How

[1] Abell, Derek F. (1980). *Defining the Business: The Starting Point of Strategic Planning.* Englewood Cliffs, NJ: Prentice-Hall.

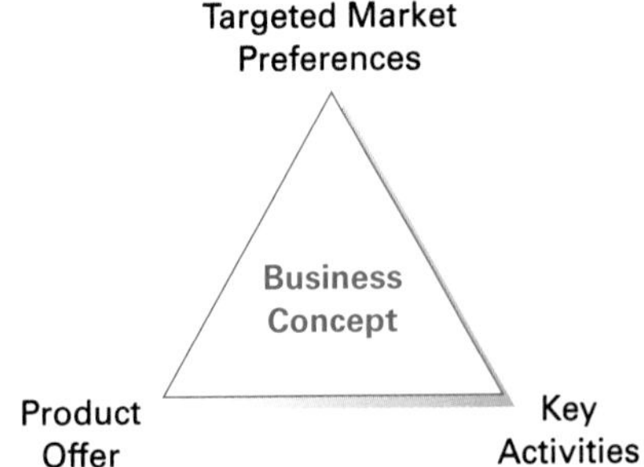

FIGURE 6.2 The Three Elements of the Business Concept

As suggested in Figure 6.2, we will build on these fundamental insights into the nature of a business by defining an organization's Business Concept as consisting of its

- Targeted market preferences
- Product offers
- Key activities

We will examine each of these three elements of the Business Concept in some detail, and then consider two *system design principles* that strategic managers must honor when they define the Business Concept of an organization. We also consider three types of "generic" product strategies to illustrate Business Concepts consistent with the two system design principles.

6.1 TARGETING MARKET PREFERENCES

Deciding which customers to serve

As we mentioned in our discussion of the nature of organizations (Chapter 1), all organizations depend on flows of resources—including financial resources—for their survival. Businesses gather financial resources by providing goods and services to customers willing to pay the price asked by a given business. Not-for-profit organizations, including government agencies, obtain funding from contributors or taxpayers who want to provide goods and services to targeted groups of people or to society at large. In either case, an organization must provide goods or services that are perceived as valuable by some targeted group of customers. A fundamental decision in strategic management is therefore deciding *which kinds of customers* an organization will try to create value for, given the resources and capabilities available to it.

Managers are often advised to "stay close to your customers" and to keep current customers satisfied. Even though this advice may be sound in the near term, in the longer term the needs of an organization's current customers may change in ways that are simply not feasible or even desirable for the organization to continue to serve. Consider, for example, how your own needs for food, clothing, shelter, transportation, entertainment, and other essentials in life have evolved thus far. The resources and capabilities that an organization must have to serve those needs are likely to be significantly different at each stage of your personal evolution. In addition, the way your own needs evolve may be quite different from the way your friends' or colleagues' needs evolve, even though you may share similar likes and dislikes for a given kind of product at a given point in time. Thus, the near-term success of an organization often depends greatly on maintaining high levels of satisfaction among its current customers, but strategic managers concerned with the long-term success of an organization must be able to look beyond an organization's current customers. Strategic managers must focus their organization on serving a well-defined set of market preferences that various customers will have in common, both today and in the future.

Identifying Market Preferences

In deciding how an organization should create value for some set of customers, strategic thinking should be on identifying and selecting the *customer preferences* that an organization will undertake to serve well. The meaning of preferences can best be explained by starting with the basic marketing concept of **market needs.** All humans have basic needs for food, clothing, shelter, and other essentials that they try to meet through use of products and services. People of limited financial means will usually accept basic products or services, as long as they are affordable. As people acquire greater financial means, however, and as they gain experience in using various kinds of goods and services, people tend to develop preferred ways of meeting their needs. For example, individuals begin to prefer products with specific *attributes*—specific functions, features, and performance levels—that provide the greatest perceived value for each person's lifestyle and way of using that product. **Market preferences** therefore determine the specific likes and dislikes of potential customers for a given kind of good or service that influence which product they choose to purchase.

Serving specific preferences well requires specific capabilities.

Preferences are fundamentally important in strategic management because an organization must develop and use specific kinds of resources and capabilities to become competent in providing products that satisfy different kinds of preferences. Consider, for example, the different kinds of resources and capabilities that Peugeot uses to produce durable and economical compact cars, that Volvo uses in producing family cars with high levels of passenger safety, and that Porsche uses to design and produce high-performance sports cars. Or the different skills that the Danish shoemaker ECCO applies in designing its rugged, comfortable shoes "made for living," compared to the skills needed by designers of trendy, high fashion shoes for women.

It takes time—often a considerable amount of time—for an organization to develop the competence (specialized resources, capabilities, and management processes) needed to create and realize products that serve a specific set of preferences well. One of the central tasks of strategic managers is maintaining a *dynamic balance* between an organization's competence building and leveraging processes and the rate of change and evolution in its product markets. In general, the different kinds of preferences that exist in a product market tend to change much more slowly than the specific individuals who have certain preferences at any point in time. In other words, a given customer is likely to change from having one set of preferences to another set of preferences more frequently than new sets of preferences emerge or old preferences disappear in a product market as a whole. Since competences take considerable time to build, their focus should be on serving market preferences that are more stable than the tastes of any customers an organization may currently be serving. Strategic managers must therefore focus on building organizational competences that will be effective in serving evolving preferences in the marketplace in the long term, while leveraging an organization's current competences to serve those individuals who happen to have preferences the organization is capable of serving well today.

Market Segments, Mass Customization, and Product Personalization

A market segment is a grouping of customers with common preferences.

Marketing research is the branch of marketing that tries to identify the different preferences that people have with respect to a given kind of product and then to group potential customers into **market segments** composed of people with *relatively similar preferences* for that product. Thus, from a marketing perspective, strategic managers deciding the Business Concept of an organization must first determine which market segments the organization will undertake to serve now and in the future. With a clear idea as to which market preferences an organization will—and will not—try to serve, managers can begin to develop the resources and capabilities needed to create and realize products that will appeal strongly to customers with targeted preferences.

Today, new technologies for designing and producing products are making it possible to produce large numbers of product variations that can be tailored in various ways to suit more exactly the preferences of individual customers. For example, both Apple Computer and Dell Computer use modular product designs and flexible assembly methods to offer customers "menus" of components (microprocessors, memory cards, hard drives, monitors, etc.) to choose from in configuring a personal computer to meet each customer's preferences as nearly as possible. Nike offers customers a similar range of choices in sole styles, colors, trim pieces, name tags, and so on in configuring personalized shoe products. Increasingly, other firms and other industries are creating modular product designs—rather than single "one-off" product designs—and using **mass customization and product personalization** capabilities to serve more closely the individual preferences of customers currently in a targeted market segment.

Real-Time Market Research

Because markets are dynamic and market preferences emerge, strengthen, or fade away as time goes by, ongoing marketing research is essential to maintaining a clear understanding of the evolving preferences in each market segment an organization is targeting or could target. Although traditional methods of marketing research (focus groups, consumer surveys, etc.) remain important, the configurability of modular products and the flexibility of manufacturing processes today enable organizations to explore evolving market preferences in new ways. In addition to (and sometimes instead of) traditional marketing research, some firms now configure modular product variations that are brought to market in small batches to test consumer reactions to new product variations. Sony used the modular architecture of its Walkman products, for example, to configure more than 160 product models (distinguished by different combinations of functions, features, performance levels, and price points) for the North American market in the 1980s. Models that sold well at various price points were put into full production and maintained in the market, while models that did not sell well were soon replaced with new models that were similarly tested in the market before either being put into full production or dropped.

This method of using modular product designs and flexible manufacturing systems to test consumer reactions to a changing array of product models is called **real-time market research.** In product markets where preferences evolve rapidly or frequently diverge to form a growing number of market segments, real-time market research provides an important means for tracking market evolution and identifying emerging market preferences an organization must prepare to serve.

6.2 PRODUCT OFFERS

NDCV = Net Delivered Customer Value

Once an organization identifies the market segments that it would like to serve, it must develop a *product offer* that will be regarded as desirable by the customers in the market segments it has targeted. A product offer (sometimes also referred to as the "product offering" or "value proposition") represents the entire package of benefits and costs a customer imagines when he or she thinks about purchasing and using a firm's product. We will use the **net delivered customer value (NDCV)** framework for representing four kinds of benefits and four kinds of costs that consumers are likely to perceive when they interact with an organization's product offer.[2] This framework is represented in Figure 6.3.

Highlight Box 6.1 provides an example that illustrates the four kinds of perceived benefits and four kinds of perceived costs that determine the net delivered customer value of a product offer.

Four Sources of Perceived Value in a Product Offer

The four sources of perceived value in a product offer relate to the benefits a customer expects to derive from the use of a product, the service aspect of the product, the image value of the product, and any personal interactions the customer may have in acquiring and using the product. We next consider each of these four potential sources of perceived value more closely.

Product Benefits

People derive benefits from the *use* of a product. The **product benefits** or usefulness of a product will largely be determined by the functions, features, and performance levels the product provides to a user.

Functions refer to the basic things a good or service product does, or lets a user of the product do, that benefits the user. Examples of functions include the protection against cold that a jacket provides, the personal mobility that an automobile provides, the convenient communication that a mobile phone service provides, the comfort and support that a desk chair provides, and so on.

Features are enhancements of a product that enhance or add to, but cannot substitute for, the basic functions of a product. For example, the Colgate Total toothbrush features a soft rubber strip on its handle that helps provide a firm and comfortable grip while a user brushes his or her teeth (which is the basic function provided by a toothbrush). Similarly, a bank may offer 24-hour Internet access as an added feature in its financial service products. Features also include styling of products, such as the shape, color, and texture used in a hardware product or the "look and feel" of a software program when displayed on a computer monitor.

Performance levels refer to measures that describe the relative degree or extent to which a product delivers a specific function. For example, the performance level of a computer monitor can be measured by the relative resolution ("pixel" size and count) of the monitor screen, the speed of a telecommunications service by its average connection time, the sound quality of a stereo amplifier by its signal-to-noise ratio, the fuel efficiency of an automobile by its fuel consumption in liters per hundred kilometers or in miles per gallon, and so on.

Service Value

A *service* in the NDCV framework is any activity that an organization performs to assist its customers in becoming aware of, learning about, evaluating, purchasing, paying for, taking delivery of, using, maintaining, repairing, upgrading, retiring, recycling, or disposing of a product. To the extent that customers or potential customers perceive that an organization is offering services that are helpful during the life cycle of the product—from first becoming aware of a product to finally disposing of a retired product—those activities add **service value** to a product offer. As more firms around the world become capable of offering products with

[2] The Net Delivered Customer Value framework was developed by the well-known marketing professor Philip Kotler. See, for example, Kotler, Philip. (2000). *Marketing Management,* 10th ed. Upper Saddle River, NJ: Prentice Hall.

Net Delivered Customer Value (NDCV)
= Perceived Benefits – Perceived Costs
= (VALUE of Product Use + Service + Image + Personal Interaction)
– (Financial + Time + Energy + Psychic COSTS)

FIGURE 6.3 Sources of Perceived Value and Cost in a Product

HIGHLIGHT BOX 6.1

The Anatomy of a Product Offer: Shirley Smith Takes a Flight

To illustrate the four kinds of perceived benefits and four kinds of perceived costs that make up the net delivered customer value (NDCV) in a product offer, let us look at the experience of a businesswoman—let's call her Shirley Smith—as she takes a business trip on a scheduled airline from Hong Kong to Singapore.

Four Sources of Perceived Benefits

Value of the Use of the Product. Perhaps the most basic benefit offered to Shirley Smith is the ability to be transported (along with her baggage) from Hong Kong to Singapore. To this benefit we can add the comfort of the seating and other interior appointments of the airplane while Shirley is traveling, and the extent to which Shirley finds her seating arrangement conducive to working on her laptop, reading reports, taking a nap, or other activities she would like to do while making the trip. We could also add the enjoyment that Shirley derives from watching a movie or listening to music on the in-flight entertainment system, as well as her satisfaction with any meals and drinks provided during the flight.

Service Value. The service activities that the airline performs for Shirley may include helping her make a reservation and obtain a ticket for her flight, advising her in advance if a flight delay occurs, checking Shirley and her baggage in for the flight, providing any personal assistance Shirley might request during the flight or on arrival, and accurately crediting Shirley with frequent flyer miles for her trip.

Image Value. To create image value, the airline may provide Shirley with "Gold," "Platinum," or "Diamond" status in their frequent flyer program and provide a special check-in counter for passengers enjoying this status.

Personal Interaction Value. Shirley's perceptions of the friendliness, helpfulness, and professionalism of the reservations agent, ticket counter staff, flight crew, and ground staff on arrival will determine the value she derives from her personal interactions with the airline's product offer.

Four Sources of Perceived Costs

Financial Costs. The financial costs of Shirley's interaction with the airline's product offer include any charges for her call to the airline reservation office (if she does not use the Internet) and her transportation costs to and from airports, as well as the cost of her ticket for the flight.

Time Costs. Time costs would include Shirley's perceptions of the time required to make her flight reservation, get her ticket, travel to the airport, check in for the flight and board the aircraft, take the flight, deplane, collect her baggage, and travel from the arrival airport to her destination. In addition, perceived time costs may include time spent waiting for an inconvenient flight time, delays encountered during the flight, time spent filing a report of lost or delayed baggage (if any), or communicating with the airline about any aspect of her trip.

Energy Costs. Energy costs could result from Shirley's efforts to find a convenient flight schedule when making a reservation, any physical or mental exertion required to check in and board the flight, as well as to travel to or from airports.

Psychic Costs. Psychic costs result whenever Shirley worries about the safety or comfort of her flight, the possibility of flight delays that would disrupt her business schedule, the possibility of lost or delayed baggage, the failure of the airline to credit frequent flyer miles for her flight, or any other aspect of her trip that could go wrong.

world-class functions, features, and performance levels, the service components of a product offer are becoming increasingly important contributors to NDCV.

Image Value

The image dimension of a product offer relates to how a user of a product thinks other people will "see" the user (or even how the user will see himself or herself) when using the product. The **image value** of a product offer is thus the extent to which some aspect of the product offer serves a customer's desire for social recognition, status, identification, or distinctiveness. Expensive luxury goods, for example, provide customers with a means of signaling that they belong to an upper economic or social stratum—or at least that they can afford to spend money on a good or service typically favored by the rich and famous. Other people may value products that send the opposite signal—rejecting a need for status based on economic or social level—and may prefer to be identified with environmental concern, social responsibility, educational level, or other social criteria. Of course, products like fashions and automobiles provide many consumers with ways of signaling certain aspects of their personalities, whether real, imagined, or simply desired.

Personal Interaction Value

A customer or potential customer may derive a positive feeling from interacting with an organization's employees or representatives, and this derived feeling may add perceived value to a firm's product offer. When an organization's employees have a helpful and concerned attitude when interacting with a customer, and when employees are knowledgeable about a firm's products and practices and can accurately answer a customer's questions and help them solve problems in a professional way, most customers are likely to derive at least some amount of positive **personal interaction value.**

Four Sources of Perceived Cost in a Product Offer

Potential customers are likely to perceive four kinds of costs when they interact with an organization's product offer: financial costs, time costs, energy costs, and psychic costs.

Perceived costs include time, energy, and psychic costs, not just financial

Financial Costs

The perceived **financial costs** of a product offer include all the monetary costs that a customer anticipates or actually experiences in the full life cycle of the product, including learning about, purchasing, taking delivery of, using, maintaining, repairing, upgrading, and retiring a product. Although the direct cash costs of purchasing and using a product throughout its lifetime may sometimes be calculated quite precisely, different customers may have quite different *perceptions* of the financial costs of a product even when calculated cash costs are the same. Perceptions of financial costs may vary considerably according to when a cost must be incurred in the life cycle of a product. Different perceptions of financial cost may result, for example, from the relative importance that each customer assigns to the time value of money, because different individuals may apply different discount rates in valuing future costs. Different customers may also have different expectations as to their current and future financial situations, and may therefore simply prefer to incur costs later rather than now, or vice versa.

Time Costs

Most people place a value on time, and the more time they must spend in learning about, purchasing, taking delivery of, using, maintaining, repairing, upgrading, and retiring a product, the greater the perceived **time cost** of a product. The value that people place on their time, however, can vary widely. For many professional people, "time is money," and the time they spend waiting for, learning to use, or maintaining a product can be converted directly into reduced working time and lost revenues. Virtually everyone places at least some value on their time, however, and for most people sooner is generally preferable to later when it comes to purchasing and maintaining products. To the extent that a firm's product offer makes customers wait for information, delivery, supplies, repairs, or other essential aspects of using its product, most customers will perceive those time requirements in a negative way, or as a time cost associated with the product offer.

Energy Costs

Some aspects of the process of interacting with a firm's product offer may require customers to expend their energy in various ways. For example, some firms may automatically provide delivery of purchased products to a customer's home or office, while other firms leave delivery up to the customer to arrange. Other firms may require that customers bring products needing maintenance or repair to their premises, while other firms may save their customers such an effort by picking up the customer's product or performing maintenance or repairs on the customer's premises. To the extent that customers perceive that they will have to expend energy to acquire and use a product, customers will perceive an **energy cost** associated with using a firm's product offer. (Note that energy cost does not refer to the cost of energy consumed directly by a product, such as electricity or gasoline. Costs for consumed energy would be recognized as financial costs.)

Psychic Costs

To the extent that a customer worries about or has psychological feelings of anxiety about acquiring and using a product, he or she will attribute a **psychic cost** to a product offer. In general, customers are more likely to perceive significant psychic costs when they are considering major purchases, such as real estate (homes), costly consumer durables (automobiles, home appliances), or expensive services (a luxury cruise vacation).

Customers may also perceive significant psychic costs if they feel intimidated by a product. Many people are still intimidated by personal computers, for example, and resist buying one even though they know they would enjoy the benefits of using a personal computer, especially in using the Internet. Recognizing this important form of psychic cost, Apple Computer reversed an industry trend in the 1990s toward ever more complex personal computers and software by introducing the Apple iMac. Targeted primarily at anxious late adopters, the iMac was offered in a "friendly" new shape available in a range of bright colors. It also promised the simplest possible three-step process for getting connected to the Internet: (1) Take the iMac out of the box, (2) Plug it in, (3) Turn it on. Apple's skill in communicating the simplicity of the iMac reduced the psychic cost perceptions of many potential customers and helped to make the iMac a runaway success, while other personal computer makers struggled to sell their more complex—and intimidating—products.

Product Differentiation: Managing the "Bundle" of NDCV

Product differentiation is about getting the right "bundle" of NDCV for a targeted market segment.

The NDCV framework holds that customers will prefer the product offer that promises to deliver maximum available NDCV—the greatest excess of perceived benefits (product, service, image, and personal interaction value) over perceived costs (financial, time, energy, and psychic costs). Designing a product offer that will be appealing to customers in a targeted market segment therefore requires carefully selecting and "bundling" the benefits and costs of a product offer so that customers with a given set of preferences will perceive that product offer as providing the greatest possible net delivered customer value.

This bundling together of benefits and costs in a product offer is the essence of **product differentiation**—the intentional creation of differences in product offers that make a positive difference to targeted market segments. In effect, strategic managers must try to differentiate their firm's product offers in the marketplace by designing product offers that maximize perceived benefits while minimizing perceived costs for customers with targeted preferences.

Highlight Box 6.2 summarizes some aspects of Hyundai's approach to managing the package of benefits and costs in its product offer when it introduced its automobiles into the U.S. market.

Determining an optimal product offer, however, is far from a simple matter, for at least three reasons. First, the benefits and costs in a product offer are invariably interrelated in complex ways. For example, adding features and high performance levels to a product may increase the perceived benefit of the product and perhaps even increase its perceived image value, but would normally also add financial costs—and perhaps even psychic costs if customers start to worry that there are "more things to go wrong" in the product. Although marketing research provides some methods (such as conjoint analysis) for discovering how potential customers are likely to make trade-offs between various benefits and costs, deciding the optimal mix of net delivered customer value in an organization's product offers remains an imperfect science.

Second, NDCV is based on customers' subjective *perceptions* of benefits and costs, and "translating" the many benefits and costs that individual customers might perceive into a common unit of economic measure—such as dollars, Euros, or units of "utility"—is often quite problematic. This perception of value versus costs is especially nebulous when potential customers are asked to judge the benefits and costs of a new product concept with which they do not yet have direct personal experience.

Third, as increasing competition encourages firms to develop more innovative and improved products, consumer expectations are rising steadily in many product markets. When a product fails to live up to customer expectations with respect to any of the four

HIGHLIGHT BOX 6.2

Hyundai Redesigns Its Product Offer in the U.S.

Hyundai, a Korean industrial conglomerate and South Korea's largest producer of automobiles, decided to introduce its cars into the U.S. market in the late 1980s. During the 1980s consumers in the U.S. market generally perceived Japanese cars as being of high quality and reliability, but few if any consumers even knew that there were large-scale automobile producers in South Korea, and most had never heard of Hyundai.

When Hyundai entered the U.S. market, it sought to build up distribution and sales volumes by aggressively pricing its cars several thousand dollars below comparably sized and equipped Japanese car models. Although Hyundai had been a component supplier to Japanese car makers for some years and although its automobiles used major components that were identical to those used in many Japanese cars, U.S. consumers were unaware of these aspects of the quality of Hyundai's vehicles.

U.S. consumers' unfamiliarity with Hyundai as a company, with the Hyundai brand, and with the actual composition of Hyundai cars created a substantial psychic cost in the minds of most consumers, and initial sales remained at a low level. In an effort to boost sales, Hyundai sought to increase the net delivered customer value of its product offer by lowering prices even further. However, effect of lowering prices was to create even greater psychic cost in the minds of U.S. consumers—in effect prompting them to wonder, "How can a car this inexpensive be any good?"

Realizing what the actual impact of lower prices had been on consumers' perceptions of its cars, Hyundai soon returned prices to their initial level and added a new feature to its product offer—an extended, all risk, bumper-to-bumper warranty. This repackaging of Hyundai's product offer was successful in building a quality image for its cars—and in lowering consumers' psychic costs significantly. Hyundai's sales in the U.S. soon began to grow strongly.

sources of perceived benefits, what is normally regarded as a source of benefit can quickly become perceived in a negative way, in effect becoming a cost perception. For example, a manufacturer may introduce a new product with the highest performance level yet offered by that firm, but if the product fails to perform at the level expected by customers, the disappointing performance level of the product can become the psychological equivalent of a cost, not a benefit. Thus, customers' perceptions of benefits and costs are always relative to some set of customer expectations, and those expectations are often a "moving target" in many product markets.

For these reasons and others as well, strategic managers inevitably face considerable uncertainties when they must decide the kinds of product offers their organization will bring to market. In the near-term, strategic managers must take responsibility for the commercial success or failure of the bundles of benefits and costs that their organization brings to market in its product offers. Moreover, in the long term, strategic managers must also take responsibility for the competences their organization will build and maintain in order to provide specific kinds of benefits and costs in its future products. These uncertainties are part of the irreducible *causal ambiguities* in contemporary decision environments that strategic managers must learn to manage, as we discuss further in Chapter 10.

6.3 KEY ACTIVITIES

Achieving the critical success factors

The third element of the Business Concept is the key activities that a firm must perform well in creating and delivering appropriate product offers to customers with targeted sets of preferences—the activities necessary, in effect, to "get the [right] what to the [targeted] who" consistently and reliably. **Key activities** are the activities an organization must perform well to achieve the "critical success factors" in each market segment it serves. Key activities might include (i) managing a global product development network to be sure a firm can always offer its performance-sensitive customers the highest-performing products, (ii) managing a "24/7" logistics and support capability to be sure that time-sensitive customers receive the fastest possible responses to their orders and inquiries 24 hours a day, 7 days a week, or (iii) sourcing the most cost-effective materials and maintaining the most efficient production operations to supply price-sensitive customers.

The key activities in an organization's Business Concept become top priority concerns of management in designing the Core Processes in an organization's Strategic Logic. We discuss the prioritization of activities within an organization's Core Processes in Chapter 8.

6.4 SYSTEM DESIGN PRINCIPLES FOR THE BUSINESS CONCEPT

In designing organizations as value-creating open systems, strategic managers must honor certain system design principles. Two system design principles directly apply to the design of a Business Concept.

System Design Principle 6.1

The three elements of a Business Concept—targeted market preferences, product offer, and key activities—must be internally logically consistent.

This system design principle reminds us that the three elements of a Business Concept must be mutually supportive to work together well and must therefore meet a test of internal logical consistency. Even though this principle may seem obvious, it is actually quite rare to find an organization that genuinely and consistently honors this system design principle in its Business Concept. Several reasons explain why the elements of an organization's Business Concept are likely over time to fail to remain mutually supportive and logically consistent.

Let us suppose that a new organization starts out with a successful, internally consistent Business Concept put together by an entrepreneur or a close-knit management team. As the organization grows, the management task will increase in magnitude, and new organizational units will normally be set up to assume responsibility for various functions in the growing business. In such situations, it would not be unusual to have a marketing group take over the task of defining and targeting market segments, a product development group take a leading role in defining the firm's product offers, and an operations group take on primary responsibility for carrying out key activities. As markets and technologies evolve, each of the three functional groups is likely to make incremental adjustments in the element of the Business Concept for which it has responsibility. As each group pursues its own objectives, the communication and coordination among the three groups will suffer. Over time, it is likely that the market segments the firm targets, the product offers it brings to market, and the key activities it maintains will start to drift apart and become less and less mutually supportive and thus less internally consistent. If the organization is also resource-constrained (as most organizations are), competition for resource allocations may lead to rivalry among the three functional groups, with further deterioration in communication, coordination, and mutually supportive objectives.

Given the common tendency of organizations to lose the internal consistency of their Business Concepts in this way, strategic managers must continually examine and adjust the current targeted market preferences, product offers, and key activities of their organization to ensure the highest possible degree of internal logical consistency and mutual supportiveness.

System Design Principle 6.2

Taken together, the three elements of a Business Concept—targeted market preferences, product offer, and key activities—must have a clear, credible rationale for superior value creation.

This system design principle reminds us that internal logical consistency of the elements of a Business Concept is a necessary but not sufficient condition for creating value. The Business Concept must also have a clear, credible rationale as to why putting the three elements of the Business Concept into action will result in successful value creation by the organization. In effect, this system design principle places the organization's Business Concept in a competitive context and demands convincing reasons why that Business Concept should succeed at least as well as—and preferably surpass—competing Business Concepts being advanced by other organizations. Again, this principle may seem obvious, but it too is rarely consistently applied in practice.

Consider the following pattern of entrepreneurial behavior observed among the pizza shops located along the commercial avenues that surround the University of Illinois campus in Champaign-Urbana, Illinois. At any given time, nearly fifty pizza shops operate in the commercial areas serving the nearly 40,000 students on this large university campus. Although some pizza shops have developed some distinctive pizza styles, appear to be quite profitable, and have remained in business for many years, large numbers of pizza shops—often as many as seven or eight per year—go out of business. These shops typically serve rather plain "generic" pizzas that offer minimal quality, large quantity, and low price. Curiously, when such pizza shops fail, they are soon replaced by new pizza shops that closely emulate the pizzas offered by the recently failed pizza businesses—minimal quality, large quantity, and low price. Inevitably, within a year or two, these pizza shops also fail, and are replaced by yet more new pizza shops that also closely emulate the pizzas of the businesses they are replacing, and soon fail. This cycle of failing pizza businesses has continued for decades around the campus.

The point of this story is that many businesses, whether started by individual entrepreneurs or large corporations, are often launched after they solve the practical problems of how to organize the new business—which they often do by emulating another business. In many cases, however, the new business will be started without a clearly defined rationale as to why the product offers of the new business will be perceived as offering superior net delivered customer value compared to competing product offers already in the marketplace. Given the observable absence of a clear rationale for superior value creation in many businesses, strategic managers must continually question and critique the Business Concept of their organization. Strategic managers must be sure that there are clear and convincing reasons why putting a given Business Concept into action will result in product offers that customers in targeted market segments will perceive as offering greater net delivered customer value than competing product offers available in the marketplace.

6.5 THREE TYPES OF "GENERIC" PRODUCT STRATEGIES

We now consider three types of generic product strategies that illustrate Business Concepts that honor the two system design principles discussed in the preceding section. The three product strategies are illustrated in Figure 6.4.

Focused Differentiation Product Strategy

Some organizations may choose to focus on understanding and serving the preferences of customers in a single market segment better than competing organizations. They will devote considerable energy to developing detailed knowledge of customers in a targeted market segment and will work hard to establish and maintain close customer relationships. The understanding they develop about the preferences of customers in the targeted market segment will be used to define and finely tune product offers to provide benefits that customers in the targeted market segment will perceive as extremely attractive. Competence building will be focused on developing the specialized resources, capabilities, and management processes needed to create and realize these finely tuned product offers. Organizations pursuing this focused differentiation product strategy will generally try to avoid direct price competition. Instead, prices will be set at levels that provide significant net delivered customer value for the targeted market segment, while also supporting high levels of investment in developing new resources and capabilities to serve targeted customers even better.

SAAB, the Swedish automobile maker now owned by General Motors, provides an example of a successful focused differentiation strategy. SAAB focuses on designing a limited line of cars that emphasize superior safety, exceptional handling and road performance, outstanding ergonomics, "high-tech" yet comfortable interiors, and aerodynamic styling. Customers for SAAB's cars are typically well-educated, successful professionals who appreciate safety, performance, technical sophistication, and the characteristic SAAB approach to design and styling. SAAB carefully trains its dealers to cultivate long-term relationships with such customers. The firm also closely manages its communications with its customers to consistently project an image of intelligent design, thoughtful attention to detail, and outstanding technical competence. SAAB's

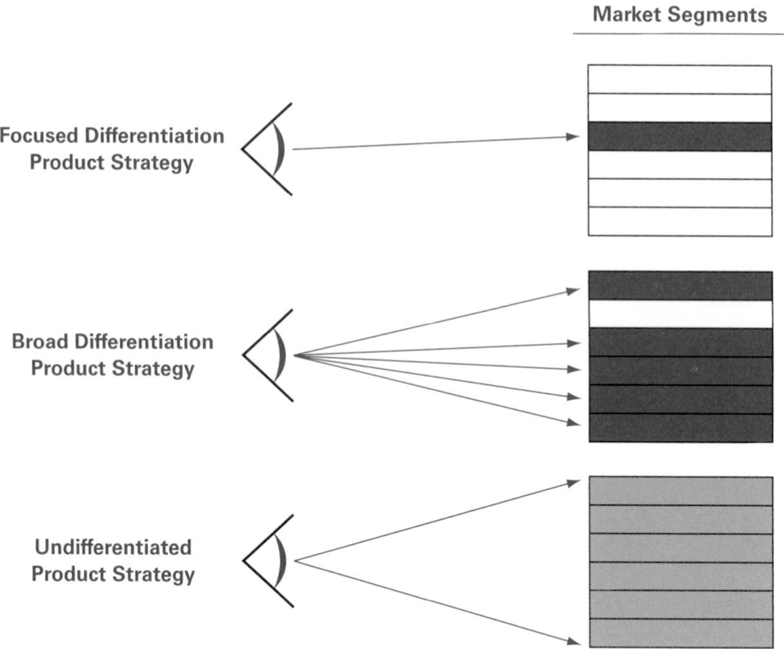

FIGURE 6.4 Three Types of "Generic" Product Strategies

consistent and clear focus on serving the preferences of its targeted market segment has earned the brand one of the highest levels of customer loyalty and repeat purchases in the automobile industry.

Broad Differentiation Product Strategy

Organizations pursuing a broad differentiation product strategy try to understand and serve the preferences of several market segments in a product market. The most ambitious broad differentiators may try to serve the preferences of all or nearly all of the market segments in a product market. Firms pursuing this strategy usually adopt a multidivisional structure that lets each division or business unit focus on a single market segment. At the same time, a central management function will seek out *synergies* across its divisions—opportunities to coordinate the activities of the various divisions in ways that can create advantages for each division that it could not obtain as a freestanding, independent business activity. A typical way of achieving synergy, for example, combines the common production activities of two or more divisions to increase economies of scale and lower unit costs of production. (We consider other ways of achieving synergies across multiple business units later in this text, when we discuss corporate strategy.)

TietoEnator, a leading Scandinavian information services firm, provides an example of a successful broad differentiation product strategy in services. TietoEnator works closely with key customers in a number of targeted industries—such as banking, telecommunications, forest products, oil and energy, health care, and the public sector—to develop leading-edge information systems for managing their businesses and "mission-critical" processes. When the company develops information systems that provide clearly superior results for its customers in those industries, it then uses its industry-specific expertise to develop information systems and services that it can then market to other firms in those industries.

General Motors Corporation is another example of a broad product differentiator—in this case, one that tries to compete in virtually every market segment for automobiles in its major markets of North America, Europe, and Asia. General Motors' product strategy is an outgrowth of its early CEO Alfred Sloan's idea of producing a range of branded automobiles "for every purse." Under Alfred Sloan, General Motors developed a portfolio of brands that would appeal to many market segments with different price and performance sensitivities. Alfred Sloan also reorganized General Motors to implement the other important aspect of a broad differentiation strategy—the realization of synergies across its brand-based business units. While the designs of each brand of General Motors cars' bodywork and interiors were managed to be distinctive, nondifferentiating components such as chassis, gear boxes, and suspensions were designed to be used in common across all or many product models to lower development and production costs. The combination of well-differentiated brands with distinctive designs and low production costs catapulted General Motors from a collection of struggling small automobile companies to one of the largest industrial enterprises in the world within a period of 20 years.

The experience of General Motors in the 1980s and 1990s, however, illustrates the inherent challenge in the broad differentiation strategy of trying to focus on and compete effectively in many different market segments. In recent years General Motors has had difficulty maintaining distinctive, appealing, contemporary identities for some of its brands. After years of declining sales, for example, in 2000 the firm decided to terminate its Oldsmobile brand, one of the oldest American automobile brands in existence and once one of General Motors' best-selling product lines.

Undifferentiated Product Strategy

An undifferentiated product strategy is one that undertakes to create a product that will appeal to customers in all or many market segments. In essence, in this product strategy an organization tries to define and design a new product that reliably meets the basic needs of consumers for a given type of product. The organization then produces the product at low cost and offers it to the market at such an attractive price that virtually all consumers will purchase the product—at least from time to time—regardless of their actual "first preferences" for that type of product.

An example of this product strategy is Bic Corporation's ubiquitous plastic pens and pencils. These products are designed to provide only the essential functions of a writing instrument, but to do so reliably. Bic pens and pencils are mass-produced at very large scale and correspondingly low unit costs, are priced well below other writing products that offer more elegant styling or additional features, and are distributed widely to most supermarkets, drug stores, office supply stores, convenience stores, and airport kiosks in the geographic areas Bic serves. Because of the basic but reliable performance of Bic's pens and pencils, their low price, and convenient availability, many different users of pens and pencils buy a package of Bic pens or pencils from time to time, even if their "usual" preference is for a more elegantly styled or prestigiously branded pen or pencil.

Occasionally a firm develops a new product targeted at a specific market segment, only to realize subsequently that the product has strong appeal to customers in many other market segments as well. In effect, a firm may fortuitously discover that its product can be the basis for a successful undifferentiated product strategy. Perhaps the most heralded example of a fortuitously successful undifferentiated product strategy is the introduction of the original Volkswagen Beetle in the U.S. market in the 1950s and 1960s. Originally positioning the Beetle as a low-cost, economical car intended for the most cost-sensitive customers in the U.S. automobile market, Volkswagen was quick to discover that many different kinds of customers were buying the Beetle for a number of other reasons. Many customers were buying the Beetle because it was "cute," "unusual," or just "fun to drive." In many cases, people who could afford to buy virtually any car they wanted—and who already owned an automobile of their first choice—were buying a Beetle as an inexpensive, fun-to-drive second car. In one of the classic advertising campaigns of all time, Volkswagen promptly revamped its advertising and positioning of the Beetle in the U.S. market to communicate the distinctive design and driving fun—as well as low-cost—aspects of its product to customers in all market segments.

KEY TERMS AND CONCEPTS

market needs Basic requirements for food, shelter, clothing, and other essentials for living that all consumers have to some extent.

market preferences Preferred ways of satisfying basic needs that are usually determined by consumers' lifestyles and economic situations.

market segments Groupings of potential customers with similar preferences.

mass customization and product personalization The use of modular product designs and flexible manufacturing systems to offer products that can be configured and produced to meet an individual customer's preferences.

real-time market research The use of a configurable modular product to explore customer preferences in real time by offering customers a range of product variations and letting customers choose which variations they prefer to buy.

net delivered customer value (NDCV) In a customer's perception of a product offer, the excess of the perceived value derived from the product and its associated services, image, and personal interaction over the perceived costs of money, time, energy, and psychic concern.

product benefits The perceived value of the functions, features, and performance levels of a product that enable a user of the product to do things they could not otherwise do, or could not do as well.

service value The perceived value of all the activities that a firm performs for a customer.

image value The perceived value of the image that a user believes will be signaled to others (or possibly to himself or herself) by using a product.

personal interaction value The perceived value of a customer's interactions with the people involved in selling, delivering, servicing, and supporting a product.

financial costs The perceived total monetary costs of a customer's purchase, use, maintenance, and retirement of a product.

time costs The perceived costs of the time a customer must spend to acquire, use, maintain, and retire a product.

energy costs The perceived costs of the energy a customer must expend to acquire, use, maintain, and retire a product.

psychic costs The perceived costs of the worry or anxiety felt by a customer as they think about acquiring, using, maintaining, and retiring a product.

product differentiation The "bundling" together of the four perceived value components and four perceived cost components in a way that is intended to provide the greatest perceived net delivered customer value for customers in a targeted market segment.

key activities The activities that are critical in successfully delivering the net delivered customer value of a product offer to customers in a targeted market segment.

REVIEW QUESTIONS

1. What are the three elements of a Business Concept?
2. Why is a Business Concept focused on serving specific *preferences* rather than specific customers?
3. When is it desirable to use real-time market research to discover preferences?
4. According to our system design principles for a Business Concept, what must be the two characteristics of the three elements of a Business Concept?
5. What is a focused differentiation product strategy?
6. What is a broad differentiation product strategy?
7. What is an undifferentiated product strategy?

CHAPTER 7

THE ORGANIZATION CONCEPT: RESOURCES, ORGANIZATION DESIGN, AND CONTROLS AND INCENTIVES

INTRODUCTION

The previous chapter described the first building block in an organization's Strategic Logic—its Business Concept. We now consider the next essential building block in a Strategic Logic—the **Organization Concept** developed by strategic managers for carrying out the Business Concept. In this chapter we examine the three critical organizational issues that strategic managers must understand and address:

- What *resources* will be used by our organization?
- What *organization design* will we use to coordinate those resources?
- How will we monitor, evaluate, and reward providers of resources that are used in carrying out our Business Concept (i.e., what *controls and incentives* will we use)?

As suggested in Figure 7.1, strategic managers' answers to these questions define the three essential elements of an Organization Concept. Just as the Business Concept sets boundaries on the customer preferences an organization will try to serve, defines the nature of the product offers the organization will create, and identifies key activities it must undertake, the Organization Concept determines the boundaries of an organization, greatly influences the kind of organization it will be, and defines the key internal activities of the organization. Similarly, while the Business Concept summarizes an organization's strategy for competing in *product markets,* the Organization Concept determines an organization's strategy for competing in *resource markets.* In effect, the Organization Concept determines the kinds of resources an organization will try to attract and the kind of organizational environment and rewards it can offer to providers of resources that contribute to the organization's value-creation processes.

We next consider in some detail each of the three elements of an Organization Concept—resources, organization design, and controls and incentives—as well as the system design principles that strategic managers must observe in order to create an Organization Concept that is an effective element of a Strategic Logic. We then consider the relative abilities of a Business Concept and an Organization Concept to be a source of sustainable competitive advantage.

7.1 DEFINING AN ORGANIZATION'S ESSENTIAL RESOURCES: ASSETS, CAPABILITIES, AND KNOWLEDGE

Resources include anything tangible or intangible that would be both useful and available to an organization in carrying out its value-creating activities. Organizations require resources of many types, and a central and ongoing concern of strategic managers is deciding what

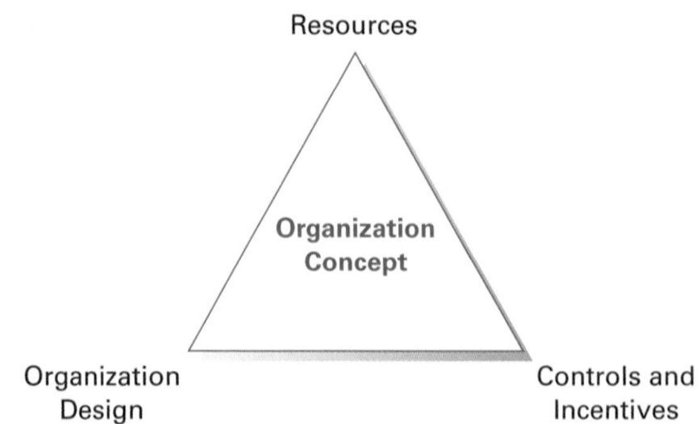

FIGURE 7.1 The Three Elements of the Organization Concept

Deciding what resources an organization will use to create value

kinds of resources their organization will need to use in order to carry out its value-creation processes in the most effective way. The resources an organization can use may be either *firm-specific* or *firm-addressable.* Firm-specific resources are resources that are internal to an organization—its employees, the machines, buildings, and land it owns, and the intellectual property it possesses. Firm-addressable resources are resources that an organization does not own, but that it can access through market transactions or other means to be used when needed. Firm-addressable resources include employees that can be hired when needed, materials and services that can be purchased from suppliers, equipment and facilities that can be rented or leased, money that can be borrowed from financial institutions or obtained from investors, and so on.[1]

Managers must be able to identify and acquire or arrange the use of three important kinds of resources—assets, capabilities, and knowledge—and to configure those resources into effective systems and processes for creating value. We first examine these three kinds of resources, and then consider the relative advantages of using *flexible resources* or *specific-use resources.* We next discuss the criteria managers should consider when deciding whether to internalize a resource or to use market transactions to assure the use of a resource when needed. We then consider the importance of developing an organization's *coordination flexibility* to respond to changing market opportunities by quickly configuring resources into effective value-creating processes.

Assets

An *asset* is anything that would be *useful* to an organization in achieving its goals. Thus, an asset will generally be something that could contribute in a clearly definable way to an organization's value-creation activities. Assets may be tangible (like machines and buildings) or intangible (like ideas, reputations, and relationships). When an asset is *available* to a firm to use in its value-creating activities, the asset can be considered a *resource* that can be used in configuring an organization's systems for creating value.

Some assets contribute directly to an organization's ability to carry out its Business Concept through its value-creation activities, and others play a more indirect—but nevertheless often important—role in helping an organization create value through its Business Concept. Assets like good product designs, quality-oriented production systems, and a respected brand can help an organization create value by increasing the *perceived value* of

[1] A firm may also access the resources in other firms by merging with or acquiring other firms. We discuss the acquisition of new resources through merger and acquisition in Chapters 11 and 12.

an organization's products and thus the price that customers are willing to pay for the products offered by the organization. Other assets, like effective engineering designs and efficient production and distribution systems, can reduce the costs an organization incurs in providing its products to customers. An organization's potential for creating value through its Business Concept therefore depends significantly on its managers' ability to identify and arrange the use of the best possible assets for increasing the perceived value of an organization's products and reducing the costs of creating and realizing its products.

Capabilities

Capabilities are "repeatable patterns of action" in an organization.

Capabilities are an organization's *repeatable patterns of action in the use of assets.* Capabilities are therefore an *action-based resource* that occupies a middle position in the hierarchy of abilities an organization may have, as shown in Table 7.1. At the most fundamental level, individuals may have *skills,* which represent the actions an individual knows how to perform reliably in carrying out a given task. *Capabilities* arise in an organization when groups or teams of individuals are able to coordinate their skills in carrying out a process of importance to an organization's overall value-creating activities. For example, a team of production workers who can consistently manufacture high-quality products or a group of marketing people who can create and manage effective advertising campaigns bring important capabilities to an organization. We previously defined *competence* (see Chapter 1) as the ability of an organization *to sustain coordinated deployments of assets and capabilities in ways that help the organization achieve its goals.* Competence is therefore an organizational characteristic that arises when the capabilities of the various groups and teams of people in the organization can be coordinated to work together in a way that enables the organization to achieve its goals.[2]

Knowledge

Knowledge provides the foundation for every action that an organization undertakes. Knowledge is therefore a resource that is essential to every organization, and strategic managers must be able to identify and help their organization acquire or access the many kinds of knowledge necessary to sustain its value-creation processes. In carrying out their key *knowledge management* role, strategic managers need to understand some fundamental characteristics of knowledge, including the following:

TABLE 7.1 Hierarchy of Abilities: Individuals, Groups, and Organizations

Individuals	Individuals develop *skills* in performing specific tasks.
Groups, Teams	Groups and teams develop *capabilities* in coordinating the skills of individuals in *repeatable patterns of action.*
Organizations	Organizations have *competence* when they can sustain coordinated deployments of assets and capabilities that help achieve the organization's goals.

[2] In human resources management, the term competency is often used to denote what we refer to here as an individual's skills. For example, an individual's competency profile in human resources terminology would correspond, in our terminology, to an individual's set of skills in performing a range of tasks. We can also make an important distinction between an individual's competency in a human resources management framework and an organization's competence in our strategic management framework.

- Conceptual differences between data, information, and knowledge
- Some key forms of knowledge: know-how, know-why, and know-what

Data, Information, and Knowledge

Data are observations.

Data are observations about events and entities, and may include both qualitative descriptions and quantitative measures. For example, data could include qualitative observations made in a salesperson's report of a meeting to discuss a customer's reaction to a new product, as well as quantitative sales figures indicating the number of units of the new product shipped to the customer in the most recent quarter. Because data are just observations, they do not themselves have much meaning until they are interpreted in some way. Interpretation usually involves comparing data gathered in one time period with the same type of data gathered in another time period (e.g., sales of a new product in this quarter compared to sales in the previous quarter). Interpretation may also include comparing data about one situation with data about one or more similar situations (e.g., comparisons of the reactions of similar kinds of customers to a newly introduced product).

Information is meaning derived from the interpretation of data.

Information is created when the interpretation of data indicates that some situation of interest to a person or organization either is constant or is changing in some significant way. For example, if sales data gathered by a firm are compared and indicate that sales in the current quarter are greater than sales in the same quarter last year, we may derive the basic but important bit of information that sales of the firm are growing. Similarly, comparing interviews with a sample of customers may indicate that all interviewed customers are satisfied with a new product, or alternatively may indicate that some customers are happy with the new product, while others are not. Information derived from comparisons of data over time or across situations becomes the basis for the development of knowledge.

Knowledge is a set of beliefs about causal relationships.

Knowledge is the set of beliefs that an individual has about causal (cause-and-effect) relationships in his or her environment. In effect, knowledge is the beliefs that each of us has about what kinds of *actions* lead to what kinds of *outcomes* in various situations. We form these beliefs by evaluating information about various situations to discover *repeated patterns* of events and circumstances. When we notice repeated patterns of events and circumstances—for example, that maintaining high levels of television advertising has consistently been accompanied by high levels of sales—we may infer a cause-and-effect relationship between television advertising and sales. We may then want to test that causal relationship by hypothesizing that increasing television advertising would lead to increased sales. If we increase television advertising and sales subsequently increase, our belief in a causal relationship between television advertising and sales is likely to be strengthened, and we will start to believe we "know" at least one effective way to increase sales. On the other hand, if increased advertising fails to increase sales, our belief in a causal relationship between television advertising and sales is likely to be weakened, and we may even start to doubt whether maintaining high levels of advertising has actually helped to maintain high sales levels. We may then even try reducing television advertising to see whether that action has a negative impact on sales.

Through processes of comparing data to discover patterns of possible cause-and-effect relationships and then testing hypotheses based on those relationships, people form beliefs about what kinds of actions cause what kinds of outcomes. In this way, the accumulated observation and interpretation of events in our environment lead to the formation of the sets of beliefs about causal relationships that we call *knowledge.*

(The processes of knowledge formation in organizations—and the challenge to strategic managers of managing these processes effectively—is discussed further in Chapter 10.)

Know-How, Know-Why, and Know-What

Three important forms of knowledge

Knowledge can of course be about many different kinds of causal relationships, but three forms of knowledge—know-how, know-why, and know-what—are of particular importance to an organization's value-creating processes and thus deserve careful attention by strategic managers. These three strategically important forms of knowledge are summarized in Table 7.2.[3]

Know-how is practical "hands-on" knowledge about *how* an organization's current systems and processes work and is therefore the form of knowledge that is essential to maintaining the efficiency and reliability of an organization's current operations. Know-how is knowledge that individuals develop and use in performing specific tasks within an organization. Important forms of know-how include the knowledge of production workers about how to maintain machine settings to achieve a consistent quality level on a production line, the knowledge of a customer account manager about the specific forms of service that must be performed well to keep various customers satisfied, the knowledge of a logistics manager about how to maintain just-in-time delivery to a key industrial customer, and so on.

Know-why is theoretical knowledge about *why* a given system or process design works and is the form of knowledge required to significantly modify a current system or process design or to create a new system or process design. Know-why knowledge is normally acquired by individuals through study of the science, technology, and design principles used in designing various kinds of systems and processes. Know-why may also be developed by individuals who develop insights into why current systems and processes either work well or do not work well. Know-why is the kind of knowledge required to design new kinds of products, new kinds of production processes, new logistics systems, new information systems, new kinds of control systems, new processes for managing customer relationships, and the like.

Know-what is strategic knowledge about the uses to which the know-how and know-why knowledge within or available to an organization can be applied. Know-what is the form of knowledge that enables strategic managers to recognize value-creation opportunities that their organizations can respond to and develop effectively. In essence, the know-what of an organization's strategic managers is the source of its "corporate imagination" that can conceive of new or improved Business Concepts the organization could pursue.

Identifying, accessing, and using the know-how, know-why, and know-what knowledge resources needed to enable an organization to achieve its goals is the essence of

TABLE 7.2 Three Forms of Knowledge: Know-How, Know-Why, Know-What

Know-How	Practical "hands-on" knowledge that enables people to maintain an existing system or process in good working order
Know-Why	Theoretical knowledge that enables people to design new systems and processes
Know-What	Strategic knowledge of the purposes to which available know-how and know-why can be applied

[3] Two other forms of important knowledge are know-who and know-when. *Know-who* is knowledge about "who knows what" within or outside an organization. Know-who becomes a useful form of knowledge when information about "who knows what" can be used to identify people whose knowledge can help an organization accomplish some task. *Know-when* is knowledge about the most appropriate timing for launching (or ending) an organization's initiatives. Know-when knowledge may require both "demand-side" understanding of the best time to begin or end market initiatives and "supply-side" understanding of the time an organization will need to begin carrying out a new process or task.

knowledge management. The key role of strategic managers in knowledge management processes is discussed in more detail in Chapter 10. For now, we note that both the boundaries of an organization and the interorganizational relationships an organization seeks to develop and maintain are increasingly influenced by the know-how, know-why, and know-what knowledge resources that strategic managers believe are needed to sustain an organization's value-creation processes. Thus, knowledge resources have become a critical cornerstone of the Organization Concept and now exercise considerable influence on the decisions strategic managers make about overall organization design and about the controls and incentives the organization will adopt.

7.2 CREATING ORGANIZATIONS AS ADAPTIVE RESOURCE SYSTEMS: COMBINING RESOURCE FLEXIBILITY AND COORDINATION FLEXIBILITY

As open systems, organizations must gather and use resources in ways that allow them to respond successfully to the changing opportunities and demands of their environments. The *strategic flexibility* of an organization to respond effectively to a dynamic environment thus depends both on the inherent flexibilities of its available resources and on the flexibility of its managers to coordinate new combinations of resources in new ways. We next consider the properties of resources that increase *resource flexibility* and the managerial capabilities required to achieve *coordination flexibility* in an organization.[4]

Resource Flexibility

The flexibility of an organizational resource can be described by three properties:

Resources have varying degrees of flexibility.

- The *number of different uses* to which the resource can be applied
- The *cost* to the organization of switching the resource from one use to another
- The *time* required to switch the resource from one use to another

The flexibility of a resource increases with the number of different uses to which a resource can be applied. Some tangible resources like computers are flexible because they can be used for many purposes, from running accounting systems to providing computer-aided design (CAD) systems for designing products. By contrast, some tangible assets like dedicated production machines are inherently inflexible *specific-use resources* because they can only do one task, although they may do that task at high speed and low cost. Similarly, the flexibility of intangible resources like knowledge or brands increases when such resources can be applied to more than one product. Human resources are flexible when people have skills that are useful in performing a variety of tasks, and when they are able to learn new skills that expand the kinds of tasks they can perform. By the same token, human resources are inflexible when they are unwilling or unable to perform more than one kind of task.

When a resource has the flexibility to be applied to more than one purpose, its flexibility may still be limited in practice when it has large *switching costs,* that is, when an organization must incur large costs to redeploy the resource from one use to another use. Similarly, the flexibility of a resource may be limited when it takes an organization a long time to switch the resource from one use to another, because there may be a significant opportunity cost when the organization cannot respond quickly to an opportunity or demand in its environment.

[4] Sanchez, R. (1995). Strategic Flexibility in Product Competition. *Strategic Management Journal, 16 (summer special issue),*135-159.

Coordination Flexibility

Coordination flexibility is the ability to identify, configure, and deploy new resources.

The flexibility of an organization's managers to coordinate resources effectively depends on their capabilities in the following areas:

- *Identifying* new (as well as currently available) resources that can be effectively applied in responding to new opportunities and demands
- *Configuring* those resources into an effective system
- *Deploying* the system of resources to new purposes

To be able to identify important new resources, managers must be able to imagine how new kinds of resources could be used, perhaps even in new kinds of processes that may not currently exist in their organization. In addition, managers must be able to imagine how resources that are currently available to the organization could be used in new ways that increase their effectiveness.

The next task of managers is to configure resources into an effective system for responding to new opportunities or demands. Performing this task well requires that managers understand the kinds of interactions that will have to take place between new and preexisting resources in the organization's processes and that they support and facilitate those interactions so that the resources work together smoothly and reliably. Managers must then be able to deploy the new system of resources effectively—to set clear goals for the organization's new processes and to provide performance measures and incentive systems that enable the new system of resources to focus on achieving those goals.

We next consider further the key task of configuring resource systems, which we refer to as *organization design* in our model of the Organization Concept. We then consider the essential role of *controls and incentives*—the third element in our Organization Concept—in achieving effective deployments of resource systems.

7.3 ORGANIZATION DESIGN: DECIDING TASK ALLOCATIONS, AUTHORITY DISTRIBUTION, AND INFORMATION FLOWS

Once strategic managers have determined the resources that will be used to carry out an organization's Business Concept, they must then determine the most effective way to configure those resources in the organization's value-creation processes. In effect, managers must create an **organization design** that determines three essential aspects of a system of resources:

- Task allocations (who will do what)
- Authority distribution (who will decide what)
- Information flows (who will know what, when, and why)

Let us consider the key choices and challenges that strategic managers face when deciding these three aspects of an organization design.

Task Allocation

Task allocation assigns responsibility for performing specific tasks in an organization.

In order for an organization as a system of resources to work well together, the overall value-creation process of the organization must be decomposed into specific tasks, and different people in the organization given the responsibility to carry out specific tasks. The various tasks to be performed in the organization may then be further decomposed into subtasks and so on, and responsibilities assigned to subunits of the organization for each subtask or smaller part of a task. **Task allocation** refers to this process of decomposing an organization's value-creation processes into specific tasks and assigning responsibilities for those tasks to individuals, groups, and teams within the organization.

Three "traditional" approaches are commonly used to decompose value-creation processes into specific tasks and areas of responsibility, and at least two new approaches are now being used in many organizations. Each approach to assigning responsibilities focuses the attention of people assigned a given responsibility on managing certain aspects of the organization's value-creation processes. The particular focus that each approach brings to managing results in both strengths and weaknesses—or pluses and minuses—that are characteristic of each approach. Strategic managers must weigh the relative strengths and weaknesses of each approach to task allocation, and then decide which approach will, on balance, bring the greatest net benefits.

Functions

Three "traditional" approaches may be used in assigning tasks and responsibilities: functions, products, and regions.

Perhaps the oldest and most traditional way of decomposing an organization's value-creation processes is by functions that require specific kinds of expertise and skills to perform. Functional decomposition is the basis of the specialization of labor in Adam Smith's famous example of the pin factory.[5] Under the craft system of production, each worker performed all the steps involved in making a pin. With the advent the specialization of labor in factory production systems, however, each worker in the pin factory focused on one step in the pin-making process. By specializing in only one step in a production process, each worker avoided the loss of time that would result when the worker switched from one task to another throughout the production process. In addition, by performing the same kind of task repeatedly, workers in the factory would develop greater skill and efficiency in performing each task, with the effect that the overall production process became much more efficient than a craft-based production system.

Functional task allocations enable a "deepening of expertise" in performing each task.

Today, decomposing an organization's value-creation processes into functional tasks and management responsibilities focused on functional tasks is thought to bring not only cost efficiencies, but a "deepening of expertise" as both workers and managers focus on and develop greater competencies in performing a specific kind of activity. Thus, in order to focus on continuously improving both efficiency and capabilities in key processes, many organizations today allocate tasks and responsibilities by key "functional areas" like research and development, marketing, logistics, finance, accounting, and so on.

The potential disadvantage of giving managers a functional focus, however, is the infamous "silo effect" in which functional area managers may become overly focused on their functional area and lose sight of the role of that function in the overall value-creation process of the organization. Communication and coordination across functional areas may then become quite difficult, leading to loss of effectiveness in the organization's systemic ability to sustain value-creation processes.

Given these potential strengths and weaknesses, task allocations by functions may work best when used by organizations in fairly stable market environments in which both the market preferences to be served and the technological means to serve those preferences are well understood and unlikely to change, and in which cost reductions achieved through productivity improvements are the key to increasing profitability. Strategic managers may then be able to define, assign, and coordinate tasks in such a way that each functional area can focus on performing its assigned responsibilities more and more efficiently, without a loss of overall effectiveness in the organization's value-creation processes. Companies that produce commodity products like petrochemicals or basic metals typically face stable market preferences and technologies of production, and as a result often use functional task allocations quite successfully to achieve continuous efficiency improvements and cost reductions.

[5] Smith, Adam. (1776). *The Wealth of Nations.* New York: Random House, 1977.

Products

Product-based task allocations clearly focus functions on specific products.

Another traditional approach to assigning tasks and responsibilities is by products or product lines. This approach became common as companies grew in size and scope in the late 1800s and began to diversify into the production of many kinds of products. As large companies began to produce more kinds of products, it became increasingly difficult for managers and other employees working in a given functional area to develop the expertise needed to effectively support a broad range of products. Decomposing an organization into units responsible for a specific type of product, however, made it possible for functional subunits (like research and development or production) within a product unit to focus on deepening their expertise in support of a given type of product.

Today the advantages of a product-based approach to allocating tasks remain much the same. Especially in product markets like computers, consumer electronics, and other "high-tech" products, competitive success depends on providing products with leading-edge performance and cost effectiveness. In such markets, most companies use product-based organization to focus management attention on deepening and coordinating the various functional expertise needed to create and realize world-class products of a given type.

A potential disadvantage of a product-based organization, however, is duplication of functions across several product-focused business units, with resulting high costs of performing such functions in the overall organization. One of the main challenges to strategic managers in allocating tasks by product is therefore to correctly determine which tasks should be operating positions focused on supporting specific products, and which tasks should be staff positions allocated to supporting specific kinds of activities across many or all product units. Most companies that use products as the primary basis for allocating tasks and responsibilities are "hybrid" organizations in which some functional expertise is allocated to supporting specific products, while some expertise is allocated to central staff units serving the broader organization.

Regions

Regional task allocations create a focus on understanding regional preferences and conditions.

The third traditional approach is to allocate tasks and responsibilities by region. Regional organizational units appeared as the geographic expansion of companies in the 1800s exceeded the ability of the limited communication and transportation infrastructures of the time to support centralized coordination from a single headquarters. Today, however, regional units are most typically established to focus organizational units on understanding and serving the preferences of customers in different countries or regions of the world. Regional organization is thus most often found in product markets in which the preferences of consumers vary significantly across regions or in service markets in which close attention to local customers is essential to competitive success.

The potential disadvantage of regional organization is of course the duplication of functions across regions, with resulting higher costs to the overall organization. In addition, a regional focus to some knowledge-intensive activities like research and development may lead to reduced learning opportunities and thus reduced "deepening of expertise" compared to organizing such activities by functions on a global basis. As in product-based organizations, to avoid these disadvantages most contemporary regional organizations will actually be hybrid organizations, with some functions performed in regional operating units and some functions (or some activities within a given function) performed in a central staff unit.

Key Customers

A more contemporary approach to allocating tasks in an organization is to focus at least some units on serving important *key customers*. In this approach, the manager of a key customer unit must focus on understanding the needs of a specific customer in detail and on developing and coordinating the functional expertise required to meet those needs in a superior way. A key customer approach to organization is also used to improve communication with the key customer by creating one point of contact between the organization and the customer's organization.

As in product and regional organizations, a potential disadvantage of the key customer approach is duplication of functions across organizational units. In addition, an exclusive focus on developing the expertise needed to serve a given customer's needs particularly well may lead to a narrowing of expertise within key customer units, with a resulting fragmentation of expertise within the overall organization.

Projects

Projects to launch important initiatives have become an increasingly common feature of many organizations. Projects often bring together people with different kinds of expertise to focus on a new opportunity or demand facing an organization. In some cases, projects are focused on developing new expertise and on introducing new methods and ways of working in an organization based on newly developed expertise.

Successful projects may even become more or less permanent units within organizations. A project team organized to launch a new product or to enter a new market overseas, for example, may become the core of a permanent unit with responsibility for the new product or regional business. In other cases, a project to introduce a new process capability like total quality management into a company may become a permanent staff function in support of the organization's operating units.

The Hierarchy of Task Allocations

All organizations have functional tasks to perform and products or services to provide. Many organizations also have operations in more than one geographic region, serve at least some key customers, and have projects of various types underway that may take on permanent or semipermanent status. As a result, most organizations will need several kinds of task allocations in their value-creation processes. In such organizations, it is common to find a multilevel hierarchy of task allocations, as suggested by the familiar "organization chart" illustrated in Figure 7.2.

> The hierarchy of task allocations influences managers' priorities.

In deciding the hierarchy of task allocations to be used in an organization, strategic managers are in effect creating a set of priorities for managing the organization's value-creation processes. The basis of task allocations adopted for the first level of the task allocation hierarchy will determine the primary focus of management attention at the highest level of the organization. This focus will in turn influence the priorities that managers at that level set in performing their tasks. This focus will be reinforced when managers in the

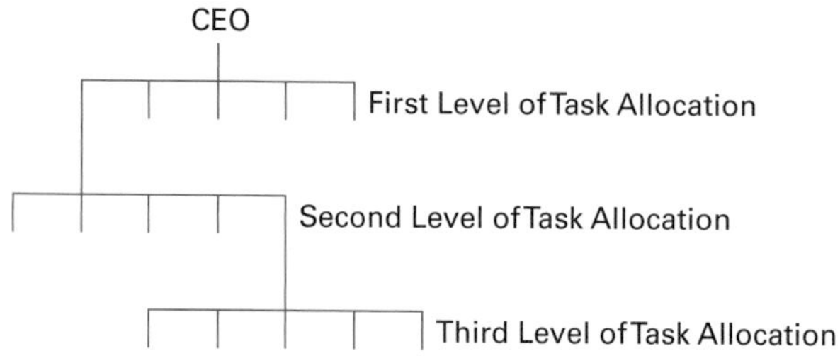

FIGURE 7.2 The Multilevel Hierarchy of Task Allocations in an Organization

first level of the hierarchy are given "bottom line" responsibility for the financial performance of their organizational unit. For example, if the first level of the organization allocates management responsibilities by product, managers at that level will as a first priority work to maximize the success of the product or product line they have responsibility for, and will pay less attention to improving functional expertise of broad use to the organization or to developing business in regions that would not significantly affect the success of their products. Similarly, if managers at the first level of the organizational hierarchy have responsibilities for functional areas, they will tend to give priority to deepening the expertise related to their functional area and will pay less attention to contributing to the success of any specific product or region.

In a similar manner, the task allocations used in the second level of the organization hierarchy will determine the second level of management priorities in the organization, and so on down to the lowest level of task allocations used in an organization. Thus, in creating a multilevel hierarchy of task allocations, strategic managers must decide which approach to task allocation should be used at which level of the organization in order to focus managers' attention and set management priorities in a way that will, on balance, produce the best results for the organization's value-creation processes. Moreover, as an organization's competitive environment changes over time, the hierarchy of task allocations used in the organization may also need to change in order to realign management focus and priorities with the organization's changing circumstances. Thus, periodic reorganization—e.g., changes in the basis of top-line task allocations—is often an essential element in maintaining an organization's ability to create value in a dynamic environment.

Primary Task Allocations in Matrix and Hybrid Organizations

Matrix and hybrid organizations seek a superior balance of management focus and priorities.

Organization design is a creative process in which strategic managers may explore alternatives to the traditional multilevel hierarchy of task allocations shown in Figure 7.2. Two such alternatives include matrix and hybrid organization designs. Both the matrix organization's use of two "primary" task allocations and the hybrid organization's mix of approaches to primary task allocations represent efforts to achieve the best possible balance of management focus and priorities in an organization's value-creation processes.

Matrix Organization Design

In a matrix organization design, strategic managers create a "two-dimensional" organization structure based on two approaches to allocating tasks and responsibilities to top managers.[6] As illustrated in Figure 7.3, a matrix structure creates both "horizontal" and "vertical" first-levels of management task allocations, each with its own responsibilities for functions, products, regions, key customers, or projects. Common combinations of horizontal and vertical task allocations include functions and products, products and regions, functions and regions, and (more recently, especially in industrial markets) products and key customers.

A matrix organization design tries to improve on a traditional "one-dimensional" organization design (such as the one in Figure 7.2) by focusing top management attention on some combination of functions, products, regions, or key customers—and thereby elevating two aspects of an organization's value-creation processes to the status of equal priority within the organization. In this way, a matrix organization provides a system of management checks and balances intended to improve consistency and coordination in carrying out the organization's overall Strategic Logic for value creation. For example, if

[6] A few organizations even tried to adopt a three-dimensional matrix design, which creates an even greater need for effective dispute resolution processes.

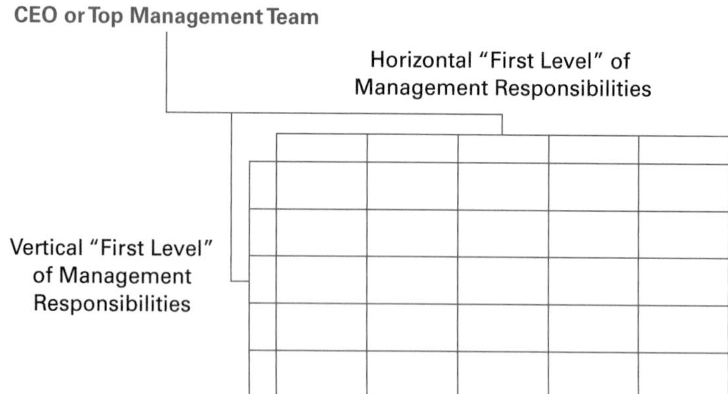

FIGURE 7.3 Two Dimensions of Primary Task Allocations in a Matrix Organization

strategic managers set goals for developing a new regional market as well as for maintaining profitability of current product lines, a regional-product matrix structure would assign a top manager the task of developing sales in the new region. The manager would then assume responsibility for ensuring that the products with the best potential for sales in his or her region are made available and marketed in the most effective way within the region. Any hesitancy by a product line manager to support the marketing of his or her products in the region would come to the attention of the regional manager, who would then have to work with the product manager to resolve his or her lack of support for developing sales in the new region. Conversely, the product manager may find that a regional manager is less than enthusiastic about marketing a new product in his or her region, and would need to resolve the regional manager's lack of support for the product in that region.

Use of a matrix organization design requires an effective dispute resolution process.

As the foregoing examples suggest, a matrix structure can be an effective device for uncovering inconsistencies in the way an organization's Strategic Logic is being executed. However, to work well in this role, strategic managers need an effective dispute resolution process that can be used to intervene when horizontal and vertical managers within the matrix structure cannot resolve differences in their objectives for their units. This dispute resolution process must lead to refinements in the definitions of each manager's responsibilities (and in the incentives to perform those responsibilities, as discussed later in the chapter) in order to achieve a better realignment of objectives within the horizontal and vertical management processes of the organization.

Hybrid Organization Design

An alternate approach to achieving an effective balance in an organization's management focus and priorities is a hybrid organization design that mixes primary task allocations in any combination of functions, products, regions, key customers, and projects that may be considered most appropriate to carry out the organization's Strategic Logic in its current situation. Thus, first-level managers will be given task allocations and responsibilities for certain functions, product lines, regions, key customers, or projects that are considered most critical to achieving success in executing the Strategic Logic of the organization, while other tasks and responsibilities regarded as less critical are attended to by managers in the second or third level of the hierarchy.

As suggested in Figure 7.4, a hybrid organization design brings a variety of tasks to the attention of the top managers of the organization. In effect, hybrid organizational designs are a kind of selective multidimensional matrix structure in which certain activities in an organization receive the direct guidance, problem-solving, and dispute-resolution attention of an organization's strategic managers. Because of the variety of primary task allocations in a hybrid organization design, a hybrid organization design

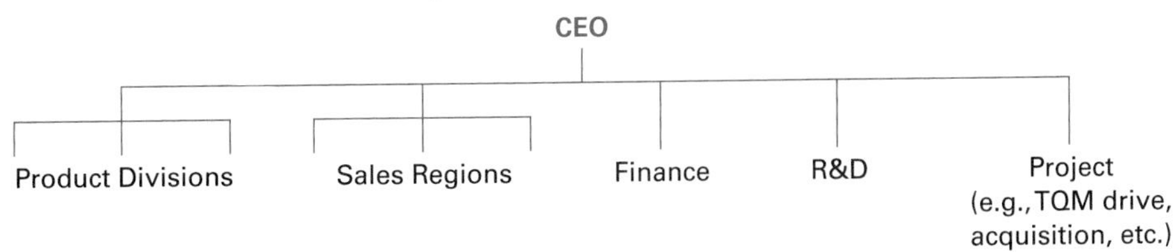

FIGURE 7.4 Example of a Hybrid Organization Design

may create a complex decision-making environment for top managers. In some cases, too much variety in top-line task allocations may lead to cognitive overload and loss of a clear view of the organization's overall Strategic Logic. Thus, a hybrid organization design should be used carefully and selectively to focus top management attention only on the key challenges facing the organization at any point in time. If used in this way, the task allocations in the first level of a hybrid organization will also tend to evolve over time. Some first-level tasks and responsibilities may even be devolved to second-level managers as successful policies and methods are developed and implemented at the top management level. In their place, new coordination challenges involving new tasks may be elevated to the first level of top management attention.

Aligning the Hierarchy of Task Allocations with Strategic Logic

Matrix and hybrid organizations seek a superior balance of management focus and priorities.

As we already discussed early in this text, a Strategic Logic is an organization's operative rationale for achieving its goals by carrying out specific value-creation processes. Achieving success in an organization's overall value-creation processes will usually depend on achieving superior performance in some especially critical activities (such as the key activities in the Business Concept). Because the hierarchy of task allocations within an organization greatly influences the priorities that managers set in allocating their attention to specific activities, strategic managers must maintain a close alignment between an organization's hierarchy of task allocations and the activities that are most critical to achieving success in the organization's value-creation activities. The most critical activities must receive the highest level of attention, while activities that are less critical to the organization's value-creation processes should receive lower-level management attention. We now state this need to maintain such an alignment in the following system design principle for an organization design:

System Design Principle 7.1

The hierarchy of task allocations must be aligned with an organization's Strategic Logic so that activities that are most critical to the organization's value-creation processes receive the highest level of management attention, while less critical activities receive a correspondingly lower level of management attention.

Authority Distribution

Authority is the formal power to acquire and allocate resources in an organization.

Authority is the formally recognized and allocated power within an organization to make decisions about certain matters. Managers make decisions about many different kinds of things, including setting goals, allocating budgets, hiring and firing, giving staffing assignments, and so on. In the most fundamental sense, however, all managerial decisions are about *acquiring and allocating resources* in one form or another. Thus, authority is fundamentally the formal power of managers to acquire and allocate an organization's resources in some area of activity.

Although authority is normally given to individual managers (or in some cases to a group of managers working closely together), managers differ greatly in the way they exercise that authority to make decisions within an organization. Some managers assert their authority by taking a "top down" approach to making decisions, essentially making decisions on their own and expecting compliance with those decisions by the people working under their supervision. Other managers use a more consultative approach to decision making, soliciting the views of some key employees in their organizational unit before making decisions. Still other managers try to create a participatory decision-making process in which all employees may express their views and ideas and then work together to reach decisions by consensus.

Whatever the process used by managers to make decisions in an organization, engaging in actions to carry out decisions requires organizational resources (people, time, money, etc.). Managers who are assigned responsibility for carrying out a given task must therefore be given the authority required to acquire and allocate the resources needed to perform that task well. This necessity is reflected in the following system design principle for aligning tasks, responsibilities, and authority in an organization design:

System Design Principle 7.2

Task allocations, managerial responsibilities, and authority distributions must be aligned so that all managers assigned the responsibility for the performance of a given task also are given the authority required to acquire and allocate the resources needed to perform that task well.

Information Flows

The design of information flows essentially considers who within an organization is supposed to know about some aspect of the organization or its environment, when they should learn about it, and why they need to know about it.

Information flows determine who knows what, when, and why.

Strategic managers differ greatly in their attitudes toward the distribution of information, and as a result organizations tend to have highly variable cultures and practices with respect to the internal processing and sharing of information—a subject we will revisit later in this chapter. Nevertheless, all organizations create and process information internally, and most also gather information from various external sources. Thus, a key part of organization design is deciding how information will be created and distributed in an organization.

Recall the definitions of data, information, and knowledge from our discussion of resources earlier in this chapter. *Data* are observations about internal aspects of an organization and its environment. *Information* is meaning that is derived from data through some process of comparison, either comparison of similar kinds of data over time or comparisons of data across similar situations. Figure 7.5, which represents an organization with a multilevel management hierarchy, illustrates the processes of gathering and interpreting data within an organization. Data are gathered at the working level of the organization (the bottom level of the hierarchy), and may include sales data generated by salespeople, output data gathered from the production department, inventory data gathered from logistics processes, and so on. Information is created through processes of compiling data in ways that make it easy to make comparisons over time (e.g., sales this quarter compared to sales last quarter) or across situations (comparisons of productivity rates in two or more factories).

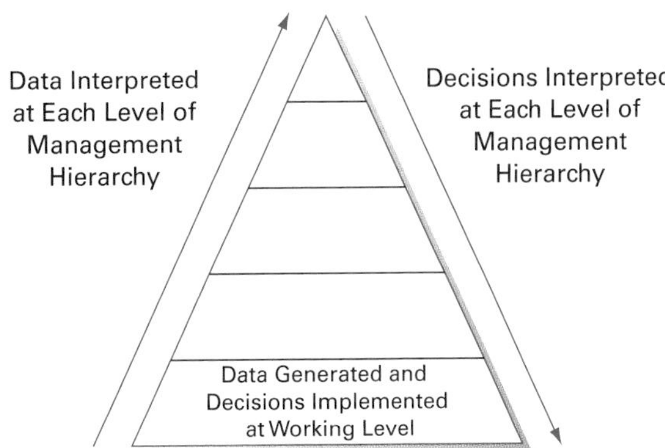

FIGURE 7.5 Interpretations of Data and Decisions in a Management Hierarchy

At each level of the management hierarchy, managers must decide what kinds of data are important and what kinds of comparisons to make in order to represent the important aspects of the organization's internal condition and external environment. Thus, managers both select and interpret data at each level of the organization. This *selective interpretation* of data is also a process of *abstraction* that sends on to the next higher level of management a condensed and "filtered" representation of the organization and its environment. Through this process, managers at one level greatly influence the impressions that managers at the next higher level form about the organization and its environment.

Information is likely to undergo a number of transformations as it works its way upward through the various levels of a management hierarchy. Both information loss and information distortion may occur, and each kind of transformation of information may be unintended or intended.

Information loss and distortion can be unintended or intended.

Information loss occurs when information that exists at one level of management does not flow upward to the next higher level of management. A certain amount of information loss is inherent in the process of selective interpretation and abstraction. A regional sales manager may read monthly sales reports from a number of salespeople, for example, and then prepare a summary report that includes the most significant events of the month, but leaves out other events judged to be of lesser importance and thus not worth bringing to the attention of the next higher level of management. Unintended loss of information may occur when a manager simply forgets or overlooks some information and does not forward that information on to higher management. A more insidious intended loss of information can occur when managers conceal information, which may occur when there is some problem or difficulty that a manager at one level does not want to come to the attention of higher management in the organization.

Information distortion occurs when the meaning of information is changed in some way as it flows from one level of management to another. Unintended information distortion can occur when a manager pays more attention to reporting some aspects of a situation than other aspects because of his or her professional training or personal interests. A product manager with a strong interest and background in building up distribution channels, for example, may emphasize successes in attracting important distributors for a new product, while paying less attention to the effectiveness of the ongoing advertising campaign to introduce the product. Such unintended biases in preparing and forwarding information may create impressions in higher management that do not adequately reflect the organization's current situation.

In a similar way, intended information distortion can create inaccurate impressions when a manager consciously tries to put a positive or negative "spin" on his or her reporting of a current situation. For example, a manager may try to put a positive spin on a report of a recent project for which he or she had responsibility, or a negative spin on a report of an investigation into proposed outsourcing arrangements to which he or she is opposed. Similarly, as also suggested in Figure 7.5, managers may put into action their own preferred interpretation of higher management directives as decisions move downward through the management hierarchy.

A consequence of both unintended and intended loss and distortion in the upward flows of information in an organization is that top managers often receive only highly abstract information about the organization and its environment. The progressive abstraction of information as it moves upward in the management hierarchy tends to provide top managers with a preponderance of quantitative measures and little if any qualitative assessments of situations facing the organization. In addition, the information that top managers receive is often heavily "sanitized," because information about problems and difficulties may be filtered out and an overly positive or negative spin put on reports about events in the organization. As a result, over time some top managers may begin to feel that they are losing touch with actual events and situations in their organization and its environment.

Faced with a growing sense of losing touch with their organizations, top managers may respond in a variety of ways. Some managers, especially top managers of large organizations, may decide that they lack both the information and the expertise needed to substantively participate in or even to qualitatively assess the ongoing processes of the organization at the working level. They may then define their role as top managers primarily in terms of setting quantitative goals for financial performance or market growth, of monitoring quantitative measures of performance judged to be important in reaching those goals, and of enforcing an organizational discipline in meeting those performance objectives.

A retreat by top managers to "managing by the numbers," however, may create a fundamental problem for an organization. Given their nature, financial performance objectives cannot and do not constitute a Strategic Logic of an organization, which must include both a broader statement of the goals of the organization and an "operative rationale" as to how the organization intends to accomplish those goals. Unless top managers also clearly articulate these substantive aspects of a Strategic Logic, an organization whose top managers are preoccupied with monitoring and enforcing financial performance measures can lose its sense of direction and of the broader purposes it is trying to serve.

To avoid losing touch with the fundamental concerns and challenges facing their organization, strategic managers in some companies adopt methods for receiving unfiltered flows of information directly from employees, customers, suppliers, and other stakeholders. The practice of "managing by walking around," for example, was adopted by top managers of computer and instruments maker Hewlett-Packard in the 1980s. To keep informed about Hewlett-Packard's current processes and problems, Hewlett-Packard managers would spend some time each week talking directly with employees developing new products, working in production factories, selling the company's new products, and carrying out other activities on the front line of the organization. Another executive in a large home appliance company spends one day a month working as a customer service representative in the firm's customer call center, receiving phone calls from customers and resolving their complaints. Such "hands on" experiences enable top managers to maintain direct communication with people at all levels of an organization. They also receive concrete, unfiltered information about current conditions in the organization that would not be likely to survive the information loss and distortion that typically occurs in the processing of information upwards in the management hierarchy.

7.4 CONTROLS AND INCENTIVES

Once strategic managers have determined the organization design that will be used to coordinate an organization's resources, they must then determine the most effective way to monitor the performance of the various resources in the organization's value-creation processes and to reward good performance (and perhaps to punish poor performance). To detect both good and poor performance of resources in an organization, strategic managers must design effective *control systems*. Managers must also define *incentive systems* that are effective in encouraging and rewarding good performance and in discouraging inadequate performance or inappropriate behaviors. Moreover, the ways an organization monitors and rewards performance must be designed to be mutually consistent and supportive. We therefore consider three key system design principles for achieving effective control and incentive systems.

Control Systems

Control systems monitor performance in an organization's value-creation processes.

Control system is the term we will use to refer to the various ways in which managers try to determine the current condition of an organization's resources and the performance of individuals, teams, and groups in the organization's value-creation processes. Broadly speaking, four basic types of control mechanisms can be used in designing a control system:

- *Market* control mechanisms
- *Output* control mechanisms
- *Bureaucratic* control mechanisms
- *Culture* control mechanisms

We next discuss each of these types of control mechanisms and the need to combine several types of control mechanisms to create "checks and balances" in an organization's overall control system.

Market Controls

Market signals come from many kinds of markets.

Organizations interact with many kinds of markets. Organizations try to sell their outputs in markets for products or services, and they try to obtain their inflows of resources from markets for equity funds, debt, labor, suppliers, and location. The potential customers and suppliers of an organization in each of these markets send a variety of signals to an organization that express their opinions about the current products and capabilities of the organization and its prospects for success in the future. **Market control mechanisms** are organizational processes that gather signals from these markets to provide strategic managers with an external perspective on the competence leveraging and building processes of an organization. Let us consider several kinds of signals that markets can send to an organization.

Product markets provide opportunities for potential and actual customers to signal their satisfaction with an organization's products and services through their decisions to buy the organization's outputs or to purchase products and services from competing organizations. In the aggregate, consumers' purchase decisions are indicated by rising or falling sales figures, increasing or decreasing market shares, percentage of repeat customers in overall sales, and other sales-based measures. Most organizations also monitor customer satisfaction through periodic customer satisfaction surveys. More qualitative data are also available when managers talk directly to current customers, to potential customers who do not do business with the organization, and to customers who have recently stopped doing business with the organization to understand the ways in which the organization has succeeded or failed in meeting customer expectations.

Financial markets form opinions about the riskiness of both near-term and long-term financial performance of an organization, and those opinions are reflected in the price investors are willing to pay for a firm's shares or the interest rates a firm must pay to arrange debt financing through bond issues or bank loans. Rising share prices and a high price-to-earnings (P/E) ratio for its industry are indicators that investors in equity markets believe a firm is creating significant strategic options for future growth and earnings increases. Falling share prices and a low P/E ratio suggest investors believe the firm lacks significant potential for growth and profitability. Similarly, when providers of debt financing demand high interest rates to lend funds to an organization, lenders are signaling their concern that the organization may not have the cash-generating capability to meet all its future debt repayment obligations. Some privately owned and controlled firms—for example, United Parcel Service—list some portion of their shares on a major stock exchange in order to receive signals from the financial markets about the current value and performance of the firm.

Labor markets provide human resources of all types to an organization. Attracting the best human resources is often essential for an organization's future success, but it is also a key indicator of what potential employees think about the organization as a place to work and make a career. Signals from labor markets include the list of organizations that new university graduates most admire and would like to work for (a widely published statistic in Japan, for example), the percentage of people who actually accept job offers from the firm, and the annual rate of turnover in employees. More qualitative signals may be available to strategic managers when they make a policy of interviewing key managers and technical staff who leave the organization.

Supplier markets are composed of all the companies capable of supplying an organization with inputs of materials, parts, components, and services. The ability of an organization to attract the "best-in-industry" suppliers of each type of input to its value-creation processes is an indicator that those suppliers believe the firm has a good future and is worth investing in building a supplier-customer relationship. Difficulty in attracting good suppliers indicates suppliers' lack of confidence in the firm as a long-term customer.

Location markets exist when national, state, or local governments try to attract organizations to locate their operations in a given geographic area. Efforts to attract an organization to locate in its area indicate that government perceives the organization as a good "corporate citizen" capable of creating significant benefits for the community without imposing unwanted "negative externalities" like air or water pollution, noise, traffic congestion, unattractive facilities, and the like.

Output Controls

Output control mechanisms gather various kinds of output measures that indicate the efficiency and effectiveness of an organization in producing its products and services. Measures such as labor productivity (labor hours per unit produced), capital productivity (capital consumed per unit produced), capacity utilization rates, and work-in-process indicate the efficiency of an organization in performing its operations. Quality measures such as yield rates (percentage of products meeting specifications) and defect rates indicate the effectiveness of an organization in producing its outputs.

Bureaucratic Controls

Bureaucratic controls include budgets, schedules, and standard operating procedures that are intended to support an organization's various activities planned or anticipated by managers. Budgets, schedules, and standard operating procedures function as **bureaucratic control mechanisms** when a situation arises that causes or requires a departure from an established budget, schedule, or procedure. For example, a marketing program that begins to run over budget, a product development project that falls behind schedule, or an inability to handle a given situation through standard operating procedures all signal to managers that something unanticipated is occurring. Such exceptions should then attract management attention to investigate and resolve the exceptions, or to modify the plans of the organization to take into account some unanticipated circumstances.

Culture Controls

When managers convincingly establish certain norms of behavior and certain values as those that the organization wants to adhere to in its activities, those norms and values help to define an organizational culture. A visible, frequently discussed set of norms and values establishes a standard of behavior and performance against which each employee's behavior and performance can then be compared. For example, the U.S. department store chain Nordstrom's uses "hero stories" to communicate examples of outstanding service provided to customers by certain employees. Through such examples, all Nordstrom's employees are encouraged to provide similar levels of service to their customers.

In much the same way as a bureaucratic control works, organizational culture works as a **culture control mechanism** when an individual's behavior and performance appear to depart from the established norms and values of the organization. Such exceptions in behavior and performance invite management attention to resolve any apparent conflicts between the norms and values of the organization and those of individuals in the organization.

Designing Checks and Balances in Control Systems

Control systems need checks and balances.

Given the complexity of the many resources and activities that make up an organization's value-creation and value-distribution processes, it is unlikely that any single type of control mechanism can provide managers with an adequate representation of the current condition of an organization. Managers who rely exclusively on market controls, for example, would have little personal knowledge of what is currently happening internally inside their organization. Conversely, managers who rely only on internal measures, such as output, bureaucratic, and culture controls, would lack the external view of the organization's performance that is provided by markets. Similarly, the quantitative measures used in market and output control mechanisms need to be supplemented by the qualitative assessments provided by bureaucratic and culture control mechanisms. Thus, a well-designed control system will typically draw on all four types of control mechanisms to create a set of "checks and balances" that give managers a balanced, multidimensional understanding of the current condition of an organization and its interactions with its environment.

Incentive Systems

Incentive systems provide rewards for good performance and punishments for poor performance.

Incentives refer to the rewards and punishments for individuals and groups that managers establish in an organization. The rewards and punishments used in an organization become an **incentive system** when they are consistently and coherently interrelated with appropriate and well-defined performance measures. In this section we consider some common and not-so-common forms of rewards and punishments used in organizations. In the following section we identify four system design principles for interrelating performance, controls, and incentives in designing effective control and incentive systems.

Rewards

An organization may reward good performance in many ways. Financial rewards include salary increases, bonuses, profit sharing, stock options, and perquisites (for example, a company-provided automobile). Nonfinancial rewards are also important and widely used. They include both formal rewards, such as a promotion in the management hierarchy or recognition as "Employee of the Month," and informal rewards in the form of praise from managers during performance reviews or in group meetings. For some employees, especially an organization's crucial "knowledge workers," some managers develop innovative reward systems that give employees time and other resources to deepen their expertise and develop new knowledge and skills. To reward its outstanding research scientists, for example, IBM awards the life-time status of "IBM Scientist" to its most outstanding researchers each year. Along with that recognition also comes several years of time and research funding to support each IBM Scientist's research into leading-edge science and technology development. More informally, many organizations today reward their most creative and productive knowledge workers by letting them choose their own work hours and location. This flexible approach enables those employees to avoid wasting time in daily commuting, to work during the hours of the day when they feel most productive, to spend certain times of the week with their families, and so on.

Punishments

Organizations may punish poor performers in a variety of ways. The ultimate punishment (except in cases of illegal behavior) is expulsion from an organization by being fired. Less drastic punishments include reassignment to a less prestigious or less important position in the organization, demotion in rank, reduction in salary, increased supervision or reporting requirements, more frequent performance reviews, or cautionary comments from managers.

Designing Effective Control and Incentive Systems

Designing effective control and incentive systems requires aligning performance measures and incentives.

Control systems monitor an organization's performance, and incentive systems encourage good performance. When control and incentive systems are not well designed to work together, management processes become ineffective, motivation declines, and performance by individuals, groups, and ultimately the organization can fall to low levels. When well-designed control and incentive systems work together effectively, however, they can provide both a self-managing capability to individuals and groups in an organization and a high level of motivation to provide superior performance in their tasks.

In spite of the central importance of having effective control and incentive systems, broadly speaking, most organizations labor under poorly conceived, inadequately defined, and largely uncoordinated control and incentive systems. Perhaps the main reason for this chronic weakness of organizations is that designing effective control and incentive systems is a significant intellectual challenge, and one with which many managers have little experience and may be reluctant to experiment. We therefore introduce four system design principles that strategic managers should clearly understand and follow when designing control and incentive systems. These system design principles address in turn the importance of having adequate definitions of what good performance means, how performance will be measured, how incentives will be related to performance measures, and how incentives will be related to the time frame within which performance can be realized and assessed.

Defining Good Performance

What constitutes "good performance" must be clearly defined.

Just as strategic managers must decompose the overall value-creation process of the organization into specific tasks to be allocated to each unit of the organization, they must also define what kinds of performance are critical as each unit carries out its task effectively. Thus, an essential aspect of managing "part-whole relationships" in organizations[7] is defining what "good performance" means for each group and individual. Strategic managers also have a fundamental responsibility to assure that the

[7] Van De Ven, A. (1986). Central Problems in the Management of Innovation. *Management Science,* 32(5).

performance objectives defined for each group and individual in the organization are systematically complementary, so that achieving good performance by individuals and groups will add up to good performance by the organization as a whole in carrying out its Business Concept. This necessity is reflected in the following system design principle for defining and aligning performance for the various elements of an organization as a value-creating system:

System Design Principle 7.3

What constitutes "good performance" must be clearly defined for each task allocated within an organization, and good performance in all allocated tasks must be systemically interrelated so that good performance by the various individuals and groups in the organization will result in good performance by the overall organization in carrying out its Business Concept.

Defining Measures of Good Performance

Measures of performance must also be clearly defined.

When strategic managers define what good performance means in carrying out each task in the organization, they must also define appropriate measures to be used in control systems for monitoring the level of performance being achieved in each task. Those measures must incorporate their own kind of "checks and balances" to be sure that good performance is being adequately represented and assessed by the measures adopted for each task.

For example, what constitutes good performance by salespeople? For most businesses, good performance means more than just generating current sales revenues. It also includes building long-term customer relationships and maintaining high levels of customer satisfaction to generate repeat sales. Thus, good performance for a salesperson would have to be defined by more than just measures of current sales, but rather would include measures of customer satisfaction, growth in sales made to each customer over time, and so on.

Obviously, in most cases, performance measures need to be defined and agreed to by both managers and the people with responsibility for performing each task. If performance measures are simply imposed by managers on an organization in a "top-down" process, managers may overlook important indicators of performance that may be suggested by employees closest to each task. Moreover, employees may lack commitment to achieving performance measures that they feel do not fully or accurately indicate what good performance means in the task for which they are responsible. Consultations between mangers and employees in defining performance measures are therefore normally essential to designing appropriate checks and balances into control system measures and to building organizational commitment to achieving high performance.

These requirements lead to the following system design principle for defining appropriate performance measures to be used in the control system of an organization:

System Design Principle 7.4

Measures of performance must be clearly defined to adequately represent and assess performance levels achieved in carrying out each task within an organization, and those measures of performance must be understood and agreed to by each group and individual with responsibility for carrying out each task.

Relating Incentives to Performance Measures

Incentives should be based only on agreed performance measures.

Once good performance is defined for each task to be carried out within an organization and appropriate measures of good performance are agreed by managers and employees, incentives must be defined and aligned to be directly and exclusively based on the agreed performance measures applicable to each task. In essence, rewards and punishments must be based *directly* on the performance measures applicable to each task in order to create *clarity* about how each person and group will be evaluated and rewarded by the organization.

In addition, all rewards and punishments used in the organization must depend *only* on the agreed performance measures to be used for each task. Basing rewards and punishments solely on defined performance measures creates *transparency and equity* in the way the organization evaluates and rewards its people. If only part of an employee's performance evaluation is determined by defined performance measures, while a significant part of an employee's evaluation depends on undefined or undisclosed assessments made by a manager, employees may regard the allocation of rewards and punishments in the organization as arbitrary, subjective, or a way for managers to perpetuate "personal control" over employees. To maintain high levels of commitment to and respect for an organization, performance assessments should not be left to the discretion of individual managers, as is the common practice in many "traditional" organizations, but rather all rewards and punishments should be based only on clearly defined and agreed performance measures.

These concerns lead to the following system design principle for aligning rewards and punishments in an organization's incentive system with the defined performance measures used to assess performance in the organization's control systems:

System Design Principle 7.5

All rewards and punishments used within an organization should be allocated only on the basis of the performance measures defined for each task and agreed to by both managers and the people with direct responsibility for carrying out the task.

Aligning Incentives with the Time Required to Achieve and Verify Good Performance

Incentives should be timed to coincide with the realization of good performance.

The time required to perform and assess the many tasks that need to be done in an organization can vary considerably. Some tasks can be performed quickly, and the performance of the task can be assessed immediately. For example, the production of parts in a factory is usually done within a matter of minutes or at most a few hours, and the conformance of those parts to quality standards (a key performance measure) can be verified in a comparably short period of time. However, other tasks in an organization inherently require a longer time to carry out and to assess. The task of improving the capabilities of an organization in some key activity, for example, may take a year or even several years to accomplish, and the performance level actually achieved in the task may not become apparent until a significant period of time has passed after completing the task.

Effective design of incentive systems therefore also involves aligning incentives with the time required to achieve and evaluate good performance. Because improvements in productivity on the shop floor may be determined soon after such improvements are realized, for example, rewards for productivity improvements may be based on short-term productivity measures. For example, the mini-mill steel producer Nucor rewards productivity improvements made during one week in its steel truss factories with productivity-based bonuses paid the following week, thus achieving a close temporal alignment of employees' efforts to achieve good performance and the organization's distribution of rewards for good performance achieved. Tasks that take longer to perform and to assess require rewards that are realized and distributed only after the performance of the task can be adequately determined. For employees with responsibility for launching new business initiatives whose success can only be determined in the long term, for example, a long-term reward would be appropriate, perhaps in the form of stock options with exercise dates several years in the future.

These concerns lead to the following system design principle for aligning the timing of incentives with the time required to achieve and verify good performance:

System Design Principle 7.6

The payment of incentives used within an organization should be aligned with the time required to carry out each task and with the time required to adequately assess performance achieved in carrying out each task.

7.5 SYSTEM DESIGN PRINCIPLES FOR THE ORGANIZATION CONCEPT

In addition to the system design principles discussed thus far in this chapter, we now add two further principles that should be applied in deciding the overall Organization Concept. First, as with the Business Concept, the three elements of the Organization Concept—the resources to be used in the organization, the organization design for coordinating resources, and controls and incentives to monitor and reward performance—must be logically consistent with each other. Although this requirement may seem obvious, it nevertheless often occurs that the three elements of an Organization Concept lose their coherence as an organization evolves over time. Resources used and the tasks they are asked to perform may change, for example, but control and incentive systems may not be modified to reflect the new tasks that need to be performed in the organization. Such misalignments of elements in the Organization Concept virtually assure that sub-optimal performance will be "designed into" the way the organization functions. Thus we emphasize the need for ongoing checks of internal logical consistency in the Organization Concept through the following system design principle:

System Design Principle 7.7

The three elements of the Organization Concept—resources, organization design, and controls and incentives—must be logically consistent with each other at all times.

The second concern is that the Organization Concept must always be consistent with the Business Concept it is intended to support. This requirement may also seem obvious, but just as an Organization Concept can lose its internal logical consistency over time, the Organization Concept can "drift" over time in ways that break down the complementarity of the two Concepts. For example, it is not at all unusual for an organization to change its Business Concept in some significant way, but then to neglect to make changes in the resources, coordination methods, and controls and incentives that are necessary to support the new Business Concept effectively. For this reason we emphasize the need for continuously maintaining logical coherence between the Business Concept and the Organization Concept in the following system design principle:

System Design Principle 7.8

The Organization Concept must be logically consistent with and effectively support an organization's current Business Concept at all times.

KEY TERMS AND CONCEPTS

Organization Concept The definition of the resources an organization will use, the organization design through which resources will be coordinated, and the controls and incentives that will be used to monitor and motivate the people who will participate in the organization's value-creation processes.

resources Anything tangible or intangible that is both useful and available to an organization in carrying out its value-creation activities.

capabilities Repeatable patterns of action in the use of assets by an organization.

organization design The definition of which tasks will be performed by whom in an organization, how authority will be distributed, and what information will flow from whom to whom within the organization.

task allocation The decomposition of an organization's value-creation processes into specific tasks and the assignment of responsibilities for performing those tasks to specific persons, groups, or teams.

control system Systems through which managers monitor the condition of an organization's resources and the performance of individuals, groups, and teams in carrying out their assigned tasks.

market control mechanisms Processes for gathering signals from various kinds of markets about the perceived condition and performance of an organization.

output control mechanisms Processes for measuring the efficiency and effectiveness of an organizations operations, based on various measures of an organization's outputs.

bureaucratic control mechanisms Budgets, schedules, policies, and standard operating procedures that signal to managers when an unanticipated situation has arisen that cannot be managed by the organization's established plans or methods.

culture control mechanisms Processes that establish organizational values and norms against which an individual's behavior and actions can be compared.

incentive systems A coherent set of rewards and punishments, based on well-defined performance measures, that is intended to motivate certain kinds of performance.

REVIEW QUESTIONS

1. In what sense does an Organization Concept define an organization's strategy for competing in resource markets?
2. What are firm-addressable resources?
3. How are data transformed into information, and information into knowledge?
4. What are the differences between know-how, know-why, and know-what forms of knowledge?
5. What are resource flexibility and coordination flexibility, and why are they important in an organization?
6. What are the relative advantages and disadvantages of each of these bases for making task allocations: functions, products, regions, key customers, and projects?
7. What are the potential advantages of a matrix organization design?
8. What is authority in an organization?
9. What are information loss and information distortion, and why are they important issues to be managed in an organization design?
10. Why are checks and balances needed in the design of control systems and incentive systems?
11. Explain the reasoning behind System Design Principle 7.2 for relating allocations of managerial responsibilities and distribution of authority within an organization.
12. Explain the reasoning behind each of the system design principles (7.3 to 7.6) applicable to controls and incentives.
13. What must be the relationship of an Organization Concept to a Business Concept in a Strategic Logic?

CHAPTER 8

CORE PROCESSES: PUTTING THE BUSINESS CONCEPT AND ORGANIZATION CONCEPT INTO ACTION

INTRODUCTION

We have so far considered two of the three elements of an organization's Strategic Logic: the Business Concept, which is the way an organization intends to create value in product markets, and the Organization Concept, which is the way the organization intends to attract and coordinate resources in its value-creation processes. Both the Business Concept and the Organization Concept are *designs* for value creation and distribution that must ultimately be put into *action*. The third element of a Strategic Logic is an organization's Core Processes—the essential activities the organization must undertake to put its ideas for value creation and distribution into action on a sustained basis.

As suggested in Figure 8.1, the Core Processes of an organization are of four basic types:

- Product creation
- Product realization
- Stakeholder development
- Transformative processes

Some organizations engage in product creation on a continuous basis, others create new products from time to time, and some organizations create a product once and then give little thought to updating current products or creating new ones. All organizations must realize products on an ongoing basis, however, because they must produce, market, distribute, and support their products at some level of activity to sustain resource inflows of sales revenues (or in the case of nonprofit or government organizations, contributions or funding). Like creating products, developing the ability of stakeholders to provide essential resources to an organization is an activity that some organizations do continuously, some occasionally, and some almost never. Transformative processes are fundamental changes in the way an organization works. Thus, transformative processes affect important aspects of an organization's other three Core Processes.

In this chapter, we consider each of the four Core Processes and their key roles in an organization's overall value-creation and value-distribution activities.

8.1 PRODUCT CREATION

Product creation defines, designs, and develops new product offers.

Product creation includes all the activities through which an organization *defines* the new product offers it will bring to market, *designs* its new products and processes, and *develops* the materials, parts, or components needed in its new products and any new process capabilities needed to produce, ship, and support its new products.

FIGURE 8.1 The Core Processes of an Organization

In dynamic product markets in which consumer preferences change frequently or in which technologies for serving customer needs and preferences rapidly change, an organization may have to sustain continuous processes for defining new and improved products simply to maintain a viable Business Concept based on competitive product offers. Philips, like other major players in dynamic consumer electronics markets worldwide, maintains continuous processes for defining the characteristics of future generations of its current kinds of products and of new product concepts that it will introduce in two, three, or more years. In markets with more stable customer preferences and technologies, an organization's product creation process may be periodic, and resulting changes in products may be quite incremental. Whatever the rate of change in market preferences and technologies, a central concern for strategic managers is that the pace of product creation in their organization must always at least keep up with the rates of change in market preferences and technologies. Failing to maintain product creation processes at an adequate level eventually leads to obsolescing products that can reduce or destroy the value-creation potential of a Business Concept.

Let us now consider each of the key product creation activities of definition, design, and development in turn.

Defining New Product Offers

Product definition determines the intended NDCV of a new product offer.

A fundamental step that must be taken at least once by all organizations is defining the product offer or product offers it will bring to market, a process known as **product definition.** As discussed in Chapter 6, a product offer includes eight ways in which a consumer may perceive value or cost in judging the net delivered customer value (NDCV) of a product or service. Defining a product offer therefore means deciding the specific ways in which an organization will try to create NDCV in each of the four dimensions of perceived value (product, service, image, and personal interaction) and in each of the four dimensions of perceived cost (financial, time, energy, and psychic costs). The objective of product definition is to define a product offer that will be perceived as delivering superior NDCV by people with preferences the organization has targeted and will try to serve through its product offers.

In addition to differences in the frequency with which organizations create new product offers, organizations differ greatly in the creativity of their approaches to defining the NDCV of their product offers. Some organizations will try to create highly innovative product offers—in effect, new combinations of value and cost that attain new levels of NDCV—while other organizations will essentially try to imitate all or part of the NDCV of successful product offers that other organizations have already brought to market. An organization must therefore not only define what customer perceptions it will try to create in each of the eight dimensions of the product offer, but also the ways in which it will be innovative or imitative in each of those eight dimensions.

Product Functions, Features, and Performance Levels

A *product concept* is a unique bundle of functions offered by a product to a user. When an organization creates a new product, it must first decide what the product will do for the customer and the kind of benefits the customer should derive from the use of the product. Will the new product be innovative and bring the customer a new bundle of functions not previously available in the market? Will the product be an improved version of an existing product concept that offers some features or performance levels different from those of currently available products? Or will the new product be a "me too" product that basically replicates the functions, features, and performance levels of existing products from other organizations?

Service

All elements of a new product offer must be defined, not just the product.

Defining a product offer also involves determining the activities that an organization will perform to help its customers become aware of, learn about, purchase, take delivery of, use, maintain, repair, retire, recycle, or dispose of a product. In effect, defining a product offer includes defining the "package of services" the organization will offer to customers along with the basic product. Enhancing the perceived value of the service package that comes with a product may also be a major source of innovation and differentiation. For example, some automobile makers offer 24-hour roadside repair and assistance to purchasers of certain vehicle models as a way of differentiating their products.

Image

Defining a product offer also includes deciding the intended image value of a new product. Image value may be created through appropriate styling of a product, the way a product is advertised to position it in the minds of consumers, and the distribution channels through which a product is presented to the market. A potential way of differentiating a new product is by "adding image value" to an ordinary product. For example, in the 1990s many specialty clothing companies with well-known brands or logos extended their brands and logos to a range of accessories and personal items (socks, key chains, wallets, mobile phone cases, etc.) that were not previously commonly sold as branded products.

Personal Interaction

An organization must also analyze how customers will interact with the people in its various service activities throughout the lifetime of the product, and how each kind of interaction should contribute to the customer's perception of value derived through ownership and use of the product. Improving personal interaction value in an activity that is often a source of dissatisfaction for consumers (like improving the way repair and maintenance service workers interact with customers) can be an important source of differentiation in a product offer.

Financial Costs

An organization must also decide the stream of costs that a customer must pay to purchase, use, maintain, and retire a product. In effect, the costs incurred during the lifetime of a product must be "engineered" to be aligned as advantageously as possible with the cost sensitivities of customers with preferences that the organization is trying to serve. For example, consumer durables like refrigerators and stoves that are targeted at lower-income market segments might be marketed with little or no down payment required and "low monthly payments" (although the payments may then extend over a considerable period of time).

Time and Energy Costs

The time and energy that a customer must expend in learning about, purchasing, taking delivery of, using, maintaining, and retiring a product must also be defined and aligned with the time and effort sensitivities of the targeted market segment. Product offers targeted at busy professionals and businesspeople, for example, may include fast delivery of a new product to the customer's home or office and on-site repair and maintenance services to minimize perceived time and energy costs.

Psychic Costs

An organization must also analyze the various ways in which a targeted customer could worry or be concerned about some aspect of the new product and its supporting services. Steps must then be defined that would be effective in minimizing a potential customer's possible worries and concerns about each aspect of acquiring, using, and maintaining a product. Free training classes, 100 percent satisfaction guarantees, and comprehensive service and maintenance plans may be included in a product offer to reduce such psychic costs.

Designing New Products and Processes

To deliver NDCV to customers requires both a product (whether hardware, software, or service) and processes for realizing the product. The next activity after defining a new product offer is therefore designing the product and the processes that will be needed to produce, distribute, and support the product.

Product design is the process of "translating" the product definition into a technical solution for products and processes that will create the desired "package" of NDCV. The defined objectives for creating NDCV through the product offer must be translated into a set of *functional components* that will provide the desired functions, features, and performance levels in the product. Similarly, the service aspects of the product offer must be translated into a supporting set of activities or "process components" for realizing the product offer. In addition, designers must also determine how the product components will work together in the product as a system and how the process components will work together as a system. Designers must therefore also specify the *component interfaces* that define how the components in a product or process design will interact or "interface" with each other. The design steps of decomposing a product or process into functional components and then specifying how the components will interact in the product or process creates an *architecture* of a product or a process.[1] These steps are shown in Figure 8.2.

The **product and process architectures** an organization creates must be designed to be as effective as possible in delivering the desired "package" of NDCV to targeted market segments over some strategically determined period of time. When both market preferences and technologies that can be used in products for serving those preferences are expected to be stable during the intended commercial lifetime of the product offer, product and process architectures may be optimized to *minimize costs* incurred in realizing the product. In markets with changing market preferences and technologies, however, product and process architectures may be optimized to *maximize the flexibility* of the architectures to support the upgrading of key components and processes over time as better components and process capabilities become available. Highlight Box 8.1 explains the

[1] Sanchez, R. (1999). Modular Architectures in the Marketing Process. *Journal of Marketing,* 63 (Special Issue), 92–111.

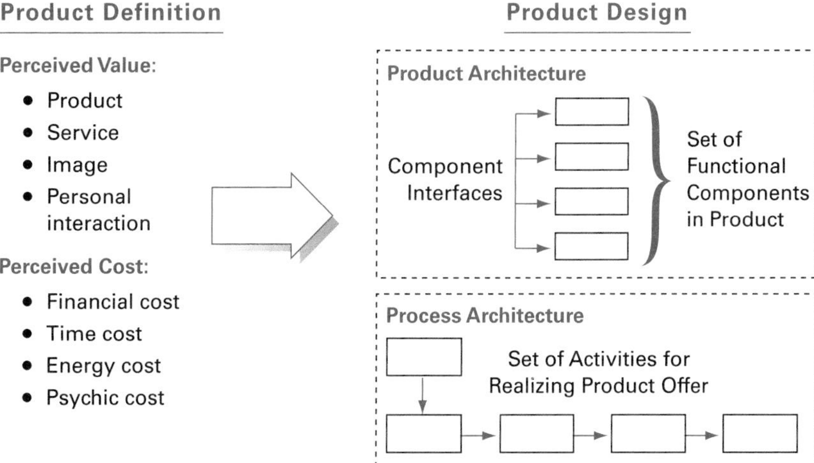

FIGURE 8.2 Product Design "Translates" the Product Definition into Product and Process Architectures

HIGHLIGHT BOX 8.1

Creating Strategic Flexibilities through Modular Architectures

Modular architectures are architectures in which component interfaces have been specified to allow the "substitution" of a range of component variations into the architecture without having to change the designs of other functional components in the architecture. This flexibility of the interfaces in a modular architecture allows the "mixing and matching" of different "plug and play" component variations within an architecture to configure specific product variations. The substitutability of a range of component variations within modular product and process architectures is suggested in Figure 8.3.

Perhaps the most familiar example of a modular product architecture is the personal computer, which makes possible the ready configuration of many different personal computer models from various combinations of microprocessors, memory cards, hard disks, and other components. Analogously, modular process architecture permits the mixing and matching of a number of process component variations within the same process architecture. For example, various kinds of development, production, distribution, and support activities may be performed by a firm's own functional groups or provided by external suppliers, but all activities can "plug and play" within the same process architecture.

The adoption of modular product and process architectures can bring a firm significant *strategic flexibilities.* Product component variations can be mixed and matched to configure many product variations to serve many market segments and customer preferences. Modular product architectures can also support rapid upgrading of product performance by "designing in" upgradeability of key components as technologically improved components become available. Creating modular process architectures helps a firm to outsource value-adding activities and to reconfigure its supply chain for developing, producing, and supporting products to meet a changing and diverse array of market demands.

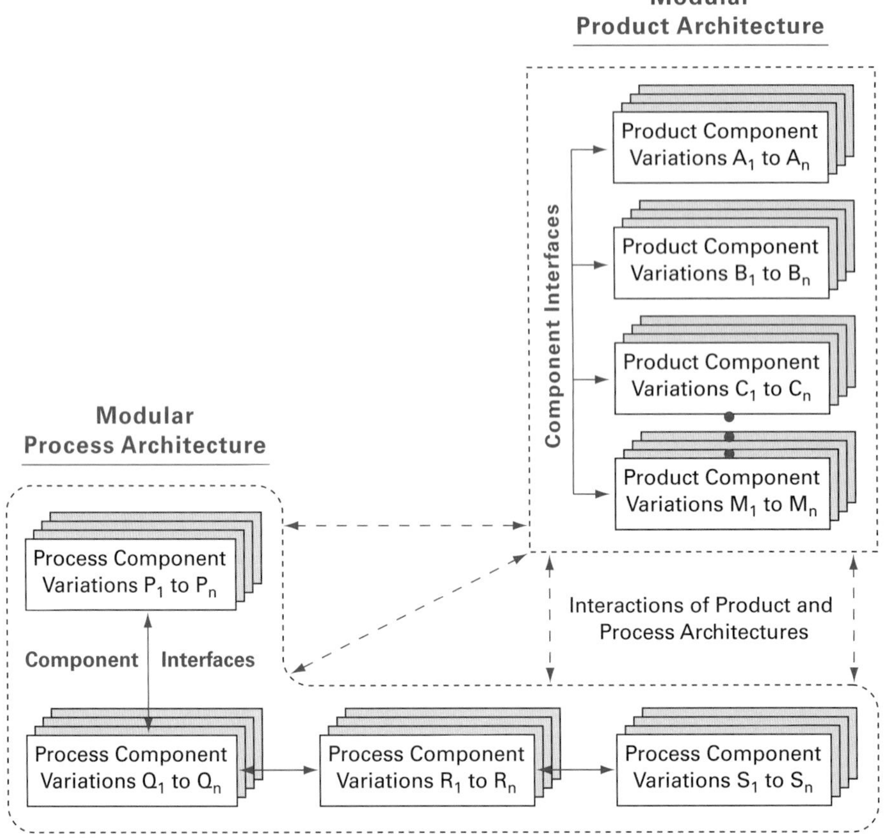

FIGURE 8.3 Modular Product and Process Architectures

growing use of **modular product and process architectures** to create key forms of strategic flexibility in an organization's products and processes.[2]

Developing New Products and Processes

Product development creates detailed designs for product components and process activities.

Once an organization creates a product architecture for its product and a process architecture to support the realization of the product offer, the next step is to *develop* detailed designs for each of the functional components in the product architecture and each of the activities in the process architecture. **Product development** activities identify alternative technologies that can be used in creating required product components and decide which technical solution offers the best means to achieve the cost and performance targets for each component. Similarly, alternate ways of designing and coordinating each of the

[2] For more on modular product and process architectures, see Sanchez, R. (2003). *Modularity, Strategic Flexibility, and Knowledge Management*. Oxford: Oxford University Press. Also see Garud, R. and A. Kumaraswamy. (1993). Changing Competitive Dynamics in Network Industries: An Exploration of the Sun Microsystems Open Systems Strategy. *Strategic Management Journal,* 14 (5), 351–369; Sanderson, S. and V. Uzumeri. (1997). *Managing Product Families.* Chicago: Richard D. Irwin; Sanchez, R. and J. Mahoney. (1996). Modularity, Flexibility, and Knowledge Management in Product and Organization Design. *Strategic Management Journal,* 17 (Winter Special Issue), 63–76; and Sanchez, R. (1999). Modular Architectures in the Marketing Process. *Journal of Marketing,* 63 (Special Issue), 92–111.

activities in the product realization process will be evaluated to decide the best overall design for the "supply chain" and service infrastructure needed to support the product realization process.

In earlier times, development activities were often carried out within a single organization, especially within large organizations. Today, however, virtually no organization in any industry is able to develop and apply well all the technologies that could be used in its product designs or all the capabilities that could be used in its process designs. Increasingly, to create the best possible products and supporting processes, product and process development activities may be carried out through global development networks of firms, which may be located in various parts of the world.

Many organizations, especially those that do not have large development staffs and resources, are nevertheless able to achieve low costs and good performance in their products through judicious use of "industry standard" components. Personal computer makers, for example, typically use product designs composed largely of industry standard components (microprocessors, memory chips, hard disk drives, etc.) developed and produced by leading component suppliers. These firms then focus their own development efforts on a few components that may be sources of differentiation, such as components that provide distinctive features and styling.

A detailed process design must also be developed for each activity in a process architecture, and people trained (or sometimes computers programmed) to perform those activities to create intended customer perceptions of value. Development of the activities in a new process architecture may also take advantage of "industry standard" activities, such as using the in-bound and out-bound logistics services of world-class specialist firms like Federal Express, Airborne Express, United Parcel Service, DHL, or TNT.

8.2 PRODUCT REALIZATION

Product realization produces, distributes, and supports product offers.

Product realization includes all the activities through which an organization *produces* its product offers, *distributes* its products to customers, and *supports* its products in the marketplace. Product realization thus includes most of what are usually referred to as the *operations* of an organization.

Production

Both tangible and intangible products require production processes.

All products—whether tangible or intangible—must be produced in some manner. Physical products may be produced through a variety of processes, depending on the type of product and the quantity being produced. Some physical products such as custom furniture, specialized machinery, and clothing may be produced either one at a time or in a *batch process* that produces a relatively small number of units of the product. Batch process production is often carried out by teams of craftworkers who perform all required production tasks from beginning to end. Many physical products such as computers and automobiles are produced through *assembly line processes,* in which the various components making up a product are brought together and assembled into the final product by workers who typically perform a single assembly task. Other products such as petrochemicals are produced through *continuous flow processes,* in which a factory (e.g., an oil refinery) processes a continuous flow of raw materials and produces a continuous flow of finished product or products (gasoline, diesel fuel, heating fuel, etc.).

Service products, although intangible, must also be produced through some kind of activity performed by people (e.g., a teller at a bank) or machines (e.g., an automated cash machine). Service products are often said to be distinguished from physical products by the fact that production and consumption of a service product are simultaneous events. A close analysis of the production process for a service, however, is likely to reveal that many steps are involved in preparing a service for "delivery" to a customer. In such cases, consumption of a service product occurs simultaneously with only the last step of the service production process. For example, when an attorney offers legal advice to a client, significant legal research (not to mention legal education) may have to be undertaken before the simultaneous delivery of a legal opinion by the attorney and its "consumption" by the client. Similarly, production of a service product such as automobile repair requires several steps (inventorying parts, maintaining repair equipment and tools) before delivery and consumption of the repair service for a given customer.

Marketing and Distribution

All products—whether tangible or intangible—must also be marketed and distributed to customers. The marketing process manages the "four Ps" in creating and realizing an organization's product offers: product, price, promotion, and place.[3]

Marketing and distribution jointly manage the "mix" of product, price, promotion, and place in product offers.

Marketing plays an essential role in defining *new product offers* by researching the various preferences that are emerging in the marketplace and grouping them into defined market segments—identified groups of customers with similar preferences. In product design and development, marketing helps to define the product functions, features, and performance levels that should be most effective in serving identified customer preferences and in deciding which customer preferences the organization is most capable of serving well. In organizations that want to maintain the appeal of their product offers, these marketing activities will be ongoing and will drive incremental improvements and extensions to existing product offers, as well as the periodic definition of new kinds of product offers.

Marketing also includes deciding the *pricing* strategy for an organization's product offer. In price-competitive markets for products with little or no differentiation, prices will effectively be set by prevailing market prices. When an organization has a well-differentiated product offer, however, price becomes a strategic variable to be decided by management. Pricing strategies may seek to build up market share rapidly in targeted market segments by offering relatively low prices, or may seek to maintain high profit margins by charging premium prices. Most commonly, pricing strategies lie somewhere between these two extremes and try to serve goals for building market share as well as goals for maintaining profitability.

The *promotion* activity in marketing manages the ways in which an organization's product offers will be communicated to the market. Promotion determines the ways in which a product will be advertised, works to secure desired locations for the product in retail establishments, develops point-of-sale support materials, and manages other aspects of the way a product offer is presented to targeted customers. Promotion also organizes campaigns intended to encourage trial, greater consumption, customer loyalty, or other marketing objectives during the life cycle of a product.

Deciding the *place* a product will be made available to customers is part of the process of designing and managing distribution channels. The distribution of physical goods in many countries follows a "two-step" or "three-step" process. In a two-step distribution process, manufacturers produce goods "to inventory," and inventories of goods are held in national or regional distribution warehouses for delivery to retailers as they place orders. In a three-step distribution process, the flow of goods goes from distribution centers to wholesalers and then to retailers. (In the case of industrial products, shipments by distribution centers or wholesalers often go directly to end customers without passing through retailers.)

[3] Kotler, P. (1997). *Marketing Management.* Upper Saddle River, NJ: Prentice Hall.

Distribution of some tangible and intangible products is becoming more personalized.

With the advent of flexible manufacturing systems and low-cost door-to-door delivery services, many firms are now converting to a "one-step" distribution process. Manufacturers produce "to order" as orders are received from individual customers, and ship directly to the customer's home or place of business. Producing to order and shipping door-to-door can virtually eliminate inventories of finished goods, thereby freeing working capital invested in inventories, eliminating costs of carrying inventory, and significantly reducing indirect costs resulting from excess stocks of individual items and obsolescing of items in inventory.

Service products are also distributed. A fundamental decision in designing service distribution, for example, is whether to deliver a service to the customer's home or place of business, or require customers to come to the service provider's place of business. At one time medical doctors in the United States used to visit patients' homes to provide medical care, but such "house calls" are a rare event today. Now health care services are generally distributed through centralized facilities like hospitals and clinics, and patients must find a way to get to those facilities to receive medical care. A similar shift to centralized facilities for distributing services can be seen in many other service product markets, including insurance, financial counseling, home improvement, and grocery retailing.

An important exception to the trend toward centralized distribution of services is the growing use of the Internet for distributing information-based services (education, financial services, travel bookings, and communication) and electronic entertainment services directly to individual customers. To the extent that all or part of a service product can be produced by a computer and delivered by the Internet or some other communication network, services can be distributed to individual customers wherever they happen to have access to a Web browser.

Support Activities

Many products, both tangible and intangible, require a variety of activities to support customers in their use of a product after taking delivery. Customers for goods such as appliances, computers, mobile phones, automobiles, and other complex products often have questions about the best way to use or maintain a product. Some firms rely on local retailers to answer such questions, but many firms are now maintaining customer "call centers" with trained staff to answer customers' most frequently asked questions (FAQs) about their products. In addition, firms must often assist customers in arranging maintenance or repairs of products, either by scheduling an appointment with the firm's own repair staff or an authorized repair service, or by suggesting an independent repair facility that is qualified to perform a needed maintenance or repair service. Some firms whose products can be recycled or must be disposed of in a controlled manner also maintain facilities for recovering products from customers at the end of their life cycle, or provide assistance or advice to customers about recycling or retiring their products.

8.3 STAKEHOLDER DEVELOPMENT

Stakeholder development improves the quality and flows of the resources an organization needs.

Stakeholder development refers to all the processes through which an organization tries to improve the ability of its resource providers to provide more, better, or lower-cost resources, or to provide required resources more quickly. When a resource provider makes investments of financial, human, and intellectual capital that give it a superior ability to meet the specific resource needs of an organization, the investment by the resource provider creates a bona fide stake in the organization. In effect, the resource provider acquires an interest in the benefits the organization will derive from the superior resources provided, and thus a right to expect some form of repayment or compensation from the organization in return for the resource provider's investment. Thus, one of the Core Processes of an organization is developing stakeholders—working with resource providers to improve the resources they can provide—to create a shared stake in the success of the organization.

Several different kinds of resource providers may become stakeholders. Let us consider the kinds of activities an organization may undertake to develop stakeholders in employees, suppliers, customers, governments, communities, and shareholders and debt holders.

Employees

Employees may become stakeholders when they develop special abilities that improve the capabilities of an organization to create value through its current or future Business Concepts. An organization may work to improve the abilities of its employees in at least three ways.

An organization may work to improve the *education* of its employees, by helping its employees learn to read, reason logically, and do mathematics, and to expand their knowledge of science, history, geography, or more specialized fields. An organization may provide *training* that improves the skills of an employee in performing a specialized task. An organization may also provide *development* programs for some employees, especially its managers, that challenge their existing assumptions and ways of thinking about the organization and its environment, and that provide new perspectives and conceptual frameworks. Through any of these three processes, an employee's ability to contribute to the value-creation process of the organization may be improved. When an employee then effectively applies his or her superior ability to the organization's value-creation processes, he or she becomes a legitimate stakeholder in the organization.

Suppliers

Just like employees, suppliers may become stakeholders when they develop special abilities to provide inputs that improve the capabilities of an organization to create value through its current or future Business Concepts.

Since the 1980s, many organizations around the world are working to develop cooperative, collaborative relationships with key suppliers who have the potential to develop superior resource supply capabilities. For example, Chrysler, the U.S. automotive arm of DaimlerChrysler, works closely with one or two suppliers of each component it needs for its automobiles. Chrysler engineers assist those suppliers in designing components and production processes that can result in high-quality components at continuously falling costs. As a supplier succeeds in improving efficiency in producing components for Chrysler, the cost savings realized are shared by Chrysler and the supplier. Thus, Chrysler works with its suppliers to develop specialized capabilities that will generate future cost reductions and profit gains, and then gives its suppliers a stake in future profit gains through mutual sharing of the cost savings realized.

Customers

Customers become stakeholders when they develop special skills in using an organization's products or in interacting with the organization, and when as a result they derive a special benefit from use of the organization's products and have a strong interest in continuing to be a customer of the organization. A customer who makes an investment in learning to use an organization's products or services may not only become a repeat customer, but also lower an organization's costs of doing business with that customer. Repeat sales to experienced customers lower marketing costs and assure more stable flows of financial resources (revenues) to an organization.

An organization may try to develop customers as stakeholders in several ways. It may develop products that are especially effective in meeting a given customer's needs. It may provide training, support services, or other ways of enhancing the desirability of its product for a customer or lowering the customer's cost of using the product.

Customer loyalty programs provide a widely used approach to developing customers into stakeholders. These programs typically offer free or reduced price products and services as a reward for a customer's prior purchases, and may also offer enhanced service and recognition to repeat customers when they are interacting with the organization. When these programs succeed in creating the perception of a superior product or service in the eye of an individual customer, they do more than effectively differentiate the organization's product in the marketplace. They also develop a customer who feels and acts like a stakeholder in the organization. Such customers are more likely, for example, to communicate with managers of the organization when they encounter something unsatisfactory in the organization's products or activities, thereby providing important information resources to managers that they would not normally receive from customers who do not feel like stakeholders.

Government

Governments too may become stakeholders in an organization when they develop special ways of supporting an organization's value-creation processes. National and state governments may create laws, regulations, tax policies, or subsidy programs that are favorable to an industry or even to specific organizations. Local government may bear all or part of the costs of developing infrastructure and other resources required to support an organization's facilities and staff. When governments at any level in effect invest the public's funds in or otherwise extend advantages to an organization on behalf of the public, they are putatively helping an organization to succeed and thus have a reasonable basis to expect some benefits in return.

An organization may work to convert governments into stakeholders by promising some direct economic benefits, such as superior employment opportunities for citizens and growing tax revenues from the organization's future profits and from its employees' salaries. Larger firms may also offer more indirect but potentially attractive benefits to governments. For example, a large manufacturer may commit to recruiting suppliers and other firms to locate in an area in order to build up a "critical mass" of businesses that will set in motion a virtuous circle of growth and development for a region.

Communities

Communities may become stakeholders in organizations when the people who live, work, or engage in other activities near the places an organization operates develop a favorable attitude toward the organization. Such positive social capital may create valuable strategic options for an organization. For example, members of the community may be supportive of, or at least may not oppose, future expansions of the organization's operations in their community.

An organization may create stakeholders in the local community by being a "good corporate citizen" and sponsoring or participating in activities that benefit members of the community. An organization may make financial contributions to charities and other social programs that address special needs in the community, and employees of the organization (including managers) may contribute their time, energy, and expertise to such causes on behalf of the organization.

Shareholders and Debt Holders

Shareholders and other kinds of direct investors have obvious financial stakes in an organization that are usually accorded rights of ownership by most legal systems in the world. Most legal systems also extend to legal owners of firms the rights of *residual claimants*—the right to claim any net financial value of the organization after it has paid its legally recognized debts and other financial obligations. Debt holders also have a financial stake in an organization—the right to be repaid any principal advanced and interest due under loans made to the organization.

An organization can improve its ability to attract providers of equity funds by creating growth opportunities that promise share price appreciation to shareholders or by establishing a track record of earning profits that will provide attractive dividend flows. An organization's growth opportunities and dividend payment record must also be communicated to investors and financial market analysts—a process that is a major responsibility of the public relations function in most companies. An organization can also improve its ability to attract providers of debt funds by establishing a record of reliable, prompt repayment of principal and interest, and by maintaining the financial capacity of the organization to repay its debts.

The perceived integrity of an organization's managers also affects the willingness of financial investors and lenders to become stakeholders. In countries with limited securities markets regulation and frequent instances of managers' diverting an organization's financial resources to their own pockets, few if any investors or lenders are willing to become stakeholders by entrusting their funds to an organization, no matter what its business prospects may be. In such situations, persuading investors and lenders to become stakeholders may require special efforts by an individual organization to implement open, reliable, honest accounting and reporting processes. As the corporate accounting scandals in the United States in 2001 and 2002 attest, even in countries with well-established security markets regulation and accounting standards, top managers must nevertheless conduct and report the financial condition and affairs of the organization in an open and honest manner. Otherwise providers of financial resources will not be interested in being stakeholders in the organization, and offering its shares and debt to financial markets will not attract flows of financial resources, at least certainly not on favorable terms.

8.4 TRANSFORMATIVE PROCESSES

Transformative processes change the way an organization thinks and acts.

From time to time an organization may undergo important transformations in the way it carries out its Core Processes of product creation, product realization, and stakeholder development. Such transformations necessarily affect the organization broadly and thus do not happen by accident. Rather, they are the result of purposeful, coordinated, systematic changes in the way the organization thinks and acts. We refer to such periodic changes as **transformative processes,** and they are vital to improving and maintaining the competence of an organization. We next briefly consider three such transformative processes that continue to have a profound impact on organizations around the world.

Total Quality Management (TQM)

Beginning in the 1980s, many organizations in the advanced economies implemented TQM programs that significantly changed the way they create and realize products. TQM largely embodies ideas originally developed by Dr. W. Edwards Deming in the 1950s about keeping an organization clearly focused on creating value for customers in every activity that can directly affect the customer's perception of the value of the organization's product offer. In the 1950s and 1960s, Dr. Deming's ideas were embraced and put into practice by many Japanese firms that subsequently developed global reputations for producing high-quality products and services.

In the 1980s and later, organizations in North America, Europe, and elsewhere also began to adopt TQM methods and practices in their product creation and realization processes. Firms reinvented the way they define and design products to become more effective in creating customer perceptions of quality through superior execution of the aspects of a product that the customer cares most about. Production processes were reorganized to define new material and manufacturing standards and new processes for maintaining and even increasing those standards over time. All "customer-facing" activities were reevaluated from the customer's point of view and redesigned to deliver superior performance in the dimensions of service of greatest concern to customers.

Adoption of the TQM framework also called for intensive development of new skills and capabilities by an organization's employees and suppliers. Employees learned new techniques like the "House of Quality" for defining customer sensitivities and translating them into engineering design criteria. Production employees learned to use new methods, such as statistical process control to improve conformance of manufacturing processes to specifications and "quality circle" meetings to generate and act on employee suggestions for reducing costs and improving speed and predictability of manufacturing processes.

In some organizations today, "quality"—in the form of systematic use of TQM practices—is now deeply embedded in every activity. Continuous improvement of quality is now understood to be a primary management objective in the organization. Managers generate and review quality measures of many types on a regular basis, and consistently recognize and reward outstanding performance in achieving objectives for quality improvement and maintenance. Such systematic embedding of quality awareness and practices creates a "culture of quality" that broadly transforms the way an organization thinks and acts.

Business Process Reengineering (BPR)

In the 1980s and early 1990s, many organizations also underwent a transformative process of business process reengineering (BPR) in which they redesigned or "reengineered" many of their business processes. The BPR process first "maps" the way an organization works. Process maps make visible in graphic form the activities an organization undertakes and how those activities interact with each other in supporting product creation and realization. Each activity is then examined to determine its costs and the ways in which it contributes to the organization's creation of value for its customers. Activities that cost more than the value they create for the customer, or activities whose contribution to value creation cannot be clearly defined, are either dropped or outsourced to a subcontractor with capabilities that can make an activity net value-adding. Interactions between key value-adding activities are then reevaluated and redesigned to more directly, efficiently, and effectively support the organization's value-creation process.

Through process mapping and evaluation of how each activity is or is not adding value, BPR improves the clarity with which an organization "sees" itself as a value-creation system. By continuously applying the test of net value creation to each activity it undertakes, BPR also systematically challenges traditional practices and processes in an organization, and improves or eliminates activities that have lost their ability to create value or that have become net value subtractors. Thus, BPR can profoundly transform the way an organization thinks about and evaluates its processes of product creation and realization.

Environmental Quality Management (EQM)

As concern for the environment and ecosystems of the earth increases among consumers, employees, governments, and the public at large, many organizations are reexamining their products and practices to understand more fully and to reassess their impacts on the environment. Bringing a more comprehensive, thorough, and systematic view of the environmental impacts of an organization's products and processes into its management processes can significantly change the way an organization thinks and acts in creating and realizing its products.

Today, many organizations are redesigning their products to be more reusable, recyclable, biodegradable, or capable of being disposed of in a way that minimizes undesirable environmental impacts. In Scandinavia, for example, paper cartons for packing and shipping food products to supermarkets have largely been eliminated and replaced by reusable plastic containers that are returned to manufacturers after unpacking at supermarkets. In many countries, assembled products as diverse as automobiles and home appliances are being redesigned to increase the content of recyclable components and materials. Nonrecyclable materials in packaging are being converted to biodegradable materials or to combustible materials that can be incinerated without emitting harmful air pollutants or producing toxic ash.

The processes an organization undertakes to realize its products are also being redesigned to become environmentally "clean" or at least self-contained. Clean processes are designed not to generate toxic, contaminating, or otherwise undesirable by-products or wastes. When it is not technically possible to avoid generating pollutants or contaminants altogether in a process, wastes may be reprocessed to remove toxic or objectionable materials before solids, fluids, or gasses are released into the environment. In some cases, continuous inputs such as water or air are technically necessary and unavoidably become polluted or contaminated in a production process. In such cases, flows of air or water may be reprocessed and returned to reusable condition, thereby creating a "closed system" that does not release pollutants into the environment.

Improving EQM by creating environmentally benign products and processes requires that employees and suppliers develop a number of new capabilities. Suppliers must develop new materials that are recyclable, biodegradable, or fully combustible. Both in-house development employees and suppliers must learn to design components that can be easily disassembled for recycling. Product designers may have to learn to design products whose useful lifetimes can be extended by replacing or upgrading only a few key components. Industrial engineers must learn how to design clean processes, and operations staff must learn how to monitor and maintain the environmental performance of production processes. Thus, EQM typically requires substantial stakeholder development to improve the environmental performance of product creation and realization processes.

8.5 CREATING EFFECTIVE, SELF-MANAGING CORE PROCESSES

Core Processes encompass the central activities in the value-creation and value-distribution processes of an organization. In most organizations, managing the details of these processes on a daily basis typically consumes the majority of managers' time and attention. Yet this is not the case in some organizations, and in principle need not be the case in any organization. In this section we introduce a fundamentally important system design principle for Core Processes that suggests why managers in most organizations spend so much time "solving problems" in operations—and also how the management resources of an organization can be liberated and refocused on more effective ways of creating value.

Some common organizational and operational problems arise in Core Processes.

Problems of many types arise in the operations of an organization for a virtually inexhaustible number of reasons. In a fundamental sense, however, many problems arise in an organization because one or more of the system design principles for Business Concepts and Organization Concepts that we discussed in Chapters 6 and 7 are not being followed in an organization. Not following the system design principles creates specific organizational and operational problems that will continue to occur over and over again in various forms and circumstances as long as any of the system design principles are being violated.

Some common failures to honor the system design principles for Business Concepts and resulting organizational problems are as follows:

- *Failure of logical consistency in the elements of the Business Concept.* An organization's market and financial performance is poor or deteriorating because it creates product offers that are not appropriate for serving the market preferences it has targeted, or because it is not performing effectively the key activities in getting its product offers to targeted customers.
- *Failure to have a clear rationale for value creation in the Business Concept.* An organization's products are not selling well to customers whose preferences the organization has targeted because its products offer no clear benefits of "better, cheaper, or faster" than competitors' products.

Some common organizational problems that arise from failure to honor the system design principles for Organization Concepts are as follows:

- *Failure to align task allocations with the right level of management attention.* Major market and organizational issues facing the organization are not addressed because top management is preoccupied with details of the organization's current operations.
- *Failure to align responsibilities with the authority to allocate the resources needed to carry out those responsibilities.* Managers who identify opportunities or needs in the organization cannot respond to them because they do not have authority to allocate the resources needed to respond, or because they cannot communicate adequately the importance or urgency of the opportunities or needs to people in the organization who do have the authority to allocate such resources. Managers may become passive in the face of perceived opportunities and needs because they feel no resources will be made available to respond appropriately.
- *Failure to adequately define what "good performance" means.* People are unsure about which aspects of their jobs are most important to the organization and should therefore receive top priority and emphasis in their work. Employees and even suppliers may fail to perform in ways that would systematically benefit the organization's value-creation process, even though they are willing and able to do so.
- *Failure to define clear and appropriate measures of performance.* People work hard in an organization, but neither they nor their managers are able to judge to what extent their efforts are currently contributing effectively to the organization's value-creation process or are improving over time. Eventually, people have little motivation to try to improve their work because they are not sure what "improvement" means or how it could be demonstrated.
- *Failure to base incentives directly on defined performance measures.* Efforts by individuals and groups to contribute to the organization through their work are

often not recognized or rewarded by managers. In the absence of objective measures of performance, managers' subjective judgments of performance are used to assess performance of employees or suppliers. Some managers may distribute rewards and punishments in what appear to be arbitrary, biased, or self-serving ways. Motivation of people in the organization may be at a low level or deteriorating because they see no clear and consistent relationship between the efforts they make and the rewards the organization distributes.

- *Failure to align timing of rewards with timing of demonstrated results.* Managers with responsibility for achieving long-term objectives are evaluated and compensated on the basis of near-term results. Managers focus on delivering high performance in the short term and neglect long-term responsibilities.
- *Failure to align resources, organization design, and controls and incentives.* The human resources needed to perform well are available in an organization, but are not given the right tasks to perform, are not coordinated in appropriate ways, do not receive the information they need to perform their tasks, or are not evaluated and rewarded in ways that motivate them to perform well.
- *Failure to align the Organization Concept with the Business Concept.* An organization tries to recruit resources and build knowledge and capabilities that are not effective in creating value in the ways defined by its Business Concept. An organization takes a clear approach to organizing its activities, but that approach is not an effective way to coordinate its resources in carrying out its Business Concept. The controls that an organization uses, its definitions of performance, and the rewards it allocates internally do not clearly focus on creating value in the way defined by its Business Concept.

Getting to the "root cause" of organizational problems

In effect, these and other organizational problems arise because strategic managers have not performed adequately their primary responsibility to design a Business Concept and Organization Concept that can form the foundation for a viable, coherent Strategic Logic. The consequence is an organization in which managers and other employees continually struggle with the kinds of problems just mentioned. As a result, such an organization will not work well as a system for value creation and distribution. When this situation exists, and it often does, even top managers will spend most or all of their time continually dealing with the myriad problems of an organization struggling to function under a flawed or inadequately developed Strategic Logic. In some cases, managers fall into a trap of devoting so much of their attention to "solving problems" that they fail to recognize and correct the fundamental flaws in the organization's Strategic Logic that are generating the organization's problems. As a common American management aphorism states, "It's hard to think about draining the swamp when you are up to your elbows in alligators."

Organizations whose managers fall into this trap are likely to begin a downward spiral of deteriorating performance from which they may be unable to escape. These organizations eventually fail in their markets because of inadequate value creation through their Business Concept, or disintegrate internally because of inappropriate approaches to coordinating resources and distributing value in their Organization Concept, or fall victim to both types of failures of Strategic Logic.

To break out of a cycle of expending management resources on recurring operational problems, in effect, strategic managers must stop treating the symptoms of flawed Strategic Logics and begin to diagnose and cure the disorders in their Strategic Logic that give rise to the symptoms. Strategic managers as system designers of organizations must continuously and systematically assess whether the system design principles we have discussed are being followed in the organization's Strategic Logic. When operational problems of various types do arise, strategic managers must focus on finding the "root causes" of the problems (i.e., on analyzing which system design principles are not being followed, and in what ways). They must then make changes in the Business Concept and Organization Concept to ensure that the system design principles are being followed. Making sure that an organization's Strategic Logic continuously honors the system design principles is a fundamental responsibility of strategic managers.

Core processes can become self-managing processes.

When strategic managers create system designs for an organization based on a Business Concept and an Organization Concept that carefully follow the system design principles we have discussed, everyone in an organization should clearly understand how the organization is trying to create value, what role each person and group plays in that process, and how they and the overall organization are performing. Such organizations are rare, but some do exist, and in such organizations the Core Processes become essentially **self-managing processes.** Strategic managers focus on defining and communicating a clearly articulated and viable Strategic Logic, and others in the organization support the Strategic Logic by performing their respective roles in the organization's value-creation processes. Management resources do not need to be expended in solving recurring problems resulting from a flawed Strategic Logic, because such "system design problems" are diagnosed and eliminated at their root causes.

With this view of what is possible—and has actually been achieved in some organizations—we introduce the following system design principle for Core processes:

System Design Principle 8.1

When the system design principles applicable to an organization's Business Concept and Organization Concept are consistently followed in designing an organization as a system for value creation and distribution, the Core Processes of the organization can become largely self-managing processes that need only limited or occasional management intervention.

KEY TERMS AND CONCEPTS

product creation The definition, design, and development of new product offers.

product definition Defining the specific ways that an organization will try to create value for a targeted market segment through a new product offer.

product design The translation of a product definition into appropriate product and process architectures and technical solutions that will deliver the intended net delivered customer value to the targeted market segment.

product and process architectures The decomposition of product and process designs into functional components and the full specification of the component interfaces that determine how the components will work together as a system.

modular architectures Product and process architectures in which the component interfaces have been defined to allow the substitution of a range of component variations to readily configure product and process variations.

product development The creation of detailed designs for each of the functional components in a new product's product and process architectures.

product realization All the activities through which an organization produces, distributes, and supports its products.

stakeholder development Processes through which an organization tries to improve the abilities of its stakeholders to provide more, better, or lower cost resources, or to do so more quickly.

transformative processes Purposeful, coordinated, and systematic changes in the way an organization thinks and acts in carrying out its value-creation and value-distribution activities.

self-managing processes Value-creation processes in which each participant understands how an organization is trying to create value and what their role is in the organization's value-creation process, and therefore can effectively manage their own activities for contributing to the performance of the organization in value creation.

REVIEW QUESTIONS

1. How do modular product and process architectures help to improve the strategic flexibility of an organization?
2. What role does marketing play in the product realization process?
3. What criteria determine who becomes a stakeholder in an organization?
4. How has each of the following transformed organizations in recent years?
   a. Total quality management (TQM)
   b. Business process reengineering (BPR)
   c. Environmental quality management (EQM)
5. What are some common forms of management failures that become visible in the Core Processes of an organization?
6. Why is it necessary to solve organizational problems at the "root cause" before an organization can create self-managing processes?

CHAPTER 9

BUSINESS UNIT STRATEGY AS A "SITUATIONAL PUZZLE": ALIGNING STRATEGIC LOGIC WITH MACROENVIRONMENT, INDUSTRY, AND PRODUCT MARKET EVOLUTION

INTRODUCTION

In the preceding chapters, we discussed the fundamental responsibility of strategic managers to define and implement a clear Strategic Logic for creating and distributing value in an organization. To define a successful Strategic Logic, strategic managers must create, in effect, a *system design* for an organization that is capable of sustaining value-creating processes in its environment. Creating a system design that will enable an organization to create value is like solving a "situational puzzle." Strategic managers must take into account many factors in an organization's competitive environment in order to identify opportunities for creating value and effective processes for taking advantage of those opportunities.

As an organization's environment changes in significant ways, the Strategic Logic of an organization must also change to maintain a viable system design for value-creating processes. In this chapter we consider three frameworks for identifying and understanding aspects of an organization's environment that are important in the design of a Strategic Logic. Because most organizational environments are dynamic in at least some respects, strategic managers must be able to recognize strategically important changes in the environment and adapt their organization's Strategic Logic to enable the organization to sustain its ability to create value. We therefore also consider ways in which an organization's Strategic Logic may have to be modified as its environment undergoes various kinds of change.

We first consider five kinds of changes in the *macroenvironment* of an organization that may call for changes in an organization's Strategic Logic. We then consider five aspects of the *industry environment* of an organization in which various kinds of change can have significant impacts on a Strategic Logic. Finally, we examine an organization's *product market* context and some important ways in which the evolution of a product market calls for evolution of an organization's Strategic Logic.

9.1 CHANGES IN AN ORGANIZATION'S MACROENVIRONMENT

Forms of macroenvironmental change

The **macroenvironment** of an organization includes all the factors outside the organization's industry and product market that can have a significant impact on the organization's ability to sustain successful value-creation and distribution processes. We can generally place such numerous factors in one of five categories of strategically significant macroenvironmental change, as suggested in Figure 9.1.

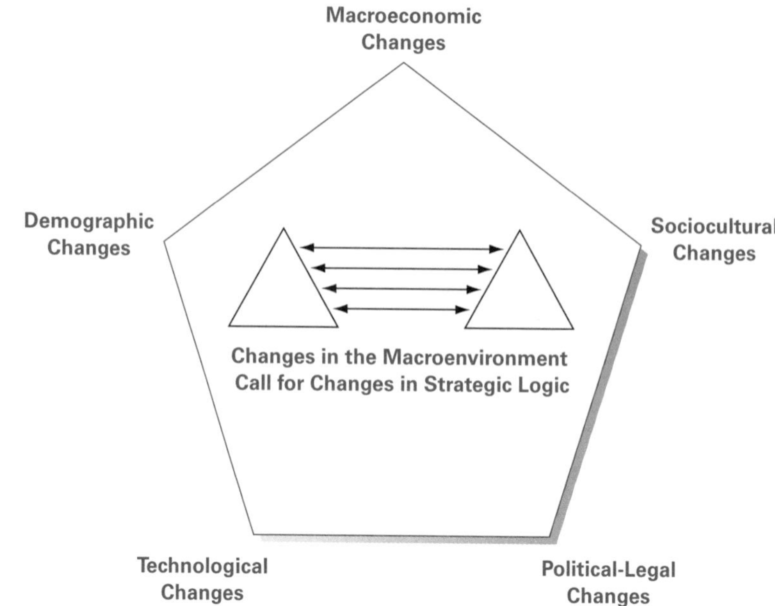

FIGURE 9.1 Kinds of Change in the Macroenvironment of an Organization

- Macroeconomic change
- Demographic change
- Sociocultural change
- Political-legal change
- Technological change

Macroenvironmental factors are beyond the control of any single organization.

Generally speaking, macroeconomic, demographic, and sociocultural changes are societal effects that are beyond the ability of any organization to influence directly. Such changes may bring new opportunities for value-creation, or may threaten existing value-creation processes. Strategic managers must be able to recognize such changes as they begin to happen and to react with appropriate and timely changes in Strategic Logic. Political-legal and technological changes in the macroenvironment will in most cases be beyond the control of any organization, but may sometimes be influenced by an organization—for example, through its efforts to lobby governments and through its research and development activities. Strategic managers must therefore be alert both to react to emerging political-legal and technological changes by modifying a Strategic Logic and to proactively seek such changes that will benefit their current or future Strategic Logic.

Macroeconomic Changes

Macroeconomic changes include changes in important aspects of the economy of a city, nation, or region of the world, or in the global economy at large. Changes in gross national product (GNP) indicate changes in a country's overall economic activity, for example, while changes in the rate of inflation, currency exchange rates, and interest rates charged to businesses and consumers typically affect current and future levels of economic activity. Strategic managers must be able to understand how such changes will affect the competitive environment of an organization and impact its Strategic Logic. Let us consider how the macroenvironmental changes just mentioned could call for changes in the Strategic Logic of organizations in some selected industries.

Changes in GNP

Economies expand and contract, and changes in the overall level of economic activity in an economy can lead to significant shifts in consumer preferences and purchasing behavior that may call for modifications in an organization's product offers. When an economy is expanding, both employment and wages tend to increase, and consumer confidence is likely to be high. Consumers who feel confident about their jobs and income level tend to buy more of some kinds of goods, like consumer durables (refrigerators, automobiles), luxury goods (expensive watches and clothes), and leisure and entertainment (vacations in foreign countries, dinners in restaurants). Many consumers will also begin to purchase higher-performing, more fully featured, and thus more expensive versions of many kinds of products. Therefore, in an expanding economy, as overall demand grows, consumer preferences for many products often shift noticeably "upmarket," while demand for "downmarket" goods may actually decrease.

When economic growth slows or an economy begins to contract, consumer confidence may fall sharply. Consumers then begin to defer purchases of more costly goods or to buy cheaper versions of products. Consumers may, for example, defer purchasing a new automobile and instead may prefer to maintain and repair their current automobile. As a result, demand for new cars and other kinds of durable goods will fall, but demand for repair and maintenance services will increase. When an economy slows or contracts, firms in the automobile business may need to shift the emphasis in their value-creation activities from production of new cars to providing parts for repair and maintenance services.

Cycles of macroeconomic expansion and contraction can result in especially large impacts on firms that supply equipment and basic materials to an industry. As suggested in Figure 9.2, swings in demand levels tend to become amplified as they work their way up the supply chain of an industry. Changes in demand for personal computers, for example, tend to lead to even greater swings in demand for semiconductors for microprocessors and memory chips, and to even greater fluctuations in demand for the pure silicon used to make semiconductors, and even greater fluctuations in the equipment like photolithography

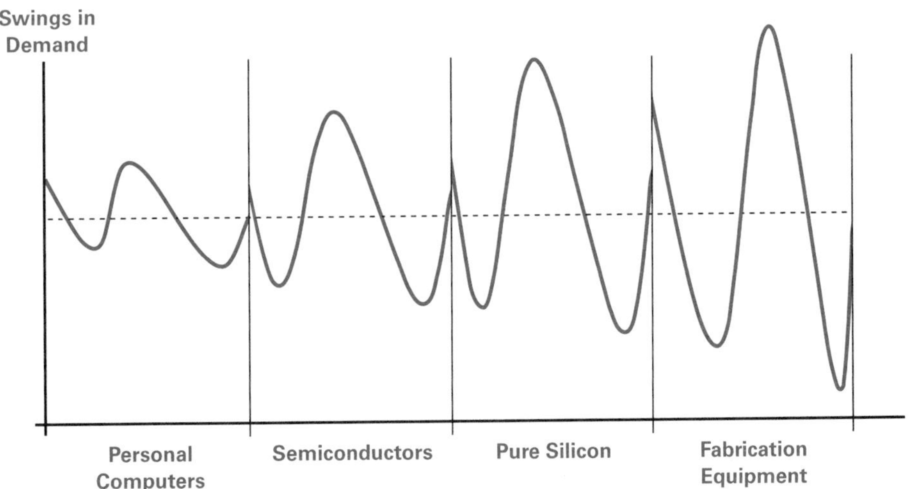

FIGURE 9.2 Increasing Amplitude of Fluctuations in Demand for Upstream Products in an Industry

machines used to make semiconductors. Thus, the further upstream in an industry is the market for a firm's products, the more the firm needs to be able to quickly ramp up or wind down production of its products. Strategic managers must design the firm's value-creation processes to have the flexibility to make appropriate adjustments in output levels.

Economic cycles are becoming more closely linked as major economies become more interconnected.

Moreover, because of the export and import trade that increasingly links the major regional economies of the world, macroeconomic changes in one major regional economy tend to precipitate macroeconomic reactions in other regional economies. Fluctuations in the rate of growth of the U.S. economy, the world's largest economy, typically lead to similar variations in the growth rates of Asian and European Union (EU) economies, the major trading partners of the United States. As flows of goods and services between major economic regions of the world expand and their economies become more interdependent, macroeconomic changes in one region are soon reflected in changes in demand levels in other regions. Thus, strategic managers must be aware of macroeconomic developments not just in their own national economy, but also in the regional economies of the world that have an impact on their national economy.

Changes in Rate of Inflation

When a currency inflates, prices of goods increase in an economy, and consumers receive fewer goods for a given amount of the currency. Unless wages are inflating at a comparable rate, consumers generally reduce their consumption of discretionary goods like entertainment, and often begin to buy lower-priced versions of necessary goods. In the developed economies of the world, governments through their central banks try to maintain low rates of inflation by regulating the supply of money or raising interest rates. Although these two interventions work in somewhat different ways, both have the effect of moderating consumer demand, which normally creates a counteracting downward pressure on prices.

Occasionally some economies fall into spirals of hyperinflation, with inflation rates of 200 to 2000 percent per year. Such situations create disincentives to save money or defer purchases of goods whose prices are rising rapidly. Consumer behavior then shifts toward purchasing as many goods as quickly as possible to avoid further loss of purchasing power. During the hyperinflation in Brazil in the 1980s and 1990s, for example, prices of goods were often changed on a daily basis or even twice a day. Many consumers would take time off from work to go shopping as soon as they received their salaries in the morning in order to avoid paying higher prices at the end of the workday.

In most economies, a certain level of inflation—usually between one and two percent—seems to be a "natural" part of economic expansion. However, in certain circumstances, even a developed economy may undergo deflation of its currency, as occurred in Japan in 2001 and 2002. When a currency deflates, prices of goods decrease in an economy, and consumers begin to receive more goods for a given amount of the currency. When consumers expect prices to fall, they may experience an incentive to defer purchases, especially of durable goods and real estate. As demand levels fall, manufacturers and retailers may lower prices to stimulate demand, but this approach often has the perverse effect of encouraging consumers to defer purchases even longer in anticipation of further price cuts. Some businesses may have to reduce output and lay off workers or reduce costs by cutting salaries. Workers affected by layoffs or salary reductions cut back on purchases, which further depresses demand, contributing to further downward spiraling of deflation and economic contraction. Unless governments make appropriate interventions, an unchecked deflationary spiral may lead to substantial contraction of economic activity, with broad impacts on demand levels.

Changes in Exchange Rates

Changes in the value of one country's currency relative to another country's currency usually create incentives for businesses to adjust their imports or exports from one country to the other. Suppose, for example, that the Australian dollar declines relative to the Japanese yen while exchange rates between the yen and other currencies remain constant. Businesses based in Japan and managing their finances in yen can then buy inputs to their value-creation processes in Australia at lower prices in yen terms. Japanese steelmakers would then have an incentive to expand their purchases of iron ore from Australia, and other Japanese importers would have an incentive to expand their imports of Australian-made goods. Japanese tourists will also find a vacation in Australia to be more affordable. Imports of Japanese goods, however, will be more expensive for Australian consumers, because they have to pay more Australian dollars to buy goods that are priced in Japanese yen. Exchange rate fluctuations therefore affect both export demand levels for a firm's products and the costs of any of its resources that may be imported.

Changes in Interest Rates

Increases in interest rates charged for loans to businesses and consumers in effect increase the costs of goods and services that must be financed by businesses and most consumers. Rising interest rates therefore tend to depress demand for most goods that are usually financed and to shift most demand in a market toward less costly versions of financed goods. However, people who have money to invest in bonds and debt instruments will receive higher interest rates on their money. As a result, demand for many luxury goods and the most upmarket versions of some products like automobiles may actually increase, because relatively rich people have more income from their investments to spend. Thus, rising interest rates may lead to a bifurcation in overall demand, with simultaneously growing demand for lower-priced and higher-priced items, while demand for goods in the mid-priced range declines.

Declines in interest rates, on the other hand, reduce the effective costs of financed goods and usually stimulate demand for all financed goods, including the mid-priced goods that most consumers purchase.

Demographic Changes

Demographic changes broadly impact market demand levels and preferences.

Demographic changes are changes in the composition and distribution of population. Demographic changes that are likely to have significant implications for an organization's Strategic Logic include changes in the size of a population, changes in family size, the age distribution of a population, its ethnic composition, and geographic distribution within a country or region. Some demographic changes can significantly affect consumer preferences and thus the composition and levels of demand for products, while some demographic changes have important effects on the human resources available to an organization and the terms on which those resources may be obtained.

Impacts on Demand Levels, Consumer Preferences, and Product Offers

Overall demand levels in a country or region tend to rise and fall as it gains or loses population. An important part of the "normal" increase in GNP of a country, for example, can be attributed to the "natural" rate of growth of its population. In many developed economies, however, birth rates of people already living in the country have fallen below the rate needed to maintain a constant population level. In some of those countries, such as the United States and the United Kingdom, immigration helps to offset this decline and to maintain a steady growth rate for the overall population, usually on the order of two to three percent per year. In Japan, however, a country with little or no immigration, the population level has actually been declining by a fraction of a percent per year for several years, further contributing to declining demand for goods in Japan's domestic economy.

Several kinds of demographic changes can affect consumer preferences. Changes in family size may lead to significant shifts in consumer preferences. In many developed economies, and among the more educated and affluent consumers in developing economies, family size is decreasing, and both spouses are increasingly likely to be employed. The increase in family units composed of "DINKS" (double-income, no kids) leads to increased demand for higher-quality goods for adults, because more people can afford to spend more on their own needs when they do not have children. Increasingly, when families do have children, they tend to have one or at most two children. As this trend continues, consumers planning to have a single child increasingly prefer smaller but better appointed homes. They are also likely to spend more money on high-quality children's clothing, toys with educational content, and daycare services that offer a stimulating learning environment for their child.

The more homogeneous the ethnic composition of a population, the more homogeneous consumer preferences tend to be. As immigration changes the ethnic composition of a country or region, however, consumer preferences become more diverse. In the United States, for example, immigration from Latin America, Asia, and Eastern Europe are creating considerable diversity in consumer preferences for food, clothing, and housing, as well as increasing demand for products labeled and advertised in the languages of various ethnic groups. On a regional level, immigration to Shanghai from many provinces of China is creating growing diversity in consumer preferences for food, restaurants, and many other products that must be marketed in different ways to consumers with different language dialects and cultural backgrounds.

Ethnic diversity and the cultural differences that come with ethnic diversity may also lead to changes in family size. Although family sizes are shrinking among most of the population in the United States, immigrants from Latin America tend to prefer larger families with several children. Thus, consumer preferences in regions of the United States with significant immigration from Latin America tend to include growing demand for affordable homes with several bedrooms, minivans and vans suitable for carrying large families, and less expensive clothing for families with several children but modest incomes.

Another important source of demographic change is the trend in developed economies with low birth rates and long life expectancies to have a growing proportion of elderly people, while in less-developed economies with high birth rates and low life expectancies the proportion of young people is increasing rapidly. The "aging" of the population in developed economies is creating greater demand for housing, transportation, medical care, financial services, food, and many other kinds of products, differentiated to serve the needs and concerns of elderly people. At the same time, an increasing share of world demand for music, sports clothing, athletic shoes, and fast food now comes from the many young consumers in the developing economies of Asia, Latin America, and the Middle East.

Impacts on Human Resources and Their Availability

Demographic changes may also significantly affect the human resources available to an organization and the terms on which key human resources may be obtained. Especially in developed economies with aging populations, growing shortages of younger workers—and especially young workers with the education and skills likely to be found primarily among recent university graduates—are likely to require that organizations offer increasingly attractive employment terms to be successful in attracting young employees to their value-creation processes. At the same time, the growing numbers of retired people presents an opportunity for expanded hiring of older workers. Both the fast-food chain McDonald's and the discount store operator Wal-Mart are successfully attracting older people to work one or two days a week to offset the diminishing numbers of young workers available for their businesses in several countries of the world.

As it becomes increasingly common in developed economies for both father and mother to be employed, while at the same time the number of grandparents living with their children decreases, the need for high-quality daycare services for children is becoming acute. In some countries—Sweden, for example—government often provides low-cost daycare centers for working parents, but in most areas of the world daycare services are a private sector activity and are either inadequately developed or quite expensive. To attract capable employees who are part of a double-income household, it is often necessary for organizations to provide on-site daycare services for their employees. For example, in Bangalore, India, the center of the Indian information technology industry, many companies that want to recruit programmers and software developers now offer on-campus daycare centers staffed with qualified nurses and teachers. Some Indian IT firms even install video cameras that enable employees to monitor their child in the daycare center while they are working at their desks.

Sociocultural Changes

Sociocultural changes can lead to major changes in both product and resource markets.

Sociocultural changes are changes in the values and behavioral norms of a society. Like demographic changes, sociocultural changes may have significant impacts on both the demand side (Business Concept) and the supply side (Organization Concept) of a Strategic Logic.

Impacts on Consumer Preferences and Product Offers

Sociocultural changes may include changes in the environmental awareness, social values, health consciousness, and other concerns and priorities of people in a society. Increasing awareness of and concern for the impacts of products on the environment typically lead consumers to prefer products and packaging that are recyclable or biodegradable. Firms whose product realization processes generate environmental pollution may find that they are the objects of protests or boycotts by pro-environment consumers, while firms with good environmental performance may be able to build on that performance to create greater customer loyalty to their products.

Consumers' concerns for their social environment may also undergo changes. Consumers may become more aware of and concerned about the working conditions of workers who make the products they are offered by various companies. In the late 1990s, for example, news media in the United States and Europe carried reports of children working long hours at low wages and under unpleasant conditions in companies in Southeast Asia that were subcontractors for the production of Nike shoes. Several consumer groups began to organize protests in front of the Nike corporate campus in Beaverton, Oregon, that received widespread attention from the news media. Fearing loss of consumer support for its products, Nike eventually adopted a policy of regularly inspecting its subcontractors' operations and enforcing more socially acceptable working conditions, including payment of higher wages and elimination of child labor and excessive working hours.

Of course, Nike originally became a successful business in large part because of another major shift in sociocultural values—the rise of health and physical fitness consciousness in the late 1970s and 1980s, especially in the United States. As American consumers became more interested in staying physically fit, they took up jogging, aerobics, tennis, and other physical activities in record numbers, and Nike created a growing array of athletic shoes designed specifically for each activity. Nike's famous slogan "Just Do It" also encouraged consumers to try new kinds of sports—and of course to buy another pair of Nike shoes designed for that sport. Eventually, Nike expanded its business into a broad line of athletic wear and sports accessories to fully outfit anyone interested in sports and outdoor activities. Other companies also built large businesses during this shift in sociocultural values by selling exercise machines, health club memberships, and sports and recreation equipment.

Along with the American "fitness craze" in the 1980s came a dramatic shift in consumer preferences for more healthful foods. Consumers began to shun foods with high fat and cholesterol content. Many consumers reduced their consumption of beef and increased their consumption of fish and chicken, which are meats that are relatively low in fat. Many consumers also began to prefer low-fat, low-calorie, and low-salt versions of many kinds of foods. Demand for "natural" and "organic" foods increased, as did demand for vitamin supplements and various natural herbs thought to benefit health.

Impacts on Resources, Organization Designs, and Controls and Incentives

Shifts in sociocultural values may also affect the terms on which human resources are available to an organization, the ways in which those resources are coordinated, and the kinds of incentives that can be effective in attracting and motivating human resources.

In recent years in the United States, for example, many of the "baby boomers"—the generation of people born during the high birth rate years of the late 1940s to early 1960s—have experienced a shift in values. Many are now giving up the pursuit of careers in corporate America in favor of less demanding but more flexible work arrangements in small firms, in not-for-profit organizations, or as self-employed free-lancers. Many baby boomers retired early or work only part-time, trading reduced income for more time to spend with family or on personal interests. Changes such as these in the priorities of some of the most educated and experienced people in the American workforce mean that organizations in the United States need to become more flexible in the design of jobs, and in many cases firms must now offer changing work assignments that keep life interesting for such people. Incentive structures must also be redesigned to offer greater intangible rewards—like flexible time schedules and participation in interesting projects—and less emphasis on purely financial compensation.

Political-Legal Changes

Political changes tend to lead to changes in the legal environment.

Political-legal changes include changes in the issues being discussed and addressed through a country's political process, as well as changes in the laws and regulations adopted in a country. Political issues tend to be precursors of changes in laws and regulations. Strategic managers must therefore be able to sense shifts in the political climate of a country, to identify possible changes in laws and regulations that such shifts may lead to, and to modify or prepare to modify the Strategic Logic of their organization accordingly.

A legal trend in many countries, especially in the United States, is the expansion of consumer rights and protections. The 1970s and 1980s saw the adoption of strict product liability laws in the United States that often hold manufacturers of products strictly liable for injuries suffered by consumers while using their products. These laws, coupled with large damages awards to plaintiffs in personal injury lawsuits, led many firms to make changes in their product designs to make them "idiot proof" and safer to use.

Protection of the environment became an important political issue in most developed economies in the 1970s and 1980s (and remains so today). In recent years, most developed countries passed environmental protection laws and set up agencies to develop and enforce detailed environmental regulations for many industries. These laws and regulations required many companies to redesign their products and production processes to reduce or eliminate pollutants, and many firms made major investments in new product designs and new production equipment to "clean up" their factories and plants. Instead of cleaning up their processes, however, some companies try to "export their pollution" by relocating their most polluting processes to countries with little or no environmental regulation. In many cases, however, those countries have also begun to adopt stricter environmental regulations, although a few countries remain legal havens for polluters and are today experiencing serious degradation of their natural environments.

Political-legal changes may also include changes in laws and regulations affecting employment. In many countries of Europe, for example, social legislation extensively defines the relationship between employer and employee in ways that are steadily expanding the rights of employees and their claims on the organizations they work for. Recent labor legislation in France, for example, makes it difficult and costly (if not impossible) for a firm to reduce the number of its employees if it is still operating profitably, and also raises the costs of discharging employees for firms not operating profitably. In addition, in an effort to create more jobs, France established a maximum 35-hour workweek. Instead of hiring more workers, however, many French firms redesigned their work processes to "do more with less" labor time, or in some cases to establish new operations in other countries with more flexible labor laws.

Technological Changes

Changes can occur in product, process, and coordination technologies.

Technological changes may occur in *product technologies, process technologies,* or *coordination technologies.*

Changes in product technologies make possible new kinds of products with new functionalities, improved products with higher performance levels, or more cost-effective products. Changes in product technologies primarily take the form of new kinds of components that add new functionalities to a product (like floppy disk drives that enabled programs to be downloaded into early personal computers), or improved components that improve product performance (such as higher power density batteries that enable longer operating times for mobile phones and laptop computers). Technological improvements in materials may also make it possible to produce components and products at lower costs. When product technology changes make possible new and improved products at lower costs, firms must be prepared to upgrade their products technologically to maintain the competitiveness of their product offers.

Changes in process technologies include new and improved production methods. Advances in process technology are often necessary to realize new products based on new product technologies. For example, the invention of microprocessors was an important change in product technology, but the reliable production of microprocessors required substantial development of new process technologies for growing pure silicon crystals, etching micron-sized circuits onto silicon wafers, and packaging silicon wafers together in assembled microprocessors. Improvements in process technologies may also lead to lower production costs and faster response to customer orders.

Changes in coordination technologies include changes in computers and telecommunications that enable faster, more precise, and broader coordination of an organization's processes. Many production processes today are increasingly run by factory automation systems that use small computers and a network of sensors and controls to increase production speeds while maintaining accuracy of machine settings and operations. Coordination among people, often located in widely dispersed areas of the globe, is increasingly accomplished through mobile phone calls and Internet e-mail. Growing numbers of knowledge workers are able to perform part or all of their work at home or wherever they may choose to be in the world, thanks to the ability to connect computers through phone lines, mobile phone networks, and satellites. Such changes in coordination technology make possible new kinds of organization designs for coordinating work, and may call for new kinds of controls to monitor outputs and productivity of telecommuting workers.

9.2 CHANGES IN AN ORGANIZATION'S INDUSTRY ENVIRONMENT

The industry environment of an organization includes both competitive pressures and opportunities for cooperation within an industry that must be carefully evaluated in designing an organization's Strategic Logic. We first consider five kinds of competitive pressure that can reduce the profits of the firms in an industry. Then we consider ways in which the sources of the five competitive pressures may also provide opportunities for cooperation that can bring increased profits and other benefits to firms that can establish cooperative relationships.

Five Competitive Pressures

Five forms of changes in an industry's competitive environment

A **competitive pressure** is any external influence on an organization that acts to limit the profits it can earn. In defining an organization's Strategic Logic, strategic managers must take into consideration five kinds of competitive pressure that may be exerted on an organization's ability to earn profits. These five sources of competitive pressure were identified and analyzed in the 1970s by Michael Porter,[1] as indicated in Figure 9.3.

The most obvious kind of competitive pressure comes from **internal rivalry** between firms in an industry—in effect, direct competition between firms trying to sell similar kinds of products to essentially the same customers. Competitive pressure may also be exerted, however, by suppliers and buyers that have **market power,** which is the ability to dictate the terms of trade for an economic exchange. Suppliers with *supplier power* may

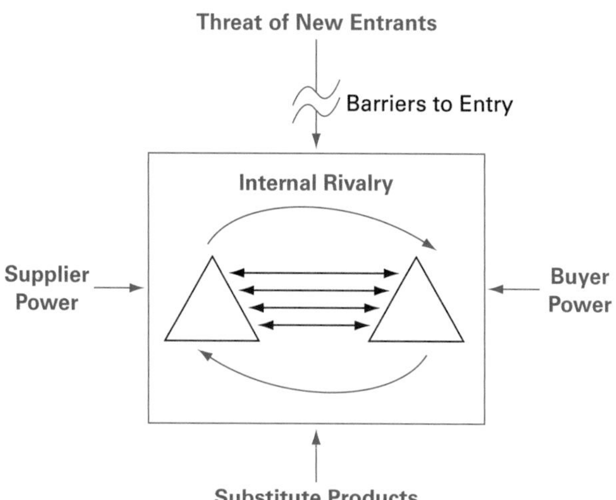

FIGURE 9.3 Five Kinds of Competitive Forces That Exert Competitive Pressure
Source: Adapted from Porter, Michael, (1979). *Competitive Strategy.* New York: The Free Press.

[1] Porter, Michael. (1979). *Competitive Strategy.* New York: The Free Press.

demand high prices for their inputs to firms in an industry and thereby diminish the profits of the firms that they supply. Similarly, buyers with *buyer power* may demand low prices and high service levels from firms in the industry that supply them, and that also acts to reduce those firms' profits. In addition, *substitute products* may limit the prices that a firm can charge for its products, thereby limiting profits. Finally, the *threat of new entrants* into an industry may also limit profits of firms already in an industry.

We next consider the circumstances under which these five competitive pressures may be significant in their impacts on firms in an industry. We also discuss the kinds of steps that strategic managers might take to create a Strategic Logic that minimizes the potential for competitive pressures on an organization from the five competitive forces.

Internal Rivalry

"Head-to-head" competition between rivals is only one form of competition.

The "head-to-head" competition between firms currently trying to sell similar products to the same customers is called *internal rivalry* within an industry. In effect, head-to-head competitors are the firms within an industry that share similar Business Concepts in their Strategic Logics. Internal rivalry will be high when many firms are selling similar products and when their intended customers can readily choose to buy from whatever firm they prefer. In such circumstances, competition between firms is likely to be intense, and may take the form of both *price competition* and *nonprice competition.* In price competition, the differences between the nonprice aspects of firm's product offers are either nonexistent or are so insignificant that offering a lower price becomes the only way to attract customers from competitors. Price competition is common among firms that offer *commodity products*—products that are essentially identical and interchangeable from the customer's point of view. Price competition limits the price that any firm can charge and thus directly limits the profits a firm can make by selling its products. Nonprice competition may also lower profits by imposing higher costs of service, advertising, and customer support as firms try to differentiate their product offers on nonprice characteristics.

To limit the competitive pressure of internal rivalry on a firm's profitability, strategic managers have two basic options. First, a firm may try to become a large-scale and efficient producer in order to achieve economies of scale in production and distribution. By achieving lower operating costs than its competitors, a firm may be able to operate profitably while selling its products at the prices that smaller, less-efficient firms must charge to stay in business. This strategy is sometimes described as one in which large, efficient producers operate profitably under *the price umbrella* of less-efficient firms. Second, a firm may try to differentiate its product offer on nonprice dimensions—by offering its products in different package sizes, with flexible delivery terms, with high levels of service and responsiveness, with close customer support, and even by advertising an image as a reliable provider of goods.

Supplier Power

Supplier power lets a supplier "dictate the terms of trade."

When a supplier can dictate the terms of trade in supplying inputs to one or more firms in an industry, that supplier is said to have **supplier power.** For example, a supplier with supplier power may be able to tell its customers how much they must pay for its products, what volumes they must buy (or must be satisfied with), and when delivery will be made. By setting high prices for its inputs into its customers' businesses, a supplier with supplier power in effect "reaches into" the profit stream of its customers to appropriate part of those profits for itself.

When will a supplier have supplier power? Essentially, when a supplier provides an input that one or more firms must have because it is important to the performance or cost basis of their products, *and* when no feasible alternate source of supply for the supplier's input is available, a supplier will have supplier power. During the mid to late 1990s, Intel held a high degree of supplier power in supplying its Pentium microprocessors to the makers of personal computers. By the 1990s Intel's microprocessors had become the *de facto* standard for the personal computer industry. Personal computers based on the Intel microprocessor architecture had become a commodity, and the only opportunity computer makers had to make profitable sales was by offering their personal computers with the latest generation of Intel's Pentium microprocessor, for which no alternate source of supply was available. During this time period, Intel's supplier power was so great that it could set virtually whatever price it wanted to charge, as well as dictate the quantities to be delivered to various personal computer makers, the time of delivery, and the terms for payment. As a result, much of the profit made in the personal computer industry was effectively appropriated by Intel, which became one of the most profitable firms in the world during this period.

Buyer Power

Buyer power lets a buyer "dictate the terms of trade."

When a buyer can dictate the terms of trade when making purchases from one or more firms in an industry, that buyer has **buyer power.** Such a buyer may be able to dictate to the firms that supply it how much it will pay, what the payment terms will be, and where and when deliveries have to be made. By offering to pay only low prices, while perhaps also demanding high levels of support and extended payment terms, a buyer with buyer power reduces the revenues and raises the costs of the firms that supply it, thereby lowering the profit levels of those firms.

Buyer power typically exists when a buyer purchases large volumes of goods relative to the total output of the firms that supply it, when it is the only large-volume customer or one of only a few large-volume customers for the firms that supply it, and when not supplying the buyer would lead to overcapacity or high unit costs of production for the firms that want to supply it. For example, General Motors often produces nearly 20 million vehicles a year worldwide, and purchases nearly 100 million tires annually—a quantity equal to the combined annual output of several modern tire factories. In order for tire companies such as Goodyear or Michelin to operate their factories at or near capacity, they essentially need to win a significant part of the tire purchases by General Motors and the other largest automakers each year. In such a situation, General Motors may be able to bargain aggressively on price and delivery terms, perhaps even offering to pay only its suppliers' variable costs of production and delivery, while encouraging its tire suppliers to recover their fixed costs from smaller auto assemblers or the after-sales market.

Large buyers like General Motors may even vertically integrate upstream into their suppliers' industry to learn the cost structure of that industry. Armed with an understanding of their suppliers' costs, and presenting a credible threat of further expansion of their own internal supply capability, large buyers may then be successful in bargaining for prices that are equal to or near their suppliers' variable costs of production and delivery.

Substitute Products

The cost of a substitute product, plus the cost of switching, limits the price a producer can charge.

A **substitute product** is any product that can provide the essential benefits offered by an industry's product, but that may impose some *switching costs* (additional costs or reduced benefits) on customers if they switch to the substitute product. The price of a substitute product, the cost of switching to the substitute, and the value of potentially reduced benefits offered by the substitute product, together determine the maximum price that firms in an industry can charge for their product. For example, electrical cable for wiring buildings is made from both copper and aluminum. Copper cable is generally preferred by most builders because it is more flexible and easier to install. The price of copper fluctuates on world markets and largely determines the cost of copper cable. However, the price that makers of copper cable can charge is limited by the current price of aluminum cable, because builders will switch to aluminum cable if the price of copper cable becomes too high, even though installing aluminum cables requires some additional work.

Substitute products are not always as obvious and close as the choice between copper and aluminum cable. As the television advertisement described in Highlight Box 9.1 illustrates, substitute products may first seem unrelated to each other. Further analysis may show, however, that an important customer benefit can be delivered through a number of different kinds of products—and therefore that those products are substitutes for each other as sources of that benefit. Because different industries may have greatly different cost structures, substitute products from other industries may be able to put severe price pressure on an industry, and perhaps even render its products noncompetitive (as we discuss further in Section 9.3 on the Product Life Cycle).

Threat of New Entrants

Incumbent firms in an industry may also feel competitive pressure from a threat that new firms may enter their industry. This competitive pressure may come in several forms. First, as new firms enter an industry that currently consists of relatively few incumbent firms, a general reduction of any market power the incumbent firms might currently enjoy is likely. As more firms enter an industry, the buyer power that incumbent firms held with respect to their suppliers may diminish, because more buyers will be competing for the inputs being offered by the industry's suppliers. Similarly, new entrants increase the number of firms that can supply the buyers of the products of the industry, and any supplier power that incumbent firms had with respect to their customers will diminish. Second, as new firms enter the industry, demand levels for the products of incumbent firms may fall, leading to reduced revenues and higher fixed costs per unit of output. Third, new entrants may bring new technologies, capabilities, and Strategic Logics that, if successful in attracting customers from incumbent firms, will impose new costs of technology development, new process development, and other changes on incumbent firms that must modify their prior Strategic Logics.

Incumbent firms in an industry may adopt several kinds of strategies in an effort to establish **barriers to entry** that will discourage potential entrants. One branch of economic theory predicts that incumbent firms will adopt a *limit pricing* strategy as a barrier to discourage potential entrants. In this strategy, incumbents set prices at a level just below

HIGHLIGHT BOX 9.1

United Airlines Fights Against Substitute Products

In the 1980s, United Airlines ran a classic advertisement on television networks in the United States. The ad starts with a CEO entering a conference room for a hastily called staff meeting. He announces to the assembled employees, "I've called this meeting because I just got a phone call from one of our oldest customers—and you know what? He just fired us. He said he doesn't know us anymore, because all we ever do is phone him or send him faxes. I think he's right. We have taken this customer and others for granted for too long. It's time get to know our customers again—and make sure they know us!"

The CEO then pulls out a stack of United Airlines tickets and starts passing them out to his staff members. "Janet, you're going to see all our clients in Chicago. Jim, you see our clients in Los Angeles. Sally, you're going to Portland...."

During the 1980s long distance phone call rates fell sharply in the United States after deregulation, and the use of fax machines was growing rapidly. United Airlines was sufficiently concerned about the impact of these low-cost substitute forms of business communication that it decided to fight back by emphasizing the distinctive benefits of direct, face-to-face business communication.

Barriers to entry discourage potential entrants from entering an industry.

the unit costs of production for new entrants, who would often have to incur large sunk costs for new factories and distribution channels that incumbent firms have already amortized. Even though limit pricing may occur in some industries, at least from time to time, more common strategies for erecting barriers to entry include investing in proprietary technologies, brand building, foreclosing distribution channels, and inviting government regulation that would restrict the number of firms in an industry.

Incumbent firms may be able to develop proprietary product or process technologies that give their products superior performance or cost benefits. When the technologies of incumbent firms can be protected through secrecy or intellectual property rights (patents or copyrights), the lack of access to those technologies may make it infeasible for a new firm to enter the industry. Similarly, incumbent firms may invest in building widely recognized and respected brands that would make it difficult for new entrants without established brands to sell their products. Incumbent firms may also try to establish exclusive distribution agreements with available distribution channels that would make it difficult for new entrants to use existing distribution channels to bring their products to market. In some cases, incumbent firms may even invite new government regulations that limit entry to an industry, either overtly or *de facto* by raising costs for new entrants. All of these strategies to erect barriers to entry seek to impose costs on new entrants that would reduce their profits below acceptable levels.

Five Sources of Cooperative Gain

The sources of competitive pressure can also become sources of cooperative gain.

By the late 1980s, many researchers and managers alike realized that the five competitive forces described by Michael Porter constitute a *zero-sum game*—a competitive environment in which one organization can benefit (increase its profit) only at the expense of another organization (by appropriating part of its profit). In the 1990s, many companies began to rethink the competitive relationships that were common among the participants in many industries in the 1970s and early 1980s, especially in the United States. An alternate view of the possible interactions between the participants in an industry emerged that emphasized the potential for creating *positive-sum games* in which cooperation can lead to "win-win" gains for all cooperating industry participants. In this section we consider ways in which the five sources of competitive pressure identified by Michael Porter may be reoriented to become sources of mutual gain through cooperation, as suggested in Figure 9.4.

Cooperation with Rivals

Several forms of cooperation among competitors can be observed in many industries today—giving rise to the term *coopetition* to describe simultaneous cooperation and competition among firms in an industry. Firms may decide, for example, to pool their resources to develop *precompetitive technologies* that make possible new kinds of products. This form of cooperation is especially common when firms must work together to establish standards that will improve consumer acceptance and lower costs of new products, such as standard grades and performance levels for products, or standards for complementary goods like batteries, fuels, tape cassettes, diskettes, and so on. Firms may also work together to develop new materials or process technologies that will improve the cost position of the industry relative to substitute products. Rival firms may also cooperate in establishing trade associations to act as advocates for industry interests to government agencies, to provide a forum for communicating with consumers and special interest groups, to promote and advertise the industry's products in ways that build consumer awareness and increase overall demand levels for the industry, and similar activities. By forming associations that speak and act for the industry as a whole, the firms in an industry can often jointly achieve higher visibility and credibility than any individual firm could attain.

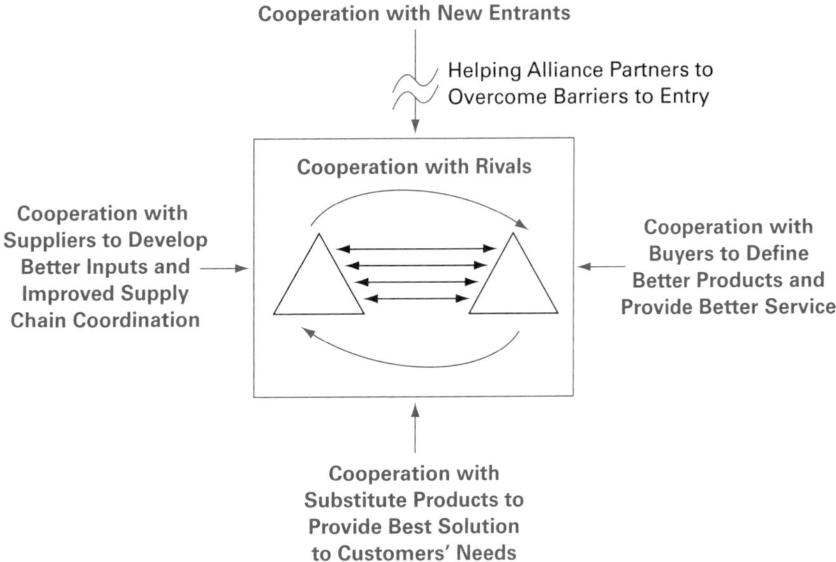

FIGURE 9.4 Five Sources of Opportunities for Mutual Gain through Cooperation

Cooperation with Suppliers

Cooperation with suppliers and buyers can create positive-sum outcomes.

Many firms today establish cooperative relationships with their suppliers that produce a number of important quality improvement and cost reduction benefits for both parties. The Chrysler Corporation in the 1990s (before its merger with Daimler to form DaimlerChrysler) extensively revamped its supplier relationships to expand their role in Chrysler's product creation and realization processes. Previously, like most American automakers, Chrysler would develop its own designs for components and then conduct competitive bidding among several suppliers to get the lowest possible prices for components. This practice sometimes led to quality problems in the supplied components, and adversarial relationships with their suppliers made it difficult to diagnose the sources of quality problems and to take corrective action. Borrowing many practices used by Japanese automobile makers, in the 1990s Chrysler began to work more closely with a few selected suppliers to develop better component designs and production methods. Key suppliers are now invited to join Chrysler's product development processes to enable a more interactive exchange of ideas for improving component quality, performance, and cost effectiveness.

Chrysler also provides financial assistance to some suppliers to improve their production process capabilities, in some cases even financing and owning the production machines used by suppliers in their own factories. Chrysler also invested in development of an ERP (enterprise resources planning) computer system that enabled key suppliers' production processes to be coordinated more closely with Chrysler's own assembly operations. Better production planning and scheduling reduced production and shipping costs for both suppliers and Chrysler. Suppliers now work much more cooperatively with Chrysler to define quality standards and targeted cost reductions for the components they supply to Chrysler. Chrysler engineers work closely with suppliers to help them meet and exceed agreed-on quality and cost targets, and any cost reductions realized above the agreed-on targets are shared equally between Chrysler and the supplier.

Cooperation with Buyers

Many of the quality improvement and cost reduction benefits that result from closer cooperation with suppliers also can be realized through closer cooperation with buyers. Like most firms in the airframe industry, Boeing Corporation had long engaged in tough bargaining with the airlines interested in buying the new airplanes it had under development. In the late 1980s, however, Boeing decided to try a different approach in launching the development of the Boeing 777 wide-body airliner. Boeing faced rising development costs of several billion dollars or more for each new airliner it introduced. The high costs of developing a new airliner made each decision to launch a new airplane a virtual "bet the company" decision, because a failure to recover development costs owing to poor sales of the airplane could lead to financial disaster for the firm. To improve its prospects for developing a new airliner that would provide the kind of performance and operational improvements its customers were most concerned about, Boeing decided to invite three of the intended major customers for the airliner to join its development process for the Boeing 777. United Airlines, British Airways, and All Nippon Airways sent members of their own technical and operational staffs to work closely with Boeing designers and engineers during the development of the 777. The resulting new airliner met the needs of its targeted customers better than any airliner the firm had previously developed. In return for their participation in the development of the 777, Boeing gave its three "lead customers" exclusive rights to fly the 777 in their respective markets for a period of time after the introduction of the 777.

Cooperation with Substitute Products

Cooperative strategies can even extend to substitute products and new entrants.

In some cases, it may be "win-win" to establish cooperative relationships with providers of substitute products. The success of IBM in transforming its business under CEO Louis Gerstner in the 1990s illustrates how this approach can work. From the 1950s until the 1980s, IBM's business was organized to support the sale of mainframe computers and software. By the 1990s, however, many new kinds of products and computing system designs became substitutes for mainframe computers and in many cases offered superior cost effectiveness. IBM maintained its commitment to mainframe-based computer systems, however, and by the late 1980s its business was rapidly declining and IBM began to post annual losses in the billions of dollars. When Louis Gerstner was hired to save IBM, he began a process of changing the Strategic Logic of IBM to focus on defining and meeting customer needs in the best possible way—whether it involved the use of a mainframe computer or not. In effect, Gerstner redefined IBM's Business Concept to make the firm a "solutions provider" that would configure the best system of computers (of any type), telecommunications, and software to meet customer needs. IBM then began to work with many firms whose products it regarded as substitutes for its mainframe computers, and through this cooperation was able find new ways to combine IBM equipment with products from other industries to provide the most cost-effective solution to its customers' needs.

Cooperation with New Entrants

New entrants are often attracted to an industry because they believe they have something new to offer that could bring them a competitive advantage, such as an existing technology that would make it possible to offer higher-performing products. At the same time, new entrants lack knowledge of the industry they might enter, and often incur large sunk costs to acquire the technology, production, distribution, and marketing assets required to operate profitably in the industry. Recognizing this situation, incumbent firms in some industries now look for opportunities to form various kinds of alliances with potential new entrants with the objective of combining and building on the strengths of both parties.

Through a cooperative alliance, for example, an incumbent firm may receive the benefit of a new entrant's new technology, while the new entrant benefits from access to the distribution system of the incumbent. In other cases, an incumbent may invite a potential new entrant to a geographic region to enter into a collaborative joint marketing arrangement that expands the geographic market coverage for both firms.

Designing a Strategic Logic to Minimize Competitive Pressure and Maximize Cooperative Gain

In designing a Strategic Logic, strategic managers must solve an ongoing puzzle: What is the best Strategic Logic design for minimizing competitive pressure on an organization and maximizing its opportunities for cooperative gain, both for the present and in the future? Solving this puzzle successfully requires making careful choices about the customers whose preferences the organization will serve, the kinds of products and services it will offer, the resources it will use in its value-creation processes, the kinds of information flows the organization should create, and the incentives it should use.

The choice of customers to serve should consider both the likely level of buyer power the organization will face in its targeted market segment(s) and the potential for involving targeted customers in various kinds of cooperative relationships that could offset and perhaps even moderate buyer power. Choosing the kinds of products and services an organization will offer should take into account the potential for effective differentiation that will limit price competition with rival firms and that may create switching costs for customers that act to moderate buyer power and limit the threat of substitute products. Decisions about the resources an organization will use, and the decision whether to internalize those resources or rely on accessing firm-addressable resources outside the firm, should carefully consider the possible levels of supplier power in alternate resource supply arrangements, as well as the potential for establishing cooperative supplier relationships that can offset or moderate supplier power. Resourcing decisions should also consider the potential for cooperation with providers of substitute products and firms currently outside an industry, as well as evaluate the possibilities for new substitute products to become available and new firms to enter the industry. Especially when an organization intends to establish cooperative relationship with buyers, suppliers, providers of substitutes, or potential new entrants, appropriate information flows need to be designed to support ongoing cooperative activities. Incentives also need to be designed to distribute appropriate rewards to all participants who cooperate in making an organization's value-creation process successful.

Moreover, as an industry environment changes—as levels of rivalry increase or decrease, as supplier and buyer power rise or fall, as substitute products enter the market, and as potential entrants appear—strategic managers must learn to anticipate such changes and to make modifications in Strategic Logic to strike a new optimal balance between sources of competitive pressure and opportunities for cooperative gain.

9.3 CHANGES IN THE PRODUCT LIFE CYCLE

Patterns of evolution in a product market

Markets for products tend to follow a fairly consistent pattern of development and growth over time. Since the 1960s, researchers have developed a number of versions of "product life cycle" models for describing the evolution of a product market. In this section, we use our version of the **product life cycle model** to identify important technological and marketing developments in the evolution of a product market, as shown in Figure 9.5. Each of the five stages in the product life cycle—embryonic, rapid growth, shake out, maturity, and renewal or decline—constitutes a different set of competitive conditions. Each stage therefore calls for a different kind of Strategic Logic to be successful.

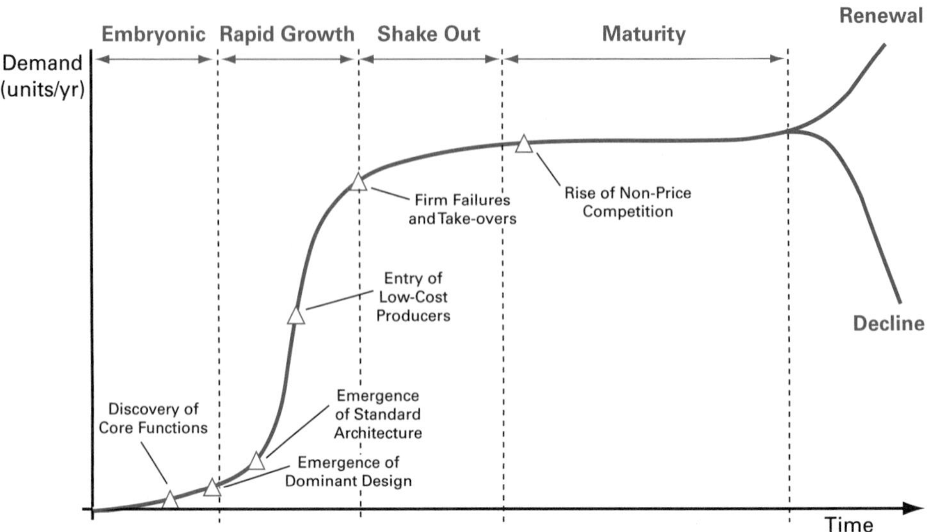

FIGURE 9.5 Five Stages and Key Events in the Product Life Cycle Model

Embryonic Stage

The embryonic stage is a period of market and technology exploration.

The embryonic stage of the product life cycle model includes the invention of a *new product concept* and the inventors' early *market interactions* with potential customers for the new product.

A new product concept is a unique new "bundle" of functionalities intended to bring new benefits to consumers or users. Many "new" product concepts are actually extensions of related product concepts. For example, in the early 1980s Sony Corporation introduced a new product concept called the "Walkman." Although related to the familiar product concept of a portable tape player, the Walkman offered the new functionalities of high-quality sound reproduction and compactness in a lightweight portable tape player. Later an additional functionality—waterproofness—was added to some Walkman models. Similarly, the development of the personal computer in the 1970s was an extension of computers already in use at the time, but the personal computer offered the additional benefits of small size and affordability to a new group of targeted customers—individual consumers.

Inventors of new product concepts usually have some kind of consumer or user in mind, and some idea how targeted consumers would use the product, but those ideas may be rather rough and at times are incorrect. The embryonic stage is therefore also a period of interactions between inventors and intended customers. Inventors must explain to potential customers what the new product concept is and what kinds of benefits using the new product could bring. Because the product concept is one that has not been available before, potential customers must try to imagine how they could use the product in their personal lifestyles, homes, or businesses. In some cases, individual functionalities included in the new product concept will not be appreciated by customers, and may need to be dropped from the product concept. In other cases, customers may ask that an additional functionality be added or the performance level of a functionality be improved in order to improve the usefulness of the product. Eventually, through such interactions of the inventors of a new product concept with potential customers, the inventors begin to discover the *core functions* of the new product concept—that is, the functionalities and their associated performance levels that must be provided by the product in order for the new product concept to gain customer acceptance and purchase. The discovery of the core functions of a new product concept is a key event in the evolution of a product market, because it essentially removes an important form of market uncertainty about whether the new product will be perceived as useful by intended customers.

Once uncertainty about market acceptance is removed by the discovery of the core functions of a new product, uncertainty still remains about the best design for delivering the core functions in the most convenient way for consumers and users. A second key event in the embryonic stage is therefore the emergence of the *dominant design* for the new product. The dominant design is the physical arrangement of the product that seems to work best and to have the greatest acceptance from customers. For example, early automobiles were made with engines in the front, rear, and middle of cars and with various kinds of steering and braking systems. By the early 1910s the dominant design for an automobile emerged—engine in front, drive train with traction at the rear wheels, steering through a steering wheel and shaft connected to a steering linkage turning the front wheels, and brakes located on all four wheel hubs. This design became the dominant design for automobiles for almost 60 years. (In the 1970s, in response to demand for more fuel-efficient car designs, the dominant design underwent an evolution that integrated the engine and drive train into one unit mounted in the front of the car, thereby converting most cars from rear-wheel drive to front-wheel drive.)

Rapid Growth Stage

The rapid growth stage is precipitated by the emergence of a *dominant design* and an *industry standard architecture.*

Once the core functions and dominant design for a new product concept are discovered in the embryonic stage, in the rapid growth stage of the product life cycle model the most cost-effective technical structure of the new product will be determined and the overall size of the market for the new product will become known.

After the emergence of the dominant design for a new product, a number of important technical issues must be resolved. The dominant design largely determines the kinds of components that will be used to provide the core functions of the product, but different firms may use different technical means to connect those components together to make the finished product. The way components work together in a product is controlled by the *interface specifications* that determine how components will interact or interface with each other. Another key event in the evolution of a product market occurs when the same interface specifications are adopted for the types of components that tend to be used by most producers. Convergence toward a standard set of interface specifications for the major components in a new product marks the emergence of an *industry standard architecture* that defines the technical structure for the new product. This key event invites component producers to begin making standard components for the new product. As various component makers ramp up their production of standard components, larger production volumes for key components lead to lower costs for the product. When producers pass these lower costs on to consumers in the form of lower prices, demand for the new product may start to increase rapidly.

The second key event in the rapid growth stage occurs when the growth of the new product market suggests that the eventual demand level for the new product will be substantial—in other words, the new product concept promises to create a large new market. At this point the new product market will typically attract the attention of some firms with capabilities in engineering products and processes to achieve large volume and low cost. One or more *low-cost producers* will then enter the market and begin to compete aggressively on price. Price competition puts pressure on the less cost-effective firms, and some or most of the original inventors and developers of the new product will fail or be taken over by the low-cost producers, leading to the next stage in the product life cycle.

Shake-Out Stage

The shake-out stage forces the exit of less cost-efficient producers.

In the shake-out stage, growth of the product market begins to slow as the new product reaches its maximum market penetration. As market growth slows, the only way a firm can sustain a high growth rate is to take market share away from other firms, and the fastest way to build market share is often to cut prices below those of competitors. Intense price competition by the low-cost producers then causes a "shake out" of less-efficient firms, driving them out of the market. By the end of the shake-out stage, the product market is consolidated around a few large, cost-efficient producers that hold dominant positions in the new market. A few smaller firms may find *niche markets,* which are market segments that have special preferences with respect to the new product and that are typically too small to attract the interest of the low-cost producers.

Maturity Stage

The maturity stage brings market segmentation and product differentiation.

In the maturity stage, which may last for several years or even decades, the market is served by a few large firms and some niche players. After demand levels stabilize, the large firms often try to shift the basis of competition from price to nonprice aspects of the product offer. Firms try to identify and serve new market segments that form as consumers become more familiar with the new product and develop preferences that can be served by different product variations. As firms identify emerging new market segments, they try to differentiate their products in the marketplace through styling, by offering their products with various features and performance levels, by expanding service, by building up new channels of distribution, or by advertising. The search to discover emerging customer preferences that can serve as the basis for differentiation of new products may eventually lead to the recognition of a large number of market segments in the product market. The automobile market in the United States, for example, today contains more than thirty well-established market segments for automobiles, and each market segment is served with differentiated products with distinctive sizes, performance, styling, and other product characteristics.

Renewal or Decline

Product markets eventually renew or decline.

Eventually, a product market goes through a further stage of significant renewal or decline. Renewal of a product market means that demand levels start to grow and reach a significantly higher level than previously. A renewal stage may be precipitated by a number of developments in the technology of the product or in the market. Improvements in materials and in the design of components may lead to significantly reduced costs and lower prices that in turn stimulate higher demand levels. Technology improvements may also increase product performance levels significantly, making the product more useful and attractive to more consumers, and lead to an increase in demand. Renewal may also happen because of changes in demographic factors or sociocultural values that lead to greater consumer demand for the product, or because of geographic expansion of marketing of the product.

Decline occurs when demand for a product begins to fall significantly or even disappear entirely. Decline may occur because of the appearance of a more attractive, higher-performing, or cost-effective substitute product, as occurred when semiconductors replaced vacuum tubes in electrical circuits. Decline may also occur because of shifts in consumer preferences or new government regulations. In the 1980s and 1990s in the United States, for example, consumer demand for food products with high content of saturated fats declined steeply as consumers became more health and weight conscious, and government regulations eliminated the market for asbestos products because of associated health risks.

KEY TERMS AND CONCEPTS

macroenvironment The macroeconomic, demographic, sociocultural, political-legal, and technological aspects of an organization's environment that are beyond its control.

competitive pressure Any influence that acts to limit or reduce the profits an organization can earn.

internal rivalry Direct, head-to-head competition between organizations competing for the same customers.

market power The ability to dictate the terms of trade in an economic exchange.

supplier power The ability of a supplier of a key input to a firm's processes to dictate the terms of trade.

buyer power The ability of a buyer of the outputs of a firm's processes to dictate the terms of trade.

substitute product A product that can provide the same essential benefits as another product, but that would impose some form of switching costs (additional costs or reduced benefits) on customers.

barriers to entry Factors like proprietary technologies, established brands, or exclusive distribution arrangements that discourage firms from entering an industry.

product life cycle model A model of the evolution of a product market through embryonic, rapid growth, shake-out, maturity, and renewal or decline stages.

REVIEW QUESTIONS

1. Give an example of each of the five forms of macroenvironmental change, and explain how each could affect the Strategic Logic of an organization.
2. What happens to fluctuations in demand as one moves upstream in the vertical structure of an industry?
3. In what ways does Michael Porter's five competitive forces model of an industry environment represent a zero-sum game?
4. How might the development of cooperation within an industry create positive-sum games for industry participants?
5. What is the key challenge for strategic managers in defining a Strategic Logic within an industry context?
6. Why are the discovery of the core functions of a new product concept, the emergence of an industry standard architecture, and the entrance of low-cost producers such important events in the evolution of a product market?

CHAPTER **10**

MANAGING MANAGERIAL COGNITION: THE UNIQUE INTELLECTUAL CHALLENGE OF STRATEGIC MANAGEMENT

INTRODUCTION

In Chapters 6, 7, and 8, we discussed in detail the three elements of an organization's Strategic Logic—its Business Concept, Organization Concept, and Core Processes. Strategic managers are ultimately responsible for designing and implementing a viable Strategic Logic for their organization. As we noted in Chapter 9, however, defining and designing a viable Strategic Logic for value creation and distribution is like solving a complex "situational puzzle."[1] Given the present external situation of an organization (its macroenvironment, industry environment, and stage in its product life cycle), strategic managers must define market opportunities for creating value that the organization can respond to effectively, given its internal situation (its current and feasible future resources and capabilities, including both firm-specific and firm-addressable resources). Managers must also correctly design the organization, by applying the set of system design principles discussed in preceding chapters, in order to put in place management processes that can effectively coordinate and motivate firm-specific and firm-addressable resources in the organization's value-creation processes.

Defining and designing a viable Strategic Logic for value creation and distribution would be an intellectually challenging task even if the external and internal environment of an organization were stable. Of course, for most organizations and situations, external and internal environments are not stable. Rather, they are dynamic, and they often change in imperfectly predictable ways. Thus, the challenge to strategic managers is twofold—both to design a Strategic Logic that can create value in today's world, and to imagine, design, and prepare to implement future Strategic Logics that can create value in tomorrow's possible worlds.

Carrying out their responsibility to solve this evolving *dynamic situational puzzle* presents strategic managers with a unique intellectual challenge. Strategic managers must provide **intellectual leadership** for organizational cognitive processes for discovering market opportunities and designing value-creation and distribution processes that can exploit targeted market opportunities. Providing intellectual leadership does not mean that strategic managers must decide everything themselves—quite the contrary. In fact, the complexity of the decisions that have to be made in most organizations today, and the uncertainty that must be recognized and dealt with in making those decisions, would quickly overwhelm the intelligence of even the most brilliant human being. Because strategic managers nevertheless have responsibility for the decisions made in their organizations, they must provide

[1] Bogaert, I., R. Martens, et al. (1994). Strategy As a Situational Puzzle: The Fit of Components. In G. Hamel and A. Heene, (Eds.), *Competence-Based Competition.* Chichester, England: John Wiley & Sons Ltd., 57–74.

intellectual leadership by designing and supporting organizational cognitive processes that draw on the *collective intelligence* of employees and others who can contribute intellectual resources to solving the dynamic situational puzzle of the organization.

To provide this essential form of intellectual leadership in their organizations, strategic managers must understand the inherent limits of human cognitive processes in complex and uncertain situations, and then learn how to *manage their own cognitive processes* in strategic decision making. In this chapter, therefore, we discuss some important cognitive aspects of the decision-making environment of strategic managers, and some fundamental approaches to improving strategic decision making. We first consider some important differences between *strategic and operational decision-making environments.* We then explore the nature and consequences of *bounded rationality* and *satisficing* in strategic decision making, and we discuss some *new organizational forms* that more effectively distribute decision making within an organization and thereby help to overcome the problem of bounded rationality and satisficing in strategic decision making. Finally, we explain the fundamental need for strategic managers to carefully balance and integrate *commitment and flexibility* in their strategic decision making.

10.1 THE NATURE OF STRATEGIC VS. OPERATIONAL DECISION MAKING

A traditional basis for distinguishing strategic from operational management[2] holds that *operational management* is concerned with improving an organization's **operational effectiveness.** An organization is considered operationally effective when it achieves performance levels in executing the activities in its value-creation processes that at least equal—and if possible surpass—the performance levels achieved by its competitors in those activities. Operational effectiveness contributes to an organization's value-creation processes by identifying and implementing operating practices that help an organization realize product offers that are perceived by targeted market segments as cheaper, better, or faster than competing product offers. Operational management is therefore focused on the following:

- *Reducing the costs* of current ways of using resources in any operation
- Finding better ways of using resources and capabilities to *improve the perceived quality* of the product offers the organization brings to market
- Coordinating the use of resources and capabilities to develop, bring to market, and support product offers *faster* than rivals

The task of operational managers to improve the cost, quality, and speed of an organization's current operations and product offers can be carried out in a decision-making environment with relatively low causal ambiguity. As we discussed in Chapter 4, relatively precise and reliable data can be gathered through lower-order control loops about an organization's current operations and the tangible assets used in those operations. The availability of relatively precise and reliable data on operations helps managers to discover cause-and-effect relationships that can lead to many kinds of managed improvements in operations. Thus, the kinds of data that an organization can gather through its lower-order control loops usually support effective decision making at the operating level.

The responsibility of strategic managers to define, design, and put into action a viable Strategic Logic for an organization, however, means that their work must be undertaken in a different kind of decision-making environment. The decision making of strategic managers must generally be carried out under high levels of structural complexity,

[2] Porter, M. E. (1996). What Is Strategy? *Harvard Business Review,* 74 (6), 61–89.

dynamic complexity, incomplete and imperfect information, and irreducible uncertainty. Let us consider briefly each of these characteristics of the strategic decision-making environment and the cognitive challenges that they pose for strategic decision makers.

Structural Complexity

Strategic decision making requires coping with structural and dynamic complexity.

In Chapter 4, we discussed some basic structural properties of an organization as a system. We defined a *system* as consisting of entities that interact with each other and create interdependencies between the entities as system elements. We also introduced the notion of a boundary that distinguishes between the entities within a system and the entities outside a system. However, the boundary of an organization as system is not perfectly impermeable, and at least some system elements of an organization also interact with entities outside the organization. The interactions of an organization's system elements with external entities effectively embed an organization in a set of increasingly larger systems—the organization's product and resource markets, its strategic group of competitors, its industry, its economy, and its society. Thus, all organizations as systems have both an internal structure determined by the interactions between its internal system elements and an external structure determined by the interactions between its own system elements and entities beyond the boundary of the organization.

The *structural complexity* of an organization as a system arises in the first instance from the number of elements that make up the organization as a system and from the number, nature, and intensities of interactions between the elements. To this internally generated structural complexity we must add the additional structural complexity that arises from system elements that interact with entities outside an organization, and from the number, nature, and intensities of those interactions. The **structural complexity of a system** increases with the number of interacting elements inside and outside the system *and* with the number and variety of significant interactions between them. Structural complexity increases faster than the rate of increase in the number of interacting system elements, as shown in Figure 10.1. For example, two interacting system elements A and B will have two interactions A→B and B→A, but three interacting system elements A, B, and C will have six interactions (A→B, A→C, B→A, B→C, C→A, and C→B), four interacting system elements will have twelve interactions, and so on.[3]

Most organizations have significant structural complexity, with perhaps tens of interacting system elements generating hundreds of important interactions and interdependencies. Strategic managers, especially of larger organizations, may be severely challenged even to create a "mental map" of all these interactions, much less to really understand and know how to manage these interactions. Coping with the high levels of structural complexity of most organizations today is therefore a key cognitive challenge in strategic decision making.

Dynamic Complexity

The **dynamic complexity of a system** arises when changes in one or more elements of a structurally complex system precipitate chain reactions of changes in other system elements. When a system element is significantly influenced by interactions with several other system elements, determining the net effects of changes in other system elements on the first system element is likely to be difficult. The inability to predict how a given system element will behave when other system elements that it interacts with undergo change

[3] More formally, the total number of potential interactions between n structural elements of a system will be $n(n-1)$.

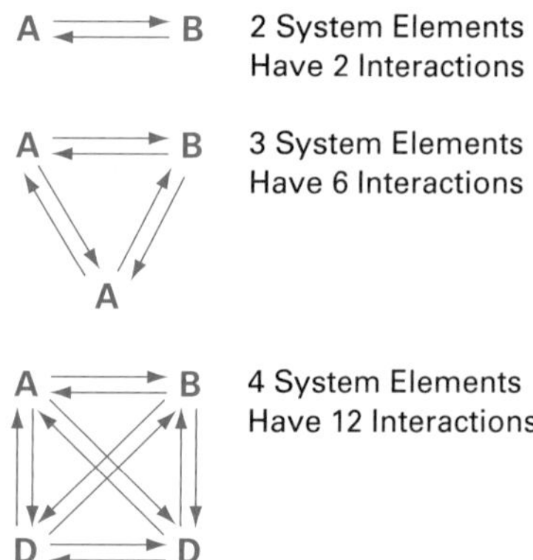

FIGURE 10.1 Structural Complexity Increases Rapidly As the Number of System Elements Increases

makes it difficult for strategic managers to discover cause-and-effect relationships that would be useful in managing the system elements and interactions in their organization.

Moreover, dynamic complexity increases greatly when a system has varying *time delays* in the influences that system elements exert on each other. When system elements are subject to influences from other system elements that operate at different speeds, the behavior of a given system element can become *nonlinear.* In other words, the behavior of a system element may not follow a consistent trend upward or downward, but may appear to vary chaotically, even when other system elements undergo "smooth," steady changes in their states. Even systems with relatively simple structures can exhibit nonlinear behaviors and exhibit behaviors that are unexpected and counterintuitive,[4] leading to "situations where … the effects over time of [managerial] interventions are not obvious."[5]

Dynamic complexity therefore further limits the ability of strategic managers to understand, predict, and manage how their organization will actually behave as a system. Dynamic complexity constricts the ability of strategic managers to make decisions about their organizations with a high level of confidence about the outcomes of those decisions.

Incomplete and Imperfect Information

Strategic decisions must be made even when information is incomplete and imperfect.

Strategic managers must base their decisions on some kind of information about their organization and its environment. As we discussed in Chapter 7, *information* is the meaning derived from some interpretation of some data.[6] When the data available to strategic managers are incomplete, imprecise, or not perfectly reliable, the information that managers can extract from data will consist of **incomplete information** or **imperfect information** (i.e., not perfectly correct), or both. As we mentioned here and in Chapter 4, the data about the lower system elements of an organization that are gathered by lower-order control loops may be relatively precise and reliable. However, the data gathered about higher system elements through higher-order control loops usually lack frameworks for making precise measurements and often rely on selective, subjective evaluations. Thus, the information that strategic managers must use in making decisions about Strategic

[4] Warren, K. (2002). *Competitive Strategy Dynamics.* Chichester: John Wiley & Sons.

[5] Senge, P. M. (1990). *The Fifth Discipline.* New York: Doubleday, 71.

[6] Sanchez, Ron (Ed.). (2001). *Knowledge Management and Organizational Competence.* Oxford: Oxford University Press.

Logics and management processes is invariably incomplete and imperfect—yet strategic managers must nevertheless find ways to make specific decisions that can lead to the best possible chance for achieving the goals of the organization.

Irreducible Uncertainty

Structural and dynamic complexity, coupled with imperfect and incomplete information, create *irreducible uncertainty*.

The concepts of uncertainty and ignorance are inextricably interrelated. Uncertainty about a situation exists when we do not understand a situation well enough to explain how the situation came to be or to predict what will happen next in that situation. Just as there are degrees of ignorance, there are degrees of perceived uncertainty. In understanding the impact of uncertainty on strategic decision making, it is useful to distinguish three levels of ignorance and their resulting forms of uncertainty.

The most profound form of ignorance is being completely unaware that something exists that could affect a situation. This form of ignorance is about factors that engineers call the "unknown unknowns." This form of ignorance leads to "surprises" that are completely unexpected in a given situation, because no one involved in managing the situation could imagine that such factors exist and would influence the situation. The best preventive measure against being surprised by unknown unknowns is drawing on a broad cross-section of expertise in evaluating strategic decision situations in order to identify the full range of factors that might be significant in a given situation.

The effort to develop a broad view of a decision-making situation is what Hamel and Prahalad described as using a "wide angle lens" to gain a better understanding of the factors that may be involved in a strategic decision situation.[7] To create this wide-angle view, strategic managers may invite consultants to evaluate or participate in their decision-making process. Managers may be hired from outside the firm or its industry to bring a new perspective and experience set to management's deliberations. Scenario planning may also be used to help strategic managers identify factors that could significantly affect future situations their organization might face.[8] Scenario planning and related techniques can help strategic managers to develop clearer alternative visions of the future and of the possible Strategic Logics they might create for their organization in those futures. (See Highlight Box 10.1.)

A lesser form of ignorance exists when decision makers are aware of a factor that could affect a situation, but do not know how to assess the possible impact of that factor on the situation. This level of ignorance enables decision makers at least to identify the "known unknowns" in a situation. This type of ignorance calls for further investigation to try to understand more clearly the nature of a factor's influence and then to develop ways to assess its likely impacts.

A lesser level of ignorance exists when a factor is known to have an influence on a given kind of situation, the extent of its influence is known to vary over some range of values, and those values can be represented by some kind of probability distribution. This lower level of ignorance enables us to characterize a given factor as posing a certain *risk* in a given situation. Unlike unknown unknowns and known unknowns, ways can sometimes be found to manage or hedge well-defined risks involved in strategic decision making. The

7 Hamel, G. and C. K. Prahalad. (1994). *Competing for the Future: Breakthrough Strategies for Seizing Control of Your Industry and Creating the Markets of Tomorrow.* Boston: Harvard Business School Press.

8 Ringland, G. (1998). *Scenario Planning: Managing for the Future.* Chichester: John Wiley & Sons; Fahey, L. and R. M. Randall (Eds.). (1998). *Learning from the Future: Competitive Foresight Scenarios.* New York: John Wiley & Sons; Van der Heijden, K. (1996). *Scenarios: The Art of Strategic Conversation.* Chichester: John Wiley & Sons; and de Geus, A. (1997). *The Living Company: Growth, Learning and Longevity in Business.* London: Nicholas Brealey Publishing.

HIGHLIGHT BOX 10.1

Tools and Techniques for Developing Visions of the Future

Hamel and Prahalad suggest that strategic managers take the following steps to develop better "visions" of the future and to gain better understanding of the uncertainties they may face in their organization's future:

1. Escape the myopia of the currently served market and enlarge the organization's opportunity horizon by thinking of the organization as possessing a portfolio of capabilities that can be applied to a variety of purposes.
2. Escape the myopia of the organization's current products by thinking of the functionalities the organization can offer to markets.
3. Challenge existing assumptions in the organization about feasible price-performance relationships and radically rethink price-performance targets.
4. Behave like little children and be naïve; question the unquestionable.
5. Develop a deep and boundless curiosity. Step out of the traditional worldview of top management to imagine other possible worlds.
6. Be humble enough to speculate. Look beyond the issues on which the top management team can claim expertise.
7. Value eclecticism. Look for the future in the intersections of changes in technology, lifestyles, regulation, demographics, and geopolitics.
8. Search for and study metaphors and analogies from other industries. The future of your industry may already be taking shape there.
9. Be a contrarian. Break the rules. Think the unthinkable.

Source: Adapted from *Competing for the Future* by Gary Hamel and C.K. Prahalad.

risk of market acceptance of a new product, for example, may be managed at least in part by test marketing and making modifications suggested by consumers participating in the test. The risk of foreign currency fluctuations can usually be hedged through futures or options contracts on the foreign currencies in question.

To make good strategic decisions, strategic managers must work to reduce all three forms of uncertainty. However, important factors in virtually all strategic decisions will involve some level of **irreducible uncertainty**—uncertainty that cannot be reduced by gathering and analyzing further information. For example, the eventual size of the market for a new kind of product will almost always be subject to a significant level of irreducible uncertainty, no matter how much marketing research an organization carries out. Similarly, the state of the macroeconomy a year or two in the future remains stubbornly unpredictable and thus is subject to significant irreducible uncertainty. Nevertheless, strategic managers must find ways to make important decisions about an organization's current and future Strategic Logics—even though many factors in an organization's internal and external environment remain subject to high levels of irreducible uncertainty.

10.2 BOUNDED RATIONALITY AND SATISFICING IN STRATEGIC DECISION MAKING

As the discussion in the previous section made clear, strategic decisions must always be made under conditions of significant structural and dynamic complexity, incomplete and imperfect information, and irreducible uncertainty. Even if all relevant information were reliable and made available to a strategic decision maker, however, extensive studies in cognitive psychology demonstrate that the quality of the human decision-making process would not necessarily be better than the quality of decision making under conditions of incomplete and imperfect information. In effect, the inherent limits of the human mind in grasping the structures and dynamic behaviors of complex systems and in reckoning with irreducible uncertainties prevent any human from fully and correctly using all available information in a decision-making process.

Most decisions are rational—but only "boundedly rational."

Herbert Simon's concept of **bounded rationality** captures these inherent limitations in human decision making. Simon observed that human decision makers generally behave rationally, but face severe limitations in exercising their rationality. As Simon noted, "The capacity of the human mind for formulating and solving complex problems is very small compared with the size of the problems whose solution is required for objectively rational behavior in the real world—or even for a reasonable approximation of such objective rationality."[9]

Simon's concept of bounded rationality suggests that decision makers behave rationally in making decisions, but they impose bounds (limits) on the information they attempt to gather and interpret in making decisions—thus the use of the qualifier "bounded" in describing human rationality. Rather than trying to gather and interpret all possible information, decision makers tend to rely on information that they found useful in their prior experiences in decision making about a similar situation.[10] Moreover, because they do not attempt to process all relevant information, decision makers do not actually try to find "optimal solutions" to problems, but rather are usually satisfied with the first "satisfactory solution" they can discover. Simon described this human tendency in decision making as **satisficing.**

The tendency of humans to exhibit boundedly rational and satisficing behaviors in decision making underlies a number of weaknesses and limitations observed in many strategic decision-making processes:

- Managers often neglect important available information in making decisions.
- Managers often selectively focus on information that would confirm their feelings or opinions about a situation, rather than seriously considering information that would appear to contradict their current views.
- Managers often accept goal-drift (a lowering of goals and expectations during decision-making processes) when an original goal seems difficult to achieve.[11]
- Managers may overlook opportunities that are as yet unexploited, even when they are recognized as potentially significant.
- Managers may prefer "new" opportunities for value creation that are conceptually close to existing, familiar value-creation processes.

To improve their organization's decision-making processes, strategic managers must devise ways to compensate for these tendencies in their own human decision-making behavior. As a fundamentally important part of managing their own cognitive processes, strategic managers should initiate broader organizational cognitive processes that can help them and other managers in their organization overcome, to the maximum extent possible, the weaknesses and limitations that bounded rationality and satisficing behavior are likely to impose on any individual manager's or management team's decision-making process. In the next section, we consider how a widely emerging new form of organization tries to address these central challenges in the cognitive processes of strategic managers.

[9] Simon, H. (1957). *Models of Man.* New York: John Wiley & Sons, 198.

[10] Johnson, P., K. Daniel, et al. (1999). Mental Models of Competition. In C. Eden and J.-C. Spender (Eds.), *Managerial and Organizational Cognition.* London: Sage.

[11] Senge, P. M. (1990). *The Fifth Discipline.* New York: Doubleday, 383–384.

10.3 NEW FORMS OF ORGANIZATION FOR IMPROVING DECISION MAKING

The enduring dilemma of hierarchical organizations is the separation of decision making from the expertise and information needed to make good decisions.

In addition to problems of bounded rationality and satisficing behavior, decision making in traditional organizations with multiple layers of management hierarchy suffers from a further problem that is an inevitable consequence of that type of organizational design.

In tall hierarchies of the type illustrated in the top of Figure 10.2, there is a *substantial separation of decision-making authority from the expertise and information needed to make good decisions.* No manager, however personally brilliant and well trained she or he may be, can have all the expertise needed to make effective decisions implementable at the working level of an organization. Moreover, as we discussed at some length in Chapter 7, the information that managers at the top of the hierarchy receive is likely to be both highly abstract in nature (e.g., tables of numbers) and may be quite distorted by the innocent omissions or self-serving interpretations of lower-level managers. Because real change in an organization is only accomplished when change actually occurs at the working level of an organization, the limited expertise and information available to strategic managers often severely constrain their ability to fully understand or significantly change what goes on in an organization at the working level. As more than one frustrated executive has observed, trying to change an organization through decisions made at the top of a management hierarchy is like "pushing repeatedly on one end of a wet noodle"—and then realizing that nothing has actually moved on the other end.

In attempts to overcome these cognitive and organizational impediments to effective decision making and organizational change, in recent years some strategic managers have redesigned their organizations to create a new form of organization that is intended to improve and accelerate processes for decision making and action taking. This new form of organization, which is illustrated in the lower part of Figure 10.2, involves a substantial *devolution of decision-making authority* to teams of people that are given broad responsibility for operational decisions in a defined activity in the organization's value-creation processes.

In this new kind of organization design, strategic managers define the *strategic direction* that will be the focus of each team's activities, like defining the new market segment that a team will then develop a new product offer to serve. Strategic managers also define essential *policies* to guide the decision making of the teams as they carry out their task. For example, strategic managers may stipulate that "all relationships with suppliers must be based on defined programs for continuous quality improvement and cost reduction." Strategic managers then delegate to the team the authority to decide how best to move forward in the strategic direction set by top management, and how best to manage their own activities. Strategic managers and teams also typically agree on budgets and timetables for accomplishing each team's task, and strategic managers commit to providing the resources agreed with each team as long as the team keeps its commitments for timely progress in their task.

New organizational forms try to align decision making with necessary expertise and information.

This new organizational form helps to compensate for both the bounded rationality and satisficing tendencies of strategic decision makers and the separation of decision-making authority from the expertise and information needed to make good operating decisions. By extending important aspects of their decision-making authority to teams that have been asked to explore and develop important new initiatives, strategic managers may overcome many of the bounds that they might unknowingly impose on their own search for and interpretation of new information. Strategic managers can also ask that teams set and achieve ambitious goals for their initiatives, which can help to counter tendencies toward satisficing. Further, if well composed, teams are more likely to have both the expertise to make good decisions and better "firsthand" information to use in making decisions, thereby overcoming the poor decisions that result when deci-

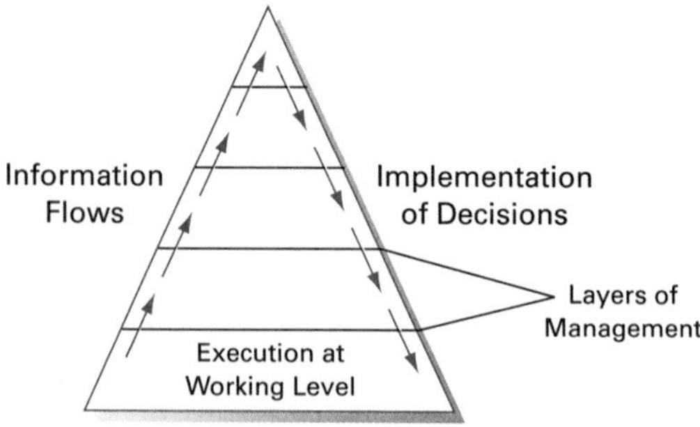

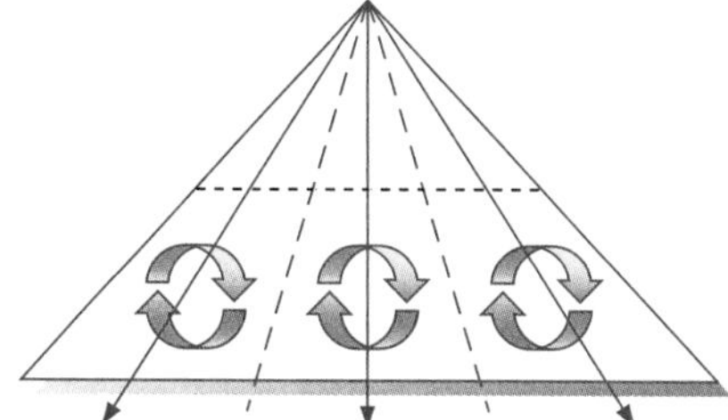

FIGURE 10.2 Traditional "Tall" Hierarchy vs. "New Forms" of Organization

sion-making authority is separated from the expertise and information needed to make good decisions.

In essence, these new organizational forms try to build a broadly distributed *collective intelligence* at the working level of the organization that can be used to improve decision making throughout the organization. These improvements come in two main forms. First, teams of workers can generally be more effective than managers in using the data gathered by lower-order control loops to identify opportunities to improve their own operating effectiveness. Second, when most operating decisions are turned over to self-managing teams, strategic managers can focus on extending and improving the data gathered through the organization's higher-order control loops, and on improving their own ability to interpret such data and use these interpretations in their decision-making processes. As such, these new organizational forms represent a major organizational innovation intended to significantly improve the cognitive capabilities of an organization by overcoming well-known psychological and organizational limitations in managerial decision-making processes.

10.4 BALANCING COMMITMENT AND FLEXIBILITY IN STRATEGIC DECISION MAKING

In the 1970s and 1980s, a widely held view among strategy theorists and managers alike was that *commitment* is the essence of strategy.[12] With the growing environmental turbulence and competitive uncertainties evident in the 1990s, however, another view of strategy emerged that emphasized the importance of creating and maintaining an organization's *strategic flexibility.* Strategic management theory and practice today are vitally concerned with both deciding when to commit an organization to a given course of action and when to create and maintain flexibilities to commit to a range of possible actions in the future. For strategic managers facing environments with significant levels of irreducible uncertainty, decision making is increasingly concerned with identifying and developing strategically important forms of flexibility that will enable an organization to take a range of possible actions in the future.

An organization's strategic flexibility is determined by its strategic options.

The **strategic flexibility** that an organization has can be defined by its set of specific **strategic options** for taking action in the future.[13] The broader the *range of* strategic options for action taking that an organization has, the more strategic flexibility the organization has. The value of an organization's strategic options also increases (i) with increases in the *speed* with which it can "exercise" its options (i.e., begin new courses of action) and (ii) with reductions in the *costs* incurred in exercising its strategic options.

In decision environments with significant levels of irreducible uncertainties, strategic managers may be fundamentally unable to determine which of a number of imaginable futures is the most likely to happen. Strategic managers are then likely to be reluctant—and with good reason—to select a single "most likely" future and to commit their organization to courses of action that are focused on preparing for that future. Committing to a single course of action under such circumstances can be quite risky and expose the organization to serious consequences if the future turns out differently from the "most likely" scenario.

Instead, when faced with significant irreducible uncertainties, many strategic decision makers today prefer to identify a range of strategic options for taking action that they would like to have available for their organization in the possible futures that they have identified through scenario planning or other methods. Then, as the future unfolds and the most advantageous course of action can be ascertained more clearly, strategic managers may then "exercise" their strategic option to commit to that course of action at the appropriate time. Thus, creating strategic flexibility in the form of specific strategic options for taking action in the future enables strategic managers to make decisions that can help their organizations prepare for the future, even when that future is currently subject to significant irreducible uncertainties.

Strategic managers can create strategic options by building organizational competences today that will enable an organization to take new kinds of competence-leveraging actions in the future. Thus, as we discussed in Chapter 3, defining and building new competences today that create new strategic options for competence leveraging in the future

[12] See, for example, P. Ghemawhat. (1991). *Commitment: The Essence of Strategy.* Cambridge: Harvard Business School Press.

[13] Sanchez, R. (1997). Preparing for a Uncertain Future: Managing Organizations for Strategic Flexibility. *International Studies in Management and Organization,* 27 (2), 71–94.

integrates key elements of both the *planning* and *emergence* approaches to strategic management. Today, strategic decision-making processes carried out under conditions of significant irreducible uncertainty are increasingly likely to focus on planning that identifies and commits to building specific competences that improve the flexibility of an organization to generate a range of emergent strategies as the future unfolds.

KEY TERMS AND CONCEPTS

intellectual leadership The essential role of strategic managers in designing and supporting organizational cognitive processes that draw on the collective intelligence of employees and others who can help to solve the "dynamic situational puzzle" of an organization in designing viable Strategic Logics for its current and future environments.

operational effectiveness Achieving levels of cost, quality, and speed in an organization's value-creation processes that at least match the levels achieved by competitors.

structural complexity of a system The complexity that arises from the number of elements in a system and from the number, variety, and intensity of interactions among the elements in a system and between those elements and entities outside the system.

dynamic complexity of a system The complexity that arises when changes in one or more elements of a structurally complex system precipitate chain reactions of changes in other system elements.

incomplete information Information that is less than full information about a situation.

imperfect information Information that is imprecise and possibly inaccurate with respect to a situation.

irreducible uncertainty Uncertainty that cannot be eliminated or reduced by gathering and analyzing further information, at least within a given time frame for decision making.

bounded rationality Rational decision-making behavior within bounds imposed by decision makers' limited ability and willingness to gather and interpret relevant information.

satisficing Acceptance of the first "satisfactory" solution to a problem instead of searching for an optimal solution.

strategic flexibility The set of strategic options that an organization has created for itself.

strategic options The courses of action that an organization can feasibly undertake now or in the future.

REVIEW QUESTIONS

1. What is operational effectiveness?
2. How is "operational management" different from "strategic management"?
3. What are some signs that decision makers are engaging in boundedly rational and satisficing behavior?
4. How do the "new forms" of organization try to overcome the separation of decision-making authority from the information and expertise needed to make good decisions?
5. How does strategic flexibility help decision makers who must cope with irreducible uncertainty?
6. How are commitment and flexibility related to planning and emergence in strategic management?

PART V

CORPORATE STRATEGY FOR MULTIPLE BUSINESS UNITS

CHAPTER 11

CORPORATE STRATEGY: THE SEARCH FOR SYNERGY AMONG MULTIPLE BUSINESS UNITS

INTRODUCTION

In previous chapters we discussed strategic management as the design and implementation of a Strategic Logic for a single business unit. Many firms today have multiple business units, however, and there are additional challenges and opportunities for strategic managers in sustaining the value-creation capabilities of multibusiness organizations. Strategic management that is concerned with improving the value-creation capabilities of multiple business units is referred to as **corporate strategy.** Strictly speaking, the term *corporate* in corporate strategy is a misnomer, because some corporations have only one business unit, while some multiple business unit organizations are not legally constituted as corporations. Nevertheless, the term *corporate strategy* is now commonly used to refer to the strategic management of organizations with multiple business units.

Corporate strategy is concerned with identifying and implementing synergies among multiple business units.

The fundamental objective of corporate strategic management is to *identify and implement synergies among multiple business units*—a task we refer to as "the search for synergy." **Synergy** is the creation of advantages for a corporate parent's business units that they would not be able to achieve if they were independent, freestanding business units. Synergy is, in effect, like combining "1 + 1" in ways that result in more than "2." As we discuss at length in this chapter, synergies achieved through a corporate parent's coordination of business units may result in (i) cost reductions, (ii) product or process improvements, or (iii) improvements in speed—all of which may increase the value of its business units' product offers. We discuss several forms of synergy, as well as various ways that a corporate parent may coordinate its business units to achieve each form of synergy.

As suggested in Figure 11.1, the coordination of business units to create synergies can include various ways of linking or combining the elements of the Strategic Logics of the corporate parent's multiple business units. Business units may be linked through elements of their Business Concepts—a shared customer base, complementary product offers, or common key activities. Business units may also be linked through their Organization Concepts—sharing or exchanging resources, information, and even incentives. In most cases, synergistic relationships between business units may involve coordination of several elements of each unit's Strategic Logic. Just as we developed a set of system design principles for designing viable Strategic Logics for individual business units, in this chapter we will discuss two fundamental system design principles for designing effective corporate strategies. These principles emphasize the need for corporate strategic management (i) to create synergies with a value greater than the added costs of corporate-level management, and (ii) to identify and implement ways of coordinating business units that create *positive-sum, self-managing interactions* between business units.

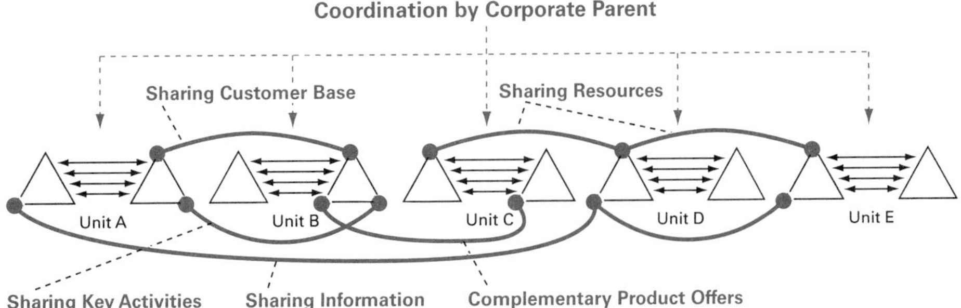

FIGURE 11.1 Examples of Synergistic Linkages between Strategic Logics of Multiple Business Units

11.1 SYNERGIES THAT REDUCE COSTS

Some of the most important and often most evident opportunities to create synergies result in significant cost reductions for business units in a corporate portfolio. We next consider four key economies that are sources of synergistic cost reduction—economies of scale, economies of learning, economies of scope, and economies of substitution.

Economies of Scale

Increasing scale can result in lower unit costs.

Economies of scale exist when the costs of performing an activity decrease as the scale of the activity increases. *Scale* refers to *capacity*—the maximum level of output that the assets used to carry out an activity are capable of sustaining. Scale may be expressed as tons of material that can be processed per year, units that can be produced per month, items that can be stored or shipped per week, accounting transactions that can be performed per day, or similar measures. Stated formally, economies of scale exist when the unit cost of producing (or distributing, or processing) at a capacity $(x + 1)$ units per time period are less than the unit cost at a capacity of (x) units per time period:

$$\textbf{Unit cost}_{\text{Scale} = (x+1)} < \textbf{Unit cost}_{\text{Scale} = (x)}$$

Economies of scale can also be expressed in the form of a declining cost curve, like the solid portion of the curve shown in Figure 11.2. Costs can fall as scale increases for two reasons. First, at a larger scale of operation, it is usually possible to achieve lower unit costs by *substituting capital for labor.* In this sense, *capital* is the economics term for tangible assets such as production machines. When machines are used to perform an activity instead of human labor, both fixed costs (amortization for machines used) and variable costs (human labor, materials, energy) may often be reduced if large quantities are produced. The substitution of machines for human labor may cover a spectrum of possibilities, from providing simple hand tools to workers to installing automated production lines that need little or no inputs of human labor. The use of the most advantageous capital-intensive versus labor-intensive methods of performing an activity is one of the most important aspects of the *technology choice* that strategic managers must make in organizing value-creation activities. A second reason why economies of scale may exist is that purchasers of the inputs into large-scale activities will often have *greater buyer power* than purchasers of smaller quantities of inputs, and they may use their buyer power to bargain for lower costs of inputs. Economy of scale curves usually fall steeply as volume increases and managers take advantage of the most obvious opportunities for improving

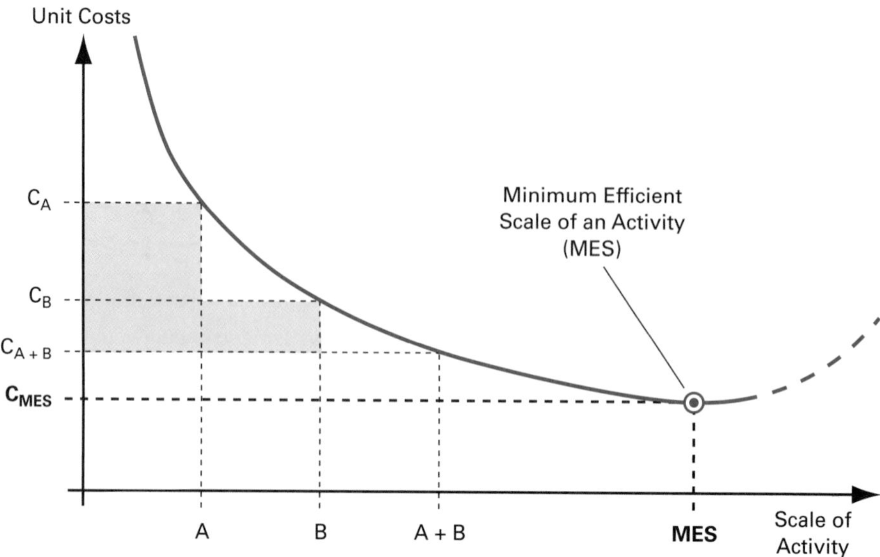

FIGURE 11.2 Economy of Scale Curve

efficiency through use of machines. Eventually, however, opportunities to achieve further economies of scale through additional use of machines or increases in buyer power will be exhausted, and the scale curve will "flatten out," as shown in Figure 11.2. Eventually, if the scale of an operation increases beyond the point of exhaustion of scale economies—the capacity level at which further cost reductions are not available through use of more machines or increases in buyer power—unit costs may actually start to increase due to rising costs of managing a larger organization, as suggested by the dashed portion of the scale curve in Figure 11.2.

Synergies in the form of lower costs resulting from economies of scale can be achieved by combining or consolidating an activity performed by two or more business units to achieve a larger scale in that activity than either business unit could sustain on its own. Suppose that Business Unit A and Business Unit B have a similar production, distribution, accounting, or other activity that would result in unit cost C_A and C_B, respectively, if carried out independently within each business unit. By combining and performing their activities in a larger-scale facility designed to process A + B units per year, unit costs for both business units will fall to C_{A+B}, resulting in a unit cost saving for Business Unit A of $(C_A - C_{A+B})$ and for Business Unit B of $(C_B - C_{A+B})$. As shown by the solid blue areas in Figure 11.2, when the capacity of the combined operation (A + B) is fully utilized, the resulting annual synergy benefit is

$$\textbf{Synergy Benefit = Annual Cost Saving = A}(C_A - C_{A+B}) + \textbf{B}(C_B - C_{A+B})$$

When searching for cost savings through consolidation of activities, corporate strategic managers must keep in mind an important competitive implication of economies of scale. As shown in Figure 11.2, every economy of scale curve will reach a point at which further increases in scale will not result in further unit cost reductions (and may even lead to increases in unit costs, as suggested by the dashed portion of the scale curve). That point defines the *maximum cost efficiency* that can be achieved in a specific activity, given the current state of technology for performing that activity. However, the point of maximum cost efficiency obtainable in a given activity is referred to as the **minimum efficient**

scale (MES) for performing that activity. The reason is that in competitive markets, for every activity that is a significant source of costs in realizing a product, price competition may give a firm no choice but to operate at maximum cost efficiency. If a competitor in a product market can begin to operate at the point of maximum cost efficiency, that competitor may set prices for its product just above the C_{MES} level. Other competitors will then have to achieve a similar level of cost efficiency, or be driven out of business by price competition. Thus, in competitive markets, the *maximum* cost efficient scale of activity is also the *minimum* efficient scale for maintaining competitiveness in each value-creating activity of an organization. When consolidating activities of multiple business units to achieve maximum cost reductions from larger scale, strategic managers must be aware of and try to achieve the MES in each consolidated activity.

Economies of Learning

Learning through experience also leads to lower unit costs.

At any given scale of an activity, the people performing an activity may learn how to reduce the costs incurred in that activity in a variety of ways. Individual workers may invent techniques that speed up the performance of a given task, or that reduce waste of the materials and parts. The flow of materials and work-in-progress through each process in an activity may also be reengineered to minimize the time, energy, and effort required to complete the overall activity. In-plant inventories may be analyzed and fine-tuned to reduce inventory levels of materials, parts, and work-in-progress, thereby reducing carrying costs of inventories and thus unit costs. Materials that are inputs to a process may also be respecified to enable use of less costly materials or to reduce waste.

When an organization tries to learn how to increase efficiency and otherwise reduce costs in its operations, it may achieve **economies of learning.** Because each unit of output that is processed through an activity presents a new opportunity to find ways to reduce costs, the cost savings realizable through sustained organizational learning will generally increase with the *cumulative number of units processed* through an activity, as indicated in Figure 11.3. Stated more formally, economies of learning are realized when the unit cost $C_{(n+1)}$ of processing the $(n + 1)$th unit are lower than the unit cost C_n of processing the nth unit:

$$\textbf{Unit cost}_{\text{Cumulative Units }(n+1)} < \textbf{Unit cost}_{\text{Cumulative Units }(n)}$$

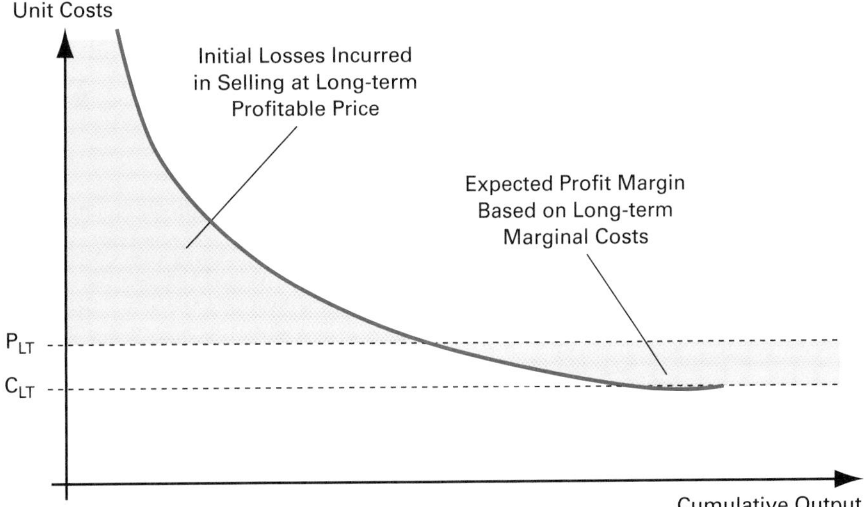

FIGURE 11.3 Economy of Learning Curve

Although economies of learning are different in nature from economies of scale, they have traditionally been achieved in a similar way—by combining operations of multiple business units to increase the number of units processed in one location, thereby increasing opportunities for workers to learn how to reduce costs. When significant cost reductions through learning are available in an industry, competition in a new product market often takes the form of a "race down the learning curve." Producers will attempt to expand output as rapidly as possible in order to maximize the rate of learning and thus the rate of cost reductions.

To generate rapid growth in demand for a new kind of product, some producers engage in "learning curve pricing." Using their organization's history of learning how to reduce costs in a given type of activity, they derive their organization's learning curve. They then calculate their long-term marginal cost for the product, and set initial prices at a level that they expect to be profitable in the long term, as indicated by the long-term profitable price P_{LT} in Figure 11.3. If competitors—who are not as confident in their ability to learn how to reduce costs—are not willing to sell their initial products at prices that will only be profitable in the long term, they will be priced out of the market. Of course, selling initially costly products at long-term profitable prices means that a firm will incur initial losses that can only be recovered in the long term if it is one of the surviving competitors in the market. This high-stakes strategy for introducing new kinds of products is often called "experience-curve pricing" and is a common form of competition in many assembled products industries with significant economies of learning, such as consumer electronics, appliances, and automobiles.

The economy of learning curve shown in Figure 11.3 is sometimes called an experience curve, because the more experience an organization has in performing an activity, the more learning about cost reductions it should be able to achieve. Experience curves are often represented in a graph that is somewhat different from the curve in Figure 11.3. By using a log scale that gives the exponential power of accumulated production on the horizontal axis, the curve of Figure 11.3 becomes a straight (or nearly straight) line, such as those indicated in Figure 11.4. This graphical representation makes it easier to see that a certain percentage of cost reduction is being achieved every time cumulative output of an activity doubles. Thus, as suggested in Figure 11.4, a "15% experience curve" represents an activity in which an organization can learn how to reduce costs another 15 percent every time cumulative output doubles. Many operations that organizations commonly perform have experience curves in the 5 percent to 30 percent range, making the development of organizational learning abilities in reducing costs an important source of competitive advantage.

Economies of Scope

Sharing the use of flexible productive assets lowers unit costs.

Value-creation activities must be performed on machines, in buildings, or through use of other assets. The costs of obtaining assets therefore contribute to the costs of performing activities, often in the form of fixed costs for amortization of equipment and real estate. Some activities may be performed on specific-use, "dedicated" assets designed specifically for producing or processing a specific product. Some assets, however, may be flexible-use assets in the sense that they can be used in the production or processing of more than one product. Specific-use assets may be designed to obtain the highest possible cost efficiencies in producing a given product. When two or more products may be produced or processed on a flexible-use asset, however, the fixed cost of the asset may be allocated to more than one value-creating activity. Thus, when an organization may not be able to fully

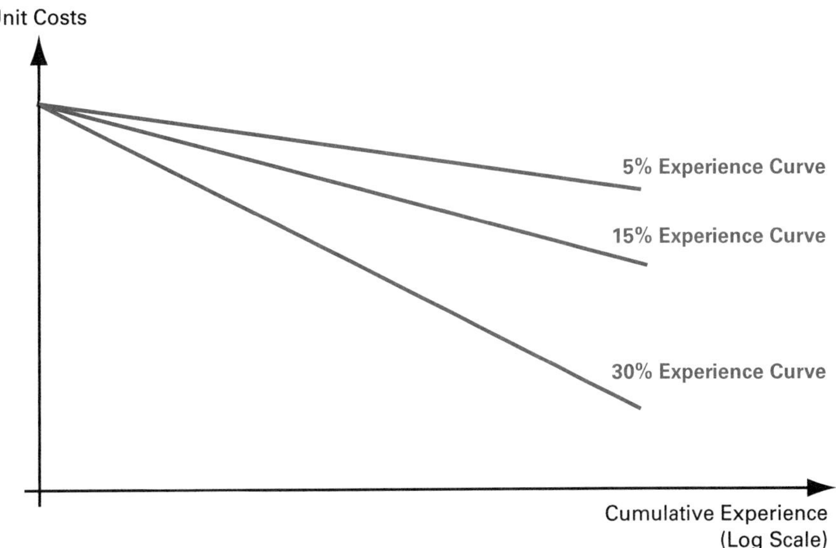

FIGURE 11.4 Experience Curve

utilize an asset in the production or processing of a single product, it may be more economical to produce or process more than one product on a flexible-use asset.[1]

Stated formally, **economies of scope** exist when the unit costs of producing or processing two or more products A, B,…*N* on a flexible-use asset $F_{A,B,\ldots N}$ are less than the unit costs of producing or processing products A,B,…*N* on specific-use assets D_A, D_B,…D_N. Economies of scope in the production of two products A and B are illustrated in Figure 11.5. By producing products A and B on flexible asset F_{A+B}, an organization may obtain lower average unit costs for producing A and B than the unit costs for producing product A on dedicated asset D_A and product B on dedicated asset D_B. When two or more products can be produced or processed on a flexible-use asset, a firm that engages in such activities may be able to achieve economies of scope by combining its production or processing on one flexible-use asset instead of using two specific-use assets. Computers are important kinds of flexible-use assets, for example, and in many firms accounting, engineering, and other computation-intensive activities are combined and carried out on one computing system. Distribution assets such as trucks and warehouses may also be used to achieve economies of scope by distributing more than one product line. Frito-Lay Corporation, for example, uses its fleet of delivery trucks to distribute not just its Fritos corn chips and Lay's potato chips, but also salsa and other kinds of dips for its chips. Intangible assets like knowledge and brands may also be sources of economies of scope when they can be used in the development, production, or marketing of more than one product.

Economies of Substitution

As we discussed in earlier chapters, to be useful in an organization's value-creation processes, resources must be systemically interrelated and coordinated with other resources. Similarly, the interactions of component parts of products must also be coordinated by the

[1] In addition, when demand for products is uncertain, flexible-use assets also give a firm potentially valuable *real options* or *strategic options* to switch production to the products with greatest demand and profit potential. See R. Sanchez. (1993). Strategic Flexibility, Firm Organization, and Managerial Work in Dynamic Markets: A Strategic Options Perspective. *Advances in Strategic Management,* 9, 251–291.

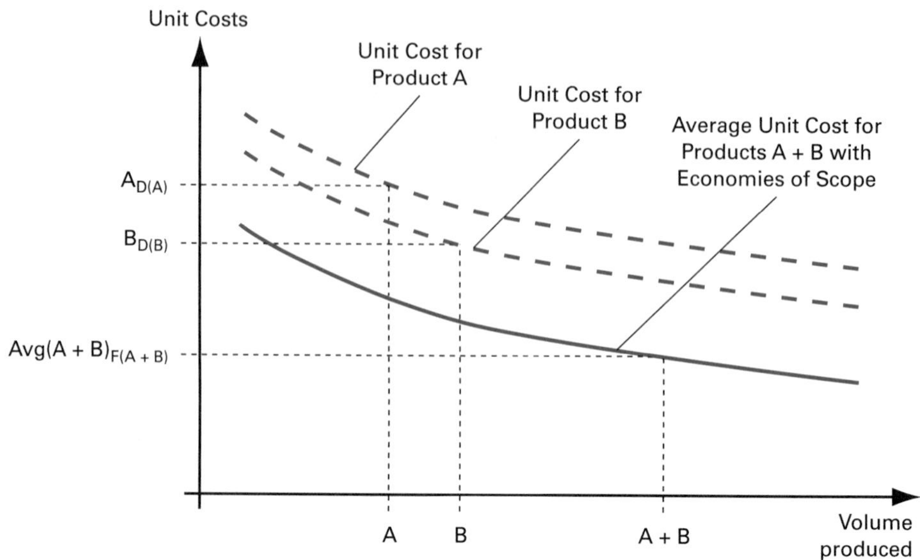

FIGURE 11.5 Economy of Scope Curve

Economies of substitution save on costs of redesigning components.

architecture of the product in order for the product to function as a system. In the designs of some organizations and products, replacing a current resource or component with another requires time-consuming and sometimes costly redesigns of the organization or product. **Economies of substitution** exist, however, when a resource in an organization or a component in a product can be replaced by another without incurring significant costs of redesigning the organization or product as a system.

As we discussed in Chapter 9, modular product architectures allow a range of component variations to be freely substituted in configuring product variations, thereby achieving economies of substitution.[2] Similarly, a "modular organization" can achieve economies of substitution by quickly incorporating alternative resources in its processes. Thus, a corporate parent may be able to achieve economies of substitution by, for example, adopting standard policies and practices across business units that enable it to transfer employees freely from a position in one business unit to a similar position in another business unit, thereby saving costs of reorienting transferred employees and "bringing them up to speed" in their new positions.

11.2 SYNERGIES THAT IMPROVE PRODUCTS AND PROCESSES

Another important set of synergies creates benefits that improve the quality, reliability, performance, appeal, market access, or other value-enhancing aspects of a firm's products or processes. We next consider how such synergies may be obtained by gaining better control of key inputs, transferring technology, sharing knowledge and capabilities, leveraging brands, and sharing key supplier and distributor relationships.

[2] See Garud, R., and A. Kumaraswamy. (1993). Changing Competitive Dynamics in Network Industries: An Exploration of the Sun Microsystems Open Systems Strategy. *Strategic Management Journal,* 14(5), 351–369; and Sanchez, R. (1999). Modular Architectures in the Marketing Process. *Journal of Marketing,* 63 (Special Issue), 92–111.

Vertical Integration to Gain Control of Key Inputs and Services

Creating and realizing high-quality products and services usually requires arranging a reliable supply of high-quality inputs, such as materials, parts, and components, as well as various services and processes. Manufacture of high-quality leather handbags and briefcases, for example, would be impossible without a supply of high-quality leather. To ensure that key inputs of the required quality and specification are available to it, a firm may purchase a key supplier or start its own internal supply unit to gain control of processes for providing key inputs. By maintaining an uninterrupted supply of key inputs, a firm may be able to improve the reliability of its realization processes. Gaining control of the business units that provide key inputs may also enable a firm to design and develop special kinds of inputs that improve the performance or quality of its products.

The supply relationships that provide the flow of inputs that sustain an industry's value-creation activities are often referred to as the *vertical structure* of an industry. As illustrated in Figure 11.6, supply relationships in a manufacturing industry—for example, the consumer electronics industry—might begin with the extraction of raw materials like iron ore or crude oil, which are then supplied as inputs to producers of processed materials, such as metals and plastics. Processed materials are then supplied to basic manufacturing firms to make parts such as metal stampings or molded plastic pieces, which are in turn supplied to producers of components such as compact disk (CD) drives and power transformers, who supply assemblers of CD players and amplifiers. Assemblers of consumer electronics products then ship their finished products to distributors, who supply dealers, who sell to consumers. In many industries, significant maintenance, service, training, and other forms of support activities are also provided to consumers after the sale of

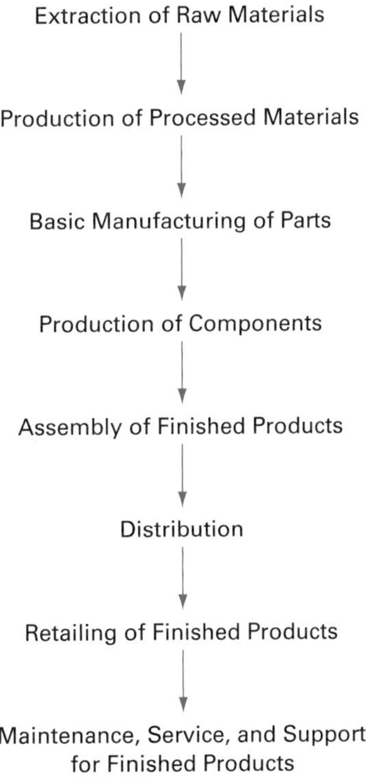

FIGURE 11.6 Vertical Structure of an Industry

finished products. Industries based on service products also have vertical structures, although these structures may be easier to understand when analyzed from the bottom up. Figure 11.7 illustrates the vertical structure of the insurance industry in the United States. At the bottom of the structure is the activity of processing claims made by insured customers—essentially the customer service and support activity in the insurance industry. These customers likely purchased their insurance policies from a network of independent insurance agents or local offices of an insurance company who are, in effect, the retailers of insurance services. The insurance services requested by prospective customers must be evaluated to determine risk levels and appropriate insurance rates to be charged for different kinds of requested insurance policies—called the underwriting process in the U.S. insurance industry. Most insurance companies, however, do not "own" the risk inherent in the insurance policies they issue. Rather, they consolidate and "package" together policies that have similar risk characteristics, and then obtain their own insurance policy for a large package of risk from what is known as the reinsurance market. The reinsurance market is composed of large reinsurance companies that essentially raise and manage risk capital that earns returns from reinsurance premiums, but must ultimately pay the claims that insured customers make under their insurance policies.

Vertical integration can be either "upstream" or "downstream."

When a firm at one stage of the vertical structure of an industry enters or "integrates" into another stage of the industry, the firm has engaged in a form of **vertical integration.** A firm may vertically integrate in two ways. *Upstream vertical integration* refers to the case when a firm at one stage of the vertical structure of an industry enters a value-creation activity that is *above* the stage it currently occupies in the vertical industry structure, such as that shown in Figure 11.6. Analogously, *downstream vertical integration* occurs when a firm enters a value-creation activity that is *below* the stage it currently occupies in the vertical industry structure. Thus, upstream vertical integration most commonly results in one or more new business units that will provide an internal supply of materials, parts, components, or products, while downstream vertical integration results in new business units that provide assembly, distribution, retailing, or customer support services. In both cases, the basic objective of vertical integration is to obtain synergies in the form of better products and services that control of key upstream inputs and downstream services can make possible.

FIGURE 11.7 Vertical Structure of the Insurance Industry

Leveraging of Technology and Intangible Assets

Leveraging of technology and other intangible assets can create important synergies.

Another form of synergy that can improve the quality and differentiation of a business unit's products and processes is the transfer—or *leveraging*—of technology or various intangible assets from another business unit.

Leveraging of technology is often most beneficial when it occurs between business units that are engaged in comparable kinds of value-creating activities (i.e., business units at the same stage of the vertical structure of an industry). For example, the numerous acquisitions of smaller automobile companies by global car producers, such as General Motors, Ford, Daimler, Volkswagen, and Renault in the 1990s, in many cases resulted in significant transfers of product and process technologies developed by the large companies to the smaller firms. In some cases, specialized technology was also transferred from smaller companies to the larger companies. The result: the performance, durability, and cost basis of the products offered by both the smaller and the larger automobile companies have in many cases improved significantly.

Leveraging of several kinds of intangible assets may also create synergies. *Market data* or *information* about trends in regional or national markets, market segments, and even individual customers may be shared between business units, as well as information about suppliers and prices of inputs obtained from various suppliers. *Knowledge*—often in the form of best practices—may be shared between business units engaged in related activities and may lead to improvements in the many kinds of value-creation processes firms undertake.

Business units may also realize synergies by leveraging a recognized *brand* of one business unit to introduce and market products from another business unit. Sony Corporation, for example, has one of the most widely recognized and highly regarded brands in the world. Sony was able to create synergies by leveraging the famous "SONY" brand of its consumer electronics business units when it established a new business unit marketing intelligent toys for children under the "My First Sony" brand. Care must be taken when leveraging a prized brand, however, to ensure that the new use of the brand is consistent with the image of the products that consumers already associate with the brand. Coca-Cola Corporation learned this lesson the hard way in the 1970s, for example, when it leveraged its famous brand—the most widely recognized in the world—to a line of casual clothing. Consumers did not perceive a connection between Coca-Cola's soft drinks and clothing products, and the company had to abandon its ill-conceived foray into the fashion business. At the same time, Caterpillar Corporation recently successfully licensed the "CAT" logo used on its bulldozers and other earth-moving equipment to a line of rugged work boots. Apparently the image of ruggedness and durability that most people associate with Caterpillar's earth-moving products provides an adequate psychological basis for using the brand on work shoe products.

Relationships are intangible assets that may sometimes also be leveraged to create synergies. It is often difficult, for example, for a firm to persuade distributors and retailers with whom it has not done business previously to begin to carry its products, because over time the most capable distributors and retailers tend to establish strong relationships with leading producers of successful products. When one business unit has established relationships with good distributors and retailers, however, it may be able to use its good relationships to encourage them to take on the products of a sister business unit within the corporate portfolio. Similarly, the best suppliers in an industry are often fully occupied with supplying existing customers, and may not have the resources or interest to begin working with a new customer. Again, a business unit that already enjoys an established relationship with good suppliers may be able to leverage those relationships to help its sister business unit establish relationships with good suppliers too. When one business unit can help other business units in a corporate portfolio obtain the best distribution and retailing services in an industry or inputs from the best suppliers, the attractiveness of the product offers of the other business units may be improved.

11.3 SYNERGIES THAT IMPROVE SPEED

In addition to helping business units create product offers that are cheaper or better, synergies may enable business units to become faster in creating and realizing products. Increases in speed may help organizations to create value in a number of ways.

In some cases, synergy from increased speed takes the form of accelerating entry into a new product market or market segment through acquisition of a new business unit. In late 2000, for example, Philips NV's Domestic Appliances and Personal Care division decided to expand its oral healthcare business. Although Philips had established a global business in affordably priced powered toothbrushes in the 1990s, Philips wanted to move its oral healthcare products "upmarket" into the premium-priced, high-performance powered toothbrush market. Conducting advanced research in oral healthcare, developing new products, establishing appropriate channels for distribution and retailing, and building a new brand identity in the premium end of the market would have required several years of effort. Instead of growing internally into this new market segment, therefore, Philips elected to purchase Optiva Corporation near Seattle, Washington, whose Sonicare brand of powered toothbrushes are based on advanced ultra-sound technology and were already recognized by the dental profession in the United States as the performance leader in dental cleaning and oral care. By buying another oral care business unit, Philips was quickly able to acquire new technology, a prized brand, and new distribution channels for premium-priced oral care products much more quickly than would have been possible through its own internal development efforts.

In dynamic markets, finding synergies that increase speed is often critical.

In product markets in which increasing speed-to-market is important in improving the chances for commercial success of a product offer, synergies that increase the speed of current product creation and realization processes may significantly improve the attractiveness of a business unit's product offers. Today, for example, Ford Motor Company develops new automobiles globally through a computer-assisted design (CAD) system that links its North American, Japanese, and European business units in a continuous, 24-hour-a-day design and development process. When, say, a suspension development team working on a new car project in Detroit in the United States finishes its design work for the day, the team's CAD file may be forwarded electronically to their counterparts at Ford's Mazda business unit in Japan to continue the design work. When the Japanese team has done its work for the day on the suspension design, the CAD file can then be forwarded electronically to Ford development centers in the United Kingdom or Germany for further work and subsequent forwarding back to the design team in Detroit. Ford's ability to coordinate multiple business units in a 24-hour-a-day "round the clock and round the world" development processes helps Ford bring new car models to market more quickly than competitors that lack the ability to coordinate such fast-paced development processes.

11.4 SYSTEM DESIGN PRINCIPLES FOR CORPORATE STRATEGY

Just as strategic managers of business units must create and implement viable Strategic Logics for their individual business units, strategic managers at the level of the corporate parent must design and implement effective corporate strategies. In this endeavor, corporate strategic managers must recognize and follow two system design principles. The first principle concerns the need for corporate strategic management to identify and create synergies with a value greater than the added costs of corporate-level management. The second principle requires that corporate strategic managers identify and implement ways of coordinating business units that create *positive-sum, self-managing interactions* between business units. Let us consider each of these principles in turn.

Earning a Positive Return on Corporate Strategic Management

Corporate strategic managers must achieve synergies in excess of the overhead costs they impose on the corporation's business units.

Fundamentally, the sales and profits of a corporate parent are generated by the activities of the individual business units, while the management activities carried out by the corporate parent generate corporate overhead costs. In order for corporate strategic management to be a net value-adding activity, corporate strategic managers must identify and realize ways to coordinate the activities of the business units that create synergies whose total value exceeds the overhead costs of corporate management. If corporate managers cannot create greater value through synergies than the corporate overhead costs they add, then corporate management is adding an unproductive and thus undesirable overhead cost to each business unit in the corporate portfolio. In that case, individual business units would be disadvantaged by belonging to the corporate parent, and they would be better off as freestanding business units.

The need for corporate strategic management to create net value added that exceeds the overhead costs of corporate management is reflected in the following system design principle:

System Design Principle 11.1

Corporate strategic management must identify and achieve synergies through coordination of business units in the corporate portfolio that exceed the added overhead costs of corporate management imposed on each business unit.

Creating Positive-Sum Interactions Between Business Units

Synergies should be achieved through self-managing, positive-sum interactions between business units.

To be as successful as possible in fulfilling System Design Principle 11.1, corporate strategic managers must also try to identify and implement opportunities to create synergies through positive-sum, self-managing interactions between business units. Positive-sum interactions are interactions between business units that are "win-win" for all involved parties. In other words, corporate managers must find ways for each business unit to realize a positive net benefit from coordinating its value-creation processes with those of one or more other business units. When the synergies to be created through such coordination are win-win for all involved business units, each business unit will have an incentive to fully exploit the identified opportunities for creating synergies between business units. In such cases, the processes within each business unit for realizing the identified synergies can become *self-managing,* thereby reducing or eliminating the need for continuing inputs from corporate strategic management staff to sustain synergistic interactions.

This objective is reflected in the second system design principle for corporate strategic management:

System Design Principle 11.2

Corporate strategic management must identify and implement synergies that can be realized through positive-sum, win-win interactions between business units in the corporate portfolio, so that coordination of synergy-creating interactions will become self-managing processes.

KEY TERMS AND CONCEPTS

corporate strategy The search for synergies among multiple business units.

synergy The creation of advantages through coordination of multiple business units that the units would not be able to achieve if they were independent, freestanding businesses.

economies of scale The lowering of unit costs with increasing scale (capacity) of a process.

minimum efficient scale (MES) The scale of a process beyond which further increases in unit scale do not result in lower unit costs.

economies of learning The lowering of unit costs with accumulated learning gathered through increasing experience in performing a process.

economies of scope The lowering of costs through the sharing of a flexible-use asset by two or more business units.

economies of substitution Replacing one resource in an organization or one component in a product with another without incurring significant costs of redesigning the organization or product as a system.

vertical integration The addition to a corporate portfolio of a business that is upstream or downstream in the vertical structure of an industry from one or more of the business units already in the corporate portfolio.

REVIEW QUESTIONS

1. Why must corporate strategic managers identify and achieve synergies among the business units of the corporate parent?
2. Why is it important to implement synergies that can lead to self-managing, positive-sum outcomes for two or more business units?

CHAPTER 12

PATTERNS AND LIMITS IN THE SEARCH FOR SYNERGY: THE LOGIC OF GROWTH THROUGH DIVERSIFICATION

INTRODUCTION

In the previous chapter we defined the fundamental task of corporate strategic management as the search for synergies that can create benefits for the multiple business units in a corporate portfolio. We explained a number of ways in which synergies can be created through coordination of multiple business units to help reduce costs, improve product quality and differentiation, and increase speed.

We now consider a number of factors that influence the choices that organizations must make as they evaluate alternative ways to achieve synergies. We will see that successful organizations often follow an underlying logic as they grow beyond a single business into a multiple-business enterprise. This logic leads to a certain pattern in the kinds of synergies that organizations seek as they grow, and in the order in which they seek those synergies, as suggested in Figure 12.1. This logic and its resulting pattern in the search for synergy lead many organizations to grow beyond one kind of business and to *diversify* into related business areas. We also consider a number of *limitations* that organizations will face as they try to develop various forms of synergies. These limitations constrain the ways an organization may grow and thereby also help to shape the patterns of growth that organizations follow as they evolve into multiple business unit enterprises.

In this chapter we discuss a pattern of growth that historically many organizations followed as they expanded. This pattern begins with domestic geographic expansion, followed by international expansion, horizontal integration, vertical integration, related diversification, and progressively less-related diversification, perhaps culminating in forms of unrelated diversification. The growth of an organization into less-related business areas, however, cannot continue forever. As we will see, for every organization there exists an *optimal extent of diversification* (i.e., the maximum overall size and diversity in mix of business units that an organization should try to manage within one corporate portfolio). We therefore also discuss several kinds of limits on an organization's ability to achieve further synergies as it grows through further diversification. Finally, we consider the increasingly important role of mergers and acquisitions in corporate growth.

Effective strategic management at the corporate level requires a clear understanding of both the potential for value creation through diversification and the limitations on the ability to create value through diversification. Only with such understanding can corporate strategic managers determine the optimal extent of diversification for a growing organization.

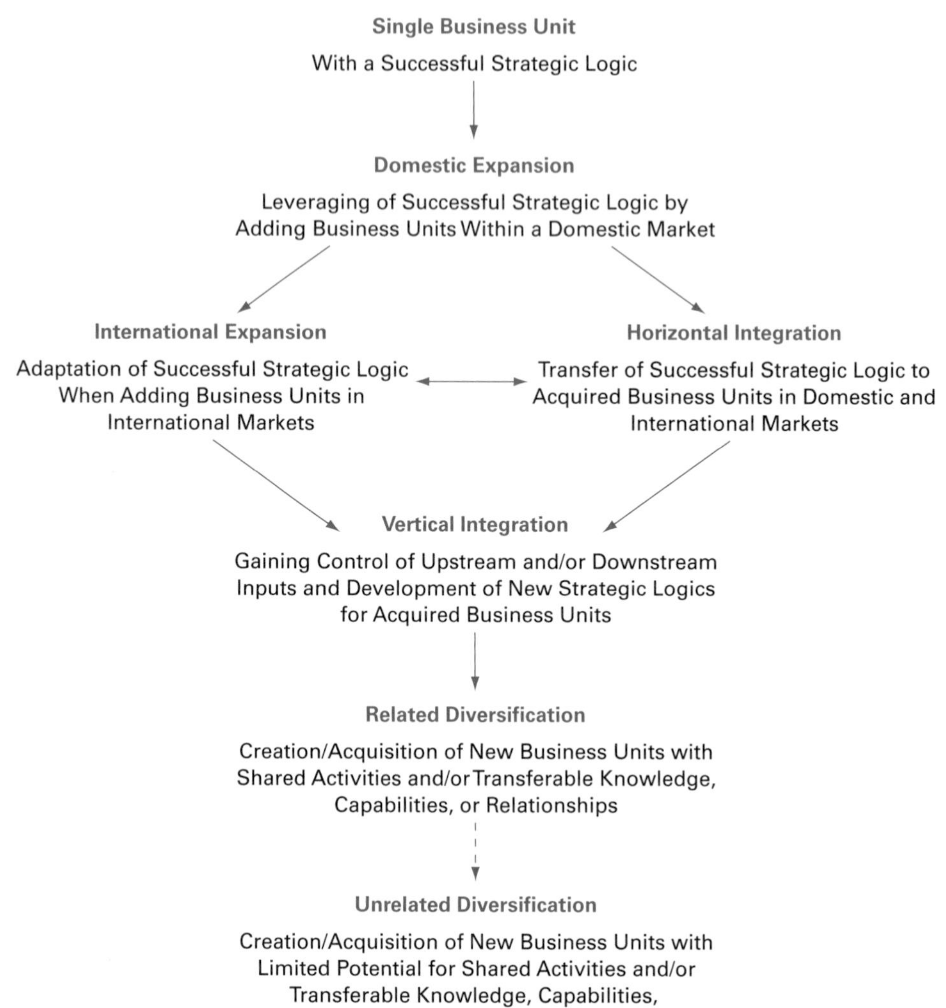

FIGURE 12.1 Common Patterns in the Growth of Multiple Business Enterprises

12.1 GROWTH THROUGH DOMESTIC EXPANSION

Imagine that an entrepreneur starts a new business, and that the Strategic Logic followed by the new business proves successful in creating value in its targeted market. How then will the business grow? For most businesses, the answer is *geographic expansion*—in effect, doing more of the same thing, but in new locations.

Growing businesses typically expand geographically within their own domestic market before attempting international growth. There are several reasons why **domestic expansion** is likely to be the most attractive growth option for a successful business. In many cases, a Strategic Logic that is successful in one part of a country can be "transplanted" successfully to other locations in the same country. The market preferences that a product offer is capable of serving well are often more similar in locations within the same country than in locations in other countries.[1] Similarly, an Organization Concept's authority relationships and incentives that work well with employees in one location are likely to be effective for employees in other locations within the same country. Other important macroenvironmental and industry factors, such as the legal and regulatory environment and the infrastructure of suppliers, are likely to be basically similar in various locations within the same country. These similarities often make it possible to "clone" or replicate a successful Business Concept to many locations within a domestic market.

Geographic expansion may be constrained, however, by both supply-side and demand-side factors. On the supply side, the main challenge many entrepreneurs will face as they grow geographically beyond a single business location is modifying their Organization Concept to be effective in carrying out the Business Concept in multiple locations. As an organization adds more people as it expands the number of locations in which it operates, new organization designs with new task allocations, information flows, and decision-making processes that span across several business locations need to be defined and implemented. New kinds of skills and coordination technologies are also often necessary to manage these new processes. In addition, new kinds of controls that monitor and evaluate performance in the growing organization's multiple business units must be defined and implemented. Many entrepreneurs, with a talent for defining a successful Business Concept and managing one or a few locations that they can supervise personally, will nonetheless fail to design a new Organization Concept capable of adequately coordinating multiple business locations.

Demand-side limits also affect the ability of a business to expand geographically within a single country. Eventually, an expanding business may occupy all the desirable locations in a domestic market not already occupied by competitors. Once this point of domestic saturation is reached, to continue growing strategic managers will generally turn to international expansion or horizontal integration.

12.2 GROWTH THROUGH INTERNATIONAL EXPANSION

After extensive growth of a business in a domestic market, an often-used approach to maintaining growth is to try to expand internationally by leveraging a successful Strategic Logic to markets in other countries. In **international expansion,** however, significant adaptations in an organization's Business Concept and/or Organization Concept are likely to be necessary.

In some cases, a Business Concept may be successfully leveraged globally or at least in many countries of the world. McDonald's Corporation, for example, successfully offers an essentially standard menu of hamburgers and related fast-food items in most countries of the world. In many product markets, however, international expansion often requires adaptation of a domestically successful Business Concept to address differences in consumer preferences that result from differences in the cultural values and norms of a country and its specific economic conditions. Products may need to be modified to reflect different usage conditions or styled differently to appeal to local tastes in design. Services may also need to be adapted to meet different levels of expectations about the support that customers will receive when they purchase a product. In Japan, for example, where every whim of a customer is usually catered to, service levels must be substantially

[1] Of course, market preferences may vary considerably within countries with diverse ethnic and cultural composition. This wide range of variation may be the case in large countries such as the United States, which has a number of important ethnic and cultural groups in its population of nearly 300 million people, but even countries with smaller populations (e.g., Belgium or Canada) may have important ethnic and cultural differences in their populations that lead to major differences in market preferences in various parts of the country.

higher than in a country where "the law of the bazaar" prevails and customers do not expect to be treated well. Expectations of personal interactions will therefore also vary considerably in different countries with different levels of expectations about customer service. However, there is always a possibility that product offers with high service and personal interaction value components may be successfully exported to countries where good service and personal interactions are not currently the norm. The success of Japanese car companies in the United States in the 1970s and beyond can be attributed not just to the high quality of their automobiles, but also to the greater emphasis that Japanese automobile companies placed on rendering customer service that was clearly superior to the prevailing customer service levels of domestic car companies in the United States at the time.

Similarly, in some cases, a domestically successful Organization Concept may sometimes be exported successfully to other cultures. Again, McDonald's Corporation has succeeded in bringing its standardized methods of training employees, managing operations, and maintaining customer service that were originally developed in the United States to many countries in the world. In some cases, however, the cultural values and norms prevailing in a country may necessitate adapting an Organization Concept to different sets of expectations by employees, suppliers, and other resource providers in different countries. Laws and regulations in different countries—for example, laws affecting the rights of employees and the costs of laying off or firing employees—may also require changes in an organization's approaches to hiring and managing employees in different countries as it expands internationally.

Strategic managers must understand which aspects of a Strategic Logic can be leveraged into another culture, and which cannot.

A fundamental task of the strategic managers of a growing international organization is to understand which aspects of a domestically successful Strategic Logic can be extended successfully to other countries, and which require adaptation to suit conditions in different countries. Such assessments are essential in determining which countries offer the greatest potential for leveraging a domestically successful Strategic Logic. In many cases, such an analysis will reveal that the best opportunities for leveraging a firm's Strategic Logic may not be the countries that are geographically closest to the firm's domestic base, but rather are the countries that are closest in terms of lifestyles and cultures. Some U.S. firms find it much easier to expand into Australia or Great Britain than into Mexico, for example, just as some Swedish firms like SAAB and Volvo found greater acceptance of their products in the United States than in many neighboring countries in Europe.

A firm that wants to expand internationally may also identify significant adaptations of its Strategic Logic that will be required to compete in markets that are otherwise attractive because of their size, the lack of significant competition, the desire to compete against foreign-based competitors in their home markets, or other reasons. Defining advantageous or necessary adaptations of a Strategic Logic and developing appropriate new product offers, key activities, resources, organization designs, and controls and incentives then become drivers for building the new organizational competencies needed to be successful in international markets.

12.3 GROWTH THROUGH HORIZONTAL INTEGRATION

Often, a successful firm will find that it has grown as much or as rapidly as it can through its own internal expansion in a given market. In such cases, another approach to sustaining growth in a successful organization is acquiring or merging with firms that are currently direct competitors in a market.

Acquiring or merging with firms that are direct competitors is called **horizontal integration,** and the origin of the term in economic theory is derived from the concept of the *structure of an industry,* discussed in Chapter 11 (see Figure 11.6). The structure of a typical manufacturing industry is illustrated in Figure 12.2, which shows that the structure of an industry has two dimensions—a *vertical structure* and a *horizontal structure.*

The vertical structure shown in Figure 12.2 follows the flow of inputs into a manufacturing industry and their progressive transformations into an output that is a finished good for some product market. The vertical structure of an industry in this case begins with the raw materials that must be processed into basic materials that are used to make parts, which are then combined into components that are in turn assembled into final products. Finished goods then enter distribution channels, are sold through retail outlets, and are maintained, repaired, and otherwise supported through an infrastructure of service activities.

The horizontal structure of an industry consists of the firms that participate in each stage in the vertical structure. At each stage of an industry, the horizontal structure may be *fragmented* (composed of many small firms), *consolidated* (composed of a few large firms), or composed of a mix of large, medium, and small firms. When firms at one stage of an industry—for example, assemblers of finished products, as shown in Figure 12.2—begin to horizontally integrate by acquiring or merging with other firms at that stage, an industry becomes more consolidated.

Horizontal integration should offer good opportunities for achieving synergies.

When one firm integrates horizontally by acquiring other firms, the acquiring firm usually intends to transfer all or most elements of its Strategic Logic to any acquired firms, or at least to achieve consistency between important elements of its Strategic Logic and the Strategic Logics of acquired firms. When the acquiring firm and the acquired firms follow similar Strategic Logics, many activities within the Organization Concepts for the firms are likely to present opportunities for achieving cost-reducing synergies through combining operations to gain economies of scale, scope, or learning. Many opportunities

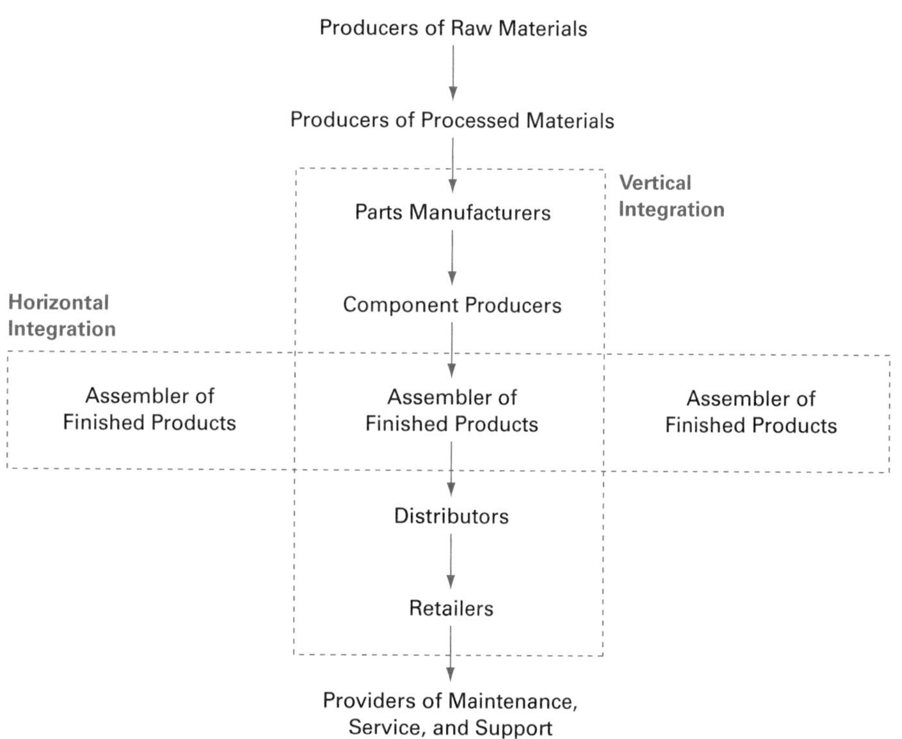

FIGURE 12.2 Horizontal and Vertical Integration within an Industry Structure

for sharing of information, knowledge, and supplier or customer relationships are also likely, as well as opportunities for transferring capabilities among the horizontally integrated business units.

Because they are competing is the same product market as an acquiring firm, acquired firms that become horizontally integrated business units of a multiple-business enterprise may show some important similarities in their Business Concepts and the Business Concept of the acquiring firm. Of course, it is usually the case that the acquiring firm is one of the more successful firms in its stage of industry, and the acquiring firm is therefore likely to seek to modify the Business Concepts of acquired firms to bring them more in line with its own successful Business Concept. Acquired firms may be refocused on the market segments the acquiring firm serves successfully. Technology or product designs may be transferred from the acquiring firm to improve the functions, features, or performance levels of the products of acquired firms. The service component of the product offer may also be improved by implementing the service practices of the acquiring firm, the acquiring firm's brand may be used to improve the image value of the acquired firms' products, employees of acquired firms that have direct contact with customers may be reskilled to improve personal interaction value, and so on. Key activities within acquired firms may be redirected to improve effectiveness in bringing the modified product offers to current or new market segments.

Horizontal integration may be limited by competition laws.

Firms seeking to grow through horizontal integration may encounter at least three kinds of limitations. First, opportunities to acquire other firms may be limited, and eventually a firm may acquire all the firms that can be acquired in a product market, either willingly through a friendly takeover or unwillingly through a hostile takeover. Second, in many countries, laws and regulations intended to maintain competition in product markets limit the market share that one firm may control in a product market. Legal permission to acquire a competitor may be denied when regulators fear a horizontally integrating firm may acquire too much market power. Third, significant growth through horizontal integration requires more than a transfer of Business Concept from the acquiring firm to the acquired firm. It also challenges the acquiring firm to devise Organization Concepts for both the acquiring and acquired firms that will be effective in implementing the coordination needed to achieve synergies. Many firms find the effective post-acquisition integration of acquired firms into the corporate portfolio to be a difficult process. In some cases firms will limit their horizontal integration initiatives because of problems with or concerns about meeting organizational challenges in the post-acquisition integration process.

12.4 GROWTH THROUGH VERTICAL INTEGRATION

As suggested in Figure 12.2, vertical integration occurs when a firm acquires or merges with one or more firms that are upstream or downstream from the stage that the firm currently occupies in the vertical structure of an industry. In Chapter 11, we explained the basic objective of vertical integration to obtain synergies by gaining control of key upstream inputs and downstream activities that can improve the quality and reliability of a firm's products and services. Upstream vertical integration and downstream vertical integration each involves its own set of issues to be managed, and we address these two modes of diversification through vertical integration next.

Successful upstream integration must overcome some significant challenges.

Upstream Vertical Integration

Growth through upstream vertical integration typically occurs after considerable growth of a business through domestic expansion, international expansion, or horizontal integration. Several reasons explain why strategic managers are likely to defer upstream vertical integration until their firm has achieved significant size. The most fundamental reason is that the minimum efficient scale (MES) of production in most industries *increases* as one goes upstream from the bottom to the top of the vertical structure of an industry. This relationship is illustrated in Figure 12.3 for the case of the automobile industry. Starting at the bottom of the automobile industry structure, the human-labor intensity of maintenance and repair activities in the automobile industry means that such services can usually be carried out economically on a small scale, perhaps servicing as few as 100–200 cars per year. In many countries, however, most automobile dealerships would have to sell several hundred automobiles per year to be economically viable. In the assembly of automobiles, the MES in a competitive open market is at least 100,000 cars per year, while the MES for an automobile engine factory is something like 500,000 engines per year. The MES for producing the iron used to make the blocks of engines would provide enough iron for many millions of engine blocks, while the MES for an iron ore mining operation would have an output of ore adequate to produce tens of millions of engine blocks.

Because of the increasing MES in the upstream direction of the vertical structure of the automobile industry, an automobile assembler that wants to control its own vertically integrated supply of engines would need to grow large enough to fully consume the outputs of an MES engine plant. In other words, the firm would have to operate several automobile assembly plants that together are capable of using 500,000 engines a year, or else face a potentially significant cost disadvantage in sourcing engines by operating its own engine plant at less than MES. American Motors Corporation (AMC) faced this dilemma in the 1960s and 1970s in the United States when it was a relatively small automobile producer trailing well behind the "Big Three" of General Motors, Ford, and Chrysler. During this time, AMC was never able to produce and sell enough cars to make it economical to

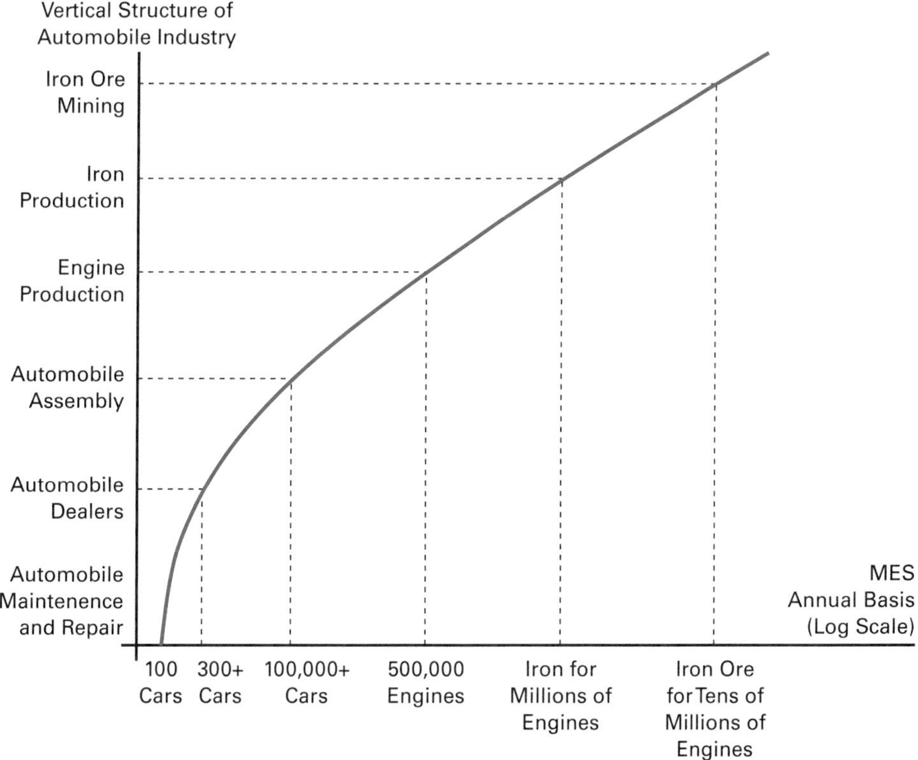

FIGURE 12.3 Increasing MES in the Vertical Structure of the Automobile Industry

have its own MES factories for engines or other major components. Automobile mechanics of the time used to say that AMC stood for "Any Maker's Components," because AMC had to design its cars to use engines and other components that it could arrange to purchase from the Big Three automakers.

An alternative to growing large enough to fully consume the outputs of an upstream vertically integrated MES supplier is to consume only part of the output of the supply unit, and to "make a business" out of the supply unit by selling the unneeded output to other customers. To make a supply unit a successful business, however, strategic managers of the corporate parent must meet two challenges. Most fundamentally, in addition to fully implementing the hoped-for synergies between the supply unit and other business units in the corporate portfolio, they must understand enough about the supply unit's business to be able to help the supply unit continue to build and leverage its own competencies. In addition, the customers of a corporate parent's upstream supply unit are generally competitors of the corporate parent, and they are likely to have concerns about sourcing key inputs from a supplier owned by a direct competitor. In this case, the corporate parent's strategic managers and the strategic managers of the supply business unit must define a Strategic Logic that both meets the supply needs of the corporate parent and enables the supply business unit to serve its other customers effectively.

Finding a Strategic Logic that can serve well both a corporate parent and the parent's competitors usually requires that the corporate parent be sufficiently large and profitable to fund ongoing investments in improving the technology and other capabilities of the supplier unit, so that the outputs of the supply unit continue to be attractive to both the corporate parent and the market at large. In addition, the Strategic Logic of the supplier unit must include the creation of a "fire wall" of absolute confidentiality separating the supplier's dealings with its corporate parent and its business with customers who are competitors of the corporate parent. Although it may be challenging to establish such separation, in many industries it has become common practice for a vertically integrated supplier to serve both its corporate parent and competitors of the corporate parent. Philips Key Components business unit, for example, supplies components for consumer electronics products not only to Philips' own consumer electronics business units, but to most other consumer electronics companies around the world, almost all of whom are direct competitors of Philips' consumer electronics business units. As a result, Philips achieves MES in the development of component technologies and in the production of components that enables it to have a profitable components business, while also assuring Philips of a cost-effective supply of leading-edge components to its own consumer electronics business units.

Finally, investing in upstream or downstream stages of an industry also generally increases business risk. When a corporate parent adds business units through vertically integrating within a single industry, it increases the sunk costs on which it must earn positive returns, as well as incurring greater fixed costs that must be generally covered from current cash flows. At the same time, because the revenues of the corporate parent are generated within a single industry, the corporate parent may become more financially vulnerable to swings in demand levels in the industry. For this reason, many strategic managers elect to diversify into related industries rather than undertake extensive vertical integration within a single industry.

Downstream Vertical Integration

Growth through downstream vertical integration is generally undertaken in response to opportunities for synergy creation that are quite different from the synergy objectives that motivate upstream vertical integration. In general, downstream vertical integration may create synergies in four ways:

- Avoiding market failures by overcoming the free-rider problem in distribution, retailing, or service and support activities
- Gaining access to distribution that may not be available through established channels
- Improving service, image, and personal interaction value in a product offer
- Gaining better understanding of market preferences by establishing direct contact with final consumers or users of a product

Overcoming the Free-Rider Problem

"Free riders" do not pay their fair share of costs.

The free-rider problem is a phenomenon long recognized in economics. In essence, a *free rider* is an economic actor who takes advantage of a benefit (usually a public good or positive externality) without paying his or her share of the costs required to create the benefit. The classic example is the person who tries to ride for "free" (i.e., without paying) on a public transit system that is funded by the fares paid by riders. If enough people become free riders, the funds required to pay for the operations of the transit system will not be collected, and the transit system may fail to be economically viable—leading to what is termed in economics a *market failure* in the creation of a public good.

The potential for a free-rider problem in distribution or retailing activities is often quite serious when a producer needs distributors or retailers to educate consumers in order to introduce a new kind of product to the market. When distributors or retailers must explain to potential consumers how a new product works or how to use a new product to obtain the greatest benefits, distributors or retailers must devote more sales time to each customer, leading to higher selling costs. If several distributors or retailers serve a given area, one or more of them may decide that it would be more advantageous not to invest in educating consumers about the new product, but rather to let the other distributors or retailers incur those costs. Then if the other distributors or retailers do invest in educating the market and thereby create demand for the new product, the free-riding distributors and retailers could still enjoy a benefit by selling to customers after the costly work of educating the market is done. The problem with this reasoning, of course, is that all distributors and retailers in a given area may have the same idea, or perhaps those who might be willing to invest in educating the market may be afraid that not enough other distributors or retailers would be willing to do so. The consequence may then be that not enough distributors or retailers make the investments needed to educate the market, and the market for the new product fails to form.

Similar problems of free-rider behavior leading to market failure may occur when retailers must invest in maintaining expensive "upmarket" sales premises or in providing a high level of customer support or training. In such cases, the maker of a product that requires extra investments by distributors or retailers may try to make contracts with distributors and retailers that commit them to making the necessary investments. However, such contracts are notoriously difficult or costly to monitor and enforce. As a result, many makers of products with potential free-rider problems opt to integrate downstream into distribution or retailing to make sure that the investments required to create and maintain the market for their products are in fact made.

Gaining Access to Distribution

Access to distribution channels may be difficult to obtain.

Another objective of downstream vertical integration by producers may be to establish distribution when existing distribution channels are not willing or able to provide distribution services. In some countries, exclusive distribution arrangements may prevent established distributors from adding new product lines from other producers (although such arrangements are increasingly seen as anticompetitive and are outlawed in some countries).

Alternatively, distributors may simply have long-standing relationships with producers that they do not wish to disturb by distributing competing products. Often, producers that are new to a product market must enter with a less than a full line of products, while incumbent producers may be able to provide their existing distributors with a full line of products. Distributors may believe that there are important economies of scope in representing full-line producers compared to representing a producer with a limited line of products. For these reasons and others as well, a producer trying to enter a new market may find that desirable established distribution channels are unwilling to accept their products. They then may have to establish their own distribution activity in order to get their products into the market.

Improving Service, Image, and Personal Interaction Value

Gaining more control of the customer experience may be critical for a producer.

In addition, some product offers may require a high level of service, image, and personal interaction value that cannot be reliably provided by established retailing channels. A producer may then have to integrate downstream into retailing to gain control of these important aspects of the product offer at the point of contact with the customer. For example, a large part of the annual sales of Louis Vuitton luggage, handbags, and other products is sold through duty-free shops in airports, especially in Asia. As independent retailers, however, few of these shops would provide an upmarket retailing environment consistent with the luxury goods image of the Louis Vuitton brand. To gain control of the retailing channels for Louis Vuitton products, in the late 1990s LVMH (the corporate parent of the Louis Vuitton business) integrated downstream by acquiring Duty Free Shoppers, the largest chain of duty-free shops in the world and a particularly strong presence in Asian airports, where most sales of Louis Vuitton goods were generated. LVMH then upgraded the retailing environment of Duty Free Shoppers locations to be consistent with the service, image, and personal interaction value of a leading luxury goods brand.

Gaining Better Understanding of Market Preferences

Maintaining direct contact with customers may also be critical.

Another incentive for a producer to integrate downstream into retailing is to gain better understanding of customer preferences by establishing direct contact with final consumers or users of its products. Especially in markets for "fast-moving consumer goods" in which specific preferences are likely to change often, firms may find that relying on conventional marketing research and on feedback through distribution channels may not provide the timely market information needed to define and develop successful new products. To gather more timely market information, firms such as Sony through its Sony Shops and Nike through its NikeTown stores have established "antennae shops" in what they regard as the trend-setting cities of the world. These retail outlets sell some currently successful products, but their emphasis is on goods based on new product ideas that are still being tested in the market to gain firsthand feedback on the response of targeted customers. The direct market feedback obtained in these antennae shops helps these firms to decide which new product ideas to put into full production, and which to drop.

12.5 GROWTH THROUGH RELATED DIVERSIFICATION

Related diversification builds on the commonalities of business units.

Diversification is the term used to refer to the form of growth that occurs when a firm starts, acquires, or merges with a business unit in a product market that is different from the product market currently served by the firm. In effect, diversification occurs when a corporate parent creates a portfolio of business units pursuing significantly different Business Concepts.

Diversification is said to be *related* when significant common activities among a corporate parent's business units enable the creation of the kinds of synergies that we discussed in Chapter 11. Recalling what we discussed in Chapter 11, in **related diversification** we would expect to find sufficient commonalities among business units to create significant synergies by

- Combining activities to achieve economies of scale, scope, or learning
- Gaining control of key inputs and services
- Sharing of useful information, knowledge, and brands
- Transferring capabilities from one business unit to another

In effect, the greater the potential for achieving synergies in these ways among business units, the more "related" is the diversification of business units within the corporate portfolio.

As a multiple-business enterprise grows, strategic managers are likely to first take advantage of opportunities to diversify into closely related businesses, because they offer the greatest and usually most evident potential for creating synergies. After fully developing the most related opportunities for growth that they can identify, strategic managers then typically pursue growth opportunities that are somewhat less related, then less related still, and so on, until a corporate parent exhausts all opportunities for growth through significant forms of relatedness. At that point, corporate strategic managers must decide whether to continue growing through *unrelated diversification,* or alternatively to limit future expansion to growth that is internally generated by the related business units already within the corporate portfolio.

In essence, the challenge facing strategic managers at this stage in the growth of a multiple-business enterprise is to determine the *optimal extent of diversification* of a corporate portfolio. To develop an approach to making this determination, we must next examine some ideas about how unrelated diversification may be able to create certain kinds of synergies. With a perspective on the potential for synergy creation through related versus unrelated diversification, we then develop a framework for identifying and evaluating the issues that strategic managers must consider in determining the optimal extent of diversification of a growing enterprise.

12.6 GROWTH THROUGH UNRELATED DIVERSIFICATION

Diversification is *unrelated* when the business units within a corporate portfolio lack commonalities that can be the basis for the creation of the "traditional" kinds of synergies we discussed in Chapter 11 and mentioned in the previous section. Instead of or in addition to pursuing these traditional forms of synergy, some strategic managers try to achieve other kinds of synergies through unrelated diversification. **Unrelated diversification** is sometimes said to be capable of creating synergies in three main ways:

- Leveraging of general management capabilities
- Avoiding market failures and inefficiencies in capital allocation by forming an internal capital market
- Diversifying away financial risk by creating a diversified portfolio of businesses

We next critically examine each of these three possibilities to assess the potential for unrelated diversification to create synergies.

Leveraging of "general management capabilities" may create synergies in some cases.

Leveraging of General Management Capabilities

Some managers and management researchers suggest that synergies can be created by leveraging general management capabilities among unrelated businesses. In effect, this idea proposes that all business—no matter how unrelated in their Strategic Logics—share a fundamental need for general management skills, and synergies can therefore be created by transferring capable managers or management methods from one unrelated business unit to another within a corporate portfolio. Some corporate parents appear to have successfully created synergies in this way, at least under certain conditions or in certain ways.

The managers of Hanson Trust, for example, created a multibillion-dollar enterprise in the 1970s and 1980s by acquiring companies in a number of unrelated traditional industries (such as brickmaking and joinery products for homebuilding) in the United Kingdom. With each new acquisition, Hanson Trust would install new managers drawn from more dynamic industries and new management methods that emphasized continuous improvement, clearly defined performance goals, and significant incentives for managers and workers to achieve higher performance and profitability. The result, sustained over almost two decades of growth through unrelated diversification, transformed a number of generally low-performing, marginally profitable or loss-making businesses into efficient, profitable businesses.

A related example is the unprecedented growth (in size and market value) of General Electric Corporation of the United States during the 1980s and 1990s. Under CEO Jack Welch, General Electric grew to include over 100 companies and put together one of the largest and most highly diversified portfolios of companies ever formed. What General Electric's strategic managers brought to this portfolio of largely unrelated businesses was essentially a common management process that demands disciplined commitment by business unit managers to achieving consistently high levels of market share and financial performance, and to maintaining a "boundary-less organization" in which all managers of business units must aggressively seek to learn from other companies and share their unit's knowledge with other business units in the General Electric portfolio. The methodical pursuit of these general management norms in all business units has apparently contributed significantly to the overall growth and success of General Electric through unrelated diversification.

These examples suggest that a nontraditional kind of synergy—an improved capacity to generate economic value—may be created in a portfolio of unrelated business units when a corporate parent implements management processes that are generally more effective than the management processes used by prior managers, or when a corporate parent imposes performance expectations that are higher than those demanded of prior managers of acquired business units. In effect, these examples suggest that market forces may not always be strong enough to force managers to extract maximum value from their business units, and that at least in some cases a demanding corporate parent may be a better institutional mechanism than markets for achieving the maximum value-creation potential of the resources in a business unit.

Of course, the potential gains from this nontraditional form of synergy must be weighed against the additional overhead costs that a corporate parent imposes on its business units. Thus, as a rule, we would expect a corporate parent that is successful in creating this nontraditional kind of synergy within a portfolio of unrelated businesses to operate with intentionally "lean" corporate management functions. The corporate parent, while imposing financial performance norms and providing general management talent where needed, would make limited demands on the financial resources of its business units and would not directly intervene in the strategic management of individual business units.

Improving Capital Allocations by Forming an Internal Capital Market

Internal capital markets may overcome capital market failures in some cases.

In finance theory, it is usually assumed that capital markets are *efficient* in the sense that investors have all available information about the value of an asset—that is, about the cash flows that can be derived from an asset now and in the future. In capital budgeting theory, it is further assumed that financial markets can correctly appraise the risk of a firm's projects to pursue growth opportunities and will efficiently fund any growth project that promises a positive net present value (NPV).

In practice, however, *information asymmetries* may exist between a firm and financial markets, and in certain circumstances, the managers of a firm may have information that investors in financial markets do not have. When such information asymmetries exist, capital markets cannot be perfectly efficient and thus may not correctly appraise the value of a firm or its projects. In such cases financial markets may not provide investment funds to a firm for its positive NPV growth projects, thus creating a *market failure* in funding positive NPV growth projects. Alternatively, with only an incomplete or perhaps even incorrect understanding of a firm's growth projects, financial markets may demand an inappropriate rate of return for investment funds, leading to *inefficient allocation of capital* to firms.

To illustrate these impacts of information asymmetry through an example, suppose that a firm discovered a new technology that can be the basis for a promising new product and that the firm needs new financial resources to fully commercialize its technology and new products. The managers of the firm may be reluctant to tell potential investors in financial markets about this new opportunity, however, because they may fear that word of the discovery would leak to competitors who could try to replicate the firm's new technology and perhaps beat the firm to market with new products. In such cases, managers may try to carry out the project using only internally generated cash flows, thereby increasing the potential for commercial failure of the project because of inadequate funding. Worse yet, they may simply abandon the project as financially infeasible, leading to a market failure in funding a positive NPV project. Alternatively, managers may provide only partial information about the project to financial markets, which may then demand a higher rate of return to compensate for a greater perceived riskiness of the project, resulting in inefficient allocation of risk capital to the firm.

Under such conditions, a second nontraditional kind of synergy may be created when corporate strategic managers use the cash flows from the corporate parent's business units to fund the most promising projects for growth and value creation within the corporate portfolio. The managers of a business unit should not fear the leaking of sensitive information to competitors if they fully reveal their new growth opportunity to the strategic managers of the corporate parent that owns their business unit. With complete information about its business units' growth projects, corporate strategic managers should be able to direct available cash flows to the most promising, greatest NPV growth projects in the corporate portfolio. In effect, corporate strategic managers should be able to use cash flows from multiple business units to create an efficient *internal capital market* that can avoid market failures and inefficiencies in funding growth projects.

Some important intrinsic limitations, however, restrict the ability of an internal capital market to function more efficiently than external financial markets. As suggested in Figure 12.4, in an internal capital market, business units in a corporate portfolio are

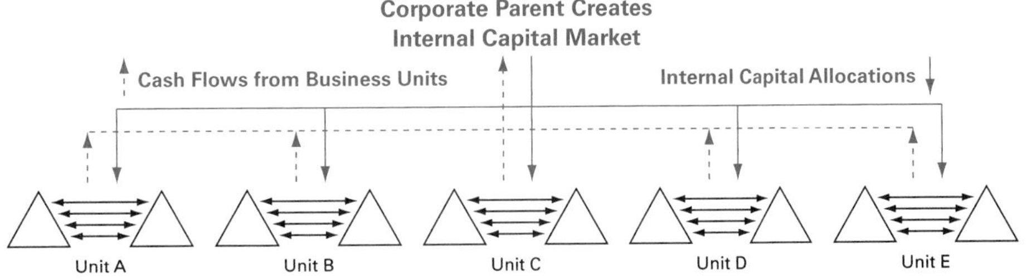

FIGURE 12.4 Creating an Internal Capital Market for Funding Growth Projects

effectively sending part or even all of their available cash flows to the corporate parent for reallocation to the most promising, greatest NPV projects in the corporate portfolio. Strategic managers of individual business units must then compete against other business units in attracting investment funds from the corporate parent to their business unit. In this situation, business unit strategic managers who want to secure corporate funds to grow their businesses have an incentive to put the best positive "spin" on their requests for investment funds. In some cases, strategic managers of business units may feel they must overstate the potential for growth and value creation of their projects in order to have any chance of securing corporate funding.

If corporate strategic managers do not have enough understanding of the product markets, technologies, and other aspects of each of the business units in the corporate portfolio to independently and correctly evaluate the investment proposals put forward by managers of business units, the risk is then that they will allocate investment funds to business units whose managers painted the rosiest picture of their growth prospects, rather than to the business units that actually have the best growth prospects. In the worst cases, an internal capital market will allocate capital to the "biggest liars" rather than to the best projects, leading to failures and inefficiencies in an internal capital market. Moreover, the potential for failure and inefficiency in an internal capital market process increases with the extent of diversification of a corporate portfolio. In effect, the less the business units in a corporate portfolio have in common, the less likely it is that corporate strategic managers can understand each business well enough to make correct evaluations of investment proposals from each business unit, and the more likely the internal capital market will experience failures and inefficiencies.

In the final analysis, internal capital markets may function more efficiently than external capital markets when (i) there are strategic reasons for maintaining information asymmetries between a business unit and external capital markets, *and* (ii) when business units in the corporate portfolio are sufficiently closely related that corporate strategic managers can understand the different businesses in the corporate portfolio well enough to make correct (efficient) internal capital allocations.

Reducing Financial Risk by Creating a Diversified Portfolio of Businesses

A third set of ideas for creating a nontraditional kind of synergy concerns the potential for reducing the financial risk faced by a corporate parent that creates a "well-diversified" portfolio of business units. The basis for diversification in this case may be *geographic diversification, diversification into countercyclical product markets,* or simply the *diversifying away of nonsystematic financial risk.* Each of these forms of diversification is intended to achieve essentially the same synergy effect—a balancing or "smoothing" of overall corporate revenues and profit streams that lowers financial risk (i.e., variability of financial returns) and provides more stable cash flows for making sustained investments in projects for growth. These approaches are sometimes espoused by some corporate managers, but several reasons encourage caution and even skepticism about the potential for achieving synergies through these approaches to diversification. Let us consider each approach in turn.

Geographic Diversification

Geographic diversification may reduce the risk of economic cycles.

We previously discussed geographic expansion within domestic markets or to international markets as the first approach to growth pursued by many firms. Geographic expansion may also be motivated, however, by the desires to reduce a firm's dependency on economic fluctuations in one geographic market and to achieve greater stability in a firm's overall business by generating revenues in more than one geographic region of the world. The basic assumption behind this approach is that different geographic markets experience different economic cycles that tend to lag each other, as suggested in Figure 12.5. When regional economic cycles do lag behind each other, a macroeconomic downturn in one region that leads to reductions in a firm's sales in that region may be offset by another region's upswing in macroeconomic conditions and a corresponding rise in sales by the firm. Overall sales and profit streams of a geographically diversified firm would then be "smoothed" or stabilized by these offsetting conditions, thereby reducing financial risk.

In some cases, geographic diversification resulted in this desired effect. In the automobile industry in the turbulent 1970s and 1980s, for example, wide fluctuations occurred in demand levels in North America and Europe, but, in general, North American macroeconomic cycles tended to lead those in Europe by 18 to 24 months. As a result, both Ford and General Motors were able to weather a number of severe downturns in the North American market because of continuing demand in their European markets, and then to offset declining sales in Europe later with a subsequent upswing in demand in North America.

Today, however, the major economic regions of the world are becoming more economically integrated, and the historic lags in one region's economic cycle relative to the other major regions are shortening or even disappearing. As the interdependencies of the world's major economic regions deepen, the potential for geographic diversification to moderate swings in a firm's overall revenues and profit streams is diminishing. Corporate strategic managers interested in diversifying away risk through geographic diversification must carefully examine recent macroeconomic cycles in various regions to determine the extent to which offsetting demand cycles still exist in those product markets.

Product Market Diversification

A second, related idea for reducing corporate risk is diversification into product markets that exhibit countercyclical patterns of demand fluctuation. For example, in the 1960s International Harvester Corporation diversified into trucks, farm equipment, and earthmoving equipment for the construction industry. Historically, manufacturing (the market sector that creates the major demand for trucks), agriculture, and construction had followed demand cycles that lagged each other by many months, and this historic countercyclical market behavior suggested a basis for diversifying away risk by participating in the three

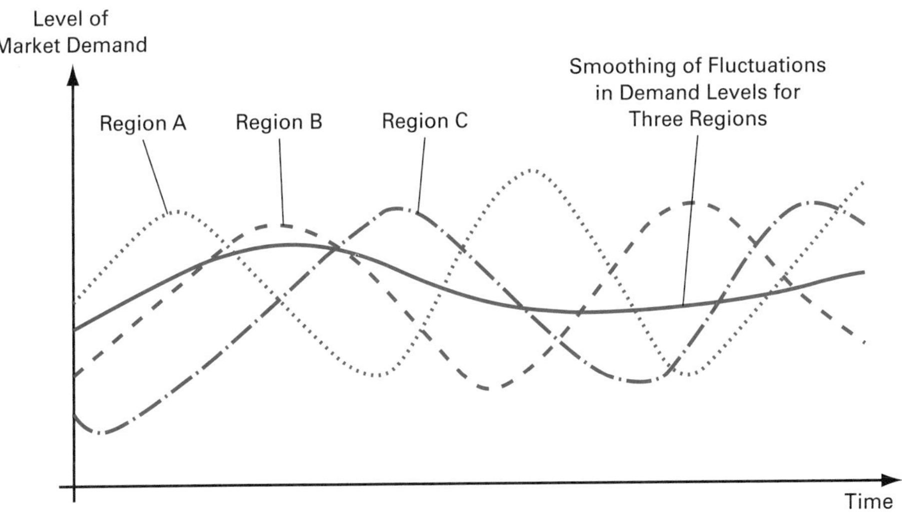

FIGURE 12.5 Smoothing of Demand Levels through Geographic Diversification

product markets. In the 1970s, however, for the first time in history, demand in all three markets declined at the same time, and International Harvester found itself ill prepared financially to cope with a decline in all three markets. As a result, the company was forced to sell off its farm and construction equipment businesses in order to continue its truck business. International Harvester's experience suggests that historic patterns of countercyclical demand behavior in product markets are not always a reliable predictor of future patterns in demand, and this lack of predictability should limit corporate strategic managers' use of product market diversification as an approach to moderating financial risk.

Diversifying Away Nonsystematic Risk

The third idea for reducing financial risk is that a corporate parent can simply form a highly diversified portfolio of companies that will diversify away the nonsystematic risk of the companies.[2] Corporate strategic managers may then create value by raising investment capital on favorable terms and making effective internal capital allocations to business units in the corporate portfolio. This idea has been discredited both theoretically and in practice. Implicit in this idea is the belief that a large diversified firm will incur a lower cost of capital than a smaller single-business firm. Let us consider the two supposed beneficial effects of size and extent of diversification in this assumption.

One might think that large firms would have a lower cost of capital than small firms because large firms have lower risk of bankruptcy—that is, a lower probability that an investment in the shares of a large firm will become completely worthless. One could argue therefore that large firms face lower risk in achieving long-term growth and share price appreciation than small firms, which tend to have high failure rates. In fact, both the risk of bankruptcy and the potential for growth of a given firm are nonsystematic aspects of the risk of investing in the shares of a firm and thus can be diversified away by investors by forming a well-diversified portfolio of shares. Thus, in efficient financial markets, investors will not have incentives to extend a lower cost of capital to a firm simply because it is large, or to demand a higher rate of return from a firm simply because it is small.[3]

Making good capital allocations to a diversified portfolio of business units is difficult.

The creation of a well-diversified corporate portfolio is also unlikely to result in an ability to attract capital at low cost or to make efficient internal capital allocations. In the first instance, to form a diversified portfolio requires investing in starting up new businesses internally or acquiring existing firms. As we discussed in Chapter 11, starting a new business internally to enter a market is likely to require making significant up-front investments in the *sunk costs* of building market share and output levels required to attain the minimum efficient scale (MES) needed for a sustainable cost position in that industry.

[2] Portfolio theory in finance holds that a portfolio of shares in unrelated businesses (in effect, shares of firms in industries whose returns are uncorrelated) can diversify away the "nonsystematic" commercial risk specific to each company, leaving only the nondiversifiable "systematic" risk of overall movement in the macroeconomy and its resulting impact on returns earned by all firms in the economy. A portfolio of 32 uncorrelated securities would, on average, diversify away virtually all the nonsystematic risk of the securities. The returns earned by this portfolio of securities would then essentially follow the movement of returns earned in the economy as a whole. This portfolio would then have a "Beta" approaching 1, which denotes a risk level identical to that of the market for all risky assets.

[3] By implication, in *inefficient and imperfectly competitive* financial markets, large firms may be able to attract capital on more favorable terms than smaller firms. For example, in the 1950s to 1990s, large firms in Japan were able to attract capital on favorable terms from a closely controlled and government-influenced capital allocation system led by a few large banks closely linked to the large firms. Smaller enterprises were often either shut out of capital markets altogether or were forced to raise investment funds at high costs outside the established financial system. However, the long-term consequences of this system of preferential capital allocation are now evident in the deep stagnation of the Japanese economy, which lacks institutions and mechanisms for efficient capital allocation to Japan's best value-creation opportunities.

Alternatively, acquiring an existing company normally requires paying an *acquisition premium*—an additional amount over current share price that must be paid to persuade current shareholders to sell their shares to an acquiring firm. In either case, corporate strategic managers must be able to find enough synergies to create the extra returns required on the capital they have invested either in the sunk costs of an internal expansion or in the acquisition premium paid in taking over an established firm.

As we discussed previously, however, corporate strategic managers are not likely to possess adequate knowledge of all the businesses represented in a well-diversified portfolio. They are therefore not likely to be able to make the optimal capital allocations needed to earn above-average returns from the many different firms that must be started or acquired to create a diversified portfolio. In fact, the track record of highly diversified corporations—especially the conglomerates of the 1960s and 1970s—in creating synergies is quite poor, and in many cases ended in major corporate failures and crises. In addition, as finance theory reminds us, individual investors could easily form well-diversified portfolios by throwing darts at the stock market pages of the *New York Times* or *Financial Times* to randomly select stocks, or perhaps more reasonably by simply buying shares in a mutual fund based on a well-diversified selection of stocks. In this way, investors can avoid paying up-front sunk costs or acquisition premiums in creating portfolios that diversify away nonsystematic risk. For these reasons, at least in economies with efficient financial markets, the notion that corporate strategic managers can create value by acting as market intermediaries in establishing diversified portfolios is essentially discredited, although one can still occasionally read statements by some managers indicating that this is what their corporate strategy intends to do.

12.7 THE OPTIMAL EXTENT OF DIVERSIFICATION

With the foregoing perspectives on both the potential for creating synergies through diversification and the limitations of various kinds of diversification, we turn now to the key issue facing strategic managers of a growing multi-business enterprise: What is the **optimal extent of diversification?** In other words, how unrelated can a corporate portfolio of business units become—and still enable synergies to be found and implemented between business units to create new value within the corporate portfolio?

Answering this question conceptually is fairly straightforward, and we do so by developing a marginal cost-benefit analysis framework for representing net value addition through diversification. Answering this question in practice, however, is usually more difficult, and the search by corporate strategic managers to discover the optimal extent of diversification often motivates an ongoing process of corporate restructuring through both acquisition and divestment of business units.

The Optimal Extent of Diversification—A Conceptual Framework

Our conceptual framework for determining the optimal extent of diversification starts with a basic comparison of the benefits and costs of adding another business unit to a corporate portfolio. In essence, diversifying into another business will create value as long as the "benefits"—the gains from the new synergies that can be created between the new business unit and the other business units in the corporate portfolio—exceed the incremental costs of adding the new business unit to the portfolio. Further, we can reasonably assume that the synergy benefits obtainable from adding a new business unit that is highly related to other business units in the corporate portfolio will be greater than the benefits that can be obtained from adding a business unit that is less related to business units already in the corporate portfolio. In addition, some incremental costs of adding another business unit to a corporate portfolio may be expected to increase as the number of business units in the corporate portfolio increases. However, some incremental costs of adding more business units may remain constant, and some incremental costs may even decrease. Let us now use Figure 12.6 to explore the implications of these assumptions and expectations in determining the optimal extent of diversification.

In Figure 12.6, the marginal synergy benefit from diversification (MSBD) curve represents the potential for obtaining synergies by adding additional business units to the corporate portfolio. The horizontal axis in Figure 12.6 starts on the left with highly related business units, moves through progressively less-related business units in the middle of the axis, and ends with completely unrelated business units on the right. The downward slope of the MSBD curve indicates that the less related a new business unit is to the other business units in the corporate portfolio, the smaller will be the potential synergies obtainable from the diversification.[4]

The two dashed marginal cost of diversification (MCD) curves in Figure 12.6 indicate the possibilities that the marginal costs of adding another business unit may increase, may remain more or less constant, or may decrease. In effect, depending on how effective corporate strategic managers are in managing the incremental costs of adding another business unit to the corporate portfolio, the MCD curve for a given firm could be anywhere in the range shown between the "MCD (Increasing) curve" and the "MCD (Decreasing) curve" shown in Figure 12.6. To understand why the MCD curve for a given firm may be anywhere in this range, we need to consider the various kinds of incremental costs that may be incurred in growing through diversification, and the potential for corporate strategic managers to manage those costs well or poorly.

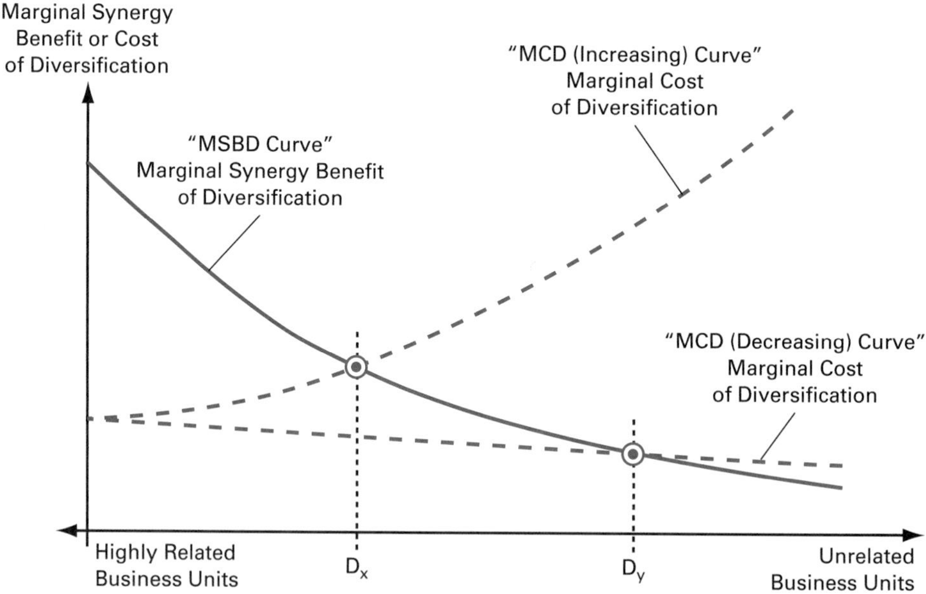

FIGURE 12.6 Marginal Cost-Benefit Analysis for Determining the Optimal Extent of Diversification

[4] This relationship, of course, follows from our assumption that the more related a new business unit is to the other business units in the corporate portfolio, the greater will be the potential synergies obtainable from the diversification.

Costs of Diversification

Several kinds of costs are incurred in diversifying.

As the number of business units in a corporate portfolio increases, several direct and indirect costs may be incurred by a corporate parent in its efforts to identify and achieve synergies among the business units. Direct costs may increase as corporate staff members are added to carry on the search for synergies and to help implement sustainable processes for achieving synergies. Direct costs also include any sunk costs incurred in an internal start-up or any takeover premiums paid in an acquisition. Having more business units may also lead to higher costs of establishing the coordination within business units needed to identify and implement synergies.

Indirect costs may also become important, especially as the business units in a growing corporate portfolio become less and less related. If corporate strategic managers try to create an internal capital market to allocate capital to unrelated business units, business unit managers competing to obtain investment funds from the corporate parent may prepare capital budgeting requests that contain distorted information. If corporate strategic managers rely on distorted information, they are likely to make ineffective capital allocations. Managers of business units that do not receive their desired level of investment funding may then lose their motivation to identify and exploit opportunities to create value within their business units. In addition, when corporate strategic managers fail to identify and achieve all the potential synergies between a newly started or acquired business unit and other business units in the corporate portfolio, the potential synergies that are not achieved represent an indirect cost of ineffective corporate strategic management.

Although it is likely that the direct and indirect costs of diversification will increase *in the aggregate* as the number of business units in a portfolio increases, it is less clear whether *incremental* costs will increase, remain more or less constant, or perhaps decrease as the size of a corporate portfolio increases. Whether direct and indirect costs of adding another business unit to a corporate portfolio increase or decrease depends greatly on the capabilities of corporate strategic managers in minimizing those costs.

Incremental direct costs of diversification may decrease when corporate strategic managers can recognize and achieve economies of learning and scope in the search for synergies by corporate staff and economies of scale in the corporate infrastructure used to help implement synergies. In essence, effective corporate strategic managers may be able to learn how to create methods and processes in their search for synergies that lead to lower incremental costs for each new business unit added to the corporate portfolio. By the same token, less effective corporate strategic managers may lack an understanding of how to organize the search for synergy efficiently, and may face rising incremental costs with each addition to the corporate portfolio. Corporate strategic managers may also realize economies of learning as they gain experience in adding new business units to the corporate portfolio. With each new start-up or acquisition, they may learn new ways to minimize the sunk costs or the takeover premiums incurred in acquiring new businesses, leading to declining startup or acquisition costs.

Similarly, corporate strategic managers of a highly diversified portfolio of businesses may realize that they are not really able to correctly evaluate capital budgeting requests from many different kinds of businesses. They may therefore decide not to establish an internal capital allocation process, but simply to consolidate all positive NPV capital budgeting requests from business units and seek capital from financial markets on more favorable terms than would be available to individual business units in the portfolio. This essentially *holding company* approach to managing the corporate capital allocation process may avoid the information distortion and managerial loss of motivation that usually results from an ineffective internal capital allocation process. Similarly, some corporate strategic managers may develop superior abilities to find and achieve synergies between new business units and existing businesses in the corporate portfolio—for example by developing superior capabilities in integrating acquired companies.

If corporate strategic managers are able to reduce the incremental costs of further diversification in these ways, then the MCD curve in Figure 12.6 will be downward sloping. In this case, the optimal extent of diversification for their firm will be greater than for firms with less capable strategic managers.

Defining the Optimal Extent of Diversification

The optimal extent of diversification ultimately depends on the capabilities of corporate strategic managers.

The optimal extent of diversification for a growing firm will depend on the capabilities of its corporate strategic managers in fully exploiting the potential synergies and minimizing the costs of diversification. Thus, the optimal extent of diversification will vary from one firm to another, as suggested in Figure 12.6. For a firm with increasing incremental costs of diversification—for example, a firm on the "MCD (Increasing) curve"—the optimal extent of diversification will be at D_x, and growth beyond a modest group of related businesses would begin to decrease value. For a firm whose strategic managers have achieved decreasing incremental costs of diversification—for example, a firm on the "MCD (Decreasing) curve"—the optimal extent of diversification will be at D_y. That firm may grow to include a large number of related and unrelated businesses before further diversification would lead to a decrease in value.

The Optimal Extent of Diversification—Some Practical Issues

In Chapter 11 and in this chapter, we surveyed the kinds of synergies that may be obtained through diversification. The conceptual framework for determining the optimal extent of diversification developed here identified a number of costs of that must be managed in diversifying. Even though both the synergies and the costs of diversifying may be readily understood conceptually, in practice fully exploiting the synergies and minimizing the costs of diversification are challenging tasks. In effect, diversification is not a science, and finding the optimal extent of diversification for a given company is often a process of trial and error. In practice, both the value of the synergies thought to be obtainable from a new business unit and the incremental costs of adding a new business unit may be difficult to determine.

Corporate restructuring is a normal part of the search for the optimal extent of diversification.

Although the need for a thorough analysis of potential synergies and costs before adding a new business unit to the corporate portfolio is clear, sometimes the actual synergies obtainable or real costs to be incurred cannot be fully ascertained until a business unit is actually added to a corporate portfolio. Thus, as firms grow through diversification, they typically go through a process of continual *restructuring of the corporate portfolio*—adding and removing business units—to converge to the optimal extent of diversification. Moreover, as a firm's macroenvironment, industry, and product markets evolve, the potential for synergies and the costs of realizing synergies are also likely to change, leading to further additions to or removals from the corporate portfolio. Thus, restructuring the corporate portfolio is a "natural" part of efforts by corporate strategic managers to discover the optimal extent of diversification for a given firm.

12.8 THE OPTIMAL EXTENT OF INTEGRATION IN MERGERS AND ACQUISITIONS

Mergers and acquisitions play an increasingly important role as mechanisms for sustaining growth through diversification. Mergers and acquisitions offer a number of advantages over starting new business units internally. For example, merging with or acquiring an existing business usually offers the advantage of speed in gaining a market position, new products, technology, customer relationships, or other resources that would normally take years to develop through an internal start-up. In some cases, especially when a market is already "saturated" with incumbent firms, it is simply not economically feasible to enter a market through a start-up, and merger or acquisition are the only options for expansion into the market.

In spite of these potential advantages, however, actually achieving net gains in synergy through mergers and acquisitions is often challenging, because corporate strategic managers must also determine the **optimal extent of integration** to pursue in a merged or acquired business unit. Corporate strategic managers must understand clearly which resources within a merger or acquisition candidate are sources of value-adding synergies. They must then identify the linkages that must be established between the merger or acquisition candidate and the business units already in the corporate portfolio in order to obtain the intended synergies. Integration efforts after the merger or acquisition must then be prioritized and focused on promptly putting in place the key linkages between business units that are essential to obtaining the intended synergies.

The optimal extent of integration is usually not total integration.

Note that this logic suggests that the optimal extent of post-merger and post-acquisition integration will not be complete integration, but rather that corporate strategic managers must follow a *selective* approach to post-merger and post-acquisition integration. Rarely, if ever, will it be necessary or desirable to integrate all activities, assets, and management processes of a merged or acquired firm with those of other business units in a corporate portfolio. In some cases, the costs of integrating an activity would simply exceed the synergy benefits that might be obtained thereby. In other cases, maintaining effective local responsiveness in the merged or acquired firm's operations is critical, as we shall see in our discussion of global strategy in Chapter 13. Thus, when using mergers and acquisitions to sustain value-adding growth through diversification, corporate strategic managers must understand clearly which resources, activities, and processes to integrate (and in what order)—and what not to try to integrate when merging with or acquiring a new business unit.

KEY TERMS AND CONCEPTS

domestic expansion Starting additional business units based on the same Strategic Logic within a single national market.

international expansion Starting business units beyond the borders of the home country of a business unit and adapting the business units' Strategic Logic to local conditions in other countries.

horizontal integration Acquisition of additional business units in the same level of the vertical structure of an industry.

diversification The addition to a corporate portfolio of a business unit in a product market that is different from the product markets currently served by the business units already in the corporate portfolio.

related diversification Creation or acquisition of business units with common activities that enable the creation of synergies through shared activities and transferable knowledge, capabilities, or relationships.

unrelated diversification Creation or acquisition of business units with limited potential for achieving synergies through shared activities or transfers of knowledge, capabilities, or relationships.

optimal extent of diversification The point in the growth of a firm through diversification at which the marginal synergy benefit of diversification by adding another business unit equals the marginal cost of diversification incurred in adding the business unit.

optimal extent of integration The integration of elements of a merged or acquired business unit with other business units in the corporate portfolio until the cost of further integration exceeds the synergy benefit achieved by further integration.

REVIEW QUESTIONS

1. Why do many firms tend to follow the historical pattern of growth shown in Figure 12.1?
2. What factors may invite a modification of a firm's Strategic Logic as it expands internationally?
3. What challenges and limitations may a firm face as it tries to grow through horizontal integration?
4. What are the key challenges in vertically integrating upstream?
5. Why do firms try to vertically integrate downstream?
6. What is the difference between related and unrelated diversification?
7. Under what circumstances might internal capital markets function more efficiently than external capital markets?
8. What problems do firms encounter in pursuing unrelated diversification?
9. Why is total integration *not* likely to be the optimal extent of integration of an acquired or merged company?

PART VI

GLOBAL STRATEGY

CHAPTER 13

THE SEARCH FOR SYNERGY IN AN INTERNATIONAL CONTEXT

INTRODUCTION

In Chapter 11, we characterized corporate strategic management as a search for synergy, and we investigated various kinds of synergies and ways that corporate strategic managers may try to achieve those synergies. In Chapter 12, we discussed some common patterns that a growing, diversifying multibusiness enterprise would be likely to follow in its search for synergy. In this chapter, we will characterize a firm's *global strategy* as its *search for synergy in an international context.* We examine in greater detail some further incentives for and constraints on achieving synergies through corporate growth and diversification into international product and resource markets.

We first describe a number of early strategy theories about why firms seek to expand their value-creation processes beyond their domestic markets to international locations. We point out several conceptual similarities in these early theories with the competence perspective on internationalizing value-creation processes that we present in this chapter. We then develop a competence-based view of why firms undertake international operations, as well as some basic reasons why firms either *centralize* or *localize* specific processes in their international operations. We discuss several sources of potential gains in synergy that may be available to firms that centralize certain of their international value-creation processes. We also consider a number of constraints that may limit the ability of an international firm to fully exploit those potential gains in synergies. We then examine some reasons why localizing certain activities may be the most effective approach—or in some cases, the only feasible approach—to creating value through international operations.

We then explain the primary task of global strategic managers as finding the *optimal balance* between centralization and localization of activities in international value-creation processes. We explain why the search to optimize the effectiveness of a firm's international value-creation processes leads to the adoption of *hybrid global organization designs* in which certain activities are carried out centrally on a global or regional basis, while other activities are carried out locally at a national level. We conclude with an example that illustrates how Caterpillar Corporation's global strategy seeks to optimize its value-creation processes through a hybrid global organization design for its international earth-moving equipment business.

13.1 EARLY THEORIES OF INTERNATIONALIZATION

Although some firms developed extensive international operations in the first half of the twentieth century, the post-World War II era from the 1950s onward was the most active period of internationalization in the history of business. American firms, which emerged from World War II with their factories and industrial infrastructure intact, actively expanded their marketing and then production activities to countries in Europe, Asia, and other parts of the world in the 1950s to 1970s. Then, as the national economies of Europe and Japan were rebuilt, firms based in those countries also joined the movement to expand broadly into international operations.

During this period of increasing internationalization, a number of theories were put forward to explain why firms were expanding internationally—or why they should do so. We next summarize some of these early theories of internationalization. We also mention some conceptual similarities of those theories to today's competence perspective on internationalization, and we consider the extent to which the theories are still applicable to international business in contemporary settings.

The Product Cycle Theory of Internationalization

The product cycle theory of internationalization is quite different from the product life cycle model of product market evolution that we discussed in Chapter 9. The product cycle theory was advanced by the international business scholar Raymond Vernon in the 1960s and sought to express a motive commonly observed in U.S. companies for expanding into overseas markets at the time.[1] This theory basically held that companies develop new products to be competitive in markets in the developed economies. As a product begins to obsolesce and gradually loses its competitiveness in those markets, according to the theory, it may still be exported to markets in less-developed economies where it would still be regarded as attractive. As the product ages further and becomes progressively more obsolete in the second-tier economies of the world, it could still be marketed in third-tier economies of the world until the end of its commercial lifetime.

In essence, the product cycle theory explains how firms can try to leverage their competences as extensively as possible by extending the marketing of their developed products to all corners of the world. This theory still has considerable validity. Many firms in advanced economies today do successfully export their older product designs to developing economies or set up factories to manufacture them there. For example, Volkswagen still produces and markets successfully its classic Beetle car in Mexico, even though sales of the model were discontinued in the United States in the mid-1970s. Volkswagen also produced a late 1970s-vintage Santana automobile model in China during the 1980s and 1990s.

Rising incomes around the world impose some new limitations on the product cycle theory.

However, there are some important limitations to this theory as well. As rising incomes in developing economies around the world bring more people in second- and third-tier economies into middle and upper-middle income levels, consumers are becoming better educated, are more likely to have worked or studied in the developed countries, and are increasingly demanding products that more nearly match the performance and quality standards of products sold in the developed economies. Such consumers are now likely to spurn older product designs and to demand affordable versions of products whose design and performance levels are more comparable to products sold in the developed economies. In India today, for example, consumers in the rapidly growing middle class demand smaller affordable cars that nevertheless provide performance and styling comparable to cars currently sold in Europe and North America, where many middle-class Indians commonly travel on work or pleasure trips. A net effect of rising affluence globally is often to shorten the commercial life cycle for products exported to second- and third-tier economies.

[1] See, for example, Vernon, R. (1966). International Investment and International Trade in the Product Cycle. *Quarterly Journal of Economics,* May, 190–207.

Maintaining a "Non-Expiring Bargain" with Host Countries

In the 1950s and 1960s, before the advent of free trade and open-door policies promoted through GATT (General Agreement on Trade and Tariffs) and its successor WTO (World Trade Organization), it was common for firms that wanted to do business in a foreign country to negotiate with governments of potential host countries to obtain licenses to operate in those countries. Even when licenses were obtained and investments in factories and other facilities were made, firms often faced an ongoing threat that their businesses could subsequently be nationalized (expropriated or otherwise taken over) by host country governments.

In this environment, the international business theorist Raymond Vernon further proposed that a firm that seeks to operate internationally must be capable of maintaining a "non-expiring bargain" with host country governments. In effect, to obtain licenses to operate in a foreign country, a firm must bargain with host country governments and convince them that it will bring them new capabilities and revenue-producing activities that would significantly benefit the host country economy. Moreover, if a firm succeeds in obtaining permission to operate in a country, to minimize the risk of a subsequent takeover of its business by a host country government, a firm must be able to continue to provide economic benefits to the host country that exceed the benefits the host country government might obtain if it were simply to take over the firm's business in the country.

Clearly, concepts of competence leveraging and building lie at the core of Vernon's theory of a non-expiring bargain. In Vernon's theory, a firm must have some competences that it can leverage in a local economy and that render it a productive and desirable addition to a host country economy. In addition, a firm must be able to improve its competences over time within a country in order to maintain a non-expiring bargain and remain a welcome participant in a country's economy.

Vernon's concept of the "non-expiring bargain" is still relevant today.

Of course, the international business environment has changed considerably since the 1950s and 1960s, but some essential aspects of Vernon's theory of a non-expiring bargain are still applicable to today's international firms. Many governments, especially in developing economies, are afraid—often with good reason—that foreign firms with advanced capabilities could drive less-capable local firms out of business, with resulting loss of local ownership and control of their economies. Most of these countries therefore maintain significant controls on the entry of foreign firms into their economies, and permission to do business in those countries is often granted only after a host government is convinced that a foreign firm will bring a significant net benefit to the national economy.

Even in more advanced economies, tax breaks and other forms of government support may be made available to foreign firms that promise to bring significant additional or new capabilities to a national economy. A firm that offers a credible prospect of valuable technology transfer to a host country—for example, by employing, training, and upgrading the skills of local engineers—may find that potential host governments of several countries will compete to persuade the firm to locate some of its design and development activities in their country.

The Transactions Costs View of Foreign Direct Investment

Building on the transactions costs theory of economic organization developed by Oliver Williamson (discussed in Chapter 2), some international business researchers proposed theories that try to explain when firms should expand internationally through market transactions based on contractual relationships, through joint ventures, or through foreign direct investment (FDI) that sets up wholly owned and managed subsidiaries. The essence of these arguments is that when the potential costs of opportunistic behavior by a party to an incomplete contract for market transactions or a joint venture in a host country are judged to be too great, firms will "internalize" those transactions by setting up their own operations in the host country. On the other hand, when transactions to be undertaken in a foreign country can be adequately specified and controlled through contracts, a firm should prefer to use the greater efficiency of market transactions to organize its business in a foreign country.

Having explicit knowledge creates contractual alternatives to internalization.

An important conceptual linkage between the transactions cost view and the competence perspective on international business concerns the ability of a firm to define, specify, and contract for various kinds of economic activities (the "transactions" in the transactions costs framework) in its global value-creation processes. Within the competence perspective, the managers of a firm that has competences should have good understanding not only about *what* the firm is capable of doing well, but also about *how* the firm is able to do well the activities that it undertakes to perform. When managers of a firm possess such explicit understanding, the firm can then define the kinds of knowledge, skills, and capabilities needed to perform a given activity, and can specify appropriate performance measures to effectively monitor the performance of a given activity. In such cases, managers' abilities to define, specify, and monitor the performance of an activity should enable greater use of contracting as a means of expanding international operations.

An example of this effect is the ability of some firms to use modular architectures to coordinate global networks of component developers in product development processes. As we discussed in Chapter 8, to be able to create a modular product architecture, a firm must be able to decompose an overall product design into functional components and then to fully specify the interfaces between the components in the product. Fully specifying the interfaces for the components to be developed for a new product creates, in effect, a complete set of system specifications for each component, and those specifications then enable a firm to contract with capable component developers anywhere in the world to develop components that meet those specifications. By contrast, if a firm cannot fully define the interface specifications for the new components it wants to have in its new products, then it must try to develop the new components internally or through some kind of strategic partnership with a component developer.

Thus, when a competent organization develops explicit knowledge about how it performs the various activities in its value-creation processes, it may choose to expand internationally through contracting with capable suppliers of specific activities around the world, rather than through foreign direct investment to establish its own internal activities in other countries.

The Opportunistic Growth Theory of International Expansion

Some researchers in international business propose that firms often do not undertake systematic rational analysis of their potential for international expansion, but rather undertake international activities opportunistically as interesting opportunities are encountered in their environments.

This observation opens up at least two interpretations. On the one hand, simply reacting to various opportunities that may be presented to a firm may be a symptom of a lack of a clear Strategic Logic for achieving synergies through international expansion. On the other hand, a firm with the capabilities and motivation needed to respond to unfolding events may be exhibiting strategic flexibilities that enable it to take advantage of unforeseen opportunities. In the first case, the lack of a clear Strategic Logic to guide its international growth may suggest that if a firm actually succeeds in achieving some benefits through opportunistic growth, it is just "lucky." In the second case, achieving synergies through opportunistic international expansion may also have an element of luck—but luck that is in the spirit of the adage, "The harder I try, the luckier I get."

From the competence perspective, the key distinction to be made in this theory of international expansion is that of *intention.* If a firm's managers first build organizational capabilities with the intent of improving a firm's ability to respond successfully to evolving international opportunities, opportunistic growth can be a form of competence leveraging. Alternatively, strategic managers may respond to unforeseen opportunities that call for building new competences "on the fly"—in effect, to learn while doing. In dynamic environments, some measure of both modes of opportunistic international expansion may be useful.

Goshal and Bartlett's Model of Innovation Processes in Multinationals

In the 1980s, Sumantra Goshal and Christopher Bartlett studied a number of multinational firms and identified several patterns in the way the firms organized their innovation processes internationally.[2] Focusing on the three activities of sensing, responding to, and implementing innovation opportunities, Goshal and Bartlett observed that these innovation activities could be undertaken either in a centralized location or in one or more local areas in which the multinationals operated. They then identified four patterns of centralization and localization of innovation activities used by the firms they studied, as summarized in Figure 13.1.

From the competence perspective, the patterns of innovation activities summarized in Figure 13.1 reflect the varying responses of international firms to two essential questions in innovation: (i) How do market preferences and thus innovation opportunities vary from one local area to another? and (ii) Where are the best resources for carrying out a given activity in innovating?

When market preferences for a given type of product do not differ from one locale to another, a central development process may be the most efficient way to create products of that type for marketing around the world. For example, Sony typically develops its new portable personal audio products (e.g., Sony Walkman) in one development center for marketing globally. In other cases, however, local market preferences may vary greatly in various areas around the globe, and the best resources for serving local preferences may also be available in each locale. Food products often meet these two criteria. In this case, innovation

Innovation Pattern	Description of Activities
Center for Global	Central marketing and R&D functions develop products for assembly and/or marketing locally.
Local for Local	Marketing, R&D, and manufacturing functions are all carried out locally.
Local for Global	Development of new products takes place locally, but products are marketed globally.
Global for Global	Local development resources are networked to develop products for global marketing.

FIGURE 13.1 Patterns of Innovation by Multinationals Observed in 1980s

[2] Goshal, S., and C. Bartlett. (1990). Managing Innovation in the Transnational Corporation. In C. Bartlett, Y. Doz, and G. Hedlund (Eds.), *Managing the Global Firm.* London: Routledge.

is likely to follow the local-for-local pattern. In some cases, a locally preferred product may gain wider market acceptance, and a local-for-global innovation process may be effective. In other cases, market preferences may be similar around the world, and good development resources may also be found in several locations of the world, as is the case for many kinds of semiconductors for personal computers and telecommunication products today. In this context, a global-for-global innovation process that coordinates development resources around the world in processes for innovating global products will often be used.

These criteria for configuring innovation processes in international firms help to introduce the contemporary competence perspective on the broader question of organizing value-creation processes in international firms. In the next sections, we extend this perspective on centralization and localization to the full spectrum of value-creation activities.

13.2 CENTRALIZING OR LOCALIZING INTERNATIONAL VALUE-CREATION ACTIVITIES

The key issue in global strategy is whether to centralize or localize an activity.

Global strategy is essentially the search for synergies among business activities carried out in an international setting. Firms may recognize opportunities to create a number of synergy benefits through centralizing certain activities, such as increasing economies of scale by consolidating production in one factory. There may also be various kinds of pressures on a firm to centralize other activities as well. For example, a key resource needed in a given activity may only be available in a specific location, and the activity requiring that resource will have to be centralized at that location. At the same time, several possible opportunities or pressures for localizing a given activity are also likely. Thus, in their efforts to optimize the synergies available to a firm through internationalizing its value-creation activities, strategic managers must weigh the relative advantages and disadvantages of performing each value-creation activity in a centralized location versus performing an activity in the local areas where the firm operates.

The trade-off between centralizing versus localizing is suggested in Figure 13.2. If the opportunities/pressures for centralizing an activity are high, while the opportunities/pressures for localizing are low, strategic managers should elect to centralize an activity. If all the activities in a firm's value-creation processes are performed in a centralized way, we would say that the firm is following a pure **centralization** strategy for internationalizing—sometimes referred to as a pure "global strategy." Conversely, if the opportunities/pressures for centralizing an activity are low, while the opportunities/pressures for localizing are high, strategic managers should elect to localize an activity. If all the activities in a firm's value-creation processes are carried out locally, we would say that the firm is following a pure **localization** strategy for internationalizing—sometimes referred to as a pure "multidomestic strategy." In fact, it would rarely if ever be the case that a firm's strategic managers would elect to carry out all the firm's value-creation activities in a centralized way or in a localized way. Normally, a firm's international value-creating processes will be a mix of centralized and localized activities as managers seek to obtain the greatest possible benefits from performing each activity in the most advantageous way. Thus, most international firms will create "hybrid" global organization designs composed of both centralized and localized activities. Hybrid designs may also include **regionalization** of an activity to serve several countries within a region of the world.

The following two sections discuss the various kinds of opportunities and pressures that firms may face for centralizing or localizing an activity. We then consider how Caterpillar Corporation's strategic managers have sought to optimize the value-creation potential of the firm's earth-moving equipment business by devising a hybrid global organization design for carrying out its value-creation activities internationally.

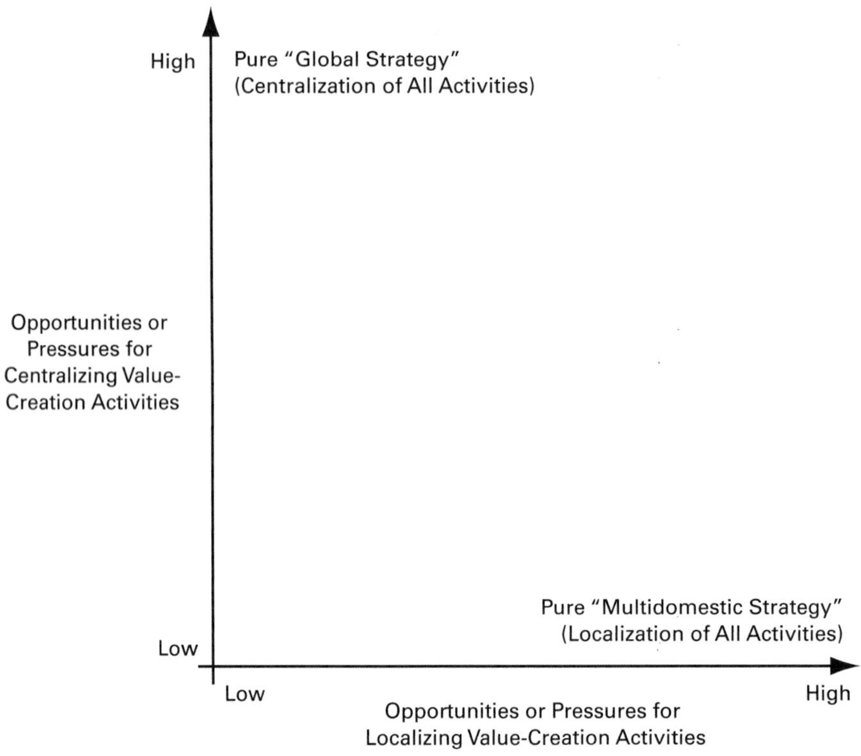

FIGURE 13.2 Centralizing vs. Localizing a Firm's International Value Creation Activities

13.3 OPPORTUNITIES OR PRESSURES FOR CENTRALIZING ACTIVITIES

Three major kinds of opportunities and pressures for centralizing an activity in an international firm include (i) opportunities to create global products; (ii) possible economies of scale, learning, or scope; and (iii) the limited availability of an essential resource in a given value-creation activity. Let us consider each of these opportunities or pressures for centralization in more detail.

Global Products

Some kinds of products can be sold in all or many countries of the world with little or no need for adaptations to meet local market preferences. Such global products include many consumer electronics products (e.g., Sony Walkman products), personal computers, automobiles, office equipment, as well as many luxury goods and industrial goods (motors, pumps, production machines, etc.). Developing global products in one central R&D center is often less costly than carrying out development activities in many local development centers. In addition, concentrating development activities for a global product in one global development center may lead to a deepening of the expertise of the development workers in that center and may help to create a unique set of development capabilities for that type of product.

Economies of Scale, Learning, or Scope

Some activities may offer the potential for achieving significant economies of scale, learning, or scope through centralization of an activity in one location. Centralizing production of a given product, for example, may make possible economies of scale that result in lower unit costs of production. Consolidating production in one central location may also help a firm to achieve economies of learning faster by accelerating the rate at which the firm can move down the learning curve in that production activity. Similarly, productive assets put in place to support a given activity may offer the flexibility to be used in one or more other activities, creating the potential for achieving economies of scope. In such cases, centralizing those other activities so that they can also be performed on the available asset may lead to lower costs for all activities that use the asset. When the potential for such economies exists, strategic managers have an opportunity to lower a firm's costs by centralizing an activity. Such opportunities may become pressures, however, when such economies are also available to competing firms, and when those firms' managers centralize an activity to take advantage of those economies. A firm may then face a competitive pressure to centralize its activities—or else face a cost disadvantage relative to its competitors.

Limited Availability of an Essential Resource

In some cases, a resource that is essential to achieving a competitive advantage in a given value-creation activity may only be available in a specific location. For example, a particularly high-grade ore for making a primary metal may only be available in one location, and centralizing a firm's extraction and refining of ore in that location may lead to cost advantages in the production of the primary metal. Alternatively, the human resources with the skills needed to perform certain activities well may be available in only one location. For example, in the 1970s the strategic managers of Toyota Corporation believed that the human skills and motivations needed to carry out the Toyota production system for assembling high-quality cars existed only in Toyota City, Japan, and in any event could not be replicated outside Japan. (Toyota's managers learned in the 1980s, however, that this belief was mistaken and that workers in the United States and elsewhere could also function effectively in the Toyota production system.) When strategic managers believe that cost, quality, or other advantages can only be obtained by using a resource available in only one location, they will try to centralize that activity to be carried out in that location.

13.4 OPPORTUNITIES OR PRESSURES FOR LOCALIZING ACTIVITIES

Several reasons also explain why localizing a given activity may be the most advantageous way to carry out that activity internationally. Localization may be the best way to perform an activity (i) when there are strong local market preferences with respect to a product, (ii) when transportation costs are high relative to economies of scale available, (iii) when the resources useful in a given activity are available in many locations, (iv) when a host government's laws or regulations require performing a given activity locally, and (v) when close and prompt customer support is critical to the competitive success of a product.

Local Market Preferences

In some product markets, the preferences of customers vary significantly from one locale to another. For example, preferences for food, clothing, personal care products, and furniture vary greatly across countries and regions of the world. In such product markets, marketing research must be undertaken locally to identify local market preferences. To serve local market preferences effectively, products must be defined and often designed and developed locally to match the specific preferences of customers in each local area. Production may also be carried out locally, especially when essential inputs to production are only available locally, as is often the case with food products. In such cases, the firm will face significant pressures to carry out these value-creation activities locally rather than in a centralized way.

High Relative Transportation Costs

Products differ greatly in their value-to-weight or value-to-volume ratios. A pallet load (approximately one cubic meter or 30 cubic feet) of microprocessors, for example, would have a market value many thousands of times greater than the market value of a pallet load of bricks. When a product has low value-to-weight or value-to-volume ratios, shipping costs may become a major part of the total cost of the product delivered to a customer. In such cases, local production that minimizes transportation costs is likely to be preferable to centralized production that would require shipping low-value products for great distances. In essence, the potential cost savings realized through economies of scale in a centralized production process must be weighed against the lower costs of shipping products that would result from localized production.

Widely Available Resources

When important inputs to product creation and realization processes are available in several locations of the world, it may be advantageous to source those inputs wherever capable, cost-effective resources are available. Local sourcing may be undertaken in several locations of the world to obtain the best raw materials for a production process. Increasingly, local sourcing may also be motivated by the desire—and competitive necessity—of accessing the best human resources possible for a firm's value-creation activities. For example, firms in high-technology businesses today commonly maintain development activities in several areas of the world where technical talent is currently located.

Host Government Laws and Regulations

Today, governments of some countries demand that firms in certain industries, seeking access to their markets, must carry out value-adding activities within their borders. Governments concerned about *import substitution*—the replacement of domestic production of goods by imported goods—may require firms to produce their goods within the country they wish to sell in. Other governments are interested in benefiting from transfers of technology from firms that want access to their markets, and may require that those firms establish research and development or other technology-intensive activities in their countries. In other cases, some governments maintain a policy of requiring foreign firms to form joint ventures with local partners to carry out activities in their country. In their concern to maintain employment and improve domestic capabilities, some host governments routinely impose these and other constraints on foreign firms to require localization of activities, even when a firm may prefer to centralize a given activity.

Speed in Providing Customer Support

In many product markets today, providing close, prompt customer support is a competitive necessity and is therefore an integral part of a successful firm's Business Concept. Customer support for an intangible, intellectual product like computer software may be provided to customers from a central location that serves customers around the world 24 hours a day. Several such centers exist in India today, for example, to provide round-the-clock customer support services to users of information systems around the world. Tangible products and services that become integrated into a customer's own processes, however, are likely to require locating customer support activities near to customers in order to maintain fast response to customer problems and requests. In some cases, an international firm may be able to subcontract with a local technical firm to provide routine support services such as scheduled maintenance and minor repairs to products. For support that is considered "mission critical" (i.e., vital to maintaining a customer's own value-creation processes), it usually may be necessary to maintain a local presence to support customers promptly wherever they may be in the world.

13.5 CREATING HYBRID GLOBAL ORGANIZATION DESIGNS FOR INTERNATIONAL VALUE-CREATION PROCESSES

Hybrid global organization designs combine centralization, regionalization, and localization of activities.

As a firm expands its activities internationally, strategic managers must weigh the benefits of centralization against the benefits or requirements of localization for each activity in the firm's value-creation activities. This process involves a series of decisions about the most advantageous way to perform each value-creation activity, and leads to a hybrid global organization design in which some activities will be centralized, some activities may be regionalized (i.e., centralized on a regional basis), and other activities will be localized. The objective of a **hybrid global organization design** is to maximize the overall benefits to a firm of centralizing or localizing each activity within the firm's international value-creation processes.

As an illustration, consider the hybrid organization design used by Caterpillar Corporation in its international earth-moving equipment business. As shown in Figure 13.3, Caterpillar has analyzed each of the activities involved in producing earth-moving equipment and supporting customers in their use of Caterpillar equipment, and decided whether on balance it would be better to centralize, regionalize, or localize each activity. Development of new technologies and new products is largely centralized in the immediate area around the company's headquarters in Peoria, Illinois, USA, because the company believes it creates world-leading technology development capabilities in the company's development centers there. Production of high-technology, high-value components such as diesel engines and hydraulic systems is also centralized in large-scale automated production facilities in the Peoria area, which enables Caterpillar to achieve significant economies of scale while maintaining extremely high quality levels.

Caterpillar's earth-moving products are designed for various kinds of uses and must perform in different climatic conditions in the various geographic areas the company serves. In Australia, for example, Caterpillar equipment is used primarily in mining operations, in Brazil for building roads and logging, and in the United States for performing various earth-moving tasks in construction projects. Because local needs and preferences for Caterpillar equipment vary considerably around the world, and because the various attachments, such as bulldozer blades and front-loader buckets required for different uses, are relatively low value-to-weight items, Caterpillar has localized the production of those attachments needed to adapt Caterpillar equipment to local use requirements.

Caterpillar equipment is typically "mission critical" in Caterpillar's customers' businesses. If a bulldozer breaks down on a construction project, for example, the interruption could cost many thousands of dollars if work is stopped and completion of a customer's project is delayed. Thus, one of the important elements in Caterpillar's Business Concept is a service guarantee that promises on-site repairs within 24 hours (or 48 hours in some

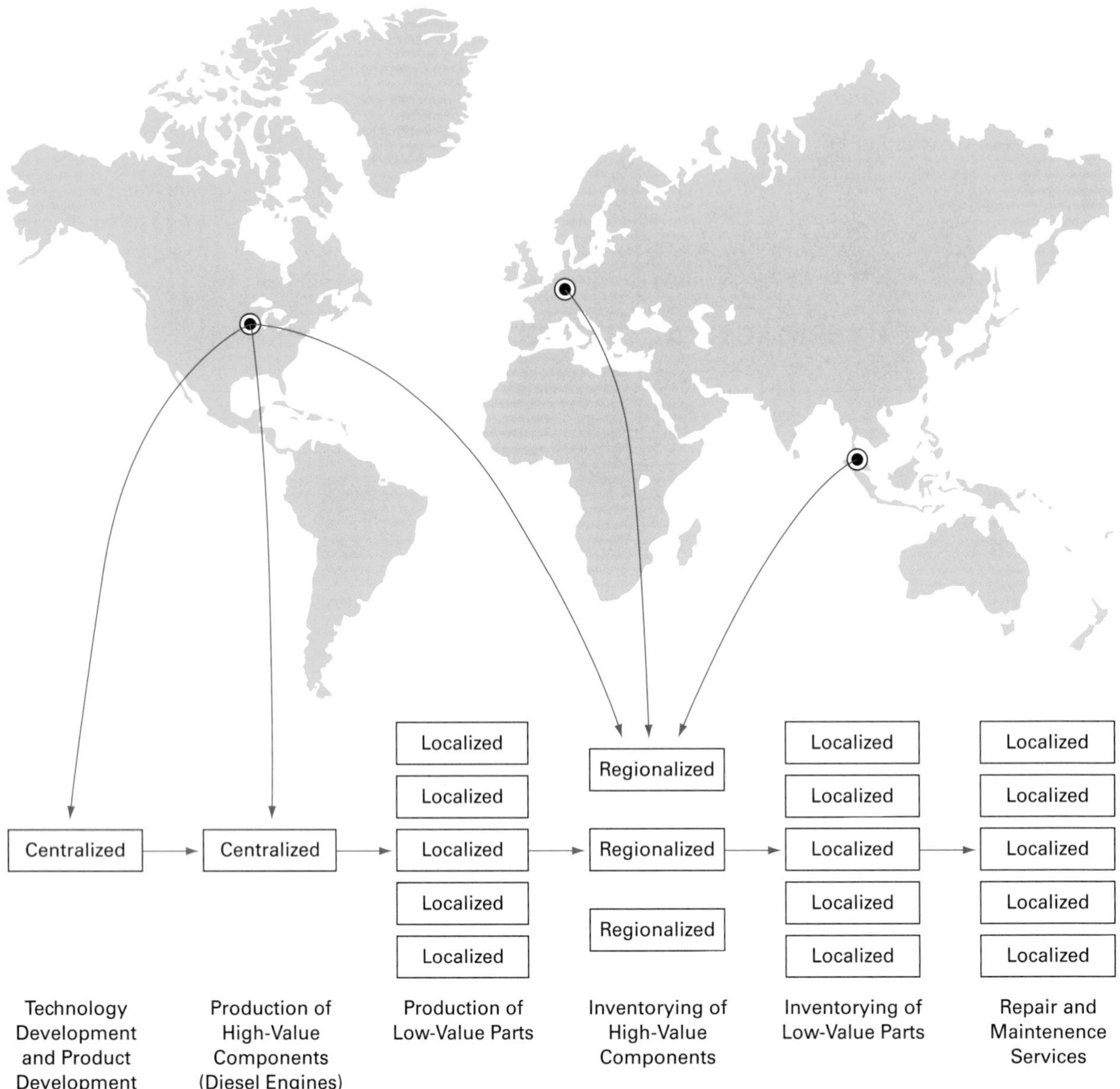

FIGURE 13.3 Hybrid Organization Design for Caterpillar's Earth-Moving Equipment Business

exceptional circumstances) no matter where a customer is using Caterpillar equipment. To deliver this level of service, Caterpillar operates a global spare-parts logistics system in which expensive, high-value parts are inventoried in a few regional parts centers around the world (so they can be shipped within 24 hours to any area within the region), while lower-value parts are inventoried by local Caterpillar dealers in hundreds of locations around the world. Local Caterpillar dealers also perform repair and maintenance services for Caterpillar equipment owners wherever they may be operating Caterpillar equipment.

Through analyses such as this, Caterpillar and other international firms create global strategies that seek to maximize the benefits of centralizing or localizing activities through hybrid global organization designs.

KEY TERMS AND CONCEPTS

centralization The concentration of an activity in one location to serve a global business.

localization The carrying out of an activity at each location where a firm does business in the world.

regionalization The concentration of an activity in a few regional centers to serve a global business.

hybrid global organization design The strategic design of a global organization to carry out the most advantageous combination of centralized, regionalized, and localized activities.

REVIEW QUESTIONS

1. What are the main propositions in each of these early theories of internationalization?
   a. Product cycle theory of internationalization
   b. The non-expiring bargain
   c. Transactions costs view of foreign direct investment
   d. Opportunistic growth theory
2. In Goshal and Bartlett's model of global innovation processes, what factors determine where innovation will occur, and for which markets an innovation will be developed?
3. What kinds of pressures or opportunities motivate centralizing an activity in a global business?
4. What kinds of pressures or opportunities motivate localizing an activity in a global business?
5. What is the objective of global strategic managers in creating hybrid organization designs for global businesses?

PART VII

STRATEGIC LEADERSHIP AND STEWARDSHIP

CHAPTER **14**

MANAGING CHANGE, RISK, AND ETHICS

INTRODUCTION

Thus far in this book, we have discussed a broad range of strategic issues that suggested some of the challenges strategic managers face in managing organizational change, risk, and ethics. In this chapter, we address these challenges more pointedly, because they constitute another central concern of strategic managers—providing what we describe here as *strategic leadership and stewardship.* We first examine the role of providing leadership in managing organizational change, and we consider two complementary kinds of leadership that strategic managers must be able to provide. We then consider the role of providing stewardship in managing organizational risk and ethics, which we characterize as the responsibility of strategic managers to conduct the affairs of the organization so as to respect and protect the interests of all stakeholders in their organization.

14.1 STRATEGIC LEADERSHIP IN MANAGING CHANGE

The concept of *strategic leadership*

As we stated in many ways throughout this book, strategic managers have the ultimate responsibility for defining, designing, communicating, and carrying out the Strategic Logic of their organization. As we also explained (especially in Chapter 9), in a dynamic world the Strategic Logic of an organization must change from time to time to respond to the changing opportunities and threats of its environment, as well as to recognize and serve the changing goals of the organization's stakeholders. Initiating and implementing changes in the Strategic Logic of an organization is also the clear responsibility of strategic managers, and it is the role of carrying out this responsibility that we refer to as **strategic leadership.**

Strategic managers must be able to provide at least two important kinds of strategic leadership. The first form of leadership is what we call *personal leadership,* and the second form we refer to as *institutional leadership.* These two forms of leadership are complementary, and both are essential in successfully leading strategic organizational change.

Personal Leadership

Much of the management literature on leadership focuses on various notions about the personal form of leadership. As suggested in Figure 14.1, leadership in both personal and institutional forms is exhibited through *vision* and *action.* In **personal leadership,** vision is provided by the strategic manager or strategic management team. The leader senses the need for a new Strategic Logic for the organization, and articulates what the new Strategic Logic should be. The personal leader, in effect, is "the man—or woman—with the plan" for the new future of the organization. The personal leader also uses personal charisma and persuasion to motivate the organization to action in carrying out the new Strategic Logic.

	Vision	Action
Personal Leadership	Leader defines and communicates new Strategic Logic	Leader used charisma and persuasion to motivate organization to adopt new Strategic Logic
Intuitional Leadership	Leader builds organizational processes for defining new Strategic Logic	Leader empowers teams to develop and carry out new Strategic Logic

FIGURE 14.1 Two Kinds of Strategic Leadership

Institutional Leadership

The institutional form of leadership defines another kind of leadership role for strategic managers. To provide **institutional leadership**,[1] strategic managers must build organizational processes in which the ideas of all stakeholders about the future can be heard, and in which a vision of the organization and its future Strategic Logic can emerge from discussions and debates among stakeholders. Of course, in such a process competing visions of new Strategic Logics may emerge from various groups of stakeholders. Strategic managers must then create organizational processes for resolving differences among competing visions of the future, for reaching agreement on a shared view of the future, and for adopting a Strategic Logic that all stakeholders can accept and support fully. To achieve action in support of the new Strategic Logic, strategic managers then empower and create incentives for teams and other units within the organization to develop and carry out their roles in implementing the new Strategic Logic.

The Complementarity of Personal and Institutional Leadership

Achieving a balanced integration of personal and institutional leadership

Personal and institutional forms of leadership should not be seen as alternative leadership styles that should be selected to suit the personality of a strategic manager. Rather, both forms are necessary and complementary in providing effective strategic leadership. Both forms of leadership offer inherent strengths and limitations. When used together effectively, the strength of each form of leadership can help to offset the limitations of the other. To be successful in leading strategic change in their organizations, strategic managers must therefore achieve a *balanced integration* of the two forms of leadership.

The most important limitation of the personal form of leadership results from the inherent complexity of an organization and its environment, and the severe cognitive challenge that such complexity poses for all managers. In effect, no single strategic manager or even team of strategic managers can possibly possess all the essential and useful insights needed to imagine the best possible future Strategic Logic for an organization. Rather than

[1] For further discussion of institutional leadership, see Van De Ven, A. (1986). Central Problems in the Management of Innovation. *Management Science,* 32(5).

relying solely on the cognitive processes of a small group of top managers—no matter how motivated they may be to provide personal leadership—most organizations would be much better off drawing on and building on the collective intelligence of all stakeholders in the organization. In essence, the collective intelligence of many people will almost always produce a broader range of good ideas than the intelligence of a single person or small group of people, no matter how brilliant or experienced they may be. Thus, providing institutional leadership by building organizational processes that draw on the collective intelligence of all participants in an organization is an essential activity of strategic managers in compensating for their own human cognitive limitations.

At the same time, the most important limitation of the institutional form of leadership is that the great diversity of ideas that may emerge within an organization may lead to difficulty in reaching organizational agreement on a shared vision of the future. In such situations, strategic managers must keep in mind that they bear ultimate responsibility for the success or failure of an organization's future Strategic Logic. Thus, strategic managers must provide the personal form of leadership required to steer organizational processes so that they converge toward a shared vision of the future and an agreed Strategic Logic that offers the best potential for successful value creation in the marketplace and for distribution of desired forms of value to all stakeholders. Finding ways to balance and integrate the competing visions of the future proposed by an organization's various stakeholders is essential to achieving their commitment in carrying out a new Strategic Logic.

The personal challenge of balancing personal and institutional leadership

In finding the right balance in integrating personal and institutional forms of leadership, strategic managers must also recognize that sometimes the most serious challenge in managing strategic change may be strategic managers themselves. Because of the responsibility they bear for the success of their organization's Strategic Logic, managers may tend to take a conservative view of the organization and its future that seeks largely to minimize risks. Some managers may even resist visions of the future that might challenge the legitimacy of their current positions of authority or leadership.[2] For example, some managers with expertise in the technologies currently used by an organization may resist accepting a vision of the future in which new technologies play major roles.

Thus, the unique intellectual challenge that strategic managers face—that of learning to manage their own cognitive processes—becomes a very personal challenge in the role of providing strategic leadership. Strategic managers must learn to be active participants in organizational processes for discussing and defining new "organizational realities" for the future. At the same time they must guard against unduly using the authority of their management positions to impose personally preferred visions of the future on their organization and its many stakeholders. The balanced integration of stakeholders' visions of the future to arrive at well-defined new Strategic Logics that build organizational commitment to action is the essence of the challenge in strategic managers' dual roles of providing personal and institutional leadership.

14.2 STRATEGIC STEWARDSHIP IN MANAGING RISK AND ETHICS

Managing risks raises both moral and practical issues.

In addition to their leadership roles, strategic managers must take on two critical **strategic stewardship** roles. The first stewardship role is managing the *risk* that an organization faces in pursuing and changing its Strategic Logic, and the second role is managing the *ethics* of the organization as it carries out its Strategic Logic. As we discuss here, these two roles are often closely interrelated.

[2] For further perspectives on the personal challenges of providing leadership of change, see Salancik, G. R., and J. Pfeffer. (1977). "Who Gets Power—And How They Hold on to It: A Strategic-Contingency Model of Power." *Organizational Dynamics,* Winter. See also Tushman, M., W. Newman, and E. Romanelli. Convergence and Upheaval: Managing the Unsteady Pace of Organizational Change. *California Management Review,* 24(1).

Managing Risks

Leading an organization in committing to a course of action based on a Strategic Logic always involves many risks, including the most fundamental strategic risks that an organization's Strategic Logic may be ill-conceived or inadequately executed, and may lead to organizational failure. Organizational failure—whether in the form of poor performance or actual extinction of an organization—leads to a loss of the legitimate interests that various stakeholders have in the organization. (Recall our discussion in Section 8.3 that only investments in creating firm-specific capital qualify a resource provider as a legitimate stakeholder of an organization.) Because strategic managers carry ultimate responsibility for the success or failure of an organization, strategic managers are obliged to recognize and serve the full spectrum of legitimate stakeholder interests in their organization. This obligation has both "moral" and "practical" implications.

One fundamental moral aspect of strategic stewardship is that *no legitimate stakeholder's interest should be ignored* in strategic managers' decisions to accept or seek specific kinds of strategic risks. In deciding to accept the risk of pursuing a new Strategic Logic, for example, strategic managers must analyze the risks that the new Strategic Logic poses for all stakeholders. Those stakeholders whose interests are likely to be diminished or eliminated under a new Strategic Logic should be given the chance to convert their current firm-specific capital into a form that can contribute to the new Strategic Logic. Skilled and dedicated workers whose jobs would be eliminated, for example, should be given the chance to reskill and become productive contributors to the organization's new way of working. Alternatively, such workers should be compensated for the loss of firm-specific human capital that they will incur as the organization moves to its new Strategic Logic.

A second moral aspect of strategic stewardship is that *the interests of a single stakeholder or group of stakeholders should not be given precedence over the interests of other stakeholders.*[3] In other words, unless a different policy is clearly articulated and communicated to all potential stakeholders *before* they become stakeholders, all stakeholders' interests should be equally respected. The strategic and moral imperative to respect and balance stakeholder interests can take many forms, two of which are illustrated in the following examples.

In the 1980s, some strategic managers of companies that had long been conservative in managing their financial structures began to issue large amounts of "junk bonds" that raised the debt-to-equity ratios of their firms to very high levels and thereby exposed their firms to much greater levels of financial risk. In many cases, bonds issued years earlier also became classified as "junk bonds" because of the elevated debt-to-equity ratio of a firm, with a resulting loss to early bondholders of much of the market value of their bonds. What made this practice especially morally objectionable is that in many cases, newly issued junk bonds were used to finance management buyouts of firms (usually referred to as a leveraged buy out, or "LBO"). In effect, some managers were willing to expose long-term bondholders to both higher financial risks and loss of market value of their bonds in order to finance their personal acquisition of controlling interests in their firms.

In the 1980s and 1990s, many strategic managers (especially in the United States) began to take the view that they must first and foremost serve the interests of their shareholders, saying in effect that the interests of financial investors would be given precedence over the interests of other kinds of stakeholders in their organization. The resulting priority given to "shareholder wealth maximization" is profoundly ironic, given that

[3] When an organization fails and enters into bankruptcy, the legal system applicable to that organization will usually establish an order of precedence to be followed in using liquidated assets to compensate various stakeholders. In this extreme case, the principle of "stakeholder equality" that we are advocating for a viable organization may be overruled by legal considerations.

shareholders are both legally and financially the *residual claimants* of a firm—that is, they are "the last in line" in asserting claims on the income and assets of an organization. However, shareholders have the right to elect boards of directors, who in turn have the legal right to hire and fire strategic managers, so it is not difficult to understand why some strategic managers would give precedence to shareholder interests. The moral dimension of this arrangement, however, is evident: Some strategic managers are willing to focus on maximizing wealth for shareholders in the near term—and thereby preserve their own jobs—rather than accepting the personal and intellectual challenge of figuring out how to serve all the interests of all the stakeholders needed to carry out a successful Strategic Logic in the long term.

Good moral performance also has "practical" benefits.

As we noted previously, the obligation to provide strategic stewardship in managing risks also involves a practical dimension. When strategic managers fail to understand and perform the moral dimension of stewardship adequately, they may greatly compromise the ability of their organization to attract and develop stakeholders whose commitments are essential to the future success of their organization. Providers of the best resources can usually choose which organization's value-creation and distribution processes they will participate in. When resource providers find reasons to think that their investments in developing human capital specific to a given organization will not be recognized and respected by an organization's strategic managers, they are not likely to be attracted to that organization or willing to make investments and commitments that can help the organization create distinctive capabilities. Thus, recognizing and respecting all stakeholder interests is not only "morally good," it is also good strategic management practice in building and maintaining organizational competences.

Managing Ethics

In addition to the moral issues involved in managing risks, strategic managers also face a fundamental obligation to define and maintain *ethical standards* of conduct in their organizations. What constitutes ethical conduct is a subject of much debate, however, and opinions vary widely across different cultures and nationalities. In some societies, for example, the "law of the bazaar" prevails, and anyone who can manage to gain an advantage by taking advantage of someone in a business transaction is simply regarded as a smart businessperson. In other societies, businesspeople may be more scrupulous about their business transactions with customers, but may nevertheless routinely publish or distribute false company financial statements. As witnessed in the United States in 2001 and 2002, some executives whose organizations published grand statements about corporate ethics and social responsibility were systematically "cooking the books" and looting the assets of their shareholders, debt holders, and employees to support their multimillion-dollar salaries, large bonuses, and lavish lifestyles.

Honesty may also be the best strategy.

In spite of the dilemma of ethical relativity and the plague of ethical duplicity, in this treatment of strategic management we take the position that a policy of honesty is in the best long-term interests of an organization. Our reason for taking this position is not a personal belief that an ethical system based on honesty is necessarily morally superior to other ethical systems. Rather, our position is based on the argument that honesty is an effective foundation for the creation of trust in a society, and a society with high levels of trust enjoys substantial positive externalities that can greatly benefit the members of that society. For example, trust can often simplify and reduce the "frictional costs" of economic exchange in a society, as when an honest person's word can be trusted enough to make detailed contracting unnecessary.

In this regard, organizations are in a real sense "microsocieties" that can create—or fail to create—trust. When strategic managers lead an organization to follow a policy of honesty and to build a culture of honesty and trust internally and a reputation for trustworthiness externally, their organization may gain several strategic advantages over organizations that lack trust. Employees who believe that their managers are honest and tell them the truth are more likely to make real commitments to contribute to their organization than employees who think their managers are dishonest and cannot be trusted. Suppliers who believe that an organization can be counted on to speak honestly and to keep its commitments are also more likely to make commitments to work cooperatively with that organization. Financial investors are also likely to be more willing to invest in a firm when they believe that its financial statements are complete, correct, and honestly prepared.

In essence, we believe that an organization that adheres to a strict norm of honesty will be better able to attract the best possible resources to its value-creation and distribution processes. We suggest therefore that the old adage "Honesty is the best policy" applies here for "practical" reasons, and that a policy of honesty is likely to be an essential part of the best strategy available to an organization.

KEY TERMS AND CONCEPTS

strategic leadership The role of strategic managers in initiating and implementing changes in an organization's Strategic Logic through a balanced integration of personal leadership and institutional leadership.

personal leadership The form of leadership in which strategic managers define and communicate a new Strategic Logic and use charisma and persuasion to motivate an organization to adopt and implement a new Strategic Logic.

institutional leadership The form of leadership in which managers build organizational processes that involve all stakeholders in defining new Strategic Logics and empower teams to develop and carry out a new Strategic Logic.

strategic stewardship The role of strategic managers in managing organizational risks and maintaining ethical standards in their organization.

REVIEW QUESTIONS

1. In what ways are personal and institutional forms of leadership complementary?
2. What does it mean to achieve a balanced integration of personal and institutional forms of leadership?
3. What is a key personal challenge that strategic managers face in balancing personal and institutional forms of leadership?
4. What are two principles that strategic managers should follow with respect to stakeholder interests in managing risks?
5. What is one important practical implication of poor moral performance in managing stakeholder interests?
6. Why might a policy of honesty be part of the best strategy for an organization?

CASES

MINI-CASE **1**

THE AIR EXPRESS INDUSTRY: FROM INCEPTION TO INTERNATIONALIZATION AND DIVERSIFICATION

The air express industry provides overnight delivery services for small parcels and document envelopes.[1] The industry as we know it today began in the United States in 1971 as the brainchild of Fred Smith, founder and longtime CEO of Federal Express, now known as FedEx. While a student at Yale University, Smith conceived of a new way of collecting, processing, airlifting, and delivering packages that would enable an "absolutely, positively overnight" pickup and delivery between most addresses in the United States (primarily in larger cities). Some thirty years later, the air express industry has evolved into a significant global industry, and its major players are beginning to diversify their portfolios of express delivery and related services they offer. The industry thus presents an opportunity to study the evolution of a new product market from inception to internationalization and diversification in little more than three decades.

BEGINNING OF A NEW INDUSTRY

Until the 1970s, firms and individuals in the United States (and elsewhere) who wanted to ship time-sensitive packages had a limited set of options, none of which was completely satisfactory. Most air cargo services were provided by passenger airlines, whose schedules for flying people during the day did not suit well the needs of most firms to ship packages at the end of a workday. Air cargo companies offered fairly fast (two- or three-day) deliveries between major U.S. cities, but their shipping schedules and processes were designed to achieve consolidation of freight to fill cargo airplanes and thereby lower operating costs, not to provide assured overnight delivery. "Air mail special delivery" available through the U.S. Postal Service (USPS) provided expedited handling of packages, but could take several days to deliver. Courier services would arrange for a courier to pick up a package, take the package on a commercial flight to its destination, and deliver the package, but at a very high cost.

Fred Smith believed that there was significant latent demand in the United States for overnight delivery of small packages (less than 70 pounds, or 32 kilograms) of time-sensitive goods such as computer parts. Smith recognized that the existing infrastructure of passenger and air cargo routes and schedules were optimized to serve other priorities, and that serving demand for overnight delivery required inventing a new kind of logistics system with a clear focus on providing reliable overnight delivery. After founding FedEx in 1971, Smith instituted a new logistics design—the hub-and-spoke system—for processing and shipping packages overnight (see Exhibit 1).

In this new design, airplanes carrying packages collected during the day (until 5:30 P.M.) would leave from major cities in the United States about 7:00 P.M., and would arrive later that evening at FedEx's hub in Memphis, Tennessee (which was near to the geographic

[1] For international air express deliveries, the additional time required to carry documents over longer distances and to clear customs at international borders usually results in deliveries within two to three days, not overnight.

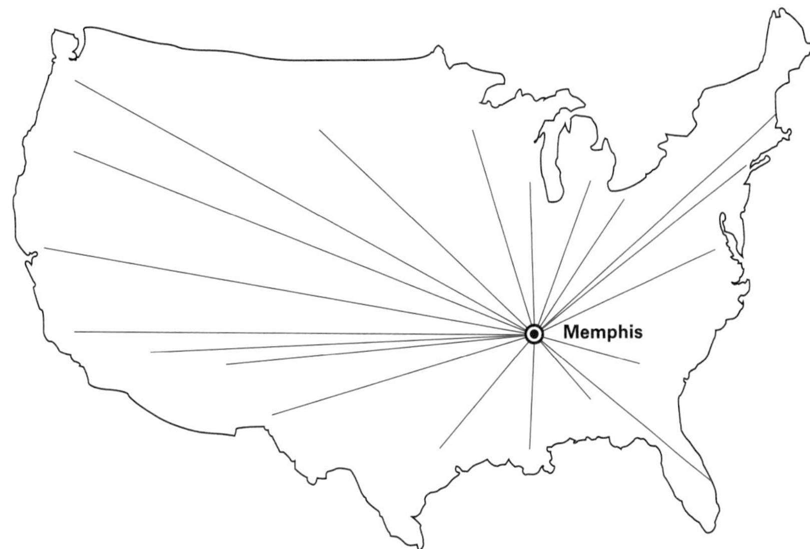

EXHIBIT 1 "Hub-and-Spoke" Logistics System for Overnight Package Delivery

population center of the United States). During the middle of the night, packages would be unloaded from each arriving airplane, sorted by destination, and then placed on the appropriate airplane heading back to the city from which it had departed. Airplanes would return to their originating cities by 7:00 A.M. or so, and packages would be unloaded and delivered to their destinations by 12:00 noon. When FedEx began operations in 1973, its innovative hub-and-spoke logistics system proved capable of providing reliable overnight delivery between major cities in the United States.

To communicate to the market that a new kind of delivery service was available, FedEx launched a major television advertising campaign in which FedEx delivery people were shown overcoming many kinds of obstacles to make their deliveries on time. Each advertisement ended with the message, "When it absolutely, positively has to get there overnight." As FedEx's new kind of delivery service became more widely known, Fred Smith's belief in significant latent demand for a reliable overnight delivery service proved correct, and by 1976 FedEx carried more than seven million packages a year between more than seventy major U.S. cities.

By the late 1970s, FedEx noticed that growing numbers of customers were shipping documents of various types, rather than time-sensitive parts or goods. As the relative importance of documents in its overall volume grew, FedEx introduced the now familiar "Overnight Letter" envelope for documents weighing less than 2 ounces (about 57 grams) and began to emphasize overnight delivery of documents in its advertising. In 1981, the first year of its introduction, FedEx delivered more than six million Overnight Letters. Subsequently, overnight document deliveries became a mainstay of the air express industry.

A CHANGING COMPETITIVE LANDSCAPE

During the 1970s, FedEx demonstrated both the existence of a significant market for overnight delivery of small packages and the ability of a well-managed hub-and-spoke logistics system to provide reliable overnight delivery. As a result, by 1980, a number of air freight companies and freight forwarders—including Emery Air Freight, Purolator Courier, and Airborne Express, among others—decided to enter the air express market. Some of the new entrants tried to "piggy-back" their air express shipments on their existing air freight routes and schedules, but often found it difficult to maintain adequate levels of reliability in making overnight deliveries. Airborne Express, however, emulated the FedEx logistics system design in establishing its own hub-and-spoke system with overnight package sorting at its hub in Wilmington, Ohio. Airborne Express was successful in launching reliable overnight delivery service to more than 100

U.S. cities. USPS also entered the market with its "Express Mail" overnight delivery service.

The entry of United Parcel Service (UPS) into the air express industry in 1982, however, profoundly changed the nature of competition. At the time, UPS was the largest package delivery service in the world, with an unparalleled network of ground delivery services to every address in the United States. In addition, the firm—which used the famous slogan "We run the tightest ship in the shipping business" in its advertising—was highly accomplished at managing and squeezing costs out of large-scale package handling systems through relentless application of industrial engineering principles and methods. When UPS entered the air express market, it offered prices that were more than 40 percent below the current prices charged by FedEx, Airborne Express, and other competitors.

FedEx's initial response to UPS price competition was to try to differentiate its service by offering next-day delivery by 10:30 A.M., instead of by 12:00 noon, the norm for the industry. This effort was unsuccessful, however, because most customers felt that a significantly lower price was preferable to a 90-minute earlier delivery time. FedEx and other competitors were soon forced to match UPS' low price. In addition, recognizing that real price competition was finally taking hold in the industry, a number of large corporations that were heavy users of air express services banded together to form buyer negotiating blocks that were successful in obtaining even deeper price reductions from FedEx, UPS, Airborne Express, and other air express firms. The advent of intense price competition forced these firms to cut costs radically by building up large volumes and adopting the latest package handling technologies to increase economies of scale, or to find a survivable niche in the industry.

With the advantage of the largest volume of shipments in the industry, FedEx managers turned their attention to getting the maximum available economies of scale and squeezing all possible costs out of their package handling system, often making major investments in the latest information technologies such as optical scanners to speed up and reduce the cost of the package sorting process. Airborne Express, lacking the financial resources available to UPS and FedEx, adopted a niche strategy focused on serving large corporate clients with significant volumes as a way to both provide customized service and achieve lower costs. Most other air express firms began to incur large operating losses, because they were unable to achieve enough volume to gain significant economies of scale, to engineer enough costs out of their package processing systems, or to identify and establish a viable niche position in the market. Between the mid-1980s and late 1980s, a number of such firms exited the air express market. By 1990, FedEx claimed about a 50 percent share of the air express market in the United States, while UPS captured a little more than a 20 percent market share. Airborne Express and USPS each held about 15 percent market share.

Beginning in the late 1980s, the major players in the air express industry began to develop and introduce a range of features and enhanced service concepts. For example, FedEx, which had tried unsuccessfully to introduce a fax service in the early 1980s, adapted the satellite communication system originally intended for its fax service to support a real-time package tracking system. When a FedEx delivery person picked up a package and scanned its bar-coded tracking number into a handheld scanner, the number was sent to a local FedEx ground station where it was beamed by satellite to FedEx's central computer system. FedEx could then track the progress of each package by further use of bar code readers at each stage of its logistics system, from pickup to delivery. This information could then be made available to customers concerned about the progress of a package, initially by phone and later by Internet. Competitors UPS and Airborne Express soon replicated this feature.

The launching of "turn-key" logistics services in the late 1980s represented a major initiative by the air express firms to enhance air express delivery services and thereby avoid pure price competition in delivering packages. These logistics services offer integrated inventory management and shipping services to mail-order retailers and other intensive shippers of time-sensitive packages. Inventories of goods are held in large warehouses adjacent to the hubs of the air express firms and equipped with the latest automated package-picking technologies. Packages can be picked from inventory as late as midnight and placed into the air express firm's sorting and logistics system for delivery by noon (12 hours later). Today, all the major competitors in the air express industry offer a range of logistics services to support companies with time-sensitive parts and goods to ship.

INTERNATIONALIZATION

In the mid-1980s, the large market for air express services in the United States attracted the interest of two large non-U.S. companies. The Australian air freight company TNT attempted to enter the U.S. air express market through a takeover of Airborne Express, but was prevented from doing so by a combination of U.S. legal restrictions on the foreign ownership of U.S. airlines (air express carriers are legally classified as airlines) and by Airborne Express' desire to remain independent. Later, in the 1990s, TNT nevertheless managed to extend its air express operations from Australia, Asia, and Europe into major U.S. cities. DHL International, at the time a Belgian air express firm with a strong base in both the European and Japanese markets,[2] also began to study possibilities for entering the U.S. air express market. It eventually added international air express services to its air cargo operations between the United States, Europe, and other destinations in the 1990s.

By the late 1980s, the U.S. domestic air express market reached saturation, and the rate of growth of demand slowed sharply from its double-digit levels of the previous fifteen years to stabilize at a modest few percentage points of growth per year. Moreover, in the 1980s, many large U.S. firms established substantial component supply, manufacturing, and marketing operations in Asia and Europe. The slowing of growth in the U.S. domestic market, combined with the increasing globalization of U.S. companies, led FedEx, Airborne Express, and UPS to seek opportunities for further growth through expansion into Europe and Asia. Each of these firms pursued its own approach to global expansion.

FedEx essentially sought to extend its mode of operating in the U.S. domestic market into Europe and Asia. In the late 1980s, FedEx acquired landing rights at major European and Asian airports in order to "clone" its hub-and-spoke logistics system in Europe and Asia.[3] Investing heavily in large-scale assets for its international routes, including new jumbo jet freighters and extensive ground delivery systems on both continents, FedEx gambled that its international air express volume would grow quickly and would soon give it a cost advantage through economies of scale. FedEx also believed that owning these assets to gain direct control of its logistics system was essential to extending its reliable air express delivery system overseas.

Airborne Express lacked the financial resources needed to match the major investments in international assets made by FedEx, however, and instead pursued internationalization through contracting and alliances.[4] Although it operates its own planes within the United States, Airborne Express negotiated contracts with major international airlines to carry its air express packages on their regularly scheduled passenger or air freight flights. Airborne Express also entered into alliances with major ground delivery companies in Europe and Asia to use their established networks to provide delivery of its air express packages.

UPS followed an approach that combined elements of both FedEx's and Airborne Express' approaches. UPS used a combination of company-owned planes and contracts with scheduled airlines to carry its air express packages to Europe and Asia.[5] In Europe, UPS invested directly in ground delivery systems that it could use for both its air express business and its less time-sensitive package delivery business. By the 1990s, the distinctive brown UPS delivery trucks were already a familiar sight in major European cities and through a series of acquisitions of ground-delivery services began to appear in major Asian cities as well.

Throughout the 1990s, DHL and TNT remained among the largest international air express firms, and continue today to occupy important positions in their home markets of Europe and Asia. As the home markets of DHL and TNT are increasingly penetrated by the extensions of FedEx, Airborne, and UPS services into Europe and Asia, however, the two firms recognize the need to substantially enlarge their businesses in the North American market if they want to remain significant long-term global players in the international air express industry. Today, those firms continue their efforts to penetrate the North American market, a stronghold of FedEx, UPS, and Airborne Express.

DIVERSIFICATION

The turn-key logistics services launched by the North American air express firms in the late 1980s and early 1990s received an enthusiastic response from U.S. companies anxious to outsource "noncore" activities such as inventory management and package delivery. The introduction of enhanced services soon became the major source of revenue and profit growth for air express firms. As more U.S. companies began to look for key suppliers capable of providing "one-stop shopping" for integrated inventory management and shipping services,

[2] Today, DHL is majority owned by Deutsche Post World Net, the privatized German post office operator, with minority partners Lufthansa Airlines and Japan Air Lines.

[3] See the full-length case "The Merger of Federal Express and Flying Tigers" in this volume for discussion of FedEx's acquisition of Flying Tigers' landing rights and operations in Asia.

[4] For further discussion of the different modes of foreign market entry adopted by FedEx and Airborne, see the "Airborne Express" mini-case in this volume.

[5] The acquisition of Flying Tiger by Federal Express in 1989 created a dilemma for UPS, since Flying Tiger was the major contract carrier for UPS's international air express packages.

the major players in the air express industry began to expand their portfolios of logistics services. The early 1990s therefore witnessed the beginning of a decade of diversification for the global air express firms. In diversifying their service offerings, each firm also sought to gain further cost reductions by increasing economies of scale and scope in the use of their logistics assets, and to further leverage their logistics capabilities and assets into related lines of business.

The acquisition by FedEx of Roadway Parcel Service, the second largest private ground delivery system in the United States after UPS, represented a major departure from FedEx's traditional focus on air express deliveries. Launched under the "FedEx Ground" brand, FedEx's ground delivery services now provide conventional package delivery services in direct competition with UPS' ground delivery services. FedEx is also actively soliciting business from traditional freight forwarders to build up volume on its main intercity overnight truck routes. In addition, FedEx now uses its FedEx Ground truck routes to provide overnight delivery for many FedEx express packages shipped between U.S. cities up to 900 miles apart. In 2003, industry analysts estimated that FedEx Ground served about 12 percent of the U.S. market for ordinary package deliveries.

Further, in a significant departure from its traditional positioning as the "reliable alternative" to USPS, in March 2003 FedEx entered into a strategic alliance with USPS. Under this arrangement, FedEx will carry USPS' Express Mail, Priority Mail, and some First Class mail on FedEx's overnight flights and truck routes. FedEx will also introduce a new "Home Delivery" service for FedEx express packages destined to residential (but not commercial) addresses in the United States. FedEx's Home Delivery service will ship express packages on FedEx's own overnight routes, but provide delivery through USPS local mail delivery services. FedEx will be permitted to install approximately 10,000 drop boxes for FedEx express packages in USPS post offices. As privatization of postal services proceeds in Europe, FedEx is planning further alliances in moving packages for and with post offices in Europe, and to this end FedEx recently concluded an alliance agreement with *La Poste,* the French post office.

In 2000, Airborne Express also launched a ground delivery service that by 2003 was carrying nearly 75 million packages a year in the United States. Following its traditional focus on large corporate customers, by 2003 Airborne Express had become the key supplier of ground delivery services for Xerox and a number of other large U.S. firms. Like FedEx, Airborne Express was also seeking alliances with USPS that would use USPS local mail delivery services to deliver the firm's express packages to residential addresses in the United States. Under its "airborne@home" program, Airborne Express picks up packages from major corporate shippers, carries them on Airborne overnight flights, and then uses local USPS mail deliveries to get the packages to their final destinations. By mid-2003, Airborne was processing more than ten million packages a year through its airborne@home program, and recently signed an agreement with the mail-order firm L.L. Bean to ship more than a million additional packages a year through this service.

UPS, as one of the oldest as well as largest package delivery firms in the world, enjoys a somewhat longer history of diversification into businesses related to its package logistics capabilities. In addition to its express, expedited (two- or three-day delivery), and regular ground delivery services, the diversified activities undertaken by UPS through 2003 include the following:

- UPS Freight Services Network designs and manages shipping systems for ordinary freight (shipments larger than 72-pound or 33-kilogram packages) for corporate clients.
- UPS Supply Chain Solutions provides logistics design, management, and information technology for managing global or regional supply chains.
- UPS Mail Innovations provides corporate clients with services that lower the cost, increase the speed, and improve the reliability of their mailings through the USPS.
- UPS Retail Services was formed in 2001 after the acquisition of 3,300 domestic and 700 overseas locations of Mail Boxes Etc. Many of the domestic locations are being rebranded as "The UPS Store" and will continue to provide mail and package receiving and shipping services for individuals and small businesses, as well as offering basic office supplies and copying services.
- UPS Consulting provides consulting in supply chain design and management.
- UPS Business Technology provides Internet-based IT solutions to companies for shipping and tracking packages and freight.
- UPS Capital provides companies with working capital through improved supply chain management and supply chain financing.
- UPS Capital Insurance Agency, Inc., provides a full line of trade-related insurance services.

DHL has recently made integrated service parts logistics the spearhead of its initiatives to establish a major presence in the North American air express market.

By 2003, the firm had established twenty-nine Strategic Parts Centers in U.S. cities to provide integrated inventory management and express delivery services for high-value, time-sensitive parts. DHL integrated these North American parts centers into its international network of 288 parts centers to provide around-the-world, around-the-clock express parts delivery for global companies. To support this effort, DHL also launched a new information technology initiative to enable integration of its parts and logistics management system with the SAP or Oracle enterprise resources planning (ERP) systems used by its customers. In addition, in 2003 DHL announced plans to offer a nationwide ground delivery service in the United States, both to build its package delivery business in North America and to provide a one-company logistics solution for U.S. companies that need to move packages to international destinations.

TNT has recently focused on building up capabilities in customizing global logistics services for strategically targeted industries. The company designs and implements global logistics solutions "to deliver the right product, at the right time, in the right condition, and at the right price"[6] for firms in the automotive, pharmaceutical and health care, high-tech and telecommunications, publishing and media, and consumer goods industries. In addition, TNT provides mail services that pick up international mail from corporate clients and move the mail to the most advantageous location in the world for final mailing.

[6] Available from the TNT Web site, at www.tnt.com.

As air express companies accelerate their diversification into ground delivery and mail-related services in the United States, several traditional ground delivery service companies have responded by launching guaranteed one-day or two-day delivery services between most major U.S. cities. Industry commentators observed that moving packages by truck is usually significantly cheaper than shipping them by air, and that many major intercity markets for express packages can be served just as quickly and reliably by overnight trucking as by overnight flights.

QUESTIONS FOR DISCUSSION

1. Identify the events that help to define the major stages in the evolution of the product life cycle for the air express industry.
2. What reasons suggest that DHL and TNT must establish significant operations in the North American market if they are to remain significant players in the international air express industry?
3. What activities do you suggest should be (a) localized, (b) regionalized, or (c) centralized in the international operations of a major air express firm, and why? (See Chapter 13.)
4. What—exactly—are the kinds of synergies that air express firms can create through the forms of diversification described in this case?
5. As the original air express firms diversify into related businesses, what new kinds of capabilities will they have to develop to achieve the synergies you identify in Question 4?

MINI-CASE **2**

AIRBORNE EXPRESS: STRATEGY FOR INTERNATIONALIZATION

Airborne Express is one of the few companies to survive the shake-out period in the evolution of the air express industry.[1] Following its motto of providing "Premium Service Without the Premium Price," Airborne Express has earned about a 15 percent market share in the United States while competing against Federal Express (now known as FedEx), with nearly 50% market share, and United Parcel Service (with about 20% market share). In international markets, Airborne Express competes against its two domestic rivals plus DHL, TNT, and international express mail.

The company positions itself as "a full-service global transportation and logistics partner to business and government agencies around the globe." To this end, the firm provides several kinds of air express service products (same day, overnight, and second-day delivery), as well as ground delivery services, air freight, and comprehensive logistics services. Through its Airborne Logistics Services division, the firm also offers customized inventory holding and management services at its Wilmington, Ohio, airport and free trade zone. In 2001, Airborne Express' revenues from its domestic activities in the United States were slightly more than US$2.8 billion, while its international operations gathered US$350 million in revenues. However, in 2001 the company posted a net loss of nearly US$20 million after earning US$120 million in 1997, US$137 million in 1998, US$91 million in 1999, and US$28 million in 2000.

After reaching the maturity phase of the air express industry in the U.S. domestic market in the early 1980s, Airborne Express and its two main U.S. rivals began to look to international markets for further growth. All three companies began to actively seek ways to extend their air express businesses into Europe and Asia. In addition to their own desire to keep growing, all three firms were serving large companies in the United States that were also rapidly internationalizing, and these companies wanted to extend their use of air express services to their European and Pacific Rim operations. Their customer companies were especially interested in using air express as an integral element in their global supply chains for moving high-value, low-weight, time-sensitive parts, components, and products between their globally dispersed manufacturing, assembly, and marketing sites. In particular, providing logistical support for makers of electronics products with manufacturing sites in Asia was seen as a market with high-growth potential.

A common concern of all three air express firms in internationalizing was to create an international air express and logistics infrastructure that could assure the same high levels of fast, reliable, on-time deliveries achieved in their U.S. operations. In this case, we first summarize FedEx's approach to meeting the opportunities and challenges of internationalizing, and then we consider Airborne Express' rather different strategy for internationalizing its business in the 1980s and 1990s.

FEDEX'S INTERNATIONALIZATION STRATEGY

As both the market innovator and the clear market leader in the United States, by the early 1980s FedEx had built up the industry's largest-scale infrastructure of modern airplanes, delivery trucks, shipping and receiving facilities,

[1] Also see the case "The Air Express Industry" by Ron Sanchez in this volume.

and tens of thousands of motivated FedEx employees throughout the United States, in addition to its highly automated overnight package sorting facility in Memphis, Tennessee. In the view of FedEx,[2] direct ownership and control of a large-scale air express infrastructure was essential both to maintain the close coordination needed to assure reliable overnight deliveries and to achieve low costs.

FedEx's approach to internationalizing was a straightforward extension of its U.S. model to the international arena. FedEx used its financial strength to purchase specially equipped Boeing 747 freighters for its new international routes,[3] to buy and upgrade a number of ground delivery companies overseas, and to recruit and train large numbers of employees to run their operations in Europe and Asia. In essence, FedEx made a large financial investment to achieve economies of scale and to achieve direct control over its air express network, but in so doing it incurred high fixed costs, both for amortization of capital equipment and for labor.

AIRBORNE EXPRESS' INTERNATIONALIZATION STRATEGY

Airborne Express had neither the financial resources nor the scale of operations of its largest rival. These constraints led Airborne Express to adopt an approach to internationalizing that differed significantly from FedEx on two key dimensions.

First, Airborne Express decided to contract as needed for cargo space on the main scheduled airlines serving Europe and Asia, rather than investing its limited financial resources in purchasing new aircraft for its international routes. Several reasons lay behind this decision. For one thing, Airborne Express was concerned that the volume of business they would develop, especially in the first years of internationalization, would be too small to achieve in practice the economies of scale that a new fleet of aircraft would make available in principle. In addition, Airborne Express was concerned about the length of time it would take to achieve a balanced flow of volumes in both directions across the Atlantic and Pacific Oceans. Their market analysis suggested that the outflow of air express packages from the United States to Europe and to Asia would be significantly larger than in the opposite directions, especially during the first years of international market development. Finally, the major airlines serving Europe and Asia were then flying with substantial unused cargo capacity, and were currently willing to offer attractive prices to Airborne Express. By Airborne Express' calculation, the unused air cargo capacity on the routes it wanted to serve in Asia and Europe exceeded the expected volume for all international air express packages for the first several years of internationalization of the industry.

Second, rather than investing in its own ground delivery facilities and equipment overseas, Airborne Express elected to form alliances with some large ground delivery operators in Asia and Europe. For example, Airborne Express entered into a joint venture called Airborne Express Japan with Mitsui Co. of Japan, one of the world's largest and (in the 1980s) most financially strong companies, and Tonami Transportation Co., to use their jointly owned Panther Express package delivery company to pick up and deliver air express packages in Japan. Mitsui also invested US$40 million to acquire about 7 percent of Airborne Express and pledged to provide financing up to US$100 million for future acquisition of aircraft. Airborne Express sought similar kinds of arrangements with other potential partners in other parts of Asia and in Europe.

In contrast to FedEx's commitment to substantial investments and high fixed costs in internationalizing, Airborne Express both sought to minimize financial investments and to incur primarily variable costs in internationalizing. This strategy was criticized by FedEx, which maintained that such a strategy could provide neither the control nor the cost basis needed to profitably operate a reliable international air express network.

QUESTIONS FOR DISCUSSION

1. Identify precisely the conditions under which FedEx's strategy could be the superior approach to internationalizing, and how those conditions would contribute to the success of FedEx's internationalization strategy.
2. Identify precisely the conditions under which Airborne Express' strategy could be the superior approach to internationalizing, and how those conditions would contribute to the success of Airborne Express' internationalization strategy.
3. What risks are inherent (a) in the FedEx internationalization strategy, and (b) in the Airborne Express internationalization strategy? What ways can you suggest to manage the risks you identified in the two strategies?
4. What general insights into the strengths and weaknesses of using firm-specific resources versus firm-addressable resources can you derive from this case?

[2] By and large, this view was also shared by United Parcel Service, which followed an approach to internationalization that was basically similar to FedEx's approach.

[3] See "The Merger of Federal Express and Flying Tiger" in this volume for discussion of FedEx's approach to internationalizing its operations.

MINI-CASE **3**

ASAHI BEER CREATES "SUPER DRY": BUILDING NEW COMPETENCES IN THE JAPANESE BEER INDUSTRY

In the late 1980s to early 1990s, the Japanese beer industry experienced unprecedented market upheaval. Through a radical change in competitive strategy, supported by the development of new organizational competences, Asahi Breweries, Ltd., was able to dislodge Kirin Beer from decades of market dominance and become a new market leader in Japan.[1]

From the 1950s to the mid 1980s, four companies—Kirin, Sapporo, Asahi, and Suntory—competed in the Japanese beer market. By the 1980s, Kirin Beer had steadily increased its share of the Japanese beer market to more than 60%, while Sapporo held a 20% share, Asahi an 11% share, and Suntory a 7% share. Kirin's hugely successful market strategy was driven by careful attention to three competitive factors:

- *Distribution.* Kirin worked hard to establish a dominant national distribution system and to persuade its nearly 100,000 distributors and retailers in Japan to sell only Kirin Beer. Kirin also used its distribution system to assure the freshness of all Kirin Beer products on dealers' shelves.
- *Production.* To serve its growing distribution channels as well as increasing consumer demand, Kirin steadily expanded its production capacity by building a new brewery nearly every two years during the 1960s and 1970s. The capacity of each brewery was selected to assure maximum economies of scale. Through this steady expansion of efficient production, Kirin became the low-cost producer of beer in Japan.
- *Brand.* By maintaining consistently high levels of advertising, Kirin succeeded in persuading most Japanese beer consumers that Kirin Beer offered "real beer taste" that was superior to the taste of other brands of beer available in Japan.

Kirin's market dominance was so significant that the price set by Kirin for its beer effectively established the maximum price for all domestic beer sold in the Japanese market. Given Kirin's highly favorable cost position, Kirin's managers priced Kirin Beer to assure that the three smaller competitors could cover their costs (at least most of the time), while allowing Kirin to enjoy strong profitability.

In the late 1970s, the smaller beer companies in Japan began to look for ways to compete more effectively against Kirin. Unable to compete on cost, they turned to new packaging concepts as a possible way of differentiating their products and building brand awareness and market share. After experimenting with beer cans shaped like rockets or labeled with cartoon characters like penguins and raccoons, all of which could be quickly imitated by any competitor, the "packaging wars" came to an end in the early 1980s without changing the relative positions of competitors. Similar efforts to define and establish "niche" markets for beers with unusual tastes also failed to change consumer preferences to any significant extent.

In the mid-1980s, facing growing cost pressures and diminishing profitability, Asahi Breweries decided to launch a "frontal attack" on the mainstream of the Japanese beer market in a perhaps final effort to wrest a profitable level of market share from Kirin. After decades of carefully controlling its brewing process to maintain

[1] For recommended full-length cases on the Asahi Beer Co., Ltd., and the Japanese beer industry, see "The Japanese Beer Industry" and "Asahi Breweries, Ltd." by Tim Craig, University of Victoria.

the same taste in its beer, Asahi's managers began to ask if that taste was what the majority of beer consumers still wanted in Japan. After doing some basic consumer research for the first time in decades, Asahi's marketing staff began to sense that the new generation of Japanese beer drinkers would be interested in a new kind of beer taste unlike the taste offered by Asahi's current beer or the "real beer taste" offered by Kirin. Describing the new taste desired by the new generation of beer drinkers (including growing numbers of young women) as "smooth but sharp," Asahi's marketing staff asked the production staff to produce new beer formulations for market testing. Asahi's brewers, however, regarded themselves as arbiters of "good" beer taste and largely resisted requests to deviate from the current taste of Asahi Beer.

Growing financial pressure led to a change in Asahi management. Asahi's new managers decided to support the frontal attack on the mainstream of the beer market proposed by the marketing staff and to promote closer cooperation between marketing and production staff. Team-building retreats were organized, as well as regular meetings of marketing and production staff. To overcome the traditional separation between marketing and production activities, a new product development team was created that brought marketing and production staff together for the first time. To emphasize the strategic importance of new product development within Asahi, the product development team was given direct access to top management, bypassing the firm's usual—and typically slow—review and approval process by several layers of middle management.

Because marketing staff used consumer terms and production staff used technical terms to describe beer, a first critical activity of the product development team was to develop a new "corporate language" for communicating about the taste of beer. After a sustained effort, marketing and production staff were able to develop a common vocabulary for describing the different tastes and sensations involved in drinking beer. As a result, the development team was able to define and develop a new beer taste that both marketing and production staff agreed was "sharper, cleaner, more refined."

The new beer was introduced as "Asahi Super Dry Beer" in 1986. The reaction of Japanese beer consumers quickly confirmed that Asahi's marketers had guessed right: The preferences of Japan's new generation of beer drinkers had indeed shifted, establishing a "new taste center" in the Japanese beer market. Super Dry was a huge hit, and Asahi quickly shifted its breweries to production of the new beer. The phenomenal consumer acceptance of the new beer soon attracted large numbers of new distributors and retailers, and Asahi's share of the Japanese beer market grew from 10.3% in 1986 to 24.8% in 1989, largely at the expense of Kirin's traditional-tasting beer.

As the success of Asahi Super Dry proved to be enduring, Kirin, Sapporo, and Suntory intensified their product development processes and began to bring a succession of new beers to market. By the early 1990s, no single beer brand dominated the Japanese market, and competition in the Japanese beer industry became centered on constant exploration of changing consumer tastes and development of new beers to serve emerging tastes. The days of one "true beer taste"—and competitive advantage based on economies in producing and distributing a dominant brand—were over.

QUESTIONS FOR DISCUSSION

1. What resources and capabilities were the basis of Kirin's competitive advantage in the Japanese beer industry prior to the 1980s? What management processes do you think were essential in developing and using those strategic resources and capabilities?
2. What new capabilities became the basis of competitive advantage in the mid-1980s? What new management processes were needed to support and deploy those capabilities in Asahi?
3. Explain the dynamic, systemic, cognitive, and holistic aspects of the new competence that Asahi developed in the mid-1980s and that enabled the firm to detect and respond more effectively to market opportunities.

MINI-CASE **4**

KENTUCKY FRIED CHICKEN'S ENTRY INTO CHINA: KEY ISSUES AND STRATEGIC CHOICES

Kentucky Fried Chicken (hereafter, KFC) is a subsidiary of Yum! Brands, Inc., of Louisville, Kentucky, USA, which owns or franchises more than 11,500 KFC, Pizza Hut, Taco Bell, Long John Silver's (seafood), and A&W All-American Food restaurants outside the United States. KFC is the largest quick-service restaurant (QSR) chain in the People's Republic of China, and in September 2002 KFC announced the opening of its 700th location in China. Samuel Su, president of Yum! Brands International–Greater China, commented on the opening: "KFC is rapidly building on its dominant position as the leading quick-service restaurant company in China. We are capitalizing on the brand's wide consumer appeal, strong infrastructure, and established processes and resources."[1]

KFC IN ASIA

KFC's popularity and visible presence in the Chinese market today, with locations in more than 150 cities, represents the successful outcome of a market entry and development process that began in 1987. At that time, KFC was a subsidiary of R.J. Reynolds Co. KFC had previously entered several Asian markets, and by 1983 had more than 400 locations in Japan and 85 franchised operations in Southeast Asia (including 20 locations in Indonesia, 27 locations in Malaysia, and 23 locations in Singapore).[2] In the 1970s, however, KFC had been unsuccessful in trying to enter the Hong Kong market. Among the problems that KFC encountered in Hong Kong was realizing too late that consumers in Hong Kong, who were used to the taste of fresh chicken typically used in Chinese cuisine, would not accept the taste of the standard frozen chickens used by KFC.

ENTERING CHINA: ISSUES AND CHOICES

When KFC was deciding in the mid-1980s whether to enter the Chinese market—and if so, how—a number of issues had to be considered.

First, a number of first-mover advantages might be gained by the first QSR chain to successfully enter the Chinese market. In particular, a successful first mover might establish its brand and menu as the "original" Western food concept in the minds of Chinese consumers, thereby potentially winning significant reputation and consumer loyalty benefits. Although no major QSR chain had yet entered China, there was speculation that KFC's arch rival McDonald's would soon move into the Chinese market. KFC wanted to be the first QSR chain to enter China, but reflecting on its experience in Hong Kong, KFC also realized that a poor initial public reaction by Chinese consumers could be difficult to overcome later. Thus, KFC was concerned that everything be "right" in its Chinese KFC restaurants from the opening of the first location.

KFC was determined not to compromise on its long-standing commitment to QSC—quality, service, and cleanliness. Every piece of chicken would have to be prepared perfectly, every employee would have to provide fast and friendly service to every customer, and every

[1] Information available at www.kfc.com/about/pr/091302.htm.

[2] For a recommended full-length case on KFC's entry into China, see "Kentucky Fried Chicken in China" by Allen Morrison and Paul Beamish of University of Western Ontario.

restaurant would have to be spotlessly clean at all times. QSC was at the core of KFC's competence and of its commitment to its customers worldwide.

However, a number of specific issues had to be resolved in deciding KFC's entry strategy for China. For example, KFC wondered whether to offer only its standard American-style menu, or whether KFC's menu in China should be adapted to Chinese taste preferences, and if so, to what extent? Clearly, the frozen chicken that was standard in KFC restaurants in the United States and that had failed in Hong Kong could not be used in China. That meant that KFC would have to learn how to source, ship, store, and prepare fresh chicken with the same consistency that it achieved through its highly developed systems for processing and cooking its standard frozen chicken. But KFC wondered whether it should add other kinds of menu items more familiar to Chinese consumers—for example, Chinese noodles or soups. Similar questions arose with respect to the decor of its restaurants. Should the restaurants in China feature the typically American decorations used in its restaurants in the United States, or should it try to reflect Chinese themes in its interior decor?

Another key issue was the location of the first restaurants to be opened. Should the first restaurants be opened in Beijing, the high-profile capital city, where it would immediately gain high visibility with Chinese government officials as well as with Beijing's trend-setting younger consumers? Or should KFC opt for Shanghai, the energetic and overtly commercial challenger to Beijing's claim as China's "first city." Or would it be better to take a more discreet approach to opening its first locations by locating them in some of the many second-tier Chinese cities with million-plus populations?

A further issue was the best form of ownership and management control to use in entering China. Direct ownership would allow complete management control, but would require heavy investment funding from KFC's parent company and would therefore pose significant financial risk. Finding the right managers to guide this process in China would also be a challenge. Moreover, approval by the Chinese government of an application to establish a wholly owned venture was not assured and could take some time to resolve. A second possibility would be a joint venture with a local partner (either private individuals or government entities). A joint venture would ease the capital investment required from KFC, but could result in sharing management control of the KFC restaurants in China with its Chinese partner or partners. However, applications to establish jointly owned restaurants in China would probably be approved by the government in relatively short time. A third possibility was franchising, which would reduce capital requirements to a minimum for KFC, but would leave most management decisions in the hands of its Chinese franchisees. Franchising was not at all common in China at the time, and it was not clear what problems the lack of familiarity with franchising might raise in attracting good franchisees or in gaining government approval for this mode of entry into China.

QUESTIONS FOR DISCUSSION

1. What are the relative advantages and disadvantages of offering the standard American KFC menu in China versus adapting the KFC menu in China to include items more familiar to Chinese consumers?
2. Should KFC open its first locations in the leading Chinese cities of Beijing or Shanghai, or select lower-profile cities?
3. Which of the three forms of ownership mentioned in the case do you think KFC should adopt for its entry into China? Why?

MINI-CASE 5

LONGS DRUGS: INFORMATION FLOWS, DECISION MAKING, AND INCENTIVES

Beginning with a modest drug store opened in 1938 in Oakland, California, the brothers Thomas and Joseph Long progressively built a chain of drug stores that by 2002 had grown to 436 stores located in six western states (California, Colorado, Hawaii, Nevada, Oregon, and Washington).[1] Corporate revenues in 2002 were US$4.3 billion, averaging close to US$10 million in sales per store per year. Corporate profits were US$69 million in 2000, but declined to US$45 million and US$47 million in the more challenging economic conditions of 2001 and 2002. Long Drugs opened 25 new stores in 2002 and planned to open up to 30 new stores in 2003. The firm also closed 19 stores in 2002 that no longer showed satisfactory long-term profit potential.

Longs Drugs pursues a distinctive strategy within the drug store industry. Longs Drugs are located in many different kinds of urban, suburban, and small town communities and serve customers with diverse income levels, education, and ethnic and cultural backgrounds. However, the mix of products offered in each of its stores is customized to serve the preferences of the people living in its local community.[2] Each Longs Drugs store continuously fine-tunes the product mix on its shelves to offer the products in greatest demand by customers in that location. Also, each store regularly offers attractively priced promotions on a range of popular products to generate frequent visits by customers. A Longs Drugs store typically generates 50 percent or more revenue per square meter of retail floor space than competing drug stores.

[1] For a recommended full-length case on Longs Drugs, see "Longs Drugs Stores" by James W. Clinton of University of Northern Colorado.

[2] Although commonly referred to as "drug stores" in the United States, Longs Drugs stores (like its large chain competitors) sell much more than drugs, which typically account for only about 20 percent of store revenues. Other items commonly offered by drug stores include cosmetics, personal care items, candy, snack foods, stationery, household items, small appliances, and even some sports goods and toys.

Longs Drugs faces several kinds of competitors. Many communities and neighborhoods have small drug stores owned and managed by a pharmacist that provide mostly prescription drugs, "over-the-counter" (nonprescription) drugs, and health care items. In urban and suburban communities, large drug store chains such as Walgreen Drugs, Osco, and Rite-Aid operate large drug stores that offer a broad, standard selection of drugs and other goods, often at discount prices. Also, large discount store chains like Wal-Mart include pharmacies that provide prescription drugs, as well as offering an extensive selection of health and personal care items within their broad range of retail merchandise. In addition, Internet-based sellers of prescription drugs delivered directly to customers by mail have begun to capture a growing share of prescription drug sales. In 2002, Longs Drugs launched a central "automated prescription fill center" that provides more than 35,000 prescriptions a week to its customers throughout the western states.

MANAGEMENT OF LOCAL STORES

Each Longs Drugs store manager has broad freedom to run his or her store within some basic corporate guidelines. For example, store managers determine the staffing needs for their store, assign tasks to employees, and set salary levels for employees, while broad corporate guidelines for human resources management determine the basic insurance, corporate profit sharing, and other benefits that each category of Longs Drugs employee receives.

Each store manager has "bottom-line" net profit responsibility for his or her store and is free to choose the mix of products and to set prices that will generate maximum profit for that location. A store manager receives a bonus based on the net profit earned by his or her store. In a store with above-average profit levels, the net-profit based bonus paid to a store manager may equal or exceed his or her base salary. As a result, Longs Drugs store managers typically feel and act like entrepreneurs in developing the profit potential of their individual stores.

Store managers also select employees to be department managers within their store. Store managers normally delegate to their department managers responsibility for deciding the mix, shelf space, and reordering rates for the products offered in their individual departments. In addition to a salary and the standard benefits offered by Longs Drugs, a department manager may earn a significant bonus based on the gross margins (sales less cost of goods sold) generated in his or her individual department.

PURCHASING, LOGISTICS, AND PRODUCT PROMOTIONS

Because net profit margins of drug stores are typically quite "thin," averaging 1 or 2 percent of total sales, most national drug store chains try to maintain and improve their profit margins by buying large volumes of each product that they offer in order to get the lowest possible prices from suppliers. To achieve large volumes, most drug store chains offer a standard mix of products in all of their hundreds or thousands of drug stores throughout the United States. The standard mix of products that would be most desirable for a chain to offer nationally is usually determined by a central marketing and purchasing office that also negotiates the lowest purchase prices with suppliers. Suppliers then ship large orders of products to the chain's central or regional warehousing and distribution centers, where products are sorted into shipments to individual stores.

In Longs Drugs, however, a store manager together with department managers monitors sales in their store and determines the profit-maximizing mix of products and stock levels for their store. Store managers may then order items for their individual stores directly from suppliers, who would then ship orders directly to individual stores. In effect, goods inventories in Longs Drugs are largely either "on the road" (i.e., being shipped by a supplier to a store) on "on the shelf" and thus available for sale. Relative to its large competitors with centralized purchasing, warehousing, and logistics, Longs Drugs incurs low costs of carrying inventories of goods. However, direct ordering and shipping to individual Longs Drugs stores may result in higher costs of goods purchased and higher shipping costs relative to similar costs incurred by the large national drug store chains. In the 1990s, in an effort to get better prices and lower logistics costs for its overall purchases from its many suppliers, Longs Drugs began to explore ways to consolidate purchases at the corporate level of the products in greatest demand by its more than 400 store managers.

In the early 1990s, Longs Drugs installed bar code readers at the cashier stations in its stores. Bar code readers scan the universal product code (UPC), or bar code, on each product that a customer is buying and automatically enters the price for the product into the running total for that customer on a cash register. In addition, as various products' bar codes are scanned by cashiers, "real-time" product sales data become available for use in reordering products to maintain desired inventory levels in each store.

Within a region with several Longs Drugs stores, store managers meet regularly (usually once a month or so) to discuss business conditions in their area, to share ideas for improving the attractiveness and performance of their stores, to share information about newly popular or fast-selling items, and to identify opportunities for undertaking regional product promotions and advertising. At their regional meetings, store managers try to identify product promotions that would be effective in attracting customers to all their stores. Store managers may decide to consolidate purchases of products that are popular in their region to negotiate lower prices with suppliers. Longs Drugs store managers typically use inserts in local newspapers and bulk mailings to local neighborhoods to advertise the special product promotions intended to generate high volumes of customer visits to their stores. In addition to sharing information about popular products, store managers look for opportunities to create advertising and promotional materials that can be used by all their stores on a regional (rather than purely local) basis. Collaboration by store managers in creating regional advertising materials and in consolidating purchasing of advertising space in local newspapers can lower the costs of advertising for each store.

QUESTIONS FOR DISCUSSION

1. What opportunities do you think exist for improving information flows within Longs Drugs, and what benefits do you think such improvements would bring?
2. What approach to consolidating purchasing of products do you recommend for Longs Drugs' corporate managers, and why?
3. Is using net profit–based bonuses for store managers and gross profit–based bonuses for department managers the most effective incentive design for supporting Longs Drugs' strategy? If so, why? If not, how do you think the design of incentives for store managers and department managers can be improved?

MINI-CASE **6**

NOVO A/S: BALANCING THE "TRIPLE BOTTOM LINE"

Novo A/S is the Danish holding company for Novo Nordisk A/S, which is the world's largest provider of insulin and insulin delivery systems for the care of diabetics, and Novozymes A/S, which produces a range of enzymes for industrial uses. The firm employs 17,000 people, operates production facilities in Denmark, the United States, China, and Brazil, and markets its products globally. Revenues in 2001 were just over US$3 billion.

Novo manages its business to produce results in three areas. The firm issues annual reports with detailed explanations of its corporate performance on social responsibility, environmental, and financial dimensions, in that order. CEO Lars Rebien Sorensen states in Novo's 2001 annual report:

> It makes a difference whether you live by your values or merely talk about them. It also makes a difference whether corporate values are consistent with your personal view of the world. Put to the test, this is the ultimate determinant of success or failure.... We are attempting to define a model for corporate social responsibility that makes sense to our shareholders and employees and to all those who benefit from our products.... Evidently, there is self-interest in this approach. To me, that is what makes it sustainable.[1]

Lisa Kingo, Novo's senior vice president for stakeholder relations, adds, "In all our day-to-day decisions, we seek a balance between being financially profitable, environmentally aware, and socially responsible."[2]

[1] 2001 Novo A/S annual report, pp. 2–3.

[2] Quoted in Henning Schwarz, "Balancing the Triple Bottom Line," *Airport Magazine* [Denmark], September/October 2001, p. 11.

SOCIAL RESPONSIBILITY

Novo defines social responsibility as "putting [our] values into action" with respect to human rights and the firm's "relationships with society at large." More specifically, the firm recognizes certain responsibilities that come with its position as the leading provider of insulin products and delivery systems for the care of people with diabetes, who are estimated to exceed 100 million in developing countries alone. The firm engages in a number of educational initiatives in developing countries to help health care professionals, educators, and families recognize the symptoms of diabetes and understand the importance of treating the disease as early as possible. In 2001, the firm also committed to contribute DKK 500 million (US$65 million) over ten years to establish the World Diabetes Foundation, whose mission is to undertake projects that will improve diabetes care in developing countries. In the same year, the firm also decided to make its products available to public health systems in the forty-nine nations defined by the United Nations as the "Least Developed Countries" at prices "not to exceed 20% of the average price in the industrialized countries of North America, Europe, and Japan."[3] This pricing policy was thought to make a meaningful difference in the affordability of the firm's products in the world's poorest countries.

ENVIRONMENTAL PERFORMANCE

Novo A/S defines the domain of its environmental responsibility as including any way in which the firm affects its external environment. Specific concerns identified by Novo include the ways the firm might affect global climate change, depletion of the ozone layer,

[3] 2001 Novo A/S annual report, p. 21.

change in biodiversity, acidification or other deterioration of soil and water quality, consumption of fresh water, consumption of fossil fuels, and waste generated by the production and use of the firm's products.

The guiding principle adopted by Novo A/S in managing its environmental performance is that the firm's growth must be realized through processes that are sustainable in the long run. The firm's 2001 annual report states, "Continued growth at the expense of nature's capital is clearly unsustainable."[4]

Novo A/S has adopted a systematic approach to reducing its consumption of natural resources (including the use of fresh water in its processing plants), to using environmentally benign materials in its products and packaging, and to optimizing its processes to minimize energy consumption and waste in all forms. Novo employees worldwide are trained to recognize environmental impacts of the firm's activities and to take personal responsibility for finding ways to improve the firm's environmental performance. Employees at all the firm's operations around the world are networked to exchange ideas for environmental improvement. Environmental impacts are defined as an essential consideration in management decision-making processes at all levels. Targets for improving environmental performance are set and published annually, and results for the current year are documented, audited, and published both internally and in the company's annual reports.

[4] 2001 Novo A/S annual report, p. 46.

FINANCIAL PERFORMANCE

Novo A/S measures its financial performance by tracking the "cash value distributions" received from or provided to all of its stakeholders each year. The firm defines its stakeholders as consisting of customers, suppliers, employees, providers of financial resources (both equity and debt), the public sector (government), and management in its role as custodians of future growth for the company. The firm's financial performance as measured by cash value distributions and reported in Novo's 2001 annual report is shown in Exhibit 1.

QUESTIONS FOR DISCUSSION

1. Does Novo A/S's "triple bottom line" reporting give a reasonably complete picture of the firm's performance as a company? Should other dimensions of Novo A/S's performance as an organization also be reported annually?
2. Could Novo A/S's concern for its social responsibility and environmental performance help or hinder its financial performance, and in what ways?
3. Suppose you received interesting employment offers both from Novo A/S and from a second drug company that explicitly emphasizes financial performance—defined only as shareholder value creation—in its annual reports. Would Novo A/S's stated concerns for its performance on social and environmental dimensions, as well as its broader stakeholder view of financial performance, make a difference in your decision as to which offer to accept? If so, why? If not, why not?

Stakeholder	Form of Cash Value Distribution	DKK Millions (%)
Customers	Cash received for products and services	23,290 (100%)
Suppliers	Cash for materials, facilities, and services	10,875 (47%)
Employees	Cash for remuneration	7,203 (31%)
Funders	Cash for dividends and interest	1,021 (4%)
Public sector	Cash for taxes	1,900 (8%)
Management	Cash to be used for future growth	2,291 (10%)
		23,290 (100%)

EXHIBIT 1 Financial Performance of Novo A/S in 2001 Measured by Cash Value Distributions

Source: 2001 Novo A/S annual report, p. 59.

MINI-CASE 7

NUCOR CORPORATION: CORPORATE CULTURE AND INCENTIVES DESIGN

The company known today as Nucor Corporation emerged from a succession of companies that began with a firm originally founded by Ransom E. Olds to produce Oldsmobile automobiles in the 1890s. By the 1950s and 1960s the main business of the company had become designing and manufacturing instruments for the nuclear and electronics industries, and the name of the company had become Nuclear Corporation of America. The company's businesses did not fare well, however, and by 1964 the company was facing bankruptcy.

In 1965 Kenneth Iverson became the new president of the company, which by then operated under the shortened name Nucor Corporation, and introduced major changes in the company's business focus and its management philosophy, especially with regard to company culture, compensation, and incentives.[1]

REFOCUSING NUCOR

On becoming president, Ken Iverson refocused Nucor on its steel joist business, which was operating profitably under the Vulcraft trade name through locations in South Carolina and Nebraska. (See Exhibit 1 for an illustration of a steel joist.) New steel joist plants were soon established in Texas and Alabama, and in 1968 the company integrated upstream into the production of steel bars to supply its growing steel joist business. With its own supply of steel bars, which were also sold to other companies in construction and manufacturing, the company was able to continue expanding its steel joist business. By 2002, Nucor had grown to include seven Vulcraft joist plants in various areas of the United States.

When it decided to begin producing its own supply of steel, the company adopted a steel production technology known as "mini-mill" technology. Rather than adopting the capital-intensive traditional method of producing steel from iron ore, Nucor recycles steel from old automobiles and other used steel products by reducing scrap steel to molten steel in electric-arc furnaces. By 2002, Nucor had established eight steel mini-mills and had become the largest recycler of steel in the United States, recycling more than ten million tons of scrap steel each year. Nucor had also become the largest producer of steel in the United States, with sales over US$4 billion annually. Its product range included heavy beams, sheet steel, steel fasteners, steel decking, and related steel products for construction and industrial metal fabrication.

Because steel is a commodity product, made in standard sizes to standard specifications, competition in the steel industry is based primarily on price. Nucor offers competitive prices for its steel products, but also offers flexibility in arranging fast deliveries of small to medium-sized orders as an added inducement for its customers. In its steel joist business, Nucor competes by offering competitive prices, while providing fast delivery of joists made to an individual customer's quantity and dimensional requirements.

COMPANY CULTURE

Nucor seeks to employ and retain capable and highly productive people in all processes and at all levels of its businesses, and then to challenge its people to help make the company the industry leader. Nucor locates its joist

[1] For a recommended full-length case on Nucor, see "Nucor in 1991" by Frank C. Barnes at University of North Carolina at Charlotte.

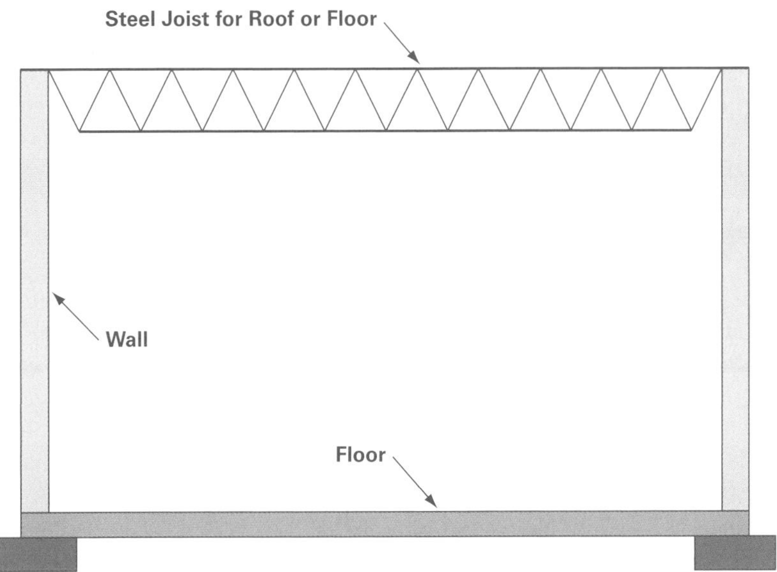

EXHIBIT 1 Illustration of Steel Joint in Building Construction

plants and mini-mills in rural areas of the United States in order to "tap the excellent work ethic of smaller towns," as Iverson once put it.

Nucor uses a simple, "flat," decentralized organization structure that encourages employees to be innovative, to make their own decisions, and to put ideas into action quickly. Below the top management team of about twelve officers are only four layers of employees: general managers (of a Vulcraft joist plant or steel mini-mill), department managers (usually five per joist plant or mini-mill), supervisors, and hourly employees.

Four principles define the employment relationship at Nucor:[2]

1. Management is obligated to manage Nucor in such a way that employees have the opportunity to earn according to their productivity.
2. Employees should be able to be confident that if they do their jobs properly today, they will have their jobs tomorrow.
3. Employees have the right to be treated fairly, and must believe that they will in fact be treated fairly.
4. Employees have a right of appeal when they feel they are being treated unfairly.

Nucor has created an egalitarian company culture in which all major benefits (profit sharing, scholarships for employees' children, insurance, etc.) are available to all employees on an equal footing. The company is also committed to having a lean corporate staff. The corporate officers and staff—fifty people in total—occupies a modest second-floor office in an unpretentious building in Charlotte, North Carolina. Corporate officers do not receive traditional perquisites like company cars, reserved parking places, corporate jets, or executive dining rooms. Further, despite his position as CEO of America's largest steel company, Ken Iverson was legendary for always flying in economy class, taking public transportation, and staying in moderately priced hotels when on business trips.[3]

Management also works hard to create a sense of "family" in the company. The cover of Nucor's 2001 annual report lists the name of each of the company's more than 8,600 employees. The company holds a number of annual events in which all employees and their families participate, from top executives to shop floor workers. Department managers also organize regular dinner events for their employees and spouses. In addition, rather than laying off some workers during dips in demand in the highly cyclical steel and joist businesses, all employees—including managers and the top management team—work a reduced schedule and receive comparably reduced compensation. The company philosophy underlying this policy is that all employees should "share the pain" in tough

[2] For more information on this and other aspects of Nucor, see the company Web site at www.nucor.com/aboutus.

[3] Ken Iverson died in April 2002 at age 76.

times, as well as "share the gains" in good times. However, Ken Iverson established a firm principle that the top managers of Nucor should have the largest part of their compensation "at risk" (i.e., based on the company's performance), because they as top managers have the greatest impact on the performance of the company.

COMPENSATION AND INCENTIVES

Nucor offers significant performance-based compensation to its employees at all levels. Approximately 10 percent of Nucor's before-tax earnings is paid to all employees, with about 15 percent of that amount paid in cash after each year and the balance put into a pension trust fund from which an employee becomes fully eligible to receive benefits after nine years of employment. However, employees are also eligible for significant performance-based compensation plans that vary with their specific jobs. Let us consider the performance incentives for three levels of employees.

Vulcraft Joist Fabrication Workers

Production workers in Vulcraft joist factories are organized into teams of workers who are given broad responsibility for fabricating steel joists in the standard or custom sizes and lengths required by individual customers (typically construction companies). Steel joists must often be produced to exact dimensions to fit a customer's building, and all welding together of steel bars in fabricating a joist must conform to a well-defined industry standard. In addition, individual customers' orders must be produced quickly in relatively small lots to be delivered to construction sites at a precisely scheduled time.

Each of the three or four fabrication teams in a Vulcraft joist plant consists of about twenty-five people and is essentially self-managing, although one team member has the title of foreman. Within a team, roles are specialized, with some workers cutting the steel bars to correct lengths, some laying out and tack-welding the steel bars together, some drilling holes or adding brackets, some doing the final welding, and some painting the joists before shipment. A final inspection is performed by a quality assurance inspector, who is not part of the fabrication team.

Joist factory workers are paid weekly bonuses based directly on the productivity of each fabrication team during the previous week. The bonus is calculated by comparing a current week's output (measured in tons of finished joists) of a fabrication team to a productivity benchmark established for Vulcraft plants in 1977. The more a team exceeds the 1977 productivity benchmark, the greater the bonus paid to the team. A newly formed fabrication team in a new Vulcraft plant might start out producing about three tons an hour, for example, but through incremental improvements that they make in their processes, the team members may eventually produce six tons of joists per hour, or more. In 2002, productivity-based bonuses for Vulcraft fabrication teams range from 80 to 150 percent of their base salaries, which are set at about 30 to 40 percent above local prevailing wage rates.

Because an improperly fabricated joist could cause a costly delay in a customer's construction schedule, or in the worst case possibly even a dangerous structural collapse, all joists must be fabricated to exact dimensions and must have correct welds before they will be shipped to a customer. If a fabrication team makes a joist that does not conform to required dimensions or that has faulty welds, the team must try to repair the joist on its own time, after work or on weekends. If a team cannot repair a faulty joist, the team must pay for the joist, in effect buying the faulty joist from Nucor, and it is then scrapped.

General Managers of Mini-Mills

Nucor mini-mills produce commodity steel products with industry standard composition, strength, shape, and size. Nucor sells steel at or near current market prices, and is profitable when it can sell steel at a market price while producing steel at lower costs than its competitors. Thus, a basic responsibility of Nucor's mini-mill managers is to maintain quality standards for its products while searching for continuous cost reductions and labor savings in their mills' production processes that would lead to a lower cost basis for Nucor. Mini-mill managers speak frequently by phone and meet three times a year to share their latest methods and techniques for cost reduction and labor savings. The firm has achieved considerable success in its cost reduction efforts. In the 1990s, for example, Nucor typically required less than four labor hours to produce a ton of steel, while leading Japanese steel mills required more than five hours of labor per ton and other U.S. steel mills more than six hours per ton.

Mini-mill managers are hired at salaries about 25 percent below the steel industry average for a mill manager. However, mini-mill managers are offered a significant bonus based on the performance of all mini-mills in the steel division. Five percent of all earnings of the steel division above 9 percent return on equity is placed in a bonus pool that is then equally divided among mini-mill managers. In good years, this bonus could equal up to 200 percent of the base salary paid to each manager. The bonus is paid in cash and stock, in roughly equal proportions. At the same time, the understanding is made clear that each mini-mill manager must achieve at least a 14 percent return on assets in his or her mini-mill to remain a manager.

Nucor's Corporate Officers

The basic responsibility of Nucor's officers is to maintain and improve the current profitability of the company, while also identifying and developing new strategic options for future growth of the company.

Nucor's corporate officers receive a base salary that is about 70 percent of the salary paid to executives in comparable positions in the industry. Moreover, they are not offered employment contracts—in effect, they can be discharged at any time without financial penalty to the company. Officers in Nucor also do not receive pension funding, special bonuses, or other perquisites that are common in many large companies. However, officers in Nucor are eligible for a significant performance-based bonus. Approximately 10 percent of the company's earnings in excess of 12 percent return on stockholders' equity is placed in a bonus pool that is pro-rata allocated to officers based on their individual salaries. Approximately half of the bonus is paid in cash after each year and half is paid in the form of deferred compensation.

QUESTIONS FOR DISCUSSION

1. How does Nucor's company culture help or hinder the firm's ability to compete effectively in its businesses?
2. Are the compensation and incentive designs for (a) Vulcraft joist fabrication workers, (b) managers of mini-mills, and (c) corporate officers effective in supporting Nucor's ability to compete in its businesses? If so, why? If not, why not, and how would you improve on these designs?
3. Should the quality assurance inspector for Vulcraft joists be made eligible to share in the joist fabrication team's bonuses? If so, why? If not, why not, and what kind of performance criteria and incentives would you recommend?
4. How would you design the "deferred compensation" portion of the bonus paid to Nucor's corporate officers? Why do you think your incentive design would be effective?

MINI-CASE **8**

PHILIPS NV: ENVIRONMENTAL TRANSFORMATIONS AND ORGANIZATIONAL EVOLUTION

Philips NV of The Netherlands is the third largest electronics company in the world and is the largest electronics company headquartered in Europe. Founded in 1891, Philips today is among the top three producers worldwide of color televisions, computer monitors, audio products, semiconductors, optical CD-R/RW drives, LCD displays, medical imaging equipment, lighting products, electric shavers, powered toothbrushes, and small household appliances (e.g., steam irons). The company employs 184,000 people in more than sixty countries around the world and posted sales of Euros 32 billion (US$30 billion) in 2001.

In the decades since World War II, Philips experienced several significant transformations of its competitive environment. It responded to these environmental changes in part with a number of reorganizations.

THE POSTWAR PERIOD

The first decade or so following World War II saw major strides in the economic rebuilding of Europe. The rebuilding of Europe was accompanied by a surge in demand for many kinds of consumer goods, that brought new levels of convenience and comfort to European households. Philips benefited greatly from this growth in consumer demand in Europe and other parts of the world, and, in the 1950s, Philips factories churned out a growing range of radios, phonographs, kitchen appliances, and other electrical products, as well as an endless stream of electric lightbulbs (its original product and a staple of its overall business). Reflecting the strong national preferences of consumers in the various countries of Europe, most consumer goods, such as radios and household appliances, were styled and produced to suit the tastes of consumers and meet the technical specifications in each country in Europe. In addition, high tariffs or strict quotas in most countries made it costly or impossible to ship goods produced in one country to another.

During this period, Philips was essentially an organization composed of about sixty national companies. The national companies that comprised Philips developed considerable independence during World War II, when Philips' corporate headquarters in Eindhoven was largely destroyed and its administrative processes disrupted. The national company structure inherited from the war years proved successful for Philips after the end of the war. Each national organization developed its own marketing processes focused on discovering and serving the preferences of consumers within its country, and each developed and produced its own products for its national market. The Philips products produced by its various national organizations became popular in their own countries, and could be sold at quite profitable prices in part because tariffs and quotas provided protection from foreign competition. Philips' national units prospered, and Philips' national-unit organizational structure became deeply entrenched in the Philips way of working globally.

THE 1960s AND 1970s

By the late 1950s and early 1960s, however, new kinds of consumer products began to emerge and developed into major product markets. Televisions, hi-fi and then stereo phonographs, and tape recorders—in both portable and home versions—became popular consumer goods. These new products differed in many important respects from the household products popular in the 1950s. The new generation of products used more sophisticated electronics technologies, and they could be produced on high-speed assembly lines that brought significant cost reductions to large-scale producers. In addition, consumers around the world readily accepted similar designs for these kinds of products, and the widespread reduction or removal of tariffs and quota restrictions imposed after World War II led to a boom in world trade in such goods.

Japanese electronics companies such as Matsushita and Sony were quick to capitalize on the new technologies and converging consumer preferences. Japanese companies invested heavily in electronics research and development, developed innovative new electronic product concepts (e.g., Sony's transistor radios and portable miniature television sets), created attractive and reliable global product designs, and built world-scale factories to obtain the greatest possible economies of scale. By the early 1970s, Japanese electronics companies had established price and performance leadership positions in consumer electronics product markets around the world.

The impact of Japanese competition on Philips can hardly be overstated. In the 1960s, each large Philips national company had its own R&D labs and national-scale production facilities. Research in the new product technologies carried out in Philips huge central research center in Eindhoven was also being replicated in several Philips national research centers around the world. In addition, the increasingly costly development of new product designs was being carried out by each national unit for its own market. Production costs in Philips national-scale production facilities were high compared to costs in the world-scale Japanese factories.

To respond to this clearly untenable state of affairs, Philips corporate management created a kind of "semi-matrix" organization structure. Several product-focused business divisions were created and given responsibility for product-related research and product development. National organizations, however, retained responsibility for production. Product strategy for each country was to be decided jointly by national managers and product division managers and carried out by the national units. Any conflicts between the national organizations and the product divisions—and predictably there were some major conflicts—were to be resolved through negotiations sponsored by a new corporate board of management.

THE 1980s

Consumer goods markets in the 1980s witnessed further technological transformations with the advent of semiconductor technology and optical media devices.[1] Within a short time, consumer electronics products became powered by semiconductors, rather than vacuum tubes and large electrical circuits. In addition, optical storage media (compact disks or "CDs") soon began to replace phonograph records and tapes as the preferred medium for audio products. The conversion of most consumer electronics products to semiconductor and optical storage technologies required massive investments in research and development, in world-scale semiconductor and CD production facilities, and in market development.

In the 1980s, Philips began to reorganize its product-related research activities into a few large laboratories, each focused on a key product technology, and consolidated production into large-scale factories producing for worldwide or at least regional markets. The reorganization placed both development centers and factories under the direction of product divisions, rather than national organizations. Philips also began to seek partners to share the growing costs of developing increasingly sophisticated but expensive new technologies, in particular initiating a long-enduring technology development partnership with Matsushita. In addition, a corporate council was created, with equal participation by national organization heads and product division heads, to decide major strategic issues.

In the late 1980s, Philips corporate management grouped most of its dozen or so product divisions into four "core" product groups focused on lighting, consumer electronics, electronic components, and telecommunication and data products. The company also began to sell off a number of peripheral product businesses. For the first time, product division managers were given bottom-line profit responsibility, and product division profitability was made the primary performance evaluation criterion for its product division managers.

THE 1990s

In the late 1980s and early 1990s, major products made by Philips and other consumer electronics firms entered a period of maturity. Products such as color televisions, video cassette recorders, home audio systems, and many personal and domestic appliances had become familiar to

[1] Most of the technology for optical storage media, such as CDs, was developed by Philips' central research facility in Eindhoven (known as the "Nat Lab" within Philips). Philips' patents on this technology generate royalties on every CD sold worldwide.

consumers around the world. In the developed economies, most consumers had already purchased such products, while in developing economies consumers were largely interested only in low-priced versions of such products. Distribution channels also began to consolidate as large chains captured more and more of the retailing of consumer electronics products. These retail chains began to bargain aggressively with producers for lower prices and began to ask that specific versions of such products be sold only through their stores. In the face of leveling demand and consolidating purchasing for such products worldwide, price competition among major consumer electronics producers became intense as they sought to remain profitable by capturing greater market share to increase their economies of scale and lower production costs.

Moreover, because the basic technologies for these products were by then essentially fully exploited and stable, product competition increasingly turned to "featuring" (adding various kinds of features that do not directly improve a product's performance) and frequent restyling, resulting in a proliferation of new product models offering incremental variations on familiar product concepts. A consumer electronics producer's "speed to market" with a stream of newly styled and featured product models became the key to attracting a larger share of consumer replacement purchases and to building market share.

To improve its cost position and speed to market, Philips created a new grouping of consumer electronics product businesses called High Volume Electronics (HVE) that cut across several of its product divisions. HVE product businesses were to cooperate in developing and operating flexible high-volume, low-cost production systems at key production centers around the world to provide a growing range of product diversity quickly and at competitive prices worldwide.

TODAY

Today, a new generation of consumer electronics products based on digital technology is coming to market and promises to reinvigorate consumer demand for many kinds of products. For example, the high resolution, precise color control, and large flat-panel screens of digital high-definition television (HDTV), coupled with the theater-quality "surround sound" for recorded movies made possible by DVD media, appears to be persuading many consumers to replace their current analog technology television sets with a new generation of "home theater" systems. At the same time, MP3 compaction technologies for audio signals, coupled with the availability of inexpensive digital memory chips for storing music in digital form, is making possible a new generation of small, lightweight portable audio products that can store thousands of songs. In addition, digital telecommunications technologies are making it possible to deliver both information and entertainment in digital form to consumers anywhere at anytime.

The ongoing convergence of personal computers, video and audio entertainment products, and telecommunications products to common digital technologies, however, is leading to a profound blurring of these traditional product categories. Today, producers from each of the three product industries are now offering new kinds of products that bundle together product functionalities that were previously available only in separate kinds of products. Moreover, because the digital technologies used in the new generation of multifunctional products are largely industry-standard "open system" technologies available to any interested producer, technological barriers to entry are low, and more and more producers will be able to offer products with essentially the same sets of multifunctional capabilities.[2]

In this emerging competitive environment, creating brands that are desired by consumers will become the critical means of differentiating a firm's products in the marketplace. Recognizing this necessity, in 2000 Philips corporate management launched a major initiative to build the Philips brand globally, especially in the North American market where the Philips brand has not been widely promoted.[3] In addition, a further reorganization of product businesses is reported to be under discussion. This reorganization would regroup a number of now unconnected product businesses to refocus them on serving the needs and preferences of important categories of consumers. One new group, for example, might consist of several portable audio and video products, as well as certain personal and domestic appliances, and would be focused on creating a coordinated suite of Philips "lifestyle products" targeted at young, mobile, and relatively affluent consumers. Coordinated advertising for the group would emphasize the message that Philips is the best source of creative products designed specifically for their lifestyles. Other regroupings would refocus several

[2] As a major developer and producer of semiconductors that provide the new digital technologies, Philips' Semiconductor division is a major supplier of "chip sets" to other consumer electronics companies, as well as to leading telecommunications companies like Nokia.

[3] Philips has maintained a major presence in North America for many years, but was previously content to market its consumer electronics products under the Magnavox brand and to provide OEM-branded products to Sears and other large retailers.

kinds of Philips products on other important groups of consumers, such as older consumers concerned about health and personal care, professionals running small businesses, and so on.

QUESTIONS FOR DISCUSSION

1. Do you think the "semi-matrix" organizational structure of product divisions and national organizations adopted by Philips in the 1960s was a good approach to meeting its competitive challenges at the time? What were the strengths and weaknesses of this approach?
2. Given the blurring of traditional product categories and the convergence toward common digital technologies in the 1990s, should bottom-line profit responsibility still remain with product division managers? If so, why? If not, why not, and where would you propose to place profit responsibility instead?
3. Given Philips' management structure in the 1990s, what organizational challenges do you foresee if Philips decides to reorganize its product businesses into groups focused on creating suites of products for specific categories of customers? How would you manage these challenges in making the transition to the new organizational structure?

MINI-CASE 9

THE RETAIL GROCERY INDUSTRY IN THE USA: A CHANGING COMPETITIVE ENVIRONMENT

The retail grocery industry in the United States includes more than 30,000 supermarkets and generates more than US$360 billion in sales annually, accounting for approximately 5% of total U.S. gross national product (GNP). After many years of relative stability and steady growth, in the 1980s and 1990s the U.S. retail grocery industry entered a period of intensifying competitive pressures and accelerating change in many aspects of its environment. These pressures and changes raise many questions about the future viability of the traditional supermarket-based Strategic Logic for competing in the retail grocery industry.[1]

INDUSTRY DEVELOPMENTS

Although groceries are sold in a variety of ways in various parts of the world, for the last four or five decades in the United States the dominant model for retailing groceries has been the supermarket. Most commonly located in an urban, suburban, or small-town shopping center, the traditional U.S. supermarket typically covers 5,000 to 10,000 square meters (approximately 50,000 to 100,000 square feet) and offers a full range of fresh, canned, and frozen foods, as well as pet food, household cleaning products, and personal care items. U.S. supermarkets also typically offer several choices of national and regional brands for most items, while large chains also offer their own store brands for most popular food items.

Ownership and management of supermarkets has traditionally included families or sole proprietors operating a single or perhaps a few supermarkets in a given urban or rural area, while supermarkets owned and operated by regional chains tend to predominate in newer suburban shopping centers built in the 1970s and later. In the 1980s and 1990s, however, a wave of mergers and acquisitions led to the emergence of several large retail grocery companies operating chains of supermarkets in several regions of the United States. By 2001, the top five U.S. grocery chains operated more than 7,400 supermarkets (about 25% of the national total), had combined revenues of more than US$145 billion, and accounted for approximately 40% of total grocery sales in the United States (see Exhibit 1). By 2000, almost all of the new supermarkets being built in the United States belonged to the largest ten grocery chains.

The 1980s and 1990s also saw the entry of two large European food retailers into the U.S. grocery market. The Netherlands-based food retailer Royal Ahold now generates approximately US$50 billion in food sales annually, of which US$30 billion is realized in Europe and US$20 billion in the United States (see Exhibit 1). In addition, Belgium-based Delhaize became a major supermarket operator in the U.S. through its acquisition of Food Lion stores.

In the 1990s, several kinds of nongrocery retailers began to enter the retail grocery industry, attracted by the exceptionally high frequency of visits that consumers typically make to supermarkets compared to other types of retailing establishments.[2] In the mid-1990s, Wal-Mart—the largest retailer in the world with sales well in excess of US$100 billion—made a determined entry into the retail grocery industry by combining its traditional discount store

[1] Information on the retail grocery industry in the United States, including some of the data used in this case, can be obtained from the trade publication *Progressive Grocer and Supermarket Business*. For a recommended full-length case on the retail grocery industry, see "The Great Atlantic and Pacific Tea Company, Inc., and the Retail Grocery Industry," by Dan Kopp, Lois Shufeldt, and Jim Kendall.

[2] In 2000, U.S. households visited a supermarket an average of 87 times a year, compared to 25 visits to a discount store, 15 visits to a drug store, and 14 visits to a convenience store.

product offerings with a large-scale supermarket to create 20,000 square meter (200,000 square foot) Supercenters selling 150,000 or more different items.[3] By 2000, Wal-Mart had opened nearly 900 Supercenters throughout the United States, while three competitors—Kmart, Target, and Meijer—between them had opened another 200 supercenter-type stores. In addition, nongrocery "category retailers"—retailers that specialize in retailing one category of goods—also began various forays into grocery retailing. For example, large drug store chains like Walgreen's (with nearly 6,000 stores), CVS (4,100 stores), and Eckerd's (2,600 stores) began to increase their offerings of some grocery items, candies, soft drinks, and snacks in an effort to increase their frequency of consumer visits.

The 1990s also saw a veritable explosion of alternative grocery retailing concepts in the United States. Warehouse clubs like Costco and Sam's Club (a division of Wal-Mart) began to offer low prices on larger-sized "institutionally packaged" products (including most essential kinds of groceries) to consumers willing to pay a modest membership fee. By 2001, more than 850 warehouse clubs operating throughout the United States were generating more than US$50 billion in total revenues, including approximately US$20 billion in grocery sales.

Another kind of grocery retailing establishment that grew rapidly in the 1990s is the limited assortment store. These stores do not try to offer a comprehensive range of grocery products, but rather use smaller stores to focus on a limited assortment of grocery items that consumers need and buy most frequently. Save-A-Lot stores (operated by Supervalu) rely on large-volume purchases and rapid inventory turnovers of a limited assortment of items to offer low prices to consumers. Aldi and Trader Joe's stores (operated by the German firm Aldi) offer aggressive pricing on a limited but continuously changing and somewhat eclectic assortment of food items. More than 2,000 limited assortment stores were operating in the United States by 2000 and were generating about US$10 billion in sales annually.

Convenience stores are also growing in importance in the retailing of groceries in the United States. There are nearly 130,000 convenience stores in the United States, typically located on high-traffic streets and highways and offering a basic selection of most frequently purchased grocery items like bread, milk, and soft drinks. The archetypal convenience store operator in the United States, 7-Eleven, operates more than 5,600 locations throughout the United States. Increasingly, the convenience store concept is being extended to include the retailing of gasoline and of snacks and fast foods prepared on the premises in kiosks operated by major fast-food companies such as Burger King, Taco Bell, and Pizza Hut. Convenience stores attached to service stations operated by Shell, Texaco, Chevron, Exxon-Mobil, British Petroleum, Phillips Petroleum, and other major gasoline retailers now number nearly 20,000 and represent the fastest growing type of convenience store in the United States. Approximately US$14 billion of grocery items were sold through convenience stores in the United States in 2001.

EVOLVING CONSUMER PREFERENCES

In addition to developments within their industry, grocery retailers also face major evolutions in consumers' lifestyles and resulting changes in consumer preferences for food products. Broadly speaking, consumers are becoming more time-constrained, are looking for the convenience of one-stop shopping, are interested in more varied and more healthful foods, are less loyal to a single store or brand of store, and are becoming increasingly price sensitive.

As more Americans began to work longer hours in the 1980s and 1990s, and especially as more women pursued careers and held full-time jobs, consumers began to have less and less time to spend on traditional family-related activities like food shopping and cooking. More U.S. consumers are now "eating out" more often, preferring to meet their need for food by buying already prepared food served in restaurants and fast-food establishments. Increasingly, when consumers do shop for groceries, many are looking for foods that require as little preparation as possible. In addition, fewer grocery shoppers are making regular weekly trips to a local supermarket to purchase a carefully prepared list of needed items.[4] Instead, more shoppers are purchasing more of their groceries on a "fill in" basis, opportunistically picking up a few items from the growing variety of retail establishments that offer some grocery products, like drug stores and gas stations with convenience stores. When they do go shopping for groceries, time-constrained consumers increasingly prefer the convenience of one-stop shopping and are attracted to supercenter-type stores

[3] Wal-Mart's Supercenters essentially emulate the "hypermarché" store concept originally developed and popularized in France by Carrefours, Auchan, and Leclerc in the 1970s and 1980s.

[4] One leading grocery retailer estimates that fewer than 30 percent of their customers regularly shop each week to purchase a predetermined list of groceries.

where they can shop for food, personal care items, hardware, garden supplies, and other kinds of consumer goods all under one roof.

More and more consumers—especially the "U.S. baby boomers" now entering their 50s and 60s—are also becoming more concerned about their health. They are looking for more healthful foods that are low in fat and salt content, low in calories, free of pesticides and other contaminants, and nutritious as well as good tasting. At the same time, in the recessionary economic conditions of 2002 and later, consumers are becoming increasingly price sensitive, less loyal to a given store or brand, and more willing to do their shopping for groceries at whatever retailer currently offers the best values on their most frequently purchased items.

THE CHANGING RETAIL ENVIRONMENT

By 2002, the retailing of grocery products in the United States was undergoing visible and far-reaching changes as operators of supermarkets—the traditional mainstay of grocery retailing—searched for new approaches to meeting the challenges posed by their evolving industry situation and changing customer preferences.

To meet the growing consumer need for the convenience of one-stop shopping, many grocery retailers are rapidly converting their traditional supermarkets to supercenters and offering an expanded mix of retail products and services, as well as grocery products. Banking, video rentals, photographic film developing, copy centers, and similar on-site services are now becoming common facets of grocery retail establishments. More grocery retailers—Jewel Osco, for example—are opening stores that combine groceries, a pharmacy, and a drug store under one roof. Other grocery retailers are building gasoline retailing services in their parking lots. Some grocery retailers have begun to partner with other kinds of category retailers like Office Depot and Toys R Us to offer boutiques with better selections of nongrocery items in their stores. In further efforts to build traffic, increase community awareness of their expanding range of products and services, and improve customer loyalty, some grocery retailers are sponsoring or hosting community events within their supercenters.

Even though the product mix offered by retail grocers is becoming broader, retailing groceries today increasingly demands continuous exploration of evolving consumer preferences for groceries and other products—and rapid responses to discovered shifts in consumer preferences. In addition, the growing ethnic, cultural, and economic diversity of the U.S. population calls for a greater ability to segment the market for grocery products more finely and to offer selections of grocery products that are fine-tuned to meet the specific preferences of targeted market segments. In this regard, a number of grocery retailers are experimenting with smaller stores that offer a more limited but tightly focused assortment of grocery products intended to serve the preferences of consumers in targeted income categories or consumers with specific kinds of preferences for food products.

In an effort to micromarket to individual consumers and thereby to rebuild customer loyalty, many grocery retailers are instituting customer membership programs (with memberships usually offered for free or at a nominal charge). These programs offer special pricing on many grocery products to customers who carry a store membership card. Use of a customer membership card when making purchases identifies each customer and allows tracking of each member's total purchases, frequency of visits, most commonly purchased items, and so on. Grocery retailers then use data gathered in this way to analyze an individual customer's purchasing habits. Targeted promotions and discounts on the items most commonly purchased by an individual customer are then sent by direct mail or e-mail to induce more frequent visits and increase total purchases.

Some of the more radical notions of micromarketing now being discussed in the industry would use advanced technologies to micromarket to individual customers within stores. For example, in one scenario of the future of grocery retailing, face-recognition technologies would identify regular customers when they enter a store. Information technologies would then match the customer's face pattern with a database of that customer's most frequently purchased items (or items for which the customer seems to have low price sensitivity). Telecommunications technologies would then send a set of personalized product promotions and offers to the customer's mobile phone while he or she is shopping.

More grocery retailers are also offering a growing array of prepared foods and devoting more floor space to "deli counters" selling prepared food to take away or to be consumed at in-store dining facilities. Increasing numbers of U.S. consumers are going to grocery retailing establishments, rather than fast-food establishments, to buy ready-to-eat food.

In response to the growing price sensitivity of consumers, most large grocery retailers are expanding their offerings of store brands that are typically sold at prices 10 to 20 percent below traditional branded products. Because grocery retailers are an essential link between food producers and food consumers, they are increasing their bargaining power with large food producers to package a growing range of food, household, and personal care products under their store brands (sometimes called "private label" goods). Today, even for large food producers with nationally known brands, gaining access to supermarket shelf space for their branded products usually requires agreeing to provide retail grocers with store-branded versions of their products. At the same time, the growing volume of lower-priced products sold under store brands is putting a further squeeze on the already razor-thin margins of grocery retailers.[5]

Finally, grocery retailers face growing difficulties in finding the right human resources to staff their new retailing environments. The strict application of child-labor laws to the grocery industry that began in the United States in the 1980s has all but eliminated the use of relatively low-wage, part-time high school students to restock goods on shelves, bag groceries, and perform other manual tasks in stores. As a result, many grocery retailers are now trying to follow Wal-Mart's lead in actively recruiting retired senior citizens to perform a variety of in-store tasks on a part-time basis. Perhaps more fundamentally, however, the retail grocery industry faces a chronic shortage of talented managers, most of whom are attracted to careers in more "glamorous" or high-profile industries. Attracting and retaining the creative and talented people needed to lead the retail grocery industry into its next era is becoming an increasingly serious challenge.

[5] Net profits of grocery retailers are typically 1 percent or less of sales.

QUESTIONS FOR DISCUSSION

1. What are the most important macroenvironmental and industry changes affecting the retail grocery industry in the United States today?
2. What kind of new Strategic Logic for retailing groceries do you think could be successful in responding to these macroenvironmental and industry changes? On what main points would the new Strategic Logic you propose differ from the traditional supermarket-based Strategic Logic in the retail grocery industry?
3. What new capabilities would a retail grocery company have to develop to carry out the new Strategic Logic you propose? Specifically, what new capabilities would be needed in the following areas:
   a. Customer relationship management?
   b. Supplier relationship management?
   c. Facilities management?
   d. Logistics?
   e. Human resources management?
4. What potential do you see for converting the competitive pressures that retail grocery firms currently face in their industry into sources of mutual gain achieved through cooperation?

Company	Number of Supermarkets[a]	Revenues (US$ billions)
Kroger Co.	2,366	43
Albertson's	1,715	31
Safeway	1,482	29
Wal-Mart[b]	908	23
Ahold USA	974	20

[a] The large supermarket companies operate stores under several brand names, generally retaining the established brand names of chains they have acquired in various parts of the United States. Kroger operates under brand names Kroger, Fred Meyer, Ralph's, Smith's, King Soopers, Dillon, Fry's, City Market, Food 4 Less, and Quality Food Centers. Albertson's operates stores under the Albertson's, Jewel Osco, and Acme Markets brand names. Safeway operates Safeway, Vons, Dominick's, Randall's Tom Thumb, and Carrs branded stores. Ahold USA operates Giant Food, Bi-Lo, Stop & Shop, and Tops supermarkets.

[b] Includes only Wal-Mart's grocery retailing activities through its grocery Supercenters and Neighborhood Markets.

EXHIBIT 1 Top Five Grocery Retailers in the United States, 2001

Source: Progressive Grocer and Supermarket Business.

MINI-CASE **10**

THE WALT DISNEY COMPANY: A SEARCH FOR SYNERGIES IN THE ENTERTAINMENT INDUSTRY

The Walt Disney Company (hereafter referred to simply as "Disney") was founded largely on the success of early animated cartoons featuring the character Mickey Mouse, created by Walt Disney in 1928. Today, Disney encompasses four major entertainment business divisions that in 2001 collectively generated revenues in excess of US$25 billion, of which slightly more than US$4 billion was earned outside the United States.[1] Disney employs more than 110,000 people around the world and is the second largest entertainment company in the world, surpassed in revenues only by AOL Time Warner. After posting profits of US$1.3 billion in 1999 and US$920 million in 2000, the firm recorded a loss of US$158 million in 2001.

Founder Walt Disney took the first steps in Disney's search for synergies soon after the company's emergence as a leading producer of animated cartoons in the 1930s, when he began to conceive of an amusement park based on his popular cartoon characters. However, it is under the direction of Michael Eisner, who became CEO of Disney in 1984, that the firm's search for synergies grew into a massive, multifaceted, global undertaking.

DISNEY'S ENTERTAINMENT BUSINESSES

In 2002, Disney's entertainment empire includes several hundred business units, most of which are grouped into four major divisions focused on movies, theme parks, television networks and Internet services, and consumer products.

Studio Entertainment

Due in large part to the huge success of its Mickey Mouse cartoon character, in the 1930s Walt Disney Studios became the largest and most sophisticated producer of animated cartoons and movies in the world. In the 1950s, Disney studios also began producing "live-action" films for family entertainment. The studio scored major financial successes with films based on popular children's books like *Treasure Island, Swiss Family Robinson, Robin Hood,* and *20,000 Leagues Under the Sea.*

Today, through its Walt Disney Studio Entertainment division, Disney produces a wide range of both animated feature films and "live action" movies for distribution through movie theaters, television, video rental stores, airline in-flight entertainment, and a variety of retail sales channels. The Walt Disney Pictures unit creates a stream of animated films featuring new cartoon characters targeted largely at children, as well as family-oriented films. Miramax Film Corp., Touchstone Pictures, and Hollywood Pictures create adult-oriented films. The studio division also distributes its films to movie theaters, video rental shops, and other channels through its Buena Vista distribution units. Live theater productions for children and adults are staged by Walt Disney Theatrical Productions and Buena Vista Theatrical Productions, respectively. The studio entertainment division also includes a music group that produces and markets music

[1] For a recommended full-length case on Disney, see "Michael Eisner's Disney Company" by Gareth R. Jones.

under the Walt Disney Records, Lyric Street, and Hollywood Records labels.

Parks and Resorts

An early dream of founder Walt Disney was to create an amusement park that would feature "live" versions of his famous cartoon characters Mickey Mouse, Donald Duck, Goofy, and others. Disney's dream was realized in July 1955 with the opening of Disneyland in Anaheim, California. Disneyland was enormously successful and soon stimulated plans for a second Disney theme park in Florida to be called Disney World. The concept behind Disney World, however, was much broader than the original idea for Disneyland. Walt Disney had observed that the hotels and restaurants around the original Disneyland were also successful and profitable—perhaps even more profitable than Disneyland itself—and he was determined to capture a larger share of the revenues to be earned from the families visiting Disney World. Disney eventually purchased a 12,000-hectare (28,000-acre) tract of land near Orlando, Florida, and in 1971 opened not just a new Magic Kingdom theme park based on Disney characters, but also a permanent display of futuristic technologies and international culture called Epcot Center. Disney also gained control of most of the vacation dollars spent by families visiting Disney World by opening a succession of large hotels within Disney World's borders. Disney also owns or licenses to major operators, such as McDonald's, all the restaurants and other concessions within Disney World.

The enormous popularity of both Disneyland and Disney World enabled Disney to raise admission fees to the parks by 45 percent in the mid-1980s. The increased admission fees, plus the revenues and licensing fees from restaurants and other concessions in the two theme parks, became the major source of profits in Disney's business in the late 1980s. Disney also began to open new kinds of theme parks adjacent to or (where possible) within its two main parks, including the water theme parks Typhoon Lagoon and Wet 'N Wild in Disney World. Disney also co-ventured with MGM studios to open Disney-MGM Studios theme park within Disney World in 1989. Building on the long-standing success of Disneyland, in 2001 Disney added California Adventure and Downtown Disney theme parks to its renamed Disneyland Resort. Where possible, Disney also bought and upgraded hotel properties in the vicinity of its Disneyland Resort parks.

The financial success of its theme parks in California and Florida led Disney to look for opportunities to open Disney theme parks outside the United States. In 1991, Disney opened EuroDisney. Located a short drive east of Paris, EuroDisney is a somewhat scaled-down version of Disney World, offering not only a Disney character theme park, but also a range of Disney hotels and other tourist services. After an initial period of low attendance, resulting financial difficulties, and restructuring in the 1990s, Disney now owns 39 percent of EuroDisney, the balance being owned by the French government and several European investors. Disney receives fees for operating EuroDisney, as well as royalties on sales generated within the park. Disney also co-developed Tokyo Disney Resort with Japanese partners and recently added an adjacent Disney Seas theme park. Disney does not actually own the two parks in Japan, but operates them and receives royalties on admission fees and other sales (estimated at US$200 million per year[2]). Most recently, Disney concluded a deal with the Hong Kong government to partner in opening a 140-hectare (300-acre) Disney theme park in Hong Kong. Disney will own 43 percent of the park and will also receive management fees and royalties on sales within the park. Shanghai and New Delhi have also been mentioned as possible sites for future Disney parks in Asia.

Disney's parks and resorts division also includes the Anaheim Angels major league baseball team and the Mighty Ducks of Anaheim professional hockey team, as well as the Disney Cruise Line.

Media Networks

Walt Disney recognized early the potential of television as a distribution channel for Disney's animated films. In 1954, Disney created a television program called "The Wonderful World of Disney" to feature Disney's animated cartoons and live-action films. In 1955, Disney brought "The Mickey Mouse Club" to American television. Both Disney television programs quickly became prominent parts of American popular culture and enjoyed great popularity and financial success for many years.

Today, television programs produced by Disney are shown on Disney's own television networks and licensed for broadcast on television networks outside the United States. Disney's Media Networks division encompasses both the ABC broadcast television network in North America and the cable television channels ABC Family, ESPN, The Disney Channel, A&E (Arts and Entertainment), Toon Disney, and SoapNet. The division also includes ten local television stations in major U.S.

[2] Jonathan Weber, "Disney, Invader," *Wired,* February 2002, pp. 70–79.

cities, as well as more than sixty radio stations. Disney programs are also regularly broadcast by television networks in Europe and Latin America. The Media Networks division is now working to expand its presence in Asia. In 2002, the Media Networks division made its first major entry into the Chinese market by concluding a contract with the state-owned China Central Television (CCTV) network to broadcast 142 Mickey Mouse cartoons to more than 225 million households in mainland China. The CCTV deal follows the successful runs in China of the *Disney on Ice* skating show and a theatrical production of *Beauty and the Beast,* both staged by the Studio Entertainment division's Theatrical Productions business unit.

In 2002, in the aftermath of the bursting of the dot-com bubble in the United States, the Media Networks division absorbed the Walt Disney Internet Group, previously the fifth business division within Disney. The Internet group maintains Web sites in more than 20 countries promoting various Disney products and services and supporting Disney's broadcast and cable television businesses through ABC.com, ABCNEWS.com, ABCSports.com, Disney.com, ESPN.com, and Movies.com. The Internet group is now developing wireless services such as leasing Disney characters to enliven mobile phone displays, a concept that has become very popular in Japan.

Consumer Products

The Walt Disney Consumer Products division creates children's toys based on Disney characters, operates a chain of Disney Stores located in major shopping malls in the United States, sells Disney goods through the direct-mail Disney Catalog and online through DisneyStore.com, and licenses Disney characters to other producers of toys, clothing, housewares, and other consumer goods. The division is now experimenting with extending the Disney brand and characters into new product categories, such as a line of Disney cereals to be produced and distributed by Kellogg (the largest producer of breakfast cereals in the United States), as well as Disney soft drinks to be produced and distributed by Coca-Cola.

The division's Buena Vista Game Entertainment Studio and Disney Interactive units create and market computer games and other software based on Disney characters. The Buena Vista Publishing Group publishes children's books, as well as the magazines *Disney Adventures, Discover, Family Fun*, and *US Weekly.*

SYNERGY SUCCESSES AND CHALLENGES

Disney's Lion King character illustrates the potential for realizing significant synergies across Disney's many business units. Since its release in 1994, the enormously popular children's animated feature film *The Lion King* has grossed over US$765 million at movie theaters worldwide. Subsequent rentals and sales of *The Lion King* videos and DVDs continue to be highly profitable. Disney also released a best-selling record album based on songs from the film and stages live theater productions of the Lion King story that continue to draw audiences in major cities of the world. A series of children's cartoons featuring the Lion King characters was launched on the Disney Channel, and a Lion King attraction has been added to Disneyland. Disney also launched an entire range of Lion King children's toys, clothing, and related items. Although Disney does not publish profit figures for products based on individual Disney characters, total profits earned by all divisions from products based on the Lion King character are thought to exceed US$1 billion to date.[3]

Successfully achieving such synergies requires coordination of marketing activities across the four Disney business divisions and their many business units. To address this challenge, in 1999 Disney created a region- and country-based management function to complement its product division structure. Country managers have responsibility for "coordinating brand strategy" across all Disney activities within a country, and regional managers have responsibility for coordinating activities of country units within their region. Country managers in Asia, for example, now meet weekly and conduct weekly conference calls with product division managers in their region to discuss upcoming releases of new Disney films and other marketing activities that should be coordinated with each film's release.

SOME CURRENT RESULTS

The US$158 million net loss in 2001 was the first loss recorded by Disney since Michael Eisner became CEO in 1984. Commentators suggested a number of possible causes. Some recent large-budget films from the Studio Entertainment division (for example, *Pearl Harbor* and *Treasure Planet*) did not do as well financially as expected. The ABC broadcast television network is

[3] Jonathan Weber, "Disney, Invader," *Wired,* February 2002, p. 75.

generally thought to be struggling, experiencing falling advertising revenues, poor ratings, a dearth of "hit" programs, and overall poor financial performance. Although its theme park operations are still a major source of profits for Disney, the decline in vacation travel in the United States after the September 2001 terrorist attacks reduced the profits contributed to Disney by its theme parks. And although more than half of the consumer products division's revenues are generated outside the United States, its sales growth both inside and outside the United States slowed in recent years.

QUESTIONS FOR DISCUSSION

1. What assets or capabilities do you think offer the greatest potential for realizing synergies across Disney's current business units? Be specific in identifying both the assets and capabilities that are important sources of synergies and the exact kinds of synergies to be obtained.
2. Has Disney achieved an optimal extent of diversification? Should it continue to add new kinds of businesses or divest some of its current businesses? Why?
3. What kind of management coordination do you think is needed to achieve maximum results in realizing synergies across Disney's four divisions and many business units?
4. If "bottom-line" profit responsibility remains with the product divisions and their business units, do you think the current product division and country manager matrix will be effective in realizing synergies across the four divisions? If so, why? If not, why not, and how would you change the allocation of profit responsibilities to improve the realization of synergies?

CASE **1**

AMAZON.COM: INTERNET BOOK RETAILING—AND BEYOND

By Suresh Kotha, University of Washington Business School

Jeff Bezos, the CEO of Amazon.com, was pleased that his three-year-old online start-up, www.amazon.com, had gone from being an underground sensation for book-lovers on the World Wide Web (WWW) to one of the most admired Internet retailers on Wall Street. To date, his attempts to transform the traditional book-retailing format through technology that taps the interactive nature of the Internet has been very successful. Although his company garnered rave reviews from respected Wall Street Analysts, Bezos clearly understood that this was not the moment to dwell on the past. In the fast-moving world of the Internet, he and his firm continued to face many formidable challenges.

This case describes how Bezos has managed to build a rapidly growing retail business on the Internet and the challenges he and his top management currently face as other industry giants such as Barnes & Noble, and Bertelsmann, the German Publishing Conglomerate, attempt to imitate his model of competition.

COMPANY BACKGROUND

In 1994, Jeffrey Bezos, a computer science and electrical-engineering graduate from Princeton University, was the youngest senior vice president in the history of D.E. Shaw, a Wall Street-based investment bank. During the summer of 1994, one important statistic about the Internet caught his attention, and imagination—Internet usage was growing at 2,300 percent a year. His reaction: "Anything that's growing that fast is going to be ubiquitous very quickly. It was my wake-up call."

He left his job at D.E. Shaw and drew up a list of twenty possible products that could be sold on the Internet. He quickly narrowed his prospects to music and books. Both shared a potential advantage for online sale: far too many titles for a single store to stock. He chose books.

> There are so many of them! There are 1.5 million English-language books in print, 3 million books in all languages worldwide. This volume defined the opportunity. Consumers keep demonstrating that they value authoritative selection. The biggest phenomenon in retailing is the big-format store—the "category killer"—whether it's selling books, toys, or music. But the largest physical bookstore in the world has only 175,000 titles. ... With some 4,200 U.S. publishers and the two biggest booksellers, Barnes & Noble and Borders Group Inc., accounting for less than 12 percent of total sales, there aren't any 800-pound gorillas in book selling.[1]

In contrast, the music industry had only six major record companies that controlled the distribution of records and CDs sold in the United States. With such control, these firms had the potential to lock out a new business threatening the traditional record store format.

To start his new venture, Bezos left New York City to move West, either to Boulder, Seattle, or Portland. As he drove west, he refined and fine-tuned his thoughts as well as his business plan. In doing so, he concluded that Seattle was his final destination. Recalls Bezos:

> It sounds counterintuitive, but physical location is very important for the success of a virtual business. We could have started Amazon.com anywhere. We chose Seattle because it met a rigorous set of criteria. It had to be a place with lots of technical talent. It had to be near a place with large numbers of books. It had to be a nice place to live—great people won't work in places they don't want to live. Finally, it had to

[1] "Who's writing the book on web business?" *Fast Company,* October–November 1996, pp. 132–133.

> be in a small state. In the mail-order business, you have to charge sales tax to customers who live in any state where you have a business presence. It made no sense for us to be in California or New York. . . . Obviously Seattle has a great programming culture. And it's close to Roseburg, Oregon, which has one of the biggest book warehouses in the world.[2]

Renting a house in Bellevue, a Seattle suburb, Bezos started working out of his garage. Ironically, he held meetings with prospective employees and suppliers at a nearby Barnes & Noble superstore. Bezos also raised several million dollars from private investors. Operating from a 400-square-foot office in Bellevue, he launched his venture, Amazon.com, on the Internet in July 1995.

As word about his new venture spread quickly across the Internet, sales picked up rapidly. Six weeks after opening, Bezos moved his new firm to a 2,000-square-foot warehouse. Six months later, he moved once again, this time to a 17,000-square-foot building in an industrial neighborhood in Seattle. To fund further expansion, Bezos attracted $8 million from Kleiner, Perkins, Caufield & Byers, a venture-capital firm based in the Silicon Valley that has funded firms such as Sun Microsystems and Netscape.

By the end of 1996, his firm was one of the most successful Web retailers, with revenues reaching $15.6 million. (Revenues for a large Barnes & Noble superstore amount to about $5 million on average per year.) With revenues surging quarter after quarter, Bezos decided to take his company public. However, just days before the firm's initial public offering (IPO) of three million shares, Barnes & Noble—the nation's largest book retailer—launched its online store and sued Amazon.com for claiming to be the world's largest bookstore. To entice customers to visit its Web store, Barnes & Noble offered deeper discounts. Bezos retaliated with a counter lawsuit of his own.[3]

On May 14, 1997, Bezos took Amazon.com public. *The Wall Street Journal* noted that: "Amazon's May 1997 debut on the Nasdaq Stock Market came with no small amount of hype. On the first day of trading, investors bid the price of shares up to $23.50 from their offering price of $18. But the shares then fell, and within three weeks of the IPO they were below their offering price."

Despite this, customers have continued to flock to Amazon.com's Web site. By October 1997 Amazon.com served its millionth "unique" customer. To keep pace with such growth, the firm expanded its Seattle warehouse and built a second 200,000-square-foot state-of-the-art distribution center in New Castle, Delaware. With these additions Amazon.com successfully increased its stocking and shipping capabilities to nearly six times its 1996 levels.

As the firm continued to expand its customer base, sales revenues have surged. The firm's revenues increased from $15.7 million in 1996 to $147 million in 1997. Sales

[2] *Fast Company,* October–November 1996.

[3] In October 1997, Barnes & Noble and Amazon.com settled their respective lawsuits by saying that they would prefer to get back to business and compete in the marketplace rather than in the courtroom.

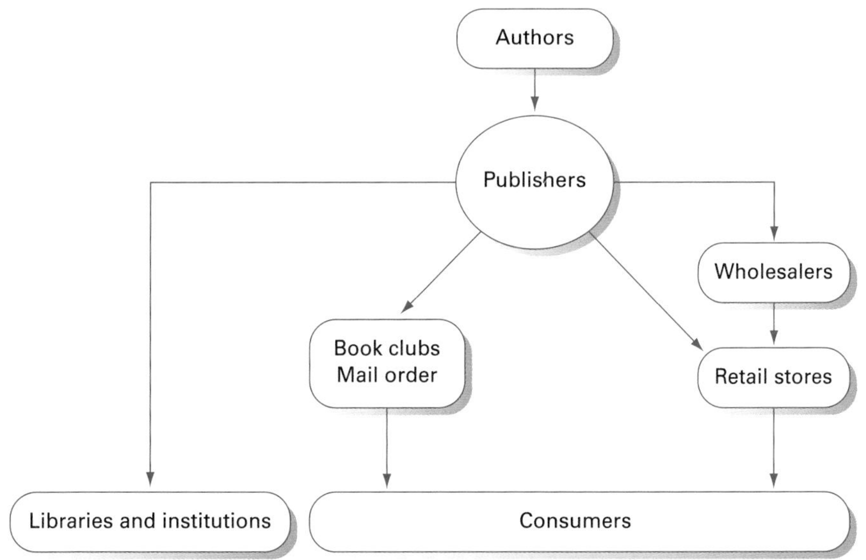

EXHIBIT 1 Book Publishing Market Structure

are now on pace to top $550 million for fiscal 1998. In response to this revenue growth, the company's stock and market capitalization have proceeded to rise as well. As of July 1998, the company's capitalization was around $6.4 billion, a number that represents the combined value of the nation's two largest retailers, Barnes & Noble and Borders Books & Music, whose combined sales are about 10 times that of Amazon.com's.

THE BOOK PUBLISHING INDUSTRY

The United States is the world's largest market for books, with retail book sales accounting for $20.76 billion in 1997. With over 2,500 publishers in the United States, the book publishing industry is one of the oldest and most fragmented industries.[4] Exhibit 1 shows the structure of the U.S. publishing industry.

Publishers

Publishers sell books on a consignment basis and assume all the risk in this industry. They also accept returns on unsold books, thus guaranteeing their distributors a 100 percent refund on all unsold books. They provide money and contracts to prospective authors and decide how many copies of a book to print. Typically a "first-run" print for a book varies from 5,000 to 50,000 copies. However, best-selling authors' first-run prints are generally set at around 300,000 copies.

In practice, however, trade (adult and juvenile books) and paperback publishers print far more copies than will be sold. About 25 percent of all books distributed to wholesalers are returned and at times these percentages run as high as 40 percent for mass-market paperbacks. According to industry experts, 20 to 30 percent for hardcover book returns is considered acceptable and 30 to 50 percent is generally considered high. Anything above 50 percent is considered disastrous. In a process known as "remaindering" (offering books to discount stores, jobbers, and other vendors) publishers drastically reduce the price after a certain period. Apart from the material cost of returns and the lost revenue they represent, publishers spend millions of dollars each year transporting books back and forth. In this industry profit margins are driven by book volume, which in turn hinges on the size of each print run. Generally about 10 percent of titles make a profit, with 90 percent barely breaking even. Exhibit 2 illustrates the margins on a typical hardcover book.

The "big three"—Warner Books, Simon & Schuster, and Pearson—accounted for 21 percent of sales in 1995. The twenty largest book-publishing companies in the United States command over 60 percent of all retail sales. Warner Books, a subsidiary of Time Warner, the U.S. entertainment giant, was the largest publisher, with sales of $3.7 billion in 1995. Simon & Schuster, a division of Viacom Corporation, ranked second with sales reaching $2.17 billion, and Pearson, a group that owns the *Financial Times,* ranked third with revenues of $1.75 billion.

Wholesalers

Wholesalers distribute books. They take orders from independent booksellers and chains, and consolidate them into lot-orders for publishers. Publishers supply wholesalers who in turn supply the thousands of retail bookstores located throughout the United States. Wholesalers accounted for almost 30 percent of publishers' sales in

[4] Much of the information discussed in this section, and the section that follows, is drawn from *Amazon.com,* a University of Washington Business School Case, by Suresh Kotha and Emer Dooley, 1997.

Book List Price	**$19.95**	**Explanation**
Revenue to publisher (i.e., price paid by wholesaler or bookstore)	$10.37	Represents 48 percent discount off suggested retail price
Manufacturing cost	$ 2.00	Printing, binding, jacket design, composition, typesetting, paper, ink
Publisher overhead	$ 3.00	Marketing, fulfillment
Returns and allowances	$ 3.00	
Author's royalties	$ 2.00	
Total publishing costs	$10.00	
Publisher's operating profit	$ 0.37	Returns amount for 3.7 percent

EXHIBIT 2 Profit Margins for a "Typical" Book

1996. Unlike publishing and retailing, wholesalers are highly concentrated, with firms like Ingram Book Co., and Baker and Taylor commanding over 80 percent of the market.

Competition in wholesaling revolves around the speed of delivery and the number of titles stocked. Ingram, for instance, receives more than 70 percent of its orders electronically and offers one-day delivery to about 82 percent of its U.S. customers. In 1994 the average net profit per book for wholesalers was less than 1.5 percent. This figure was down from the traditional margins of about 2 percent a few years earlier.[5]

Technological advances have made warehouse operations more efficient which in turn has made it possible for wholesalers to provide attractive discounts to retailers. Also, the types of books wholesalers are supplying to retailers are changing. Bookstores are increasingly relying on wholesalers for fast-selling titles and less-popular backlist books.[6] However, with the emergence of superstores, such large retailers as Barnes & Noble and Borders Books & Music are no longer using wholesalers for initial orders of major titles. For example, Borders Books & Music currently buys over 90 percent of its titles directly from publishers.

Retail Bookstores

Retail bookstores, independents, and general retailers accounted for between 35 and 40 percent of industry revenues (see Exhibit 3). From 1975 to 1995, the number of bookstores in the United States increased from 11,990 to 17,340. According to industry sources, the total sales for the nation's four largest bookstore chains—Barnes & Noble, Borders Books & Music, Books-A-Million, and Crown Books—rose 14.3 percent to $5.68 billion for the fiscal year ended January 1998.[7] This figure represented about 24 percent of all book sales. Industry analysts point out that from 1992 through 1995, superstore bookstore sales grew at a compounded rate of 71 percent while nonsuperstore sales grew at a rate of 4 percent.

With the increasing growth of these superstores, experts cautioned that in smaller markets a shakeout was inevitable.[8] Also, 1995 marked the first year in which bookstore chains sold more books than independents.[9] A spokesperson for the *American Booksellers Association,* noted:

> In the three years from 1993 to 1995, 150 to 200 independent-owned bookstores went out of business—50 to 60 in 1996 alone. . . . By contrast in the same period, approximately 450 retail superstore outlets opened, led by Barnes & Noble and the Borders Group, with 348 openings.[10]

Independent booksellers believed the growth of superstores might be reaching a saturation point. But even as Barnes & Noble and Borders entered city after city, as many as 142 U.S. metropolitan markets still did not have

[5] *Publishers Weekly,* January 1, 1996.

[6] Although the best-selling books get the bulk of the attention and marketing dollars, "backlist" books are considered the "bread and butter" of the industry. A backlist is the publishing company's catalog of books that have already appeared in print. Estimates indicated that as much as 25 to 30 percent of a publisher's revenues come from this source. Backlisted books have predictable sales with occasional bumps, such as when a subject matter loses favor with consumers or when an author dies. Since these books require no editing and little promotion, they are generally profitable. Moreover, print runs are easier to predict, resulting in fewer returns to publishers.

[7] Expected revenues for the top four U.S. booksellers in 1997 were as follows (in $ millions): Barnes & Noble, $2,797; Borders Group, $2,266; Books-A-Million, $325; Crown Books, $298. (Source: *Publishers Weekly,* March 23, 1998, p. 17.)

[8] *Publishers Weekly,* March 11, 1996. Superstores, originally confined to big metropolitan areas, were increasingly entering markets with populations of 150,000 or less. Industry estimates indicated that superstores had to make around $200 a square foot to turn a profit. For example, a typical Barnes & Noble superstore needed $3 to $4 million in sales revenues to break even. Some industry observers questioned whether such cities can support these mammoth stores and whether superstores in these locations could sell enough books to turn a profit.

[9] *Philadelphia Business Journal,* September 27, 1996.

[10] "A Nonchain Bookstore Bucks the Tide," *The New York Times,* September 8, 1996.

Channel	Percentage of Total Sales
Bookstore chains, independents, and general retailers	35%–40%
Mail-order and book clubs	21%
Sales to college bookstores	17%
Schools	15%
Libraries and other institutions	10%

EXHIBIT 3 Book Sales in 1994 by Various Distribution Channels

a book superstore. According to Amy Ryan, a Prudential Securities analyst, the current rate of expansion could continue at least through the year 2000. This is because the United States could support about 1,500 such stores.

Institutions and Libraries

There are more than 29,000 private, public, and academic libraries in the United States.[11] This market is crucial to publishers because of its stability and size. Since libraries order only what they want, this lowers the overhead costs associated with inventory and return processing, making this segment a relatively profitable one for publishers. Moreover, as hardcover trade books have become relatively expensive, many readers now borrow them from libraries rather than purchase them outright. Industry experts observed that about 95 percent of general titles published in any year sold less than 20,000 copies; of that amount, about 55 percent were purchased by libraries. Libraries also frequently repurchase titles to replace worn-out and stolen books. By doing so, they keep the "backlist" sales healthy.

Mail Order and Book Clubs

The industry is witnessing a significant drop in the mail order book business. This drop in sales was attributed to the growth of large discount-sale retailers. Publishers' book club sales on the other hand have risen steadily, gaining 9 percent in 1994 and in early 1995. This growth was attributed to the increasing popularity of specialized book clubs that focus on favorite baby-boomer interests such as gardening and computers.

The industry sells a variety of books that include trade, professional, mass market, El-Hi (Elementary-High school) and college-text books, and others, and each of these categories varied in terms of sales, competition, profitability, and volatility (see Exhibit 4).

A survey commissioned by American Booksellers Association found that some 106 million adults purchased about 456.9 million books in any given quarter.[12] The survey, which looked at book-buying habits of consumers during the calendar year 1994, revealed that six in ten American adults say they purchased at least one book in the last three months. Annually that corresponds to 1.8 billion books sold, an average of seventeen books per book-buying consumer a year. The average amount paid for the three most recent books purchased by consumers in the last 30 days was about $15. According to another report by *Book Industry Study Group*, "1996 was a year of major transition and flux in the publishing industry with buyer and seller alike reexamining standard operating procedures to work together in order to adapt to recent changes including growth of retail space and the impact of the Internet."

THE GROWING PRESENCE OF "VIRTUAL" BOOKSTORES

The two hardest challenges for book selling—physically distributing the right number of books to bookstores and getting the word about serious books out to potential readers—are getting a more than trivial assist from the new online technologies. The rapid growth of the online businesses is spreading to book publishing and retailing. According to Larry Daniels, director of information technologies for the National Association of College Stores:

> Booksellers' concern revolves around the potential for publishers to deal directly with consumers and the media on the Internet. . . . The phenomenon could mean the elimination of middlemen such as bookstores.[13]

Moreover, Daniels notes that there is also the potential for publishers to be "disintermediated," because computer-literate writers can now publish and distribute their own works online. However, the leading publishing houses are skeptical of electronic book-publishing capabilities and remain uncertain about the Internet's future with regard to physical books.

Despite industry skepticism and concern, a plethora of "virtual" bookstores are now selling books on the Internet. A cursory search on an Internet search-engine such as Yahoo! produced a listing of 475 online bookstores operating on the Web (as of August 1998). A search on Buyers Index (www.buyersindex.com), a mail order buyers' search engine, lists over 234 online bookstores. Many of these firms are relatively unknown compared to such online retailers as Amazon.com and Barnes & Noble. These two firms in particular have been growing at the self-reported double-digit rates and are fast becoming a formidable presence on the Web. Book and music sales online accounted for $156 million in 1997. Although this amount represented a small percentage of

[11] *Standard & Poor's Industry Surveys,* July 20, 1995.

[12] 1997 sales for the eight largest categories of books in the United States were as follows ($ millions): Professional books, $4,156; Trade books (adult), $4,095; El-Hi textbooks, $2,957; College textbooks, $2,670; Mass market books, $1,434; Trade books (juvenile), $1,358; Book club editions, $1,145; Religious books, $1,132. (Source: Book Industry Study Group Trends, 1998.)

[13] *The Christian Science Monitor,* September 18, 1996.

- **Trade Books.** This segment includes general interest hardcover and paperback books sold to adults and juveniles. Trade books accounted for almost 25% of book revenues in 1997. According to industry reports, books sold to adults increased by more than 30% between 1991 and 1995. Juvenile book sales showed a double-digit growth rate in the late 1980s and early 1990s. However, juvenile hardcover book sales represented a 2.3% increase in 1997 over the previous year and juvenile paperback book sales fell by as much as 18.6% during the same time period. This slow growth was attributed to a decline in the number of popular titles and increased spending by children on toys and games.

  Random House Inc., Bantam Doubleday Dell, Simon & Schuster, HarperCollins, and Penguin are some of the leading firms that compete in this product category.
- **Professional Books.** Over 165 million professional books were sold in 1997 accounting for $4.15 billion. Since 1991 professional book sales have grown at a compound annual rate of 3.0 percent (in units). Legal publishing was the largest segment of the professional-books category, with the scientific and technical category coming in second place. The long-term outlook for this category was good because employment in the medical, legal, scientific, and business profession was expected to grow strongly.

  Thomson Crop's was the largest professional-books publisher with sales of $1.99 billion. Professional book revenues comprised 31% of Thomson's total revenues. Reed Elsevier ranked second with 1994 sales of $1.63 billion, and was followed by Wolters Kluwer and Times Mirror with $1.07 billion and $775 million in sales respectively.
- **Mass-Market Books.** A large proportion of these books are sold through magazine wholesalers and outlets such as newsstands and drugstores. This category includes bestsellers that have shelf lives of about three to six weeks and in 1997 they accounted for about 7 percent of all books sold. Although the cost of acquiring the paperback rights to a best-selling hardcover title can cost millions of dollars, the per-unit fixed costs for printing are small because print runs were as large as 500,000. However, when return rates, which typically exceed 40% are factored in, profit margins tend to be less than 12%.

  The largest publishers are Random House, Bantam Doubleday Dell, Simon and Schuster, and Harper Collins.
- **El-Hi Books.** El-Hi or Elementary-High school books accounted for 14% of all books sold in 1997 (they used to represent 30 percent of all books sold in 1994). Sales in this segment rose nearly 14% in 1997 and forecasts suggest that they are likely to increase by 4.8% in 1998. El-Hi is driven by state adoption and enrollment levels and are sold to school systems on a contract basis. The development of materials for schools is a capital intensive process that typically takes up to five years to develop for most new programs. Per pupil expenditures as well as the number of students are expected to grow through the year 2000, implying moderate growth (3 to 4%) for this segment.

  The big publishers are owned by media conglomerates such as News Corp. Times Mirror, and Paramount. The largest El-Hi publisher is McGraw Hill, followed by Paramount (the parent company of Prentice Hall and Silver Burdett), Harcourt Brace, and Houghton Mifflin.
- **College Text Books.** College publishing is the most profitable category. The cost of producing a college text is lower than in the El-Hi market, because the texts are typically prepared by university faculty members and used individually. However, the unit sales tend to be small and used text book sales generally accounted for 20–40% of total sales. College textbook sales represented 12.8% of all book sales in 1997. Sales are estimated to increase 6.9% to $2.85 billion in 1998.

  Prentice Hall (owned by Paramount) is the largest college publisher, followed by HB College (owned by Harcourt General), International Thomson, McGraw-Hill, and Irwin (a division of Times Mirror).

EXHIBIT 4 The Various Product Categories

the overall retail book sales in 1997, it is projected to reach about $1.1 billion in 2001.

COMPETING ON THE WORLD-WIDE WEB

Operating a Virtual Bookstore

At Amazon.com, unlike traditional bookstores, there are no bookshelves to browse. All contact with the company is either through its Web site [www.amazon.com] or by e-mail. At the firm's Web site, customers can search for a specific book, topic or author, or they can browse their way through a book catalog featuring numerous subjects. Visitors can also read book reviews from other customers, *The New York Times,* the *Atlantic Monthly,* and Amazon.com's staff. Customers can browse, fill up a virtual shopping basket, and then complete the sale by entering their credit card information or by placing their order online and then phoning in their credit card information. Customer orders are processed immediately. Books in stock (mostly bestsellers) are packaged and mailed the same day. When their order has been shipped, customers are notified by e-mail. Amazon.com places orders for non-bestsellers with the appropriate book publisher immediately.

Shunning the elaborate graphics that clutter many Web sites on the Internet, the firm loads up its customers with information instead. For many featured books, it offers capsule descriptions, snippets of reviews, and "self-administered" interviews posted by authors. The firm has found a way to use the technology to offer services that a traditional store or catalog can't match. Notes Bezos:

> An Amazon customer can romp through a database of 1.1 million titles (five times the largest superstore's inventory), searching by subject or name. When you select a book, Amazon is programmed to flash other related titles you may also want to buy. If you tell Amazon about favorite authors and topics, it will send you by electronic mail a constant stream of recommendations. You want to know when a book comes out in paperback? Amazon will email that too.[14]

Additionally, the firm offers space for readers to post their own reviews and then steps out of the way and lets its customers sell to each other. Notes Bezos:

> There are so many things we can do on-line that can't be done in the real world. We want customers who enter Amazon.com to indicate whether they want to be "visible" or "invisible." If they choose "visible," then when they're in the science fiction section, other people will know they're there. People can ask for recommendations—'read any good books lately?'—or recommend books to others. I'm an outgoing person, but I'd never go into a bookstore and ask a complete stranger to recommend a book. The semi-anonymity of the on-line environment makes people less inhibited.[15]

Value Propositions and Customer Service

When asked why people come to their site, Bezos responds:

> Bill Gates laid it out in a magazine interview. He said, "I buy all my books at Amazon.com because I'm busy and it's convenient. They have a big selection, and they've been reliable." Those are three of our four core value propositions: convenience, selection, service. The only one he left out is price: we are the broadest discounters in the world in any product category. . . . These value propositions are interrelated, and they all relate to the Web.[16]

At Amazon.com almost all books are discounted. Bestsellers are sold at a 30 to 40 percent discount and the other books at a 10 percent discount. Points out Bezos:

> We discount because we have a lower cost structure than physical stores do and we turn our inventory 150 times a year. That's like selling bread in a supermarket. Physical bookstores turn their inventory only 3 or 4 times a year.

The firm's Seattle and Delaware warehouses are used to stock popular book items, and to consolidate and repack customer orders. Moreover, only after the firm receives a paid customer order does it request the appropriate publisher to ship the book to Amazon.com. The firm then ships the book to the customer.[17] The firm owns little expensive retail real estate and its operations are largely automated. Its distribution center in

[14] *The Wall Street Journal,* May 16, 1996.

[15] *Fast Company,* October–November 1996.

[16] Ibid.

[17] Industry observers note that although Amazon discounts most books, it levies a $3 service charge per order, plus 95 cents per book. And it can take Amazon a week to deliver a book that isn't a best-seller, and even longer for the most esoteric titles. Also, some people don't like providing their credit card number over the Internet.

Delaware, for example, uses state-of-the-art technology to consolidate and package books for shipment.

To keep customers interested in Amazon.com, the firm offers two forms of e-mail-based service to its registered customers. "Eyes" is a personal notification service, in which customers can register their interests in a particular author or topic. Once customers register with Amazon.com, they receive information about new books published by their favorite author. "Editor's service" provides editorial comments about featured books via e-mail. Three full-time editors read book reviews, pore over customer orders, and survey current events to select the featured books. These, and other free-lance editors employed by the firm, provide registered users with e-mail updates on the latest and greatest books they've been reading. These services are automated and are available free of charge and customers subscribing to these services have certain guaranteed rights (see Exhibit 5 for "Customer Bill of Rights").

According to Bezos, such services are vital for success on the Internet:

> Customer service is a critical success factor for online merchants. If you make customers unhappy in the physical world, they might each tell a few friends. If you make customers unhappy on the Internet, they can each tell thousands of friends with one message to a newsgroup. If you make them really happy, they can tell thousands of people about that. I want every customer to become an evangelist for us. About 63 percent of the book orders come from repeat customers.

Additionally, the firm's employees compile a weekly list of the twenty most obscure titles on order, and Bezos awards a prize for the most amusing. Amazon.com drums up all these orders through a mix of state-of-the-art software and old-fashioned salesmanship. When asked to differentiate his firm from potential rivals, Bezos notes:

> People who just scratch the surface of Amazon.com say—"oh, you sell books on the Web"—don't understand how hard it is to actually be an electronic merchant. We're not just putting up a Web site. We do 90 percent of our customer service by email rather than by telephone. . . . There are very few off-the-shelf tools that help do what we're doing. We've had to develop lots of our own technologies. There are no companies selling software to manage email centers. So we had to develop our own tools. In a way this is good news. There are lots of barriers to entry.[18]

Culture and Philosophy

Amazon.com had 800 employees in August 1998. A significant portion of the firm's employees manage "content" on the firm's Web site, including such tasks as Web page updating and formatting book reviews for display. The firm also employees a large number of people to develop software tools for operating on the Internet and a large group of employees do nothing but answer e-mails from customers. Notes Bezos:

> Amazon.com is committed to ingenuity and problem-solving. Almost nothing is off-the-shelf at Amazon.com: Our software engineers are developing programs that are the first of their kind; our editors create original content; our site team designs features that can't be found anywhere else. . . . Also, we have some of the best programmers, and the best servers in the world.

According to Amazon.com insiders: "This is a very driven place. Hours are typically 8 to 8 and many people work weekends. Jeff spends every waking hour on this business." Adds Bezos:

> Everyone at Amazon.com works hard, long, and smart. We act like owners because we are owners—stock options give each of us an

[18] *Fast Company,* October–November 1996.

Amazon.com's Bill of Rights claims that as a customer there is:

1. *No obligation.* Eyes & Editors Personal Notification Services are provided free of charge, and you are under no obligation to buy anything.
2. *Unsubscribing.* You can unsubscribe or change your subscriptions at any time.
3. *Privacy.* We do not sell or rent information about our customers. If you would like to make sure we never sell or rent information about you to third parties, just send a blank e-mail message to never@amazon.com.

EXHIBIT 5 Amazon.com's Customer Bill of Rights

Source: Available at www.amazon.com

> equity stake in the company. We are passionate about what we're doing. Because of that, we have fun at work, and it makes it easy for us to work hard. What we're building is unprecedented. We're not aspiring to a corporate model—we are creating the model. This to me is the most compelling reason for people to come to work here.

Continues Bezos:

> There is no Amazon.com "type." There are Amazon.com employees who have three master's degrees and some who speak five languages. We have people who worked at Procter & Gamble and Microsoft, and people who worked at *Rolling Stone* and *The Village Voice*. We have a professional figure skater, two race-car drivers, a Rhodes scholar, a set of twins, a husband and wife, and their dog. We wear jeans to work, have meetings in the hallway, and we get excited about HTML-enabled email.

Bezos describes his firm's corporate philosophy as follows:

> The Amazon.com corporate philosophy is simple: If it's good for our customers, it's worth doing. Our company mission is to leverage technology and expertise to provide the best buying experience on the Internet. Put another way, we want people to come to Amazon.com, find whatever they want, discover things they didn't know they wanted, and leave feeling they have a new favorite place to shop.

Operating Philosophy

The firm's operating philosophy is unlike traditional bookstores. At Amazon.com there are no salespeople. The firm is open for business 24 hours a day and has a global presence. Over 3 million customers from 160 countries have purchased books from the firm. The firm is devoid of expensive furnishings, and money is spent sparingly. Notes Bezos:

> We made the first four desks we have here ourselves—all our desks are made out of doors and four-by-fours. ... My monitor stand is a bunch of old phone books. We spend money on the things that matter to our customers and we don't spend money on anything else.[19]

[19] *Upside,* October 1996.

Amazon.com spends a substantial amount on Web advertising and marketing. According to Jupiter Communications, the firm spent over $340,000 for the first half of the 1996 and ranked 34th in Web ad spending. Since then, however, these expenses have gone up significantly. This is partly because Amazon.com has entered into multi-year advertising agreements with Internet aggregators, such as Yahoo!, Excite and AOL. For the most recent quarter ending June 1998, the firm spent $26.5 million on marketing, equivalent to 23 percent of sales.

Since Amazon.com is an Internet-only retailer, Web advertising gives it a unique opportunity to track the success of an ad by the number of click-throughs to the store's Web site and the number of Internet surfers who actually purchase something. Industry analysts estimate that between 2 percent and 3 percent of people who see an ad on the Web will actually click-through to see more.

The firm advertises mainly in such large-circulation news papers as *The Wall Street Journal, New York Times,* and *San Jose Mercury News,* and on Internet search-engine sites such as Yahoo!, Lycos, the Microsoft Network (MSN) and Microsoft's *Slate* magazine. Amazon.com keeps its banner ads simple, with just a few words and a Web address. Recently, the firm has started advertising on radio, and television (e.g., CNN). It also hands out discount coupons in several cities to entice customers to use its services.

The decision to locate Amazon.com in Seattle appears to be paying off. The firm has been able to attract some Microsoft veterans and many highly qualified executives. See Exhibit 6 for an illustration of how the firm is organized and Appendix A for a brief description of the firm's top management.

Growth via Micro-Franchising

The firm is currently growing at a rapid pace each quarter. Part of the reason for this rapid growth is the firm's Associates Program. The program was designed to increase traffic to Amazon.com by creating a referral service from other Web sites to Amazon.com's 2.5-million book catalog. An associated Web site, such as Starchefs—which features cookbook authors—recommends books and makes a link from its Web page to Amazon.com's catalog page for the books. The associated Web site then earns referral fees for sales generated by these links. Partners receive weekly referral fee statements and a check for the referral fees earned in that quarter. More than 90,000 sites have already signed up under this program and earn a commission sometimes up to 15 percent of the

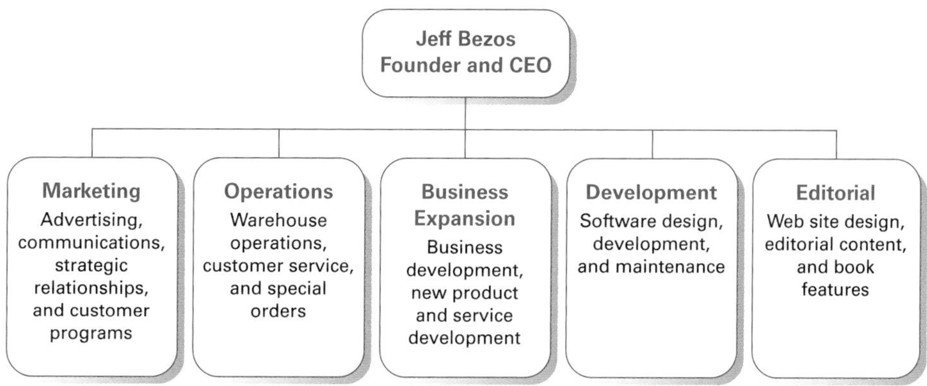

EXHIBIT 6 Company's Organizational Structure

value of books bought by the referred customer. Notes Bezos, "[The] Web technology has made it possible to set up micro-franchises, and with zero overhead."[20]

Since July 1995, Amazon.com has doubled in size every 2.4 months.[21] By August 1996, sales were growing at 34 percent a month. The firm posted revenues of $147.8 million for 1997, an 838 percent increase over the previous year. However, the net loss for fiscal 1997 was $27.6 million, compared to a net loss in fiscal 1996 of $5.8 million. When the company was founded in 1995, the plan was to be profitable in five years. The firm claims to have exceeded expectations and has made its business plan more aggressive. Despite continuing losses, Wall Street's interest in the new venture has remained strong. Further, based on cybershare (and revenues), the firm is currently acknowledged to be the largest online bookstore on the Web.

Moreover, Bezos is focused on expanding Amazon.com: "In the year 2000, our goal is to be one of the world's leading bookstores." Adds Bezos:

> We believe we're expanding the market for books. With this new way of selling books on the Web we can expose people to far more books than before. People buy books from us that they won't find in bookstores. And we're growing rapidly in this stagnant market.

CHALLENGES FACING AMAZON.COM

Although Bezos is pleased that Amazon.com is well regarded by analysts on Wall Street, he acknowledges that many strategic challenges remain. Particularly, a few important challenges demand his immediate attention. They include: finding creative ways to fend off formidable new competitors, leveraging the firm's brand name to expand beyond just books, and meaningfully integrating the new acquisitions made by the firm.

Fending off Formidable Competitors

Competition between online book merchants is likely to become even more intense, with a growing number of publishers and retailers going online. For example, Ingram and other large publishers have begun experimenting with the Web. Notes *The Wall Street Journal*: "In addition to Amazon and Barnes & Noble, publisher Random House Inc. sells books online and Viacom Inc.'s Simom & Schuster unit launched an Internet book-selling site grandly called "The SuperStore."[22]

Barnes & Noble, the largest U.S. book retailer, launched its online store in May 1997, a little less than two years after Amazon.com opened for business. Although Barnes & Noble finds itself in the unusual position of trailing a competitor, it claims that it holds the unique distinction of operating in four different channels—retail stores, the Internet, 1-800-THE-BOOK, and mail order. Notes Stephen Riggio, vice chairman of Barnes & Noble, who is presiding over the new online venture:

> How big is it [online sales] going to get? We're looking at $100 million in sales this year [1998]. We're not being speculative about that range. We're going to be there. It's going to be bigger than a billion dollar business.

[20] "Amazon.com forges new sales channel," *Web Week*, August 19, 1996.

[21] *Financial Times*, October 7, 1996.

[22] *The Wall Street Journal*, October 21, 1997.

Barnes & Noble online sales for the year ending in 1997 amounted to $14 million, a small fraction of the firm's overall retail book sales. However, according to a report in *Business Week*, Leonard Riggio, CEO of Barnes & Noble, is dead serious about the online segment:

> Riggio plans to spend $40 million to ballyhoo the service in 1998. . . . Riggio is already thinking ahead of how to integrate this technology into the shelves of Barnes & Noble. In the bookstore of the future, he says, customers could tap into millions of titles and print any part from these works on the spot. He talks about software programs that could point customers to specific lines in various books, threaded by a single topic, or ones that could ferret out and print obscure texts that never made it into book form. In short, Riggio envisions modifying what constitutes a published work.[23]

In July 1998, Borders Group Inc. (the parent corporation of Borders Books & Music) entered the fray with Borders.com, a newly formed subsidiary. At the Border's Web site customers can purchase books, music CDs, and videos. The firm's Web site described Borders' late entry as follows:

> We're not content with being just another online bookseller. We want to do it right. Anyone who's been to a Borders store knows that selling books, music, and videos isn't just a business, it's a passion. . . . At Borders.com, we aim to provide the same high level of expertise and vast selection customers have come to associate with the Borders name. No other online bookseller can offer 10 million books, CDs, and videos—in stock and available now.

In late 1997 Ingram, the largest U.S.-distributor of books, began experimenting with online retailing. It began testing an experimental service to create new online retailers. Notes *Business Week*: "All the would-be retailers had to do was lure the shoppers. Ingram handled everything else, from maintaining the Web site to taking orders, processing credit-card billings, and shipping the books. In effect the virtual bookshops became little more than a retail façade of Ingram. However, after six months of test-marketing, Ingram quietly pulled the plug in early October."[24]

Undaunted by Ingram's failure, Bertelsmann, the German media conglomerate, announced in February 1998 that it planed to open an online store (tentatively called BooksOnline) that will sell books in English, French, Spanish, German, and Dutch.[25] Bertelsmann hoped to ship books to customers in Europe and the United States through its extensive distribution in both countries. In October 1998, however, the firm announced it was buying a 50 percent share in Barnesandnoble.com for $200 million and both Bertelsmann and Barnes & Noble are expected to spend another $100 million each to strengthen their joint operation. Further, Bertelsmann will abandon the U.S. rollout of its BooksOnline service. Observes Maria Latour-Kadison, an online retail analyst at Forrester Research:

> This is a real powerhouse combination: the retail power of Barnes & Noble and the fulfillment power of Bertelsmann. . . . They already have what Amazon is spending millions to acquire [a band name and infrastructure]. There's a very steep learning curve associated with doing online retailing well, and Bertelsmann will be able to leapfrog some of it because of Barnesandnoble.com's experience.[26]

Acknowledges Bezos: "Bertelsmann can be a formidable competitor. They have 50 percent stake in AOL's German operations, over 35 million active book and music club members and significant warehousing and book distribution assets spread out internationally." However, he notes:

> We are not competitor focused but customer focused. Figuring out what the customer wants is a never-ending process. We differentiate along the following dimensions: selection (we are still the largest); ease of use; price; and discovery. Scale is important in e-commerce and so is "ease of use." Our innovations like "1-Click shopping" continue to make our Web site far more attractive than competitors. We are working with interesting features such as "book matcher," using the latest collaborative filtering technology that we acquired from Net Perceptions. We believe such things greatly enhance the customer experience at our store. Discovery

23 "The Baron of Books," *Business Week,* June 29, 1998.

24 The reason why Ingram's experimental foray into online retailing floundered was because many of the new online entrants were unable to attract enough customers. Notes *Business Week,* "Ingram stirred a backlash among its existing clientele, who were clearly not happy with the prospect of having to compete with other low-cost clones."

25 Bertelsmann AG was the world's third-largest media conglomerate with $14 billion in sales in 1997. In July 1998, Bertelsmann acquired U.S.-based Random House Publishing. This single largest publisher of English language books owns Doubleday, Bantam Books, Dell Publishing, and several other publishing companies.

26 *Internet World,* October 12, 1998.

> means understanding customers as individuals and finding ways to accelerate their discovery process while they are at the store. We are working on software that increases the odds that customers will find the right book that they are looking for when searching in our store. Discovery is powerful for customers.

Bezos's immediate concern therefore revolves around finding innovative ways to stay ahead of his competitors and he acknowledges that this will remain a continuing challenge.

Leveraging the Amazon.com Brand Name

In June 1998, Amazon.com expanded its product line to include music. The music store offers more than 125,000 titles, ten times the CD selection of the typical music store, and everyday savings of up to 40 percent. The new music store features expert and customer reviews, interviews, an essentials lists, a list of the hottest CDs from around the country and the world, music news, and recommendations. Music fans can search for their favorite music by CD title, artist, song title, or label. Bezos describes the new venture as follows:

> You can browse through nearly 300 styles ranging from Alternative to Zydeco (everything but Classical, which is on the way) or use "Essentials" (my favorite feature) to learn about the best CDs to help you start or build a collection in a particular style. And you can reduce guesswork by listening to some of our 225,000 song clips. . . . It's a music discovery machine. Using the power of technology and the Internet, we're enriching the music experience for everyone, from casual to devoted listeners alike.

More importantly, he adds:

> The music store was designed with the help of more than 20,000 customers who responded to our invitation to "build the music store of your dreams." Many of the features in our new music store are the direct result of these suggestions. Our customers told us they wanted a site that is as rich in musical selection and content as the Amazon.com bookstore—with the same great prices, features, and customer service.

The launch of Amazon.com's music store was accompanied by a major update of the firm's Web site. Bezos describes the changes thus:

> We didn't focus only on music. We've also redesigned our store to make it even easier to find the books you want. . . . The new store design permits customers to move easily between the book and music areas, making it fast and simple to find what they are looking for and to discover new titles. We now provide an integrated shopping cart, 1-Click ordering, and consolidated shipping across both books and music.

Unlike book retailing, many online music stores such as cdnow.com (www.cdnow.com) and n2k.com (www.n2k.com) have been in operations for more than a few years. Cdnow.com, for example, claims it is the world's leading online music store by offering over 250,000 music related items. N2K.com operates many music sites (called channels) including Music Boulevard on the WWW (see Exhibit 7 for a partial listing of online music stores). In response to Amazon.com's entry into the Music Business, Cdnow and N2K signed an agreement in October to merge their two companies.

Notes Bezos: "We don't really view existing online music stores as our direct competitors. We are more focused on parties that already have a large portion of music sales." Some analysts are, however, skeptical about whether Amazon.com should compete in the music business. Notes a report in *The Wall Street Journal*:

> But the move [to offer music CDs] is risky too; Cyberspace is increasingly crowded with on-line superstores set up by Amazon's physical-world counterparts, companies with more marketing clout and track records of profitability. And Amazon could lose cachet with bibliophiles if its forays into other media dilute its reputation as a destination for booklovers. . . . [M]ail-order giants Columbia House, a joint venture of Time Warner Inc. and Sony Corp., and Bertelsmann AG's BMG Entertainment have made Internet selling a top priority. Columbia House is taking orders from music-club members on one site; on a separate super-store site, Total E, it's moving straight into Amazon territory with plans to add books and CD-ROMs to its existing catalogue of videos and CDs.[27]

Some analysts point out that the music business is "somewhere between a no-margin and a low-margin business" and therefore question the firm's recent move. But notes Bezos:

> Amazon.com brand has to stand for something. For us the brand name means price, convenience,

[27] "In Looking to Branch Out, Amazon Goes Out on a Limb," *The Wall Street Journal*, May 12, 1998.

- *CDnow**—The idea for this store was conceived in the summer of 1994 and was started by twin brothers Jason and Matt Olim in their parents' basement in 1994. In 1997, the firm posted sales of $15 million. It reported averages about 18% in operating margins.
- *Music Boulevard (www.musicboulevard.com)*—Owned by N2K, Music Boulevard operates transaction sites in English, French, German, Japanese, and Spanish. Started in September of 1996, n2k.com bills itself as "the premier online music entertainment company and the Internet's only complete source for music content, community and comment." In 1997 it reported revenues of $11.7 million.
- *Musicspot (www.musicspot.com)*—According to a recent 10-000-household PC-Meter survey, CUC's musicspot ranked top among the top "Hot Storefronts."
- *Tunes.com (www.tunes.com)*—Berkeley California-based Tunes.com launched in November 1996, features 200,000 thirty-second music clips backed by collaborative filter, which matches visitors' music interests to profiles created by people with similar tastes. The company plans to have 1 million samples online by mid-1998, which will make it the largest music sampling source online.
- *Record Clubs*—Record clubs are shaping up to be the Web's most powerful retailers. An estimated 16.5 million customers belong to record clubs in the United States. Columbia House and BMG both debuted Web sites in 1995. Their sites now handle all club chores including administration, buying, status checking, and the commendable job of cyber-retailing.

*CDnow and Music Boulevard signed an agreement on October 8, 1998, to merge their two companies.

EXHIBIT 7 A Partial Listing of Online Music Stores

> customer service, and a great selection. There is a huge advantage in expanding to other product categories. The customer acquisition costs are significantly lower and so are the costs related to the lifetime value of that customer. If we can successfully expand the brand, as we think we can, then there are significant economic benefits to expansion. . . . We recognize that the music business is a different environment than books. About half-a-dozen players control the entire distribution of music in this country and the likely implication of such control is lower margins. However, we like to emphasize the incremental dollar value of music sales to our existing customers.

International Expansion and Acquisitions

Capitalizing on increased market value, Amazon.com acquired three companies, Bookpages Ltd., Telebook Inc., and Internet Movie Database Ltd. in April 1998. Notes Bezos:

> With these we have accelerated our expansion into European e-commerce and acquired a foundation for a best-of-breed video store. These acquisitions will enable Amazon.com to offer a new set of consumers the same combination of selection, service and value that we now provide our U.S. book customers. Fortunately, we were able to build an international brand name as a by-product of operating on the Internet. People in Japan, Germany, and U.K. are very familiar with the Amazon.com name (about 22 percent of the firm's sales come from outside the United States currently).

Although Bezos remains quiet about his intentions regarding Internet Movie Database Ltd., analysts speculate that The Internet Movie Database is likely to form the key underpinning for Amazon.com's eventual entry into online video sales.

In July 1998, Amazon.com signed agreements to acquire two additional firms. They include Junglee Corp. and PlanetAll. PlanetAll is a Cambridge, Massachusetts, firm that provides a unique Web-based address book, calendar, and reminder service. Junglee Corp., based in Sunnyvale, California, is a leading provider of advanced Web-based virtual database (VDB) technology that can help shoppers find millions of products on the Internet (see Exhibit 8). Discussing his firm's intention to acquire these two firms Bezos noted:

> PlanetAll is the most innovative use of the Internet I've seen. It's simply a breakthrough in doing something as fundamental and important as staying in touch. The reason PlanetAll has over 1.5 million members—and is growing even faster than the Internet—is simple: it creates

- *Bookpages (www.bookpages.co.uk)*—As one of the largest online bookstores in the United Kingdom, the firm provides access to all 1.2 million UK books in print.*
- *Telebook (www.telebuch.de)*—This firm operating through its ABC Bücherdienst subsidiary, is Germany's number one online bookstore, with a catalog of nearly 400,000 German language titles.
- *Internet Movie Database (www.imdb.com)*—Originally launched in 1990, Internet Movie Database is a comprehensive repository for movie and television information on the Internet, and is an excellent example of genuine community on the Internet.
- *PlanetAll.com (www.PlanetAll.com)*—The firm launched in November 1996 reportedly has 1.5 million members, and reports that thousands of new members are joining each day to use the secure, free service to organize and automatically update information about friends, business associates, relatives, and alumni. Users accessing PlanetAll service have complete control over their own contact information and decide what information they want to share with others on a person-by-person basis. Moreover, PlanetAll's service is compatible with personal information managers (PIMs) and personal digital assistants (PDAs), such as Microsoft Outlook and 3Com Palm Pilot. Also, it has integrated its service within the sites of a number of Internet leaders, including Lycos and GeoCities, as well as numerous universities and professional associations. Amazon.com intends to operate PlanetAll as a wholly owned subsidiary located in Cambridge. Savage and the two cofounders will remain with the company.**
- *Junglee Corp (www.junglee.com)*—The firm was founded in June 1996. The firm's breakthrough virtual database (VDB) technology is based on founders' doctoral research carried out at Stanford University. Junglee's first deployment was CareerPost.com, the Washington Post Company's online recruitment site, in January 1997. Junglee carries more than 15 million items in the Junglee Shopping Guide and over 90,000 job listings in its Job Canopy. Junglee has developed breakthrough database technology that can dramatically enhance customers' ability to discover and choose from among millions of products online. To date, two of the markets it has targeted have been online retailing and online recruitment. Junglee's customers and partners in these markets include Yahoo!, Compaq, Snap!, six of the top seven newspaper companies, and many other new-media companies. All founders of Junglee are expected to remain with the company.

* Each of the acquisitions, Bookpages, Telebook, and Internet Movie Database, will be accounted for under the purchase method of accounting. The company will incur total charges of approximately $55 million in connection with all three transactions. Consideration was comprised of cash and common stock, and the company anticipates issuing an aggregate of approximately 540,000 shares of common stock as a result of these transactions.

** Amazon.com will acquire 100 percent of the outstanding shares and assume all outstanding options of Junglee and PlanetAll in exchange for equity having an aggregate value of approximately $280 million. Amazon.com will issue approximately 800,000 shares and assume all outstanding options in connection with the acquisition of PlanetAll and anticipates accounting for this transaction as a pooling of interests. Amazon.com will issue approximately 1.6 million shares and assume all outstanding options in connection with the acquisition of Junglee and anticipates accounting for this transaction under the purchase method of accounting.

EXHIBIT 8 Recent Aquisitions by Amazon.com

> extraordinary value for its users. I believe PlanetAll will prove to be one of the most important online applications. . . . Junglee has assembled an extraordinary team of people. Together we'll empower customers to find and discover the products they want to buy.

Bezos, commenting on the recent expansion and acquisitions, argues:

> Our product extension and geographic expansion is better late than early. Why better late than early? We had to first focus on the book business and grow that until we were comfortable with it. There are always numerous opportunities to expand. We try to err on the side of being slow. Fortunately, we are not capital constrained, but we are definitely people constrained. We only pursue opportunities when the people bandwidth is not constrained. . . . The single most important criterion that we use to acquire a new company is this: Who are the people behind this venture, and what is the people bandwidth of the acquired company going to be? We are looking for business athletes indoctrinated in this space

> and companies that have a culture that is common with ours.

However, notes a report in *The Wall Street Journal:*

> In the end, though, neither specialization nor branding may determine who succeeds in the on-line sales game. In the physical world, hardcore comparison shopping has been left to a highly motivated faction of consumers willing to trudge between stores. But on the Web, it's become almost effortless. Today, a user can enter a title of a book on Yahoo! Inc.'s Visa Shopping Guide site which then queries multiple booksellers for prices and displays the result in a table. Hyperlink next to book prices lets users order the cheapest one at the click of a mouse. With comparison services proliferating elsewhere on the Web—and for dozens of other products—it's unclear whether a sterling brand like Amazon's will ultimately sway consumers when rock-bottom prices are so easy to spot.[28]

Bezos concedes that many challenges still confront him and his top management team as they ponder the future moves by his firm. Acknowledges Bezos:

> It is hard to provide great customer service and experience for the customer. It is hard to grow the business. But when you combine these two, the complexity of operating increases exponentially. We are expanding our product line and broadening our geographic reach simultaneously, and there is a lot of execution risk when you try to do this. Moreover, many of our new initiatives will continue to require aggressive investment and entail significant execution challenges. However, that is the nature of this business.

APPENDIX A: AMAZON.COM'S TOP MANAGEMENT TEAM[29]

Jeffrey P. Bezos, Founder and Chief Executive Officer

Jeff Bezos has always been interested in anything that can be revolutionized by computers. Intrigued by the amazing growth in use of the Internet, Jeff created a business model that leveraged the Internet's unique ability to deliver huge amounts of information rapidly and efficiently. In 1994 he founded Amazon.com, Inc., an Internet retailer of books and other information-based products that offers services that traditional retailers cannot: lower prices, authoritative selection, and a wealth of product information. Before heading west to start Amazon.com, Jeff worked at the intersection of computer science and finance, leading the development of computer systems that helped manage more than $250 billion in assets for Bankers Trust Company. He also helped build one of the most technically sophisticated quantitative hedge funds on Wall Street for D. E. Shaw & Co. Jeff received a degree in electrical engineering and computer science, summa cum laude, from Princeton University in 1986. He is a member of Phi Beta Kappa.

George T. Aposporos, Vice President, Business Development

George Aposporos joined Amazon.com in May 1997 as vice president of business development and is responsible for identifying and negotiating key strategic relationships for the company. Prior to joining Amazon.com, George was founder and president of Digital Brands, a strategic consulting and interactive marketing firm that has served clients such as Starbucks Coffee, Sybase, American Express, and BMG Entertainment. While at Digital Brands, he placed Starbucks in the first campaign to use animated advertising on America Online. From March 1994 to August 1995, George was vice president of I.C.E., a Toronto-based multimedia developer and corporate communications firm, where he spearheaded involvement in interactive media, including development of the company's interactive television and Internet capabilities. From 1989 to 1994, George was an independent producer in a variety of media, including television, video, and CD-ROMs. George was an Olin Scholar at Wesleyan University.

Rick Ayre, Vice President and Executive Editor

Rick Ayre joined Amazon.com in September 1996 as vice president and executive editor and is responsible for the editorial content and design of the Amazon.com Web site. Rick comes to Amazon.com from *PC Magazine*, the popular Ziff-Davis publication, where he served as executive editor for technology. Rick launched PC Magazine on the World Wide Web in March 1995. He was responsible for the print coverage of online technology, and he ran *PC Magazine*'s online services, including the *PC Magazine* Online Web site and PC MagNet, part of ZD Net on CompuServe. During his five years at *PC Magazine*, Rick also held positions as the magazine's executive editor for software and as technical director for software in *PC Magazine* Labs, where he supervised all software product testing. Before joining *PC Magazine,* Rick served as chief of information resources management at the Highland

[28] *The Wall Street Journal,* May 12, 1998.

[29] Amazon.com 1997 10-K filing with Securities Exchange Commission.

Drive VAMC, a 750-bed hospital in Pittsburgh. He began his technology career while a Ph.D. candidate in psychiatric epidemiology at the University of Pittsburgh in the early 1980s. There he learned to program in Fortran to manipulate large data sets on an early DEC time-sharing system. When the IBM PC was born, he quickly adopted one and taught himself to program in Pascal and to use dBASE. He was soon logging on to local BBS systems, and he's been working online ever since.

Joy D. Covey, Chief Financial Officer

Joy Covey joined Amazon.com in December 1996 as chief financial officer and vice president of finance and administration. She is responsible for financial and management systems and reporting, and she also manages planning and analysis, legal, administrative, investor relations, and human relations activities. Before joining Amazon.com, Joy was vice president of business development and vice president of operations, broadcast division, of Avid Technology, a leader in the digital media industry. From 1991 to 1995, she was the CFO of Digidesign, where she managed a successful IPO and eventual merger with Avid Technology. During her tenure, Digidesign achieved more than 50 percent annual growth and strong and consistent profitability and cash flow, and strengthened its dominant position in the digital audio production systems market. Before she worked at Digidesign, Joy was a mergers and acquisitions associate at the investment bank of Wasserstein Perella & Co. and a certified public accountant with Arthur Young & Co. (currently Ernst & Young). She holds both a J.D. and an M.B.A. from Harvard, where she was a Baker Scholar, and a B.S. in business administration, summa cum laude, from California State University, Fresno.

Richard L. Dalzell, Chief Information Officer

Richard Dalzell joined Amazon.com in August 1997 as chief information officer and is responsible for all Amazon.com information systems, including corporate networks, logistics, electronic buying, accounting, and data warehousing. Before joining Amazon.com, Rick was vice president of information systems for Wal-Mart Stores. He managed all merchandising and logistics systems, led the development of world-class supply chain systems, set the standard for international retailing and merchandising systems, and was instrumental in establishing the world's largest commercial decision-support and data-mining systems. From 1990 to 1994, Rick held several management positions within the information systems division at Wal-Mart. Prior to that, he spent three years as the business development manager for E-Systems and seven years as a teleprocessing officer in the U.S. Army. Rick received a B.S. in engineering from the U.S. Military Academy, West Point, in 1979.

Mary Engstrom Morouse, Vice President, Merchandising

Mary Engstrom Morouse joined Amazon.com in February 1997 as vice president of publisher affairs and became vice president of merchandising in April 1998. She is responsible for managing supplier relationships and direct purchasing. Before joining Amazon.com, Mary served as general manager of the security business unit and vice president of product marketing at Symantec Corporation, a developer of information management and productivity enhancement software. In these roles, she managed the development, production, testing, manufacturing, distribution, and marketing of Symantec's line of antivirus and security products, including the Norton AntiVirus line. From July 1989 to September 1994, Mary held several management positions at Microsoft Corporation, including group product manager for Microsoft Access, group product manager for Microsoft Project, and director of marketing in strategic relations. Mary received her B.A. in economics from the University of California, Berkeley, in 1984 and her M.B.A. from the Anderson Graduate School of Management at the University of California, Los Angeles, in 1989.

Sheldon J. Kaphan, Chief Technology Officer

Shel Kaphan has served as Amazon.com's vice president and chief technology officer since March 1997. In this role, Shel is responsible for technical architecture and directing technical efforts. From October 1994 to March 1997, Shel was vice president of research and development for the company and was responsible for developing Amazon.com's core software and maintaining the company's Web site. Shel brings more than twenty years of experience in designing hardware and software systems and services to Amazon.com. Prior to joining the company, he held senior engineering positions at Kaleida Labs, Frox, and Lucid. Shel received a B.A. in mathematics, cum laude, from the University of California, Santa Cruz, in 1980.

John David Risher, Senior Vice President, Product Development

David Risher joined Amazon.com in February 1997 as vice president of product development, responsible for developing new products and services. He was promoted to senior vice president of product development in December 1997 and now has overall responsibility for product development, marketing, editorial, and content licensing. Before joining Amazon.com, David served as founder and product unit manager for Microsoft Investor, Microsoft Corporation's Web site for personal investment. From 1991 to 1995, he held a variety of marketing and project management positions within the Microsoft Access product team, including Microsoft Access team manager. In this role he managed all aspects of the product development team including design, development, branding, advertising, and customer research to produce Microsoft Access 95. From 1987 to 1989 David was an associate at the LEK Partnership, a corporate management consulting firm. David holds a B.A. in comparative literature, magna cum laude, from Princeton University and an M.B.A. from Harvard Business School.

Joel R. Spiegel, Vice President, Engineering

Joel Spiegel joined Amazon.com in March 1997 as vice president of engineering and is responsible for all Web site software. From March 1995 to March 1997, Joel held several positions with Microsoft Corporation, including Windows 95 Multimedia development manager, Windows Multimedia group manager, and product unit manager for information retrieval. From June 1986 to March 1995, he held a variety of positions at Apple Computer, most recently as senior manager, and was responsible for new product development in the Apple Business Systems Division. Prior to that he held software product development positions at a number of companies, including Hewlett-Packard and VisiCorp. During his career, Joel has had a hand in the development and delivery of a wide range of software products, including Windows 95 Multimedia, DirectX, Macintosh System 7 File Sharing, several versions of MacDraw, AppleSearch, Smalltalk-80 for the Macintosh, and VisiON. Joel holds a B.A. in biology, with honors, from Grinnell College.

Jimmy Wright, Chief Logistics Officer

Jimmy Wright joined Amazon.com in July 1998 as vice president and chief logistics officer. He is responsible for all global supply chain activities, including managing the company's distribution centers, product purchasing, distribution, and shipping. Jimmy comes to Amazon.com with more than twenty-six years of experience in logistics management. He was recognized as one of the key logistics leaders within Wal-Mart Stores, the world's largest retailer and a company globally known for its logistics excellence. He joined Wal-Mart in 1985 and served as vice president of distribution from 1990 to his retirement in 1998. During that time he was responsible for more than thirty regional and specialty distribution centers, which accounted for 38 million square feet of retail distribution space, staffed by more than 32,000 employees. Jimmy's career in logistics management began at the Fina Oil and Chemical Company, a branch of Petrofina S.A. based in Brussels. From 1972 to 1985, he held a variety of positions, most recently as general manager of distribution. He received a B.B.A. in personnel management from the University of Texas in 1976.

CASE 2

THE MERGER OF FEDERAL EXPRESS AND THE FLYING TIGERS LINE

By Howard S. Tu and Sherry E. Sullivan, University of Memphis

It was January, 1990. Thomas R. Oliver, Senior Vice-President of International Operations for Federal Express Corporation, was on his way to meet with the members of his "Tigerclaws Committee." The operational merger of Flying Tigers with Federal Express was supposed to be concluded last August. Yet, anticipated and unanticipated problems kept surfacing. International Operations were draining financial resources and there were other problems that had to be immediately resolved.

Several days ago, Mr. Oliver met with Mr. Fred Smith, the company founder and CEO, and was assigned the job of heading a special task force. The purpose of the task force was to direct the Flying Tigers merger efforts and resolve the resulting problems. Mr. Oliver requested, and got, representatives of senior executives from every department of the company to form what he named the "Tigerclaws Committee" (see Exhibit 1). This committee had the power to cut across departmental bureaucratic lines. It had the resources of all the departments behind it to reach fast-track solutions to any problems in existence. Even with such commitments, Mr. Oliver realized what a formidable task he and his committee were facing.

EXPRESS AND FREIGHT FORWARDING INDUSTRIES

In 1990, sending documents or packages by priority mail was viewed as a necessary convenience rather than a luxury. The domestic market was led by Federal Express Corporation with 53 percent of the market, followed by United Parcel Service (UPS) at 19 percent. The U.S. Postal Service had 3 to 4 percent of the market (Curry, 1989). The overnight letter traffic was characterized by slow growth because of the increased use of facsimile machines.

The increasing competition between express delivery services and the traditional air freight industry was changing the face of international cargo transportation. Many independent freight carriers complained that big couriers and integrated carriers were poaching on their market niches. Others ignored the competition believing that the more personalized relationship provided by traditional air freight companies would keep clients coming back. Still, companies such as Federal Express were having a big effect on the air freight industry. Express couriers were building their non-document business by 25 to 30 percent a year. Proprietary consolidation and expedited treatment at customs had been the major factors influencing this growth rate. In an effort to move deeper into the cargo sector, some express companies were marketing themselves as providers of third-party logistics services (Strugatch, 1990).

Express Service in the U.S.

Federal Express, UPS, Airborne Express, and the U.S. Postal Service were quickly introducing services that promised to translate the fundamentals of speed and information into a powerful competitive edge. They were stressing good service at lower costs. For example, UPS had started offering discounts to its bigger customers and shippers that shipped over 250 pieces weekly. In addition, UPS was building an $80-million computer and telecommunications center to provide support for all operations worldwide. Airborne's chief advantage was that it operated its own airport and had begun operating a "commerce park" around its hub in Wilmington, Ohio.

Europe

The international document and parcel express delivery business was one of the fastest growing sectors in Europe. It was anticipated that its scope would grow even

Departments that are represented:
Memphis SuperHub
Business Application
Airfreight Systems
Q.A. Audits
Planning and Administration
International Clearance
Communications
Ramp Plans/Program
Hub Operations
Personnel Services
International Operations
Central Support Services
Customer Support
COSMOS/Pulsar Support System Division
COO/Quality Improvement

EXHIBIT 1 Representatives on the Tigerclaws Committee

faster when most European customs barriers were removed in 1992. Although the express business would become more important in the single European market, none of the four principal players in Europe was European. DHL, Federal Express, and UPS were U.S. companies while TNT was Australian. Europe was not expected to produce a challenger because the "big four" were buying smaller rivals at such a fast pace; the odds seemed to be heavily against a comparable competitor emerging (Arthur, 1989).

Pacific Rim

The Asia-Pacific air express market was expanding by 20 to 30 percent annually and the world's major air express and air freight companies had launched massive infrastructure buildups to take advantage of this growth. Industry leader DHL strengthened its access to air service by agreeing to eventually sell 57.5 percent of the equity of its international operation to Japan Air Line, Lufthansa, and Nissho Iwai trading company. TNT Skypak's strength was in providing niche services, and its ability to tap into the emerging Asian-East European route with its European air hub. Two new U.S. entrants, Federal Express and UPS, were engaged in an undeclared price war. Willing to lose millions of dollars annually in order to carve out a greater market share, Federal Express had already captured about 10 percent of Pacific express business and 15 percent of freight. UPS' strategy was to control costs and to offer no-frills service at low rates. All four companies were seeking to expand the proportion of parcels, which could yield about twice the profits of the express documents business (Guyot, 1990).

Major Airlines

Since the common adaptation of wide body jets, major international airlines had extra cargo space in their planes. Japan Air Lines and Lufthansa were two of the worldwide players, with most national airlines providing regional services.

Airlines were expanding and automating their cargo services to meet the challenges presented by fast-growing integrated carriers. Two strategies were being employed: (1) the development of new products to fill the gap between the demand for next-day service and traditional air cargo service, and (2) computerization of internal passenger and cargo operations (McKenna, 1989b).

THE MERGING ORGANIZATIONS

Federal Express Corporation

Frederick W. Smith, founder of Federal Express Corporation, went to Yale University, where he was awarded a now infamous C on an economics paper that outlined his idea for an overnight delivery service (Foust, 1989). After college and military service, Smith began selling corporate jets in Little Rock, Arkansas. In 1973, he tapped his $4 million inheritance, rounded up $70 million in venture capital and launched Federal Express, testing his college paper's thesis. The company turned profitable after three years.

Federal Express had always taken pride in its people-oriented approach and its emphasis on service to its customers. Mr. Smith believed that in the service industry, it is the employees that make the business (Smith, 1991). The philosophy of Smith and his managing staff was stated in the motto: People, Service, Profit. The philosophy was manifested in many ways, including: (1) extensive orientation programs, (2) training and communications programs, (3) promotion of employees from within, and (4) a tuition reimbursement program. Federal Express's "Open Door Policy" for the expression of employee concerns also illustrated the commitment of top management to resolve problems (Trunick, 1989).

As to services, Federal Express stressed the importance of on-time delivery and established a 100 percent on-time delivery goal. It has achieved a record of 95 percent on-time delivery. In 1990, Federal Express was one of the five U.S firms to win the Malcolm Baldrige National Quality Award. This award was given by the U.S. Government to promote quality awareness and recognize the quality achievements of U.S. companies.

Frederick W. Smith had a vision for the overnight express delivery business. Although Federal Express was the number one express firm in the U.S., Mr. Smith firmly believed that globalization was the future for the express business (*Journal of Business Strategy,* 1988). From 1986 to 1988, Federal Express struggled to become a major player in international deliveries. The company experienced entrenched overseas rivals, such as DHL, and onerous foreign regulations (Foust, 1989).

Frustrated with the legal processes in negotiating for landing rights that were restricted by bilateral aviation treaties (*Journal of Business Strategy,* 1988), Mr. Smith reversed his promise to build only from within and started a series of acquisitions. From 1987 to 1988, Federal Express purchased fifteen minor delivery companies, mostly in Europe. In December 1988, Mr. Smith announced the acquisition of Tiger International Inc., best known for its Flying Tigers air freight service. On paper, the merger of Federal Express and Tiger International seemed to be a marriage made in heaven. As one Federal Express executive pointed out: "If we lay a route map of Flying Tigers over that of Federal Express, there is almost a perfect match. There are only one or two minor overlaps. The Flying Tigers routes are all over the world with highest concentration in the Pacific rim countries while the Federal Express routes are mostly in domestic U.S.A." As a result of the merger, Federal Express world routes were completed. For example, the acquisition of Flying Tigers brought with it the unrestricted cargo landing rights at three Japanese airports that Federal Express had been unsuccessful in acquiring for the last three years (Calonius, 1990).

One high level Federal Express employee commented that the merger brought other benefits besides routes. He said: "We got a level of expertise with the people we brought in and a number of years of experience in the company in handling air freight. . . . You have to look at this acquisition also as a defensive move. If we hadn't bought Flying Tigers, UPS might have bought Flying Tigers."

Tiger International Inc.

Tiger International Inc., better known for The Flying Tigers Line Inc. freight service or Flying Tigers, was founded 40 years ago by Robert Prescott. Over the years, the company became modestly profitable. But in 1977, Smith won his crusade for air-cargo deregulation over the strident objection of Tiger founder, the late Robert Prescott. Heightened competition, troubled acquisitions, and steep labor costs led to big losses at Tigers. In 1986, Stephen M. Wolf, the former chairman of Republic Airline Inc., came on board at Tigers and managed to get all employees, including those represented by unions, to accept wage cuts. As Tigers rebounded financially, it was ripe to be taken over by one of the major delivery service companies. In 1988, Federal Express announced the acquisition of Tigers to the pleasure of some and dismay of others. At the announcement, some Tigers' employees shouted "TGIF—Thank God It's Federal" or "It's purple [Federal Express] not brown [UPS]—thank goodness." In contrast, Robert Sigafoos, who wrote a corporate history of Federal Express, commented that "Prescott must be turning over in his grave" (Foust, 1989).

Flying Tigers always had a distinctive culture, one that partly developed from the military image of its founders. Tigers' employees stressed "Tiger Spirit" or team work. Since Mr. Wolf took over as the chairman and CEO at an extremely difficult time, the general orientation of Flying Tigers was to keep the company flying.

In October of 1980, Flying Tigers purchased Seaboard World Line. One long-time Tiger, who had witnessed the Seaboard merger, remarked: "There was no job protection. Everyone was not offered a job. There were wholesale layoffs. There was no monetary compensation paid to any of the Seaboard employees. If you were moving with the company, they did not pay your moving expenses." Continued cost cutting was required to enable Tigers' turnaround.

THE MERGER

Federal Express announced the acquisition of Flying Tigers in December of 1988. However, because of government regulations, the actual operational merging of the two companies did not occur until August of 1989.

One top level Federal Express executive, with considerable expertise in mergers, described the process in the following way: "I think that after any merger, you go through three phases. You come in and you have euphoria. Everybody's happy. The second phase is the transition phase. In that phase, the primary qualification that every employee must have is sadomasochistic tendencies because you kill yourself going though it. . . . And then you start coming out of that into the regeneration and regrowth phase where you clean up all this hazy area without knowing exactly what you are going to do or thinking this works and trying it out. . . . In the meantime, going through all that turmoil creates a number of problems. . . . People's morale starts to dip. People start to question all the leadership. You start to see the company reorganizing, you know, trying to figure out well what's the best thing to do here or there or whatever and all of a sudden all of the confidence that ever existed in the whole world starts to diminish."

Although the two companies were supposed to now become one, problems from the merger kept surfacing. Some of these problems were to be anticipated with the merger of two companies of these sizes. However, many problems, as detailed in the next section, were not anticipated and had become very costly to the company.

Human Resource Management Problems

Unions

Federal Express had traditionally been a non-union shop while the Flying Tigers' employees were predominately unionized. During the merger, the National Mediation Board could not determine a majority among the pilots at Federal Express and Flying Tigers. The Board requires a majority to decide the union status at any firm. Because a majority could not be determined, the Mediation Board decided to allow the temporary mixed union and non-union employees until the fall of 1989 when elections would determine if there would be union representation. The ruling had created ambiguities in employee status and raised some important financial and legal issues for Federal Express, the unions, and the employees (Ott, 1989).

An executive in the international division described Federal Express's feelings on unions: "They [Flying Tigers] had a lot of unions. Tigers was a traditional company . . . and we [Federal Express] don't dislike unions. . . . Our feelings about unions are that if you get a union, you deserve it, because you have not managed your business well. We would like to think that we could keep that old family [feeling]. We realize that we can't keep the old family. It's very difficult to keep the family spirit corporatewide [after a merger]."

Job Offers

The employees of Federal Express believed that Federal Express was a great place to work mainly because of its people-oriented policies. Because of this belief, most of the managers thought that the Flying Tigers employees would "welcome the merger with open arms." A communications official said: "We tried to position Federal Express as a great place to work, a wonderful place to be—cutting edge technology, a great aircraft fleet, a great employee group, good management—all those types of things."

Flying Tigers had a rich and long history. Tiger employees prided themselves on their team spirit and their willingness to take pay cuts for the good of the Flying Tiger Line, Inc. during the lean years. Employees proudly displayed items with the Tiger logo on them.

A long-time Tiger employee, and member of one of the pre-merger Tiger committees, remarked on the job offers: "For the employees, it [the merger] was a spectrum, we've got all of them on a line. Up in front, we've got those employees for whom the merger was the best thing that ever happened to them. In the back, you've got the employees where it was the worst thing that ever happened—because of personal things, they decided to leave the company. And then there's the group of employees in the middle, which really composed the majority of Flying Tigers employees, that it really didn't matter one way or the other since they never moved. All they did was change their uniforms from Friday to Monday. They're basically doing the same jobs in the same locations. . . ." A member of his family and many friends refused to accept a job with Federal Express. He explained their refusal by saying: "Because [Federal Express] were taking the name away. You were taking the history of the Flying Tiger line away . . . because we were a small company, we were like a close-knit family. . . ." Another, middle level, former Tiger said although a lot of merger information was provided to people at headquarters in L.A., people at other locations, like Boston, received less information. She said that some Tigers refused the job offer for the following reason: "They left, I think, just because of the attitude that . . . you're taking Flying Tigers away and I don't want to go with you." Some Tigers hoped that Federal Express would permit them to keep the Flying Tiger name or change the company name to Federal Tigers.

Differences in Culture

A Federal Express executive on the Tigerclaws Committee commented on cultural differences by saying: "The difference was astounding, absolutely astounding. Federal Express employees typically seem to be younger, were all in uniforms, and enthusiastic about the company. You can walk around Federal Express and everybody can tell you what the corporate philosophy is. . . . I remember standing in the Los Angeles airport facility. . . . It's typical Federal Express. And you go over to the Tiger facility and here are all of these much older guys standing around. None of them in any type of uniform, clothes were all over the map, there was no apparent standards, whatsoever. You know, kicking some of the packages, tossing them, throwing. It was just . . . just terrible. I couldn't believe it. But, that was part of the way they did business. They referred to a lot of the cargo that they carried as big, ugly freight. And to us, . . . we go around thinking every customer's package is the most important thing we carry."

A former Tiger employee shared her perspective on the differences: "Most of the employees that you dealt with you had known for a lot of years. We used to work together side by side very closely for twenty years. And this company, Federal Express, isn't even twenty years old. You walk into a meeting or classroom or something . . . Federal Express people are introducing themselves to other Federal Express people. Tiger people found that really hard to believe that you didn't know everybody at Federal Express. . . ."

Job Assignments

During the announcement of the merger, Mr. Smith made a job offer to all the employees of Flying Tigers. Almost 90 percent of the 6,600 former Tiger employees took the offer. In a two-week period, from July 15th to the 31st, over 4,000 new jobs were to be created and Tiger employees transferred to these jobs. Many employees had to be relocated because the old Tiger hub in Columbus, Ohio, was phased out, and primarily only freight and maintenance personnel were kept at the hub in Los Angeles. Some job placements were troublesome because the human resource department had difficulty obtaining job descriptions and pay scales from Flying Tigers. During the haste, there were quite a number of mismatches of jobs and employees.

Expectations

One of Federal Express's personnel officers remarked: "I was concerned about being able to meet employees' expectations. A lot of times people coming in from outside of Federal Express have this—I mean it's a great place, but they have this picture that it's a fairy tale place, and that there aren't any real problems and that everybody gets their own way. So I was concerned about the expectations that people brought, both positive and negative. How are we going to make people feel real good about the company?"

In order to help former Flying Tigers employees determine whether to accept Federal Express's job offers, Federal Express provided the employees with detailed information about the company. Videotapes introducing Federal Express and explaining the benefits of working for the company were mailed to the homes of Tiger employees. Additionally, many Tiger employees were flown into Federal Express's headquarters in Memphis and given the "grand tour." "Express Teams," groups of four to five employees, visited Flying Tigers locations and gave them previews of what it was like to work for Federal Express.

Regarding expectations, one long-time Tiger remarked: "There's still a lot of unhappy people in Memphis that came out of L.A., because I think they expected an awful lot. They had the option of saying no to a job and being out on the street looking for something else, or they could come to Memphis and have Federal Express be their employer. And there are a lot of people that still take offense at the fact that Federal Express bought Flying Tigers. But those people have an attitude that they have to deal with." Another former Tiger remarked: "And I honestly thought that by going from a small company to a large company, I was just going to be another number. But . . . it's also their attention to people. All of the hype and promotion they did before T-day [merger day] to Flying Tiger people that they were people oriented. . . . We really didn't [know] what that meant and what it would mean to us individually until we became employees."

Operational Management Problems

Operational Procedures

Although Flying Tigers had operational policies and procedures for handling international freight, they were not being used after the official date of the operational merger. Because Federal Express was not in the traditional cargo business, it did not have such a manual. Coupled with the inexperience of most Federal Express managers at the ports of entry, many international cargo shipments were being moved before going through U.S. customs. Federal Express was fined on several occasions for such violations. Because of the lack of operational procedures, top managers could not hold anyone responsible for these mistakes

One executive on the Tigerclaws Committee made this comment about operations: "We tend to think we invented the express business. We're the best at it, and no matter what someone else has done, what their history might have taught them, we know we do it better than they know it. And we went into this merger process kind of 'big-dogging-it,' in my opinion. That's one reason Tigerclaws was formed. That Federal Express people said 'No, no, no, don't bother to tell us how you used to do things because this is how we do things, so we'll show you the Federal Express way of doing it.' That didn't go over great. You know, you can imagine, you know these people had been in the Flying Tigers business for all these years saying 'Look, we know the freight business, we know the international business, and FedEx people don't. We do know better than you do.'"

Similarly, a former Tiger employee remarked: "It's a whole different concept and there's still a lot of people within the company that don't fully understand the two concepts. I, myself don't fully understand the express concept...if there's freight left over, that's ok because we'll move it out tomorrow. That's not Federal Express' philosophy...it's like the difference between driving a Volkswagen and a Cadillac. I mean there are differences and you need to get used to them."

Computer Systems

Federal Express developed the Cosmos II Positive Tracking System. The system, one of the most famous examples of strategic information systems, was honored as the 1990 ComputerWorld Smithsonian Award winner in the transportation category. The key component of the system was SuperTracker, a hand-held computer. It could accept data from key entry, bar-code scanning, or electronic coupling and withstand rough treatment in warehouses and trucks. The system was designed to track and handle high quantity movement of small packages (Margolis, 1990).

Flying Tigers used the KIAC system. This system was designed to handle large volume cargoes with limited consignments. Unfortunately, these two systems were not 100 percent compatible and currently both systems were being used by Federal Express with limited communication between the two systems.

Maintenance of Tiger Fleet and Equipment

Federal Express discovered after the merger that most of Flying Tigers' planes were poorly maintained. Most of these planes would require considerable upgrading or face retirement.

Also, there were differences in equipment requirements. One Federal Express executive remarked: "[The hubs] had to deal with this stuff, packages that were used to flowing along 300 and 500 feet per minute; now they have a skid that might weigh thousands of pounds. You need a forklift. We didn't use forklifts. There might be a forklift here or there for equipment or engines, but it was not used to move pallets of freight around. So, all these costs, as you know, whether it was lease or buy, these things mount up. I mean, through all aspects of the company, they can say, sure, we planned for that.... There are always surprises."

Marketing Problems

Products

Federal Express moved pieces of 150 pounds or less, primarily with smaller transports. Flying Tigers' forte was heavy cargo and used primarily Boeing 747 freighter aircrafts (McKenna, 1989a). A Federal Express executive remarked: "[For] twenty-years [Tiger] people who sold nothing but freight [for them] going and talking about time-sensitive stuff is difficult. It's quick. It's overnight. It's don't make a mistake. Whereas, our people who are used to doing things quickly. I mean, they often used to hear the phrase about their freight grew hair on it. I mean the stuff would sit around...it's a cheap price but you move it when you've got the space. Well, we're not used to that. At the end of the day, we go into a station and we want that place empty. Move it. Why? Because that's what your customers want."

Customer Relations

Many of Flying Tigers' customers, including UPS, are competitors of Federal Express. Previously, they paid Flying Tigers to carry packages to countries where they had no landing rights. Freight forwarders, companies that transport cargo to and from airports, made up a good portion of the Flying Tigers' customer base. Because Federal Express handled local logistics for its operations, international freight forwarders complained that Federal Express would take away their business. Federal Express compromised by guaranteeing that it would use its own couriers and custom-clearing services for pieces weighing less than 150 pounds. Forwarders would get the business for anything heavier than 150 pounds. However, freight forwarders were still suspicious and Federal Express had been losing heavy freight business since the merger (Calonius, 1990).

Financial Problems

Federal Express's nine-month loss from overseas operations doubled to more than $200 million. The poor showing caused Federal Express to report its first-ever quarterly operating loss. Since then its stock had slipped 16 percent. With $2.4 billion in debt and heated competition at home from United Parcel Service of America Inc. and Airborne Freight Corp., Federal Express could not continue to hemorrhage overseas without damaging its domestic operation. Standard & Poor's and Moody's lowered its long-term-debt rating. The international business "doesn't have a lot of time to return to profitability" warned David C. Anderson, Federal Express chief financial officer (Pearl, 1991).

One high level Federal Express executive, and member of the Tigerclaws Committee, described the financial situation as follows: "That all of a sudden you hit this brick wall and you have to make decisions now on what we are going to do. And when you start making these decisions, you're taking your eye off other balls that you're watching out there. And, you know, we spend a lot of time debating how we're going to do this express product . . . how we're going to keep all this revenue because we couldn't afford to lose it. You could not physically shut down enough business to get out of the air freight side and still be profitable on the express side. The increments of capacity were too excessive. So you had to figure out how you were going to evolve this . . . I mean, it came painfully."

SUMMARY

Since 1985, Federal Express's international business had lost approximately $74 million and given company executives a lifetime supply of headaches (Foust, 1989). In order to improve Federal Express's competitive position with its overseas rivals and overcome the foreign regulations regarding landing rights, Frederick Smith announced, in December of 1988, the acquisition of Tiger International, Inc. Although the combined companies would have $2.1 billion in debt, Flying Tigers was expected to provide Federal Express with desperately needed international delivery routes. The Tiger acquisition would allow Federal Express to use its own planes for overseas package delivery where Federal Express used to contract with other carriers. In addition, Tigers' sizable long-range fleet could be used to achieve dominance in the international heavy-freight business that Federal Express had yet to crack.

Suppose you were in Thomas Oliver's shoes and were the head of the Tigerclaws Committee. What are the major problems and opportunities facing Federal Express? What should be the priorities of the Tigerclaws Committee? How will you solve or reduce the problems and exploit the opportunities?

REFERENCES

Arthur, Charles, 1989. "The War in the Air," *Business [UK]*, November, pp. 60–66.

Calonius, Erik, 1990. "Federal Express Battle Overseas," *Fortune,* Vol. 122, #14, December 3, pp. 137–140.

Curry, Gloria M., 1989. "Package Delivery Service: The Options Are Plentiful," *Office,* Vol. 110, #2, August, pp. 60–62.

Foust, Dean, 1989. "Mr. Smith Goes Global," *Business Week,* February 13, pp. 66–72.

Guyot, Erik, 1990. "Air Courier Fight for Pacific Business," *Asian Finance [Hong Kong],* Vol. 16, #7, July 15, pp. 22–23.

Journal of Business Strategy, July/August 1988. "Federal Express Spreads Its Wings," Vol. 9, #4, pp. 15–20.

Margolis, Neil, 1990. "High Tech Gets It There on Time," *Computer World,* Vol. 24, #27, July 2, p. 77.

McKenna, James T., 1989a. "Federal Express/Tiger Merger Would Reshape Cargo Industry," *Aviation Week & Space Technology,* Vol. 130, #1, January 2, p. 106.

McKenna, James T, 1989b. "Airlines Boost International Cargo Services to Protect Market Shares," *Aviation Week & Space Technology,* Vol. 131, #21, November 20, pp. 124–125.

Ott, James, 1989. "Board Decision Muddles Rules on Union Role After Merger," *Aviation Week & Space Technology,* Vol. 131, #9, August 28, p. 68.

Pearl, Daniel, 1991. "Innocents Abroad: Federal Express Finds Its Pioneering Formula Falls Flat Overseas," *Wall Street Journal,* April 15, p. Al.

Smith, Frederick W., 1991. "Empowering Employees," *Small Business Reports,* Vol. 16, #1, January, pp. 15–20.

Strugatch, Warren, 1990. "Air Cargo Report: Reliability Is the Buzzword," *Global Trade,* Vol. 110, #4, April, pp. 48–51.

Trunick, Perry A., 1989. "Leadership and People Distinguish Federal Express," *Transportation & Distribution,* Vol. 30, #13, December, pp. 18–22.

World Wide, 1989. "A Tiger's Eye View," Vol. 1, #5.

CASE 3

PERDUE FARMS INC.: RESPONDING TO TWENTY-FIRST CENTURY CHALLENGES

George C. Rubenson and Frank Shipper, Department of Management and Marketing, Franklin P. Perdue School of Business, Salisbury University.[1]

BACKGROUND/COMPANY HISTORY

> "I have a theory that you can tell the difference between those who have inherited a fortune and those who have made a fortune. Those who have made their own fortune forget not where they came from and are less likely to lose touch with the common man."
>
> —Bill Sterling, "Just Browsin'" column in *Eastern Shore News,* March 2, 1988.

The history of Perdue Farms Inc. is dominated by seven themes: quality, growth, geographic expansion, vertical integration, innovation, branding, and service. Arthur W. Perdue, a Railway Express Agent and descendent of a French Huguenot family named Perdeaux, founded the company in 1920 when he left his job with Railway Express and entered the egg business full-time near the small town of Salisbury, Maryland. Salisbury is located in a region immortalized in James Michener's *Chesapeake* that is alternately known as "the Eastern Shore" or "Delmarva Peninsula." It includes parts of *DEL*aware, *MAR*yland and *V*irgini*A*. Arthur Perdue's only child, Franklin Parsons Perdue was also born in 1920.

A quick look at Perdue Farms' mission statement (Exhibit 1) reveals the emphasis the company has always put on quality. In the 1920s, "Mr. Arthur," as he was called, bought leghorn breeding stock from Texas to improve the quality of his flock. He soon expanded his egg market and began shipments to New York. Practicing small economies such as mixing his own chicken feed and using leather from his old shoes to make hinges for his chicken coops, he stayed out of debt and prospered. He tried to add a new chicken coop every year.

By 1940, Perdue Farms was already known for quality products and fair dealing in a tough, highly competitive market. The company began offering chickens for sale when "Mr. Arthur" realized that the future lay in selling chickens, not eggs. In 1944, Mr. Arthur made his son Frank a full partner in A.W. Perdue and Son, Inc.

In 1950, Frank took over leadership of the company that employed forty people. By 1952, revenues were $6,000,000 from the sale of 2,600,000 broilers. During this period, the company began to vertically integrate, operating its own hatchery, starting to mix its own feed formulations and operating its own feed mill. Also, in the 1950s, Perdue Farms began to contract with others to grow chickens for them. By furnishing the growers with peeps (baby chickens) and the feed, the company was better able to control quality.

In the 1960s, Perdue Farms continued to vertically integrate by building its first grain receiving and storage facilities and Maryland's first soybean processing plant. By 1967, annual sales had increased to about $35,000,000. However, it became clear to Frank that profits lay in processing chickens. Frank recalled in an interview for *Business Week* (September 15, 1972) "... processors were paying us ten cents a live pound for what cost us 14 cents to produce. Suddenly, processors were making as much as 7 cents a pound."

A cautious, conservative planner, Arthur Perdue had not been eager for expansion and Frank Perdue

[1] The authors are indebted to Frank Perdue, Jim Perdue, and the numerous associates at Perdue Farms Inc., who generously shared their time and information about the company. In addition, the authors would like to thank the anonymous librarians at Blackwell Library, Salisbury State University, who routinely review area newspapers and file articles about the poultry industry, the most important industry on the DelMarVa peninsula. Without their assistance, this case would not be possible.

Perdue Mission 2000

Stand on Tradition

Perdue was built upon a foundation of quality, a tradition described in our Quality Policy...

Our Quality Policy

"We shall produce products and provide services at all times which meet or exceed the expectations of our customers."

"We shall not be content to be of equal quality to our competitors."

"Our commitment is to be increasingly superior."

"Contribution to quality is a responsibility shared by everyone in the Perdue organization."

Focus on Today

Our mission reminds us of the purpose we serve...

Our Mission

"Enhance the quality of life with great food and agricultural products."

While striving to fulfill our mission, we use our values to guide our decisions...

Our Values

Quality: We value the needs of our customers. Our high standards require us to work safely, make safe food and uphold the Perdue name.

Integrity: We do the right thing and live up to our commitments. We do not cut corners or make false promises.

Trust: We trust each other and treat each others with mutual respect. Each individual's skill and talent are appreciated.

Teamwork: We value a strong work ethic and ability to make each other successful. We care what others think and encourage their involvement, creating a sense of pride, loyalty, ownership and family.

Look to the Future

Our vision describes what we will become and the qualities that will enable us to succeed

Our Vision

"To be the leading quality food company with $20 billion in sales in 2020."

Perdue in the Year 2020

To our customers: We will provide food solutions and indispensable services to meet anticipated customer needs.

To our consumers: A portfolio of trusted food and agricultural products will be supported by multiple brands throughout the world.

To our associates: Worldwide, our people and our workplace will reflect our quality reputation, placing Perdue among the best places to work.

To our communities: We will be known in the community as a strong corporate citizen, trusted business partner and favorite employer.

To our shareholders: Driven by innovation, our market leadership and our creative spirit will yield industry-leading profits.

EXHIBIT 1 Perdue Mission Statement

himself was reluctant to enter poultry processing. But, economics forced his hand and, in 1968, the company bought its first processing plant, a Swift and Company operation in Salisbury.

From the first batch of chickens that it processed, Perdue's standards were higher than those of the federal government were. The state grader on the first batch has often told the story of how he was worried that he had rejected too many chickens as not Grade A. As he finished his inspections for that first day, he saw Frank Perdue headed his way and he could tell that Frank was not happy. Frank started inspecting the birds and never argued over one that was rejected. Next, he saw Frank start to go through the ones that the state grader had passed and began to toss some of them over with the rejected birds. Finally, realizing that few met his standards, Frank put all of the birds in the reject pile. Soon, however, the facility was able to process 14,000 broilers per hour.

From the beginning, Frank Perdue refused to permit his broilers to be frozen for shipping, arguing that it resulted in unappetizing black bones and loss of flavor and moistness when cooked. Instead, Perdue chickens were (and some still are) shipped to market packed in ice, justifying the company's advertisements at that time that it sold only "fresh, young broilers." However, this policy also limited the company's market to those locations that could be serviced overnight from the Eastern Shore of Maryland. Thus, Perdue chose for its primary markets the densely populated towns and cities of the East Coast, particularly New York City, which consumes more Perdue chicken than all other brands combined.

Frank Perdue's drive for quality became legendary both inside and outside the poultry industry. In 1985, Frank and Perdue Farms, Inc. were featured in the book, *A Passion for Excellence,* by Tom Peters and Nancy Austin.

In 1970, Perdue established its primary breeding and genetic research programs. Through selective breeding, Perdue developed a chicken with more white breast meat than the typical chicken. Selective breeding has been so successful that Perdue Farms chickens are desired by other processors. Rumors have even suggested that Perdue chickens have been stolen on occasion in an attempt to improve competitor flocks.

In 1971, Perdue Farms began an extensive marketing campaign featuring Frank Perdue. In his early advertisements, he became famous for saying things like "If you want to eat as good as my chickens, you'll just have to eat my chickens." He is often credited with being the first to brand what had been a commodity product. During the 1970s, Perdue Farms also expanded geographically to areas north of New York City such as Massachusetts, Rhode Island and Connecticut.

In 1977, "Mr. Arthur" died at the age of 91, leaving behind a company with annual sales of nearly $200,000,000, an average annual growth rate of 17 percent compared to an industry average of 1 percent a year, the potential for processing 78,000 broilers per hour, and annual production of nearly 350,000,000 pounds of poultry per year. Frank Perdue said of his father simply, "I learned everything from him."

In 1981, Frank Perdue was in Boston for his induction into the Babson College Academy of Distinguished Entrepreneurs, an award established in 1978 to recognize the spirit of free enterprise and business leadership. Babson College President Ralph Z. Sorenson inducted Perdue into the academy which, at that time, numbered eighteen men and women from four continents. Perdue had the following to say to the college students:

> "There are none, nor will there ever be, easy steps for the entrepreneur. Nothing, absolutely nothing, replaces the willingness to work earnestly, intelligently towards a goal. You have to be willing to pay the price. You have to have an insatiable appetite for detail, have to be willing to accept constructive criticism, to ask questions, to be fiscally responsible, to surround yourself with good people and, most of all, to listen."
>
> —Frank Perdue, speech at Babson College, April 28, 1981.

The early 1980s saw Perdue Farms expand southward into Virginia, North Carolina and Georgia. It also began to buy out other producers such as Carroll's Foods, Purvis Farms, Shenandoah Valley Poultry Company and Shenandoah Farms. The latter two acquisitions diversified the company's markets to include turkey. New Products included value added items such as "Perdue Done It!," a line of fully cooked fresh chicken products.

James A. (Jim) Perdue, Frank's only son, joined the company as a management trainee in 1983 and became a plant manager. The latter 1980s tested the mettle of the firm. Following a period of considerable expansion and product diversification, a consulting firm recommended that the company form several strategic business units, responsible for their own operations. In other words, the firm should decentralize. Soon after, the chicken market leveled off and then declined for a period. In 1988, the firm experienced its first year in the red. Unfortunately, the decentralization had created duplication and enormous administrative costs. The firm's rapid plunge into turkeys and other food processing, where it had little experience, contributed to the losses. Characteristically, the company refocused, concentrating on efficiency of operations, improving communications throughout the company, and paying close attention to detail.

On June 2, 1989, Frank celebrated fifty years with Perdue Farms, Inc. At a morning reception in downtown Salisbury, the Governor of Maryland proclaimed it "Frank Perdue Day." The Governors of Delaware and Virginia did the same. In 1991, Frank was named Chairman of the Executive Committee and Jim Perdue became Chairman of the Board. Quieter, gentler, and more formally educated, Jim Perdue focuses on operations, infusing the company with an even stronger devotion to quality control and a bigger commitment to strategic planning. Frank Perdue continued to do advertising and public relations. As Jim Perdue matured as the company leader, he took over the role of company spokesperson and began to appear in advertisements.

Under Jim Perdue's leadership, the 1990s were dominated by market expansion into Florida and west to Michigan and Missouri. In 1992, the international business segment was formalized serving customers in Puerto Rico, South America, Europe, Japan and China. By fiscal year 1998, international sales were $180 million per year. International markets are beneficial for the firm because U.S. customers prefer white meat while customers in most other countries prefer dark meat.

Food service sales to commercial consumers has also become a major market. New retail product lines focus on value added items, individually quick frozen items, home meal replacement items and products for the delicatessen. The "Fit 'n' Easy" label continues as part of a nutrition campaign using skinless, boneless chicken and turkey products.

The 1990s also saw the increased use of technology and the building of distribution centers to better serve the customer. For example, all over-the-road trucks were equipped with satellite two-way communications and geographic positioning, allowing real-time tracking, rerouting if needed, and accurately informing customers when to expect product arrival. Currently, nearly 20,000 associates have increased revenues to more than $2.5 billion.

MANAGEMENT & ORGANIZATION

From 1950 until 1991, Frank Perdue was the primary force behind Perdue Farms' growth and success. During Frank's years as the company leader, the industry entered its high growth period. Industry executives had typically developed professionally during the industry's infancy. Many had little formal education and started their careers in the barnyard, building chicken coops and cleaning them out. They often spent their entire careers with one company, progressing from supervisor of grow-out facilities to management of processing plants to corporate executive positions. Perdue Farms was not unusual in that respect. An entrepreneur through and through, Frank lived up to his marketing image of "it takes a tough man to make a tender chicken." He mostly used a centralized management style that kept decision making authority in his own hands or those of a few trusted, senior executives whom he had known for a lifetime (see Exhibit 2). Workers were expected to do their jobs.

In later years, Frank increasingly emphasized employee (or "associates" as they are currently referred to) involvement in quality issues and operational decisions. This later emphasis on employee participation undoubtedly eased the transfer of power in 1991 to his son, Jim, which appears to have been unusually smooth. Although Jim grew up in the family business, he spent almost 15 years earning an undergraduate degree in biology from Wake Forest University, a master's degree in marine biology from the University of Massachusetts at Dartmouth, and a doctorate in fisheries from the University of Washington in Seattle. Returning to Perdue Farms in 1983, he earned an EMBA from Salisbury State University and was assigned positions as plant manager, divisional quality control manager and vice president of Quality Improvement Process (QIP) prior to becoming chairman.

Jim has a people-first management style. Company goals center on the three P's: People, Products, and Profitability. He believes that business success rests on satisfying customer needs with quality products. It is important to put associates first because "If [associates] come first, they will strive to assure superior product quality—and satisfied customers." This view has had a profound impact on the company culture which is based on Tom Peters' view that "Nobody knows a person's 20 square feet better than the person who works there." The idea is to gather ideas and information from everyone in the organization and maximize productivity by transmitting these ideas throughout the organization.

Key to accomplishing this "employees first" policy is workforce stability, a difficult task in an industry that employs a growing number of associates working in physically demanding and sometimes stressful conditions. A significant number of associates are Hispanic immigrants who may have a poor command of the English language, are sometimes undereducated and often lack basic health care. In order to increase these associates' opportunity for advancement, Perdue Farms focuses on helping them overcome these disadvantages.

For example, the firm provides English-language classes to help non-English speaking employees assimilate. Ultimately employees can earn the equivalent of a high-school diploma. To deal with physical stress, the company has an ergonomics committee in each plant that studies job requirements and seeks ways to redesign those jobs that put workers at the greatest risk. The company also has an impressive wellness program that currently includes clinics at ten plants. The clinics are staffed by professional medical people working for medical practice groups under contract to Perdue Farms. Employees can visit a doctor for anything from a muscle strain to prenatal care to screening tests for a variety of diseases and have universal access to all Perdue operated clinics. Dependent care is available. While benefits to the employees are obvious, the company also benefits through a reduction in lost time for medical office visits, lower turnover and a happier, healthier, more productive and stable work force.

MARKETING

In the early days, chicken was sold to butcher shops and neighborhood groceries as a commodity, that is, producers sold it in bulk and butchers cut and wrapped it. The customer had no idea what firm grew or processed the chicken. Frank Perdue was convinced that higher profits could be made if the firm's products could be sold at a premium price. But, the only reason a product can command a premium price is if customers ask for it by name—and that means the product must be differentiated and "branded." Hence, the emphasis over the years on superior quality, broader breasted chickens, and a healthy golden color (actually the result of adding marigold petals in the feed to enhance the natural yellow color that corn provided).

In 1968, Frank Perdue spent $50,000 on radio advertising. In 1969, he added $80,000 in TV advertising to his radio budget—against the advice of his advertising agency. Although his early TV ads increased sales, he decided the agency he was dealing with didn't match one of the basic Perdue tenets: "The people you deal with should be as good at what they do as you are at what you do." That decision set off a storm of activity on Frank's part. In order to select an ad agency that met his standards, Frank learned more about advertising than any poultry man before him and, in the process, catapulted Perdue Farms into the ranks of the top poultry producers in the country.

He began a ten-week immersion in the theory and practice of advertising. He read books and papers on advertising. He talked to sales managers of every newspaper, radio and television station in the New York area, consulted experts, and interviewed forty-eight ad agencies. During April 1971, he selected Scali, McCabe, Sloves as his new advertising agency. As the agency tried to figure out how to successfully "brand" a chicken—something that had never been done—they realized that Frank Perdue was their greatest ally. "He looked a little like a chicken himself, and he sounded a little like one, and he squawked a lot!"

McCabe decided that Perdue should be the firm's spokesman. Initially Frank resisted. But, in the end, he accepted the role and the campaign based on "It takes a tough man to make a tender chicken" was born. The firm's very first television commercial showed Frank on a picnic in the Salisbury City Park saying:

> "A chicken is what it eats...And my chickens eat better than people do...I store my own grain and mix my own feed...And give my Perdue chickens nothing but pure well water to drink...That's why my chickens always have that healthy golden yellow color...If you want to eat as good as my chickens, you'll just have to eat my chickens."

Additional ads, touting high quality and the broader breasted chicken read as follows:

> "Government standards would allow me to call this a grade A chicken...but my standards wouldn't. This chicken is skinny...It has scrapes and hairs...The fact is, my graders reject 30 percent of the chickens government inspectors accept as grade A...That's why it pays to insist on a chicken with my name on it...If you're not completely satisfied, write me and I'll give you your money back...Who do you write in Washington?...What do they know about chickens?"

> "The Perdue Roaster is the master race of chickens."

> "Never go into a store and just ask for a pound of chicken breasts...Because you could be cheating yourself out of some meat...Here's an ordinary one-pound chicken breast, and here's a one-pound breast of mine...They weigh the same. But as you can see, mine has more meat, and theirs has more bone. I breed the broadest breasted, meatiest chicken you can buy...So don't buy a chicken breast by the pound...Buy

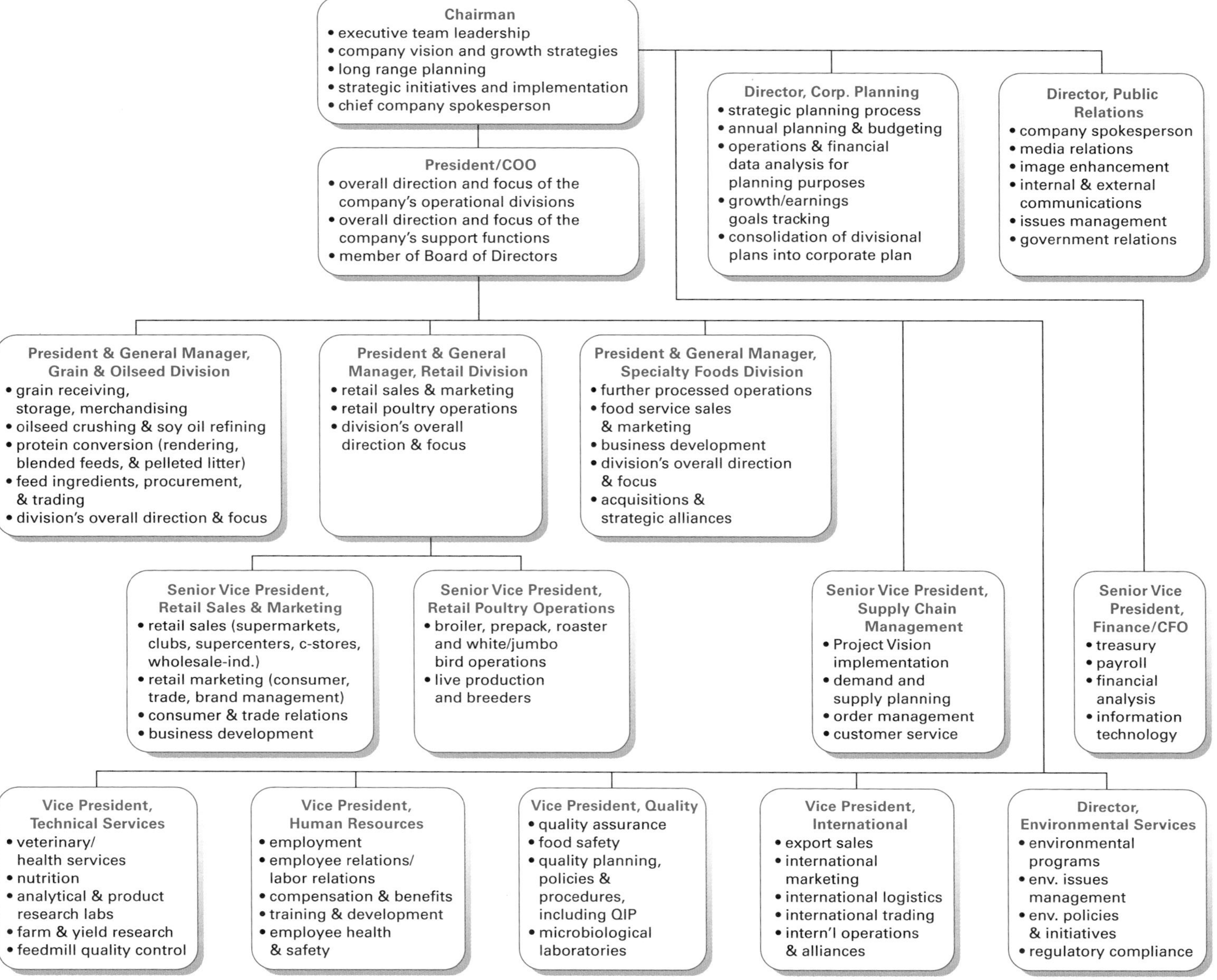

EXHIBIT 2 Perdue Farms Inc.—Senior Management

them by the name...and get an extra bite in every breast."

The ads paid off. In 1968, Perdue held about three percent of the New York market. By 1972, one out of every six chickens eaten in New York was a Perdue chicken. Fifty-one percent of New Yorkers recognized the label. Scali, McCabe, Sloves credited Perdue's "believability" for the success of the program. "This was advertising in which Perdue had a personality that lent credibility to the product. If Frank Perdue didn't look and sound like a chicken, he wouldn't be in the commercials."

Frank had his own view. As he told a Rotary audience in Charlotte, North Carolina, in March, 1989, ".... the product met the promise of the advertising and was far superior to the competition. Two great sayings tell it all: "Nothing will destroy a poor product as quickly as good advertising," and "a gifted product is mightier than a gifted pen!"

Today, branded chicken is ubiquitous. The new task for Perdue Farms is to create a unified theme to market a wide variety of products (e.g., fresh meat to fully prepared and frozen products) to a wide variety of customers (e.g., retail, food service and international). Industry experts believe that the market for fresh poultry has peaked while sales of value added and frozen products continue to grow at a healthy rate. Although domestic retail sales account for about 60 percent of Perdue Farms revenues in FY2000, food service sales now account for 20 percent, international sales account for 5 percent and grain and oilseed contribute the remaining 15 percent. The Company expects food service, international, and grain and oilseed sales to continue to grow as a percentage of total revenues.

DOMESTIC RETAIL

Today's retail grocery customer is increasingly looking for ease and speed of preparation, i.e., value added products. The move toward value added products has significantly changed the meat department in the modern grocery. There are now five distinct meat outlets for poultry:

1. The fresh meat counter—traditional, fresh meat includes whole chicken and parts.
2. The delicatessen—processed turkey, rotisserie chicken.
3. The frozen counter—individually quick frozen items such as frozen whole chickens, turkeys and Cornish hens.
4. Home meal replacement—fully prepared entrees such as Perdue brand "Short Cuts" and Deluca brand entrees (the Deluca brand was acquired and is sold under its own name) that are sold along with salads and desserts so that you can assemble your own dinner.
5. Shelf stable—canned products.

Because Perdue Farms has always used the phrase "fresh young chicken" as the centerpiece of its marketing, value added products and the retail frozen counter create a possible conflict with past marketing themes. Are these products compatible with the company's marketing image and, if so, how does the company express the notion of quality in this broader product environment? To answer that question, Perdue Farms has been studying what the term "fresh young chicken" means to customers who consistently demand quicker and easier preparation and who admit that they freeze most of their fresh meat purchases once they get home. One view is that the importance of the term "fresh young chicken" comes from the customer's perception that "quality" and "freshness" are closely associated. Thus, the real issue may be "trust," i.e., the customer must believe that the product, whether fresh or frozen, is the freshest, highest quality possible and future marketing themes must develop that concept.

FOOD SERVICE

The food service business consists of a wide variety of public and private customers including restaurant chains, governments, hospitals, schools, prisons, transportation facilities and the institutional contractors who supply meals to them. Historically, these customers have not been brand conscious, requiring the supplier to meet strict specifications at the lowest price, thus making this category a less than ideal fit for Perdue Farms. However, as Americans continue to eat a larger percentage of their meals away from home, traditional grocery sales have flattened while the food service sector has shown strong growth. Across the domestic poultry industry, food service accounts for approximately 50 percent of total poultry sales while approximately 20 percent of Perdue Farms revenues come from this category. Clearly, Perdue Farms is playing catch-up in this critical market.

Because Perdue Farms has neither strength nor expertise in the food service market, management believes that acquiring companies that already have food service expertise is the best strategy. An acquisition already completed is the purchase in September 1998 of Gol-Pak Corporation based in Monterey, Tennessee. A further processor of products for the food service industry, Gol-Pak had about 1,600 employees and revenues of about $200 million per year.

INTERNATIONAL

International markets have generally been a happy surprise. In the early 1990s, Perdue Farms began exporting specialty products such as chicken feet (known as "paws") to customers in China. Although not approved for sale for human consumption in the U.S., paws are considered a delicacy in China. By 1992, international sales, consisting principally of paws, had become a small, but profitable, business of about 30 million pounds per year. Building on this small "toehold," by 1998 Perdue Farms had quickly built an international business of more than 500 million pounds per year (see Exhibit 3) with annual revenues of more than $140 million, selling a wide variety of products to China, Japan, Russia, and the Ukraine.

In some ways, Japan is an excellent fit for Perdue Farms products because customers demand high quality. However, all Asian markets prefer dark meat, a serendipitous fit with the U.S. preference for white breast meat because it means that excess (to America) dark meat can be sold in Asia at a premium price. On the downside, Perdue Farms gains much of its competitive advantage from branding (e.g., trademarks, processes and technological and biological know-how) which has little value internationally because most of Asia has not yet embraced the concept of branded chicken.

To better serve export markets, Perdue Farms has developed a portside freezing facility in Newport News, Virginia. This permits poultry to be shipped directly to the port, reducing processing costs and helping to balance ocean shipping costs to Asia which are in the range of 2–3 cents per pound (contracting an entire ship equal to 300–500 truckloads).

Shipping poultry to Asia is not without problems. For example, in China, delivery trucks are seldom refrigerated. Thus, the poultry can begin to thaw as it is being delivered, limiting the distance it can be transported prior to sale. One shipload of Perdue Farms chicken bound for Russia actually vanished. It had been inappropriately impounded using forged documents. Although most of its dollar value was eventually recovered, it is important for firms to be aware of the possible difficulties of ocean shipping and the use of foreign ports.

Initial demand for product in Russia, Poland and Eastern Europe was huge. By the fiscal year 1998, a significant portion of international volume was being purchased by Russia. Unfortunately, the crumbling of Russia's economy has had a devastating effect on imports and sales are currently off significantly. Such instability of demand, coupled with rampant corruption, makes risking significant capital unacceptable.

Import duties and taxes are also a barrier. In China, according to the USDA, import duty rates for poultry are a whopping 45 percent for favored countries and 70 percent for unfavored countries. And, there is a 17 percent value added tax for all countries. Import duties and taxes

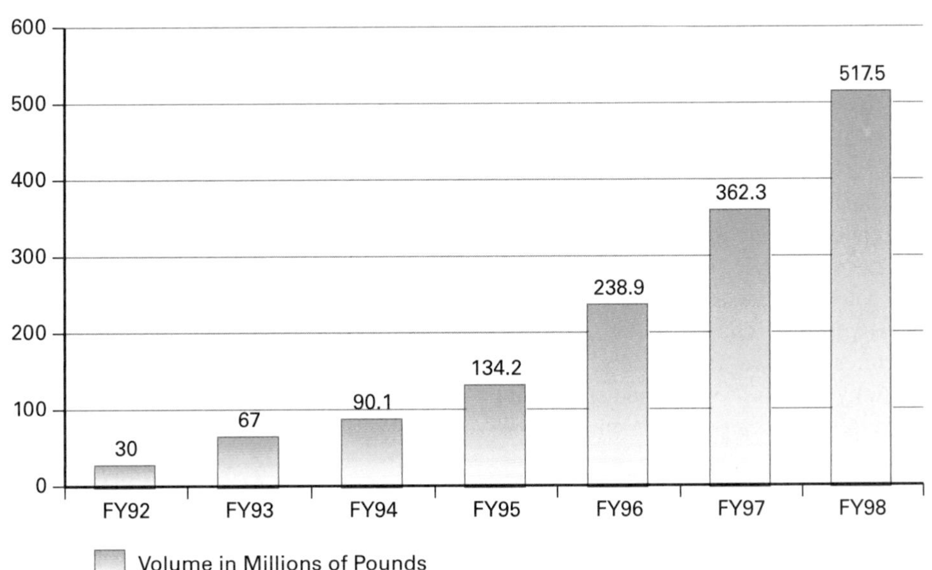

EXHIBIT 3 International Volume

in Russia have been similarly high. Hence, profits can be expected to be slim.

Perdue Farms has created a joint partnership with Jiang Nan Feng (JNF) brand in order to develop a small processing plant in Shanghai. Brand recognition is being built through normal marketing tools. The products use the first "tray pack" wrapping available in Shanghai supermarkets. This new business shows promise because the sale in China of homegrown, fresh dark meat is a significant competitive advantage. Additionally, although government regulations do not presently permit importation to the U.S. of foreign grown poultry, the future possibility of importing excess white meat from Shanghai to the U.S. is attractive since Asian markets, which prefer dark meat, will have difficulty absorbing all of the white breast meat from locally grown poultry. Perdue Farms' management believes that investments in processing facilities in Asia require the company to partner with a local company. Attempting to go it alone is simply too risky due to the significant cultural differences.

OPERATIONS

Two words sum up the Perdue approach to operations—quality and efficiency—with emphasis on the first over the latter. Perdue more than most companies represents the Total Quality Management (TQM) slogan, "Quality, a journey without end." Some of the key events are listed in Exhibit 4.

Both quality and efficiency are improved through the management of details. Exhibit 5 depicts the structure and product flow of a generic, vertically integrated broiler company. A broiler company can choose which steps in the process it wants to accomplish in-house and which it wants suppliers to provide. For example, the broiler company could purchase all grain, oilseed, meal and other feed products. Or, it could contract with hatcheries to supply primary breeders and hatchery supply flocks.

Perdue Farms chose maximum vertical integration in order to control every detail. It breeds and hatches its own eggs (nineteen hatcheries), selects its contract growers, builds Perdue-engineered chicken houses, formulates and manufactures its own feed (twelve poultry feedmills, one specialty feedmill, two ingredient blending operations), oversees the care and feeding of the chicks, operates its own processing plants (twenty-one processing/further processing plants), distributes via its own trucking fleet, and markets the products—see Exhibit 5. Total process control formed the basis for Frank Perdue's early claims that Perdue Farms poultry is, indeed, higher quality than other poultry. When he stated in his early ads that "A chicken is what it eats.... I store my own grain and mix my own feed.... and give my Perdue chickens nothing but well water to drink..." he knew that his claim was honest and he could back it up.

Total process control also enables Perdue Farms to ensure that nothing goes to waste. Eight measurable items—hatchability, turnover, feed conversion, livability, yield, birds per man-hour, utilization, and grade—are tracked routinely.

Perdue Farms continues to ensure that nothing artificial is fed to or injected into the birds. No shortcuts are taken. A chemical-free and steroid-free diet is fed to the chickens. Young chickens are vaccinated against disease. Selective breeding is used to improve the quality of the chicken stock. Chickens are bred to yield more white breast meat because that is what the consumer wants.

To ensure that Perdue Farms poultry continues to lead the industry in quality, the company buys and analyzes competitors' products regularly. Inspection associates grade these products and share the information with the highest levels of management. In addition, the company's Quality Policy is displayed at all locations and taught to all associates in quality training (see Exhibit 6).

RESEARCH AND DEVELOPMENT

Perdue is an acknowledged industry leader in the use of research and technology to provide quality products and service to its customers. The company spends more on research as a percent of revenues than any other poultry processor. This practice goes back to Frank Perdue's focus on finding ways to differentiate his products based on quality and value. It was research into selective breeding that resulted in the broader breast, an attribute of Perdue Farms chicken that was the basis of his early advertising. Although other processors have also improved their stock, Perdue Farms believes that it still leads the industry. A list of some of Perdue Farms technological accomplishments is given in Exhibit 7.

As with every other aspect of the business, Perdue Farms tries to leave nothing to chance. The company employs specialists in avian science, microbiology, genetics, nutrition, and veterinary science. Because of its research and development capabilities, Perdue Farms is often involved in USDA field tests with pharmaceutical suppliers. Knowledge and experience gained from these tests can lead to a competitive advantage. For example, Perdue has the most extensive and expensive vaccination program in the industry. Currently, the company is working with and studying the practices of several European producers who use completely different methods. The

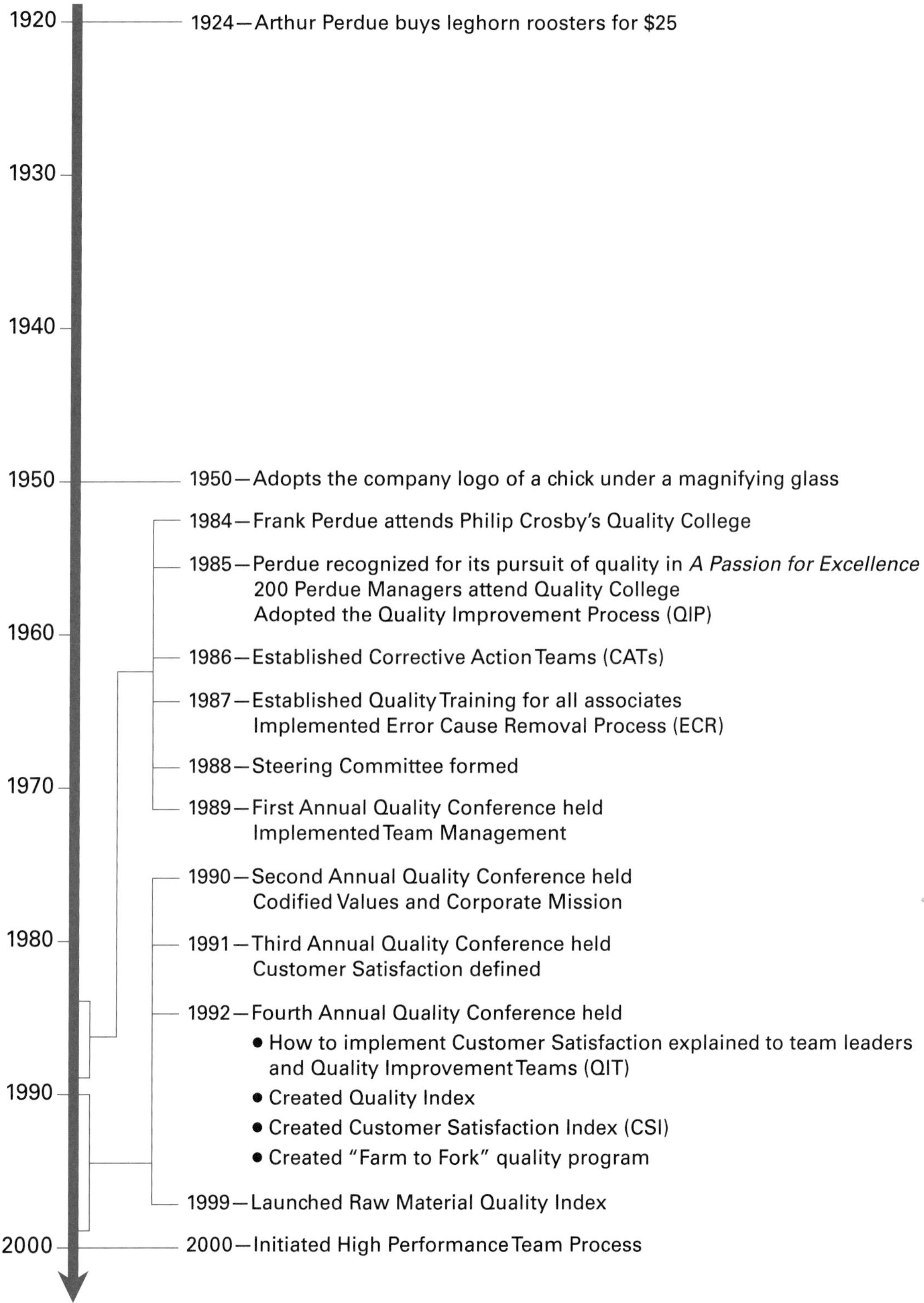

1920
1930
1940
1950
1960
1970
1980
1990
2000
1924—Arthur Perdue buys leghorn roosters for $25
1950—Adopts the company logo of a chick under a magnifying glass
1984—Frank Perdue attends Philip Crosby's Quality College
1985—Perdue recognized for its pursuit of quality in *A Passion for Excellence*
200 Perdue Managers attend Quality College
Adopted the Quality Improvement Process (QIP)
1986—Established Corrective Action Teams (CATs)
1987—Established Quality Training for all associates
Implemented Error Cause Removal Process (ECR)
1988—Steering Committee formed
1989—First Annual Quality Conference held
Implemented Team Management
1990—Second Annual Quality Conference held
Codified Values and Corporate Mission
1991—Third Annual Quality Conference held
Customer Satisfaction defined
1992—Fourth Annual Quality Conference held
• How to implement Customer Satisfaction explained to team leaders and Quality Improvement Teams (QIT)
• Created Quality Index
• Created Customer Satisfaction Index (CSI)
• Created "Farm to Fork" quality program
1999—Launched Raw Material Quality Index
2000—Initiated High Performance Team Process

EXHIBIT 4 Milestones in the Quality Improvement Process at Perdue Farms

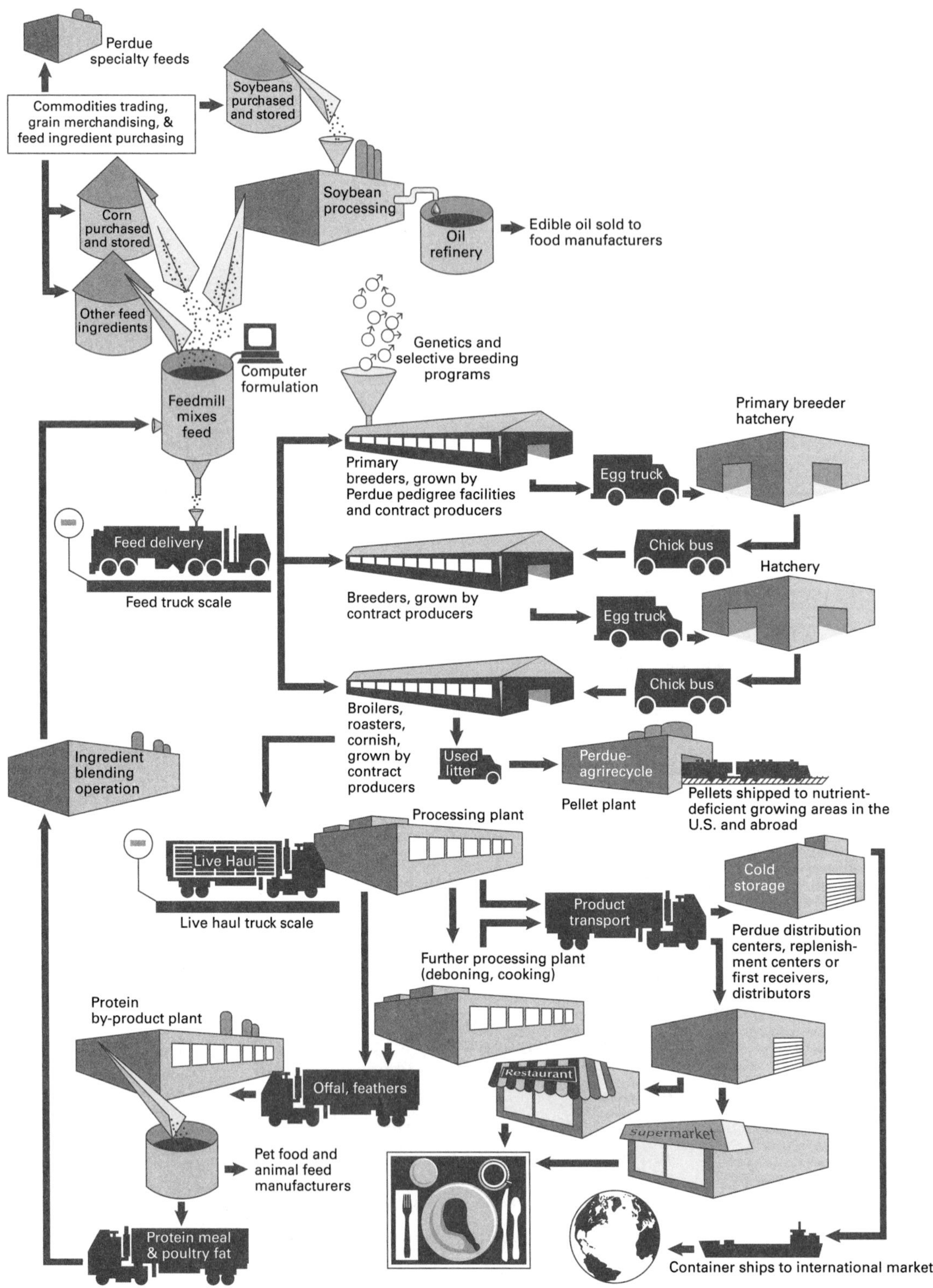

EXHIBIT 5 Perdue Farms—Integrated Operations

WE SHALL produce products and provide services at all times that meet or exceed the expectations of our customers.

WE SHALL not be content to be of equal quality to our competitors.

OUR COMMITMENT is to be increasingly superior.

CONTRIBUTION TO QUALITY is a responsibility shared by everyone in the Perdue organization.

EXHIBIT 6 Quality Policy

- Conducts more research than all competitors combined
- Breeds chickens with consistently more breast meat than any other bird in the industry
- First to use digital scales to guarantee weights to customers
- First to package fully-cooked chicken products on microwaveable trays
- First to have a box lab to define quality of boxes from different suppliers
- First to test both its chickens and competitors' chickens on fifty-two quality factors every week
- Improved on-time deliveries 20% between 1987 and 1993
- Built state of the art analytical and microbiological laboratories for feed and end product analysis
- First to develop best management practices for food safety across all areas of the company
- First to develop commercially viable pelletized poultry litter

EXHIBIT 7 Perdue Farms Inc. Technological Accomplishments

company has used research to significantly increase productivity. For example, in the 1950s, it took 14 weeks to grow a 3-pound chicken. Today, it takes only seven weeks to grow a 5-pound chicken. This gain in efficiency is due principally to improvements in the conversion rate of feed to chicken. The current rate of conversion is about two pounds of feed to produce one pound of chicken. Feed represents about 65 percent of the cost of growing a chicken. Thus, if additional research can further improve the conversion rate of feed to chicken by just 1 percent, it would represent estimated additional income of $2.5–3 million per week or $130–156 million per year.

FINANCE

Perdue Farms, Inc., is privately held and considers financial information to be proprietary. Hence, available data is limited. Stock is primarily held by the family with a limited amount held by Perdue Management. Common numbers used by the media and the poultry industry peg Perdue Farm's revenues for the fiscal year 2000 at about $2.5 billion and the number of associates at nearly 20,000. *Forbes* magazine has estimated the fiscal year 2000 operating profits at about $160 million and net profits at about $22 million.

The firm's compound sales growth rate has been slowly decreasing during the past twenty years, mirroring the industry which has been experiencing market saturation and overproduction. However, Perdue has compensated by using manpower more efficiently through improvements such as automation. For example, twenty years ago, a 1 percent increase in associates resulted in a 1.6 percent increase in revenue. Currently, a 1 percent increase in associates results in an 8.5 percent increase in revenues (see Exhibit 8).

Poultry operations can be divided into four segments: Retail Chicken (growth rate 5 percent), Foodservice Chicken and Turkey (growth rate 12 percent), International Sales (growth rate 64 percent over past six years), and Grain and Oilseed (growth rate 10 percent). The bulk of Perdue Farms sales continues to come from retail chicken—the sector with the slowest growth rate. The greatest opportunity appears to lie in food-service sales, where the company is admittedly behind, and international sales where political and economic instability in target countries make the risk to capital significant.

	Revenue	Associates	Sales/Associate
Past 20 years	10.60%	6.48%	3.87%
Past 15 years	8.45%	4.48%	4.48%
Past 10 years	7.39%	4.75%	2.52%
Past 5 years	8.39%	0.99%	7.33%

EXHIBIT 8 Annual Compound Growth Rate Through FY2000

Perdue Farms has been profitable every year since its founding with the exception of 1988 and 1996. Company officials believe the loss in 1988 was caused by overproduction by the industry and higher administrative costs resulting from a decentralization effort begun during the mid-eighties. At that time, there was a concerted effort to push decisions down through the corporate ranks to provide more autonomy. When the new strategy resulted in significantly higher administrative costs due to duplication of effort, the company responded quickly by returning to the basics, reconsolidating and downsizing. The loss in 1996 was due to the impact of high corn prices. Currently, the goal is to constantly streamline in order to provide cost-effective business solutions.

Perdue Farms approaches financial management conservatively, using retained earnings and cash flow to finance most asset replacement projects and normal growth. When planning expansion projects or acquisitions, long-term debt is used. The target debt limit is 55 percent of equity. Such debt is normally provided by domestic and international bank and insurance companies. The debt strategy is to match asset lives with liability maturities, and have a mix of fixed rate and variable rate debt. Growth plans require about two dollars in projected incremental sales growth for each dollar in invested capital.

ENVIRONMENT

Environmental issues present a constant challenge to all poultry processors. Growing, slaughtering and processing poultry is a difficult and tedious process that demands absolute efficiency in order to keep operating costs at an acceptable level. Inevitably, detractors argue that the process is dangerous to workers, inhumane to the poultry, hard on the environment and results in food that may not be safe. Thus media headlines such as "Human Cost of Poultry Business Bared," "Animal Rights Advocates Protest Chicken Coop Conditions," "Processing Plants Leave a Toxic Trail," or "EPA Mandates Poultry Regulations" are routine.

Perdue Farms tries to be pro-active in managing environmental issues. In April 1993, the company created an Environmental Steering Committee. Its mission is "...to provide all Perdue Farms work sites with vision, direction, and leadership so that they can be good corporate citizens from an environmental perspective today and in the future." The committee is responsible for overseeing how the company is doing in such environmentally sensitive areas as waste-water, storm water, hazardous waste, solid waste, recycling, bio-solids, and human health and safety.

For example, disposing of dead birds has long been an industry problem. Perdue Farms developed small composters for use on each farm. Using this approach, carcasses are reduced to an end product that resembles soil in a matter of a few days. The disposal of hatchery waste is another environmental challenge. Historically, manure and un-hatched eggs were shipped to a landfill. However, Perdue Farms developed a way to reduce the waste by 50 percent by selling the liquid fraction to a pet food processor that cooks it for protein. The other 50 percent is recycled through a rendering process. In 1990, Perdue Farms spent $4.2 million to upgrade its existing treatment facility with a state-of-the-art system at its Accomac, Virginia, and Showell, Maryland, plants. These facilities use forced hot air heated to 120 degrees to cause the microbes to digest all traces of ammonia, even during the cold winter months.

More than ten years ago, North Carolina's Occupational Safety and Health Administration cited Perdue Farms for an unacceptable level of repetitive stress injuries at its Lewiston and Robersonville, North Carolina, processing plants. This sparked a major research program in which Perdue Farms worked with Health and Hygiene Inc. of Greensboro, North Carolina, to learn more about ergonomics, the repetitive movements required to accomplish specific jobs. Results have been dramatic. Launched in 1991 after two years of development, the program videotapes employees at all of Perdue Farm's plants as they work in order to describe and place stress values on the various tasks.

Although the cost to Perdue Farms has been significant, results have been dramatic with workers' compensation claims down 44 percent, lost-time recordables just 7.7 percent of the industry average, an 80 percent decrease in serious repetitive stress cases and a 50 percent reduction in lost time or surgery back injuries (Shelley Reese, "Helping Employees get a Grip," *Business and Health,* Aug. 1998).

Despite these advances, serious problems continue to develop. In 1997, the organism Pfiesteria burst into media headlines when massive numbers of dead fish with lesions turned up along the Chesapeake Bay in Maryland. Initial findings pointed to manure runoff from the poultry industry. Political constituencies quickly called for increased regulation to insure proper manure storage and fertilizer use. The company readily admits that ".... the poultry process is a closed system. There is lots of nitrogen and phosphorus in the grain, it passes through the chicken and is returned to the environment as manure. Obviously, if you bring additional grain into a closed area such as the Delmarva Peninsula, you increase the amount of nitrogen and phosphorus in the soil unless you find a way to get rid of it." Nitrogen and phosphorus from manure normally make excellent fertilizer that moves slowly in the soil. However, scientists speculate that erosion speeds up runoff threatening the health of nearby streams, rivers, and larger bodies of water such as the Chesapeake Bay. The problem for the industry is that proposals to control the runoff are sometimes driven more by politics and emotion than research, which is not yet complete.

Although it is not clear what role poultry-related nitrogen and phosphorus runoff played in the Pfiesteria outbreak, regulators believe the microorganism feasts on the algae that grows when too much of these nutrients is present in the water. Thus, the EPA and various states are considering new regulations. Currently, contract growers are responsible for either using or disposing of the manure from their chicken houses. But, some regulators and environmentalists believe that (1) it is too complicated to police the utilization and disposal practices of thousands of individual farmers and (2) only the big poultry companies have the financial resources to properly dispose of the waste. Thus, they want to make poultry companies responsible for all waste disposal, a move that the industry strongly opposes.

Some experts have called for conservation measures that might limit the density of chicken houses in a given area or even require a percentage of existing chicken houses to be taken out of production periodically. Obviously this would be very hard on the farm families who own existing chicken houses and could result in fewer acres devoted to agriculture. Working with AgriRecycle Inc. of Springfield, Missouri, Perdue Farms has developed a possible solution. The plan envisions the poultry companies processing excess manure into pellets for use as fertilizer. This would permit sale outside the poultry-growing region, better balancing the input of grain. Spokesmen estimate that as much as 120,000 tons, nearly one-third of the surplus nutrient from manure produced each year on the Delmarva peninsula, could be sold to corn growers in other parts of the country. Prices would be market driven but could be $25–30 per ton, suggesting a potential, small profit. Still, almost any attempt to control the problem potentially raises the cost of growing chickens, forcing poultry processors to look elsewhere for locations where the chicken population is less dense.

In general, solving industry environmental problems presents at least five major challenges to the poultry processor:

1. How to maintain the trust of the poultry consumer,
2. How to ensure that the poultry remain healthy,
3. How to protect the safety of the employees and the process,
4. How to satisfy legislators who need to show their constituents that they are taking firm action when environmental problems occur, and
5. How to keep costs at an acceptable level.

Jim Perdue sums up Perdue Farms' position as follows: ".... we must not only comply with environmental laws as they exist today, but look to the future to make sure we don't have any surprises. We must make sure our environmental policy statement (see Exhibit 9) is real, that there's something behind it and that we do what we say we're going to do."

LOGISTICS AND INFORMATION SYSTEMS

The explosion of poultry products and increasing number of customers during recent years placed a severe strain on the existing logistic system which was developed at a time when there were far fewer products, fewer delivery points and lower volume. Hence, the company had limited ability to improve service levels, could not support further growth, and could not introduce innovative services that might provide a competitive advantage.

Perdue Farms is committed to environmental stewardship and shares that commitment with its farm family partners. We're proud of the leadership we're providing our industry in addressing the full range of environmental challenges related to animal agriculture and food processing. We've invested—and continue to invest—millions of dollars in research, new technology, equipment upgrades, and awareness and education as part of our ongoing commitment to protecting the environment.

- Perdue Farms was among the first poultry companies with a dedicated Environmental Services department. Our team of environmental managers is responsible for ensuring that every Perdue facility operates within *100 percent compliance of all applicable environmental regulations and permits.*
- Through our joint venture, Perdue AgriRecycle, Perdue Farms is investing $12 million to build in Delaware a first-of-its-kind pellet plant that will convert surplus poultry litter into a starter fertilizer that will be marketed internationally to nutrient deficient regions. The facility, which will serve the entire Delmarva region, is scheduled to begin operation in April, 2001.
- We continue to explore new technologies that will reduce water usage in our processing plants without compromising food safety or quality.
- We invested thousands of man-hours in producer education to assist our family farm partners in managing their independent poultry operations in the most environmentally responsible manner possible. In addition, all our poultry producers are required to have nutrient management plans and dead-bird composters.
- Perdue Farms was one of four poultry companies operating in Delaware to sign an agreement with Delaware officials outlining our companies' voluntary commitment to help independent poultry producers dispose of surplus chicken litter.
- Our Technical Services department is conducting ongoing research into feed technology as a means of reducing the nutrients in poultry manure. We've already achieved phosphorous reductions that far exceed the industry average.
- We recognize that the environmental impact of animal agriculture is more pronounced in areas where development is decreasing the amount of farmland available to produce grain for feed and to accept nutrients. That is why we view independent grain and poultry producers as vital business partners and strive to preserve the economic viability of the family farm.

At Perdue Farms, we believe that it is possible to preserve the family farm; provide a safe, abundant and affordable food supply; and protect the environment. However, we believe that can best happen when there is cooperation and trust between the poultry industry, agriculture, environmental groups and state officials. We hope Delaware's effort will become a model for other states to follow.

EXHIBIT 9 Perdue Farms Environmental Policy Statement

In the poultry industry, companies are faced with two significant problems—time and forecasting. Fresh poultry has a limited shelf life—measured in days. Thus forecasts must be extremely accurate and deliveries timely. On one hand, estimating requirements too conservatively results in product shortages. Mega-customers such as Wal-Mart will not tolerate product shortages that lead to empty shelves and lost sales. On the other hand, if estimates are overstated, the result is outdated products that cannot be sold and losses for Perdue Farms. A common expression in the poultry industry is "you either sell it or smell it."

Forecasting has always been extremely difficult in the poultry industry because the processor needs to know approximately eighteen months in advance how many broilers will be needed in order to size hatchery supply flocks and contract with growers to provide live broilers. Most customers (e.g., grocers, food service buyers) have a much shorter planning window. Additionally, there is no way for Perdue Farms to know when rival poultry processors will put a particular product on special, reducing Perdue Farms sales, or when bad weather and other uncontrollable problems may reduce demand.

Historically, poultry companies have relied principally on extrapolation of past demand, industry networks and other contacts to make their estimates. Although product complexity has exacerbated the problem, the steady movement away from fresh product to frozen product (which has a longer shelf life) offers some relief.

In the short run, Information Technology (IT) has helped by shortening the distance between the customer and Perdue Farms. As far back as 1987, PCs were placed directly on each customer service associate's desk, allowing them to enter customer orders directly. Next, a system was developed to put dispatchers in direct contact with every truck in the system so that they would have accurate information about product inventory and truck location at all times. Now, IT is moving to further shorten the distance between the customer and the Perdue Farms service representative by putting a PC on the customer's desk. All of these steps improve communication and shorten the time from order to delivery.

In the longer run, these steps are not enough due to the rapidly expanding complexity of the industry. For example, today, poultry products fall into four unique channels of distribution:

1. Bulk fresh—Timeliness and frequency of delivery are critical to ensure freshness. Distribution requirements are high volume and low cost delivery.
2. Domestic frozen and further processed products—Temperature integrity is critical, distribution requirements are frequency and timeliness of delivery. This channel lends itself to dual temperature trailer systems and load consolidation.
3. Export—Temperature integrity, high volume, and low cost are critical. This channel lends itself to inventory consolidation and custom loading of vessels.
4. Consumer packaged goods (packaged fresh, prepared and deli products)—Differentiate via innovative products and services. Distribution requirements are reduced lead time and low cost.

Thus, forecasting now requires the development of a sophisticated *supply chain management system* that can efficiently integrate all facets of operations including grain and oilseed activities, hatcheries and growing facilities, processing plants (which now produce more than 400 products at more than twenty locations), distribution facilities and, finally, the distributors, supermarkets, food service customers and export markets (see Exhibit 5). Perdue Farms underlined the importance of the successful implementation of supply chain management by creating a new executive position, Senior Vice President for Supply Chain Management.

A key step in overhauling the distribution infrastructure is the building of replenishment centers that will, in effect, be buffers between the processing plants and the customers. The portside facility in Norfolk, Virginia, which serves the international market, is being expanded and a new domestic freezer facility added.

Conceptually, products are directed from the processing plants to the replenishment and freezer centers based on customer forecasts that have been converted to an optimized production schedule. Perdue Farms trucks deliver these bulk products to the centers in finished or semi-finished form. At the centers, further finishing and packaging is accomplished. Finally, specific customer orders are custom palletized and loaded on trucks (either Perdue owned or contracted) for delivery to individual customers. All shipments are made up from replenishment center inventory. Thus, the need for accurate demand forecasting by the distribution centers is key.

In order to control the entire supply chain management process, Perdue Farms purchased a multi-million dollar information technology system that represents the biggest non-tangible asset expense in the company's history. This integrated, state-of-the-art information system required total process re-engineering, a project that took eighteen months and required training 1,200 associates. Major goals of the system were to (1) make it easier and more desirable for the customer to do business with Perdue Farms, (2) make it easier for Perdue Farms associates to get the job done, and (3) take as much cost out of the process as possible.

INDUSTRY TRENDS

The poultry industry is affected by consumer, industry and governmental regulatory trends. Currently, chicken is the number one meat consumed in the United States with 40 percent market share (Exhibits 10 and 11). Typical Americans consume about 81 pounds of chicken, 69 pounds of beef, and 52 pounds of pork annually (USDA data). Additionally, chicken is becoming the most popular meat in the world. In 1997, poultry set an export record of $2.5 billion. Although exports fell 6 percent in 1998, the decrease was attributed to Russia's and Asia's financial crisis and food industry experts expect this to be only a temporary setback. Hence, the world market is clearly a growth opportunity for the future.

The popularity and growth of poultry products is attributed to both nutritional and economic issues. Poultry products contain significantly less fat and cholesterol than other meat products. In the United States, the demand for boneless, skinless breast meat, the leanest meat on poultry, is so great that dark meat is often sold at a discount in the United States or shipped overseas where it is preferred over white meat.

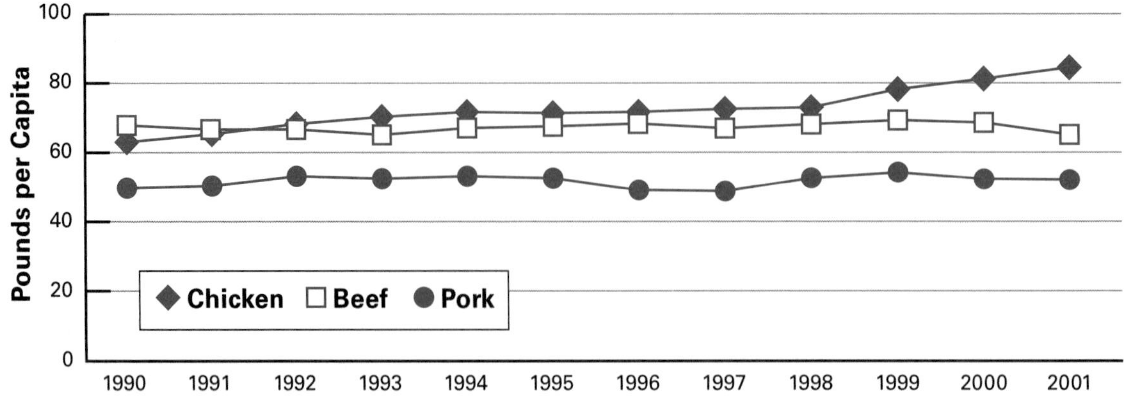

EXHIBIT 10 Consumption Per Capita of Chicken, Beef, and Pork in the 1990s and Projected Consumption for 2000, 2001

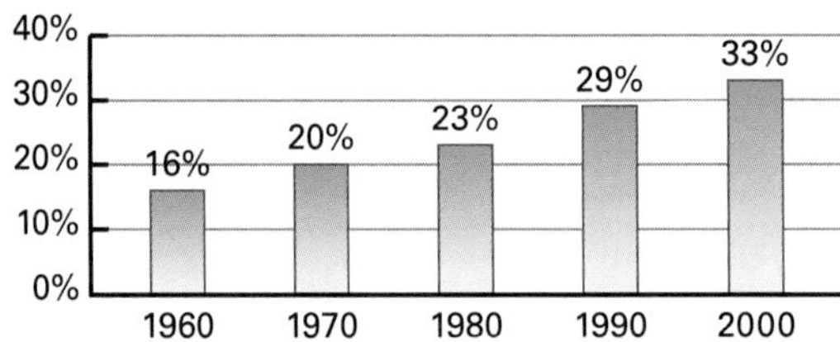

EXHIBIT 11 Going Up: Chicken as a Percentage of Overall Meat Consumption, 1960–2000

Another trend is a decrease in demand for whole birds to be used as the base dish for home meals and an increase in demand for products that have been further processed for either home or restaurant consumption. For example, turkey or chicken hot dogs, fully-cooked, sliced chicken or turkey, and turkey pastrami—which neither looks nor tastes like turkey—can be found in most deli cases. Many supermarkets sell either whole or parts of hot rotisserie chicken. Almost all fast food restaurants have at least one sandwich based on poultry products. Many up-scale restaurants feature poultry products that are shipped to them frozen and partially prepared in order to simplify restaurant preparation. All these products have been further processed, adding value and increasing the potential profit margin.

The industry is consolidating, that is, the larger companies in the industry are continuing to buy smaller firms. Currently there are about thirty-five major poultry firms in the United States but this number is expected to drop to twenty to twenty-five within the next ten years. There are several reasons for this. Stagnant U.S. demand and general product oversupply create downward price pressure that makes it difficult for smaller firms to operate profitably. In addition, pressure for efficiency improvements requires huge capital outlays. Finally, mega-retailers such as Sam's Club and Royal Ahold (the Dutch owner of several U.S. supermarket chains) do not like to manage individual contracts with numerous smaller processors. Mega-retailers prefer to deal with mega-suppliers.

The industry is heavily regulated. The Food and Drug Administration (FDA) monitors product safety. The USDA inspects poultry as it arrives at the processing plant. After it is killed, each bird is again inspected by a USDA inspector for avian diseases, contamination of feces or other foreign material. All poultry that does not meet regulations is destroyed under USDA supervision. USDA inspectors also examine the plant, equipment, operating procedures and personnel for compliance with sanitary regulations. Congress has mandated that the USDA make this information available online. Additional intensive inspections of statistically selected samples of poultry products have been recommended by the National Academy of Sciences. Thus, additional FDA regulations for product quality are anticipated.

Although poultry produces less waste per pound of product than cattle or hogs, all meat industries are experiencing increased scrutiny by the Environmental

Protection Agency (EPA) regarding the disposal of waste. In general, waste generated at processing plants is well controlled by regulation, monitoring, and fines. When an EPA violation occurs, the company that operates the plant can receive a substantial fine, potentially millions of dollars.

Still, the most difficult problems to deal with are those that occur as a cumulative result of numerous processors producing in a relatively limited area. For example, increasing poultry production in a given area intensifies the problem of disposal of manure. In man-made fertilizer, phosphorous and nitrogen exist in approximately a one-to-eight ratio whereas in poultry manure the ratio can be one-to-one. Thus, too much poultry manure can result in serious phosphorous run-off into streams and rivers, potentially resulting in aquatic disease and degradation of water quality. In 1997, an outbreak of Pfiesteria, a toxic microbe, occurred in the tributaries of the Chesapeake Bay. Although the poultry industry insisted that there were many possible reasons for the problem, the media and most regulatory spokespersons attributed it primarily to phosphorous run-off from chicken manure. After much negative publicity and extensive investigation by both poultry processors and state regulatory agencies, the State of Maryland passed the Water Quality Act of 1998, which required nutrient management plans. However, many environmentalists continue to believe that the EPA must create additional, stricter federal environmental regulations. Recent regulatory activity has continued to focus on Eastern Shore agriculture, especially the poultry industry. However, new studies from the U.S. Geological Survey suggest that the vast majority of nutrients affecting the Chesapeake Bay come from rivers that do not flow through the poultry-producing regions of the Eastern Shore. The studies also found that improved agricultural management practices have reduced nutrient runoff from farmlands. Jim Perdue says, "While the poultry industry must accept responsibility for its share of nutrients, public policy should view the watershed as a whole and address all the factors that influence water quality."

Other government agencies whose regulations impact the industry include The Occupational Safety and Health Administration (OSHA) for employee safety and the Immigration and Naturalization Service (INS) for undocumented workers. OSHA enforces its regulations via periodic inspections, and levies fines when non-compliance is found. For example, a Hudson Foods poultry plant was fined more than a million dollars for alleged willful violations causing ergonomic injury to workers. The INS also uses periodic inspections to find undocumented workers. It estimates that undocumented aliens working in the industry vary from 3 percent to 78 percent of the workforce at individual plants. Plants that are found to use undocumented workers, especially those that are repeat offenders, can be heavily fined.

THE FUTURE

The marketplace for poultry in the twenty-first century will be very different from the past. Understanding the wants and needs of Generation X-ers and Echo-boomers will be key to responding successfully to these differences.

Quality will continue to be essential. In the 1970s, quality was the cornerstone of Frank Perdue's successful marketing program to "brand" his poultry. However, in the twenty-first century, quality will not be enough. Today's customers expect—even demand—all products to be high quality. Thus, Perdue Farms plans to use customer service to further differentiate the company. The focus will be on learning how to become indispensable to the customer by taking cost out of the product and delivering it exactly the way the customer wants it, where and when the customer wants it. In short, as Jim Perdue says, "Perdue Farms wants to become so easy to do business with that the customer will have no reason to do business with anyone else."

In the poultry business, customer purchase decisions, as well as company profitability, hinge on mere pennies. Thus, the location of processing facilities is key. Historically, Perdue Farms has been an Eastern Shore company and has maintained major processing facilities on the Eastern Shore. However, it currently costs about one cent more per pound to grow poultry on the Eastern Shore versus what poultry can be grown for in Arkansas. This difference results from the cost of labor, compliance with federal and state environmental laws, resource costs (e.g., feed grain) and other variables. Clearly, selecting favorable sites for future growing and processing facilities is key. In the future, assuming regulations will permit the importation of foreign grown poultry, producers could even use inexpensive international labor markets to further reduce costs. The opportunity for large growers to capture these savings puts increased pressure on small poultry companies. This suggests further consolidation of the industry.

Grocery companies are also consolidating in order to compete with huge food industry newcomers such as Wal-Mart and Royal Ahold. These new competitors gain efficiency by minimizing the number of their suppliers and buying huge amounts from each at the lowest possible price. In effect, both mega-companies—the supplier and the buyer—become dependent on each other. Further, mega-companies expect their suppliers to do more for them. For example, Perdue Farms considers it possible that, using sophisticated distribution information programs, they will soon be able to manage the entire meat department requirements for several supermarket chains. Providing this service would support Perdue Farms' goal of becoming indispensable to their first line retail customer, the grocer.

The twenty-first century consumer will demand many options. Clearly, the demand for uncooked, whole chickens purchased at the meat counter has peaked. Demand is moving toward further processed poultry. To support this trend, Perdue Farms plans to open several additional cooking plants. In addition, a criterion for future acquisitions will be whether they support value added processing. Products from these plants will fill food service requirements and grocery sales of prepared foods such as delicatessen, frozen, home meal replacement, and shelf stable items. Additionally, the twenty-first century customer will be everywhere. Whether at work, at a sports event, in school, or traveling on the highway, customers expect to have convenient refreshment machines available with a wide selection of wholesome, ready-to-eat products.

Designing a distribution system that can handle all of these options is extremely difficult. For example, the system must be able to efficiently organize hundreds of customer orders that are chosen from more than 400 different products that are processed and further prepared at more than twenty facilities throughout the southeast for delivery by one truck—a massive distribution task. As executives note, the company survived up until now using distribution techniques created as many as twenty years ago when there were a handful of products and processing facilities. However, the system approached gridlock during the late 1990s. Thus, Perdue Farms invested in a state of the art information processing system—a tough decision because "we could build two new processing plants for the price of this technology package."

International markets are a conundrum. On one hand, Perdue Farms' international revenue has grown from an insignificant side business in 1994 to about $140 million in 1999, approximately 5 percent of total revenues. Further, its contribution to profits is significant. Poultry is widely accepted around the world providing opportunities for further growth. But, trying to be global doesn't work. Different cultures value different parts of the chicken and demand different meat color, preparation and seasoning. Thus, products must be customized. Parts that are not in demand in a particular country must be sold at severely reduced prices, used as feed, or shipped frozen to a different market where demand exists. While this can be done, it is a distribution problem that significantly complicates an already difficult forecasting model.

International markets can also be very unstable, exposing Perdue Farms to significant demand instability and potential losses. For example, in 1997, about 50 percent of Perdue Farms' international revenues came from Russia. However, political and economic problems in Russia reduced 1999 revenues significantly. This high level of instability, coupled with corruption that thrives in a country experiencing severe political and economic turmoil, introduces significant risk to future investment.

Clearly, the future holds many opportunities. But, none of them comes without risk and Perdue Farms must carefully choose where it wants to direct its scarce resources.

CASE **4**

MCC SMART: INNOVATORS MUST BREAK RULES—BUT HOW MANY?

Research Associate George Rädler prepared this case under the supervision of Professor Ulrich Steger as a basis for class discussion rather than to illustrate either effective or ineffective handling of a business situation.

> Right from the beginning, we considered the smart to be a learning exercise—a model on which we could try out lots of new ideas that we normally couldn't use on Mercedes-Benz cars. And we have learned an invaluable number of things—how to improve production and sales, for instance. What's more, some of our findings can also be applied to other brands within the company.
>
> —Jürgen Hubbert, Board Member of DaimlerChrysler, Head of Mercedes-Benz Passenger Cars & MCC smart

In late September 1999 the board of DaimlerChrysler (DC) was looking for a "fix-it" CEO and President for its controversial smart® subsidiary (refer to Exhibit 1 for a picture of the smart and its features). Sales for 1999 were far below expectations. Instead of selling 140,000 smarts as initially planned, the company was even struggling to meet its revised annual goal of 80,000 units. Losses were estimated at €200 to €400 million for the same year.

Mr. Andreas Renschler, 41, was a natural choice for leading the turnaround of the young brand. Renschler had built the first Mercedes-Benz plant outside Germany, in Alabama, USA. This plant produced the M-Class, a very popular sport utility vehicle. After the successful launch of the M-Class, Renschler had turned into one of the rising stars in DC.

Nevertheless, Renschler knew that turning around the smart was his toughest assignment to date. Realizing the impatience of his board on this matter, Renschler needed fast answers. How could he ensure the quality levels of the car? Should he change the distribution channel? The mobility concept? Push for new models (include a four-seater), or even rally for a strategic alliance with another manufacturer? Overall, the main question remained whether the smart was necessary for DaimlerChrysler to comply with future regulations for fuel consumption.

SMART: THE YOUNGEST CAR MANUFACTURER IN THE WORLD

The Idea

Mercedes-Benz (MB) had already had experiences with the mini-car segment in the 1970s and 1980s—but they never took it beyond the concept stage. However, at the beginning of the 1990s, MB felt strong competition from Japanese manufacturers in the luxury segment. The newly launched S-Class had gotten mixed reviews. The model had grown larger, but for Greenpeace, the S-Class had quickly become a symbol for the excesses of car manufacturing and fuel consumption, sparking a discussion of mobility across Europe. Over the years, sales of the S-Class had stayed below forecasts, which had eventually started a process of re-evaluating the markets served by MB. Marketing executives were also increasingly concerned about the age structure of MB drivers. In the early 1990s MB recorded an average age of 53 years for its customers.

At the MB headquarters in Stuttgart, executives looked at the possibility of entering other market segments. Potential segments had to offer volume, growth and profitability. Moreover, any move into a new market should not tarnish the value of the MB brand. The effect of stretching the MB brand image was the most important issue. The brand's premier positioning made it a natural choice for luxury vehicles (refer to Appendix A for

The smart

Standard Equipment:

- ABS
- 2 Full-size Airbags
- Power Windows
- Softip Transmission (no clutch)
- Turbo
- Power locks with a remote control
- Ability to exchange body panels

1.52 m.

1.51 m. 2.50 m.

Fuel Consumption:

4.8 liters/100 km (mixed driving) or 4.2 liters on the highway. The smart cdi diesel will have a fuel consumption of 3.4 liters/100 km. An electric engine is not planned.

The 3-cylinder engine and gearbox are designed as one unit. They are located behind the driver in the trunk.

General Data:

Top Speed:	135 km/h
Unloaded/Loaded Weight:	720 kg/990 kg
Price in Swiss Francs (incl. VAT):	12,790–16,150 (06/2000)
1 Swiss Franc = $0.61 or 0.64	

Safety Features

Rollbar:

In case the car rolls over, driver and passenger will be protected.

Retractable Steering Wheel:

In case of head-on collision, the steering wheel is moved away from the driver.

Tridion Frame:

Very strong frame with two floors (sandwich construction).

Trust Plus:

This traction and stability system monitors the traction of all wheels and regulates the gas accordingly.

Structural Enforcement:

Special steel enforced door beams.

Crash Box:

Similar to a second bumper. Installed in the front and in the back. They fully absorb crashes up to a speed of 15 km/h.

EXHIBIT 1 The smart

Source: MCC smart

background information on Mercedes). But entering new segments also carried technical and financial risks. So far, MB had only produced large, rear-wheel drive cars. Most smaller cars had front-wheel drive. Competition in the small car market was fierce and profits limited (the traditional attitude was that small cars produced only small profits).

Mr. Nicolas Hayek, founder and CEO of the Swatch Group (formerly SMH), the Swiss manufacturer of Swatch watches, was trying to change the auto industry as he had done with the watch industry. Hayek became the CEO of the newly merged SMH company in 1983 and proposed the launch of a low cost, high-tech, artistic, emotional watch in order to fight off cheap competition from Asia. Within eleven years, Hayek's new watch, the Swatch, sold over 150 million units. Hayek acquired several brands, and by 1998, SMH accounted for 22% to 25% of watches sold in the world (refer to Appendix B for a company profile of the Swatch Group).

Hayek wanted to replicate his success with cars. He presented a car that was only 2.5 meters long, and offered enough space "for two adults and two cases of beer." Nevertheless, the car had to convey the Swatch message: "High quality, low price, joie de vivre, challenge, special design and constant innovation." The care was to be powered by a hybrid engine and would thus appeal to "green customers." Buyers could change the color of their cars by buying different sets of body panels. The company also intended to make the purchasing experience more enjoyable by locating some of the showrooms, for example, in shopping malls and airports. Furthermore, Hayek wanted to offer a mobility concept by interfacing with public transport, rental companies, etc.

Hayek's company had tried to expand its marketing knowledge into new fields, such as telephones and Swatches with integrated pagers, but with only modest results. For his mini-car he had initially had Volkswagen (VW) as a partner in a 50/50 joint venture. The newly appointed CEO of VW, however, did not believe in the concept and stopped the development in 1993. So Hayek turned to MB.

Micro Compact Car (MCC)

Based on their idea of a mini-car, Swatch and MB formed a joint venture (Micro Compact Car, or MCC). The smart (named after Swatch, Mercedes and Art) would give both companies a good opportunity to combine their strengths while creating a strong brand. Hayek stated at the launch:

> I'm not a dreamer. We can make this car. Believe me. The car will be ecological without being boring. It will be modern yet affordable and will become a trendy car for young urban dwellers. This car should cost around 10,000 Swiss Francs [1 Swiss franc = $0.61 or €0.64] and should be powered by a hybrid engine.

The joint venture was set up as 51% to 49%, with MB in the driver's seat. The headquarters was located in Biel, Switzerland, while the developers were in close proximity to Stuttgart, but still in a separate location in order to challenge existing conventions. This was one of Mr. Hayek's main concerns.

In 1997 MB increased its share to 81% as Hayek's board declined to raise the equity of the company. Hayek commented to shareholders:

> Given certain open questions in connection with the start of the investment foreseen, delayed delivery dates and a few technical problems, MCC had to make a major share capital increase The SMH Group decided not to follow this line and reduced its financial commitment from 49% to 19%. One should note, however, that the Group's emotional and technological commitment in respect of design and marketing remains unchanged.

Nevertheless, MB acquired Hayek's remaining shares in 1998 (before the market introduction). As a result, the company headquarters was moved from Biel, Switzerland, to Renningen, a small village outside Stuttgart.

THE EUROPEAN MARKET FOR MINI-CARS

Mini-cars (referred to as the A-Segment) were initially defined as cars with a length of less than 3 meters (10 feet) and engine size up to 1000 cc. Typical examples included the Ford Ka, Renault Twingo and Fiat Seicento, but some of the mini-cars exceeded 3 meters. According to market researchers, the A-Segment was expected to grow by 38.5% between 1998 and 2004 (refer to Exhibit 2 for growth rates of different segments).

Mini-cars have a long tradition in Europe. The early models like the Fiat 126 offered basic transportation to lower-income groups. Mini-cars were inexpensive and easy to repair, and were mostly sold in Southern Europe. Starting in the early 1990s, a new customer segment evolved. Customers were demanding stylish mini-cars with a performance similar to large cars in terms of safety and quality.

In 1995, 556,847 mini-cars were sold in Europe. The main markets were Italy (163,000 units), France (146,000 units) and Germany (83,000 units). In 1998, 1,031,440 mini-cars were sold in Europe, surpassing the Japanese market as the world's largest market for mini-cars. However, Japanese manufacturers only played a minor role in the European market for mini-cars. Import restrictions forced Japanese manufacturers to export cars with higher profit margins (refer to Exhibit 3 for the sales figures of various brands). However, by the late 1990s, several mini-cars from Asia had entered the market. These models were not trendy, but they attracted customers due to their low prices combined with a good range of standard equipment.

According to market researchers, European consumers were buying mini-cars for the following reasons:

- *Space:* There was a need for cars that are easy to park and maneuver in confined city centers.
- *Price:* Small cars provide an opportunity for consumers to enter the new car market at a lower price point.
- *Fuel consumption:* Smaller cars use less fuel, and high fuel prices create a requirement for cars that consume less.
- *Local tax system:* Many European countries have ownership tax systems, which rise according to the size of the vehicle. This implies that owning a small car is substantially cheaper than owning a large car.

Forecasted Car Sales (Units) According to Segment for 2004 (vs. 1998 Actual)

Segment	Models	1998 Actual	% of Total in 1998	2004 Forecast	% of Total in 2004	Growth 98–04 (%)
A	Ford Ka	2.65 M	*5.7*	3.68 M	*7.0*	38.5
B	Nissan Micra	7.21 M	*15.6*	8.34 M	*15.9*	15.7
C	VW Golf	11.80 M	*25.4*	13.01 M	*24.8*	10.2
D	Ford Mondeo	10.09 M	*20.9*	10.31 M	*19.1*	2.1
E	VW Passat	2.48 M	*6.1*	2.92 M	*6.2*	17.9
F	MB S-Class	0.70 M	*1.5*	0.69 M	*1.3*	−1.3
G	Jaguar XJS	0.43 M	*0.9*	0.34 M	*0.6*	−21.4
LCV	VW Caravan	0.91 M	*2.0*	1.03 M	*2.0*	12.7
MPV	Chrysler Minivan	2.30 M	*4.9*	2.59 M	*4.9*	11.3
Pick-Up	Ford F150	3.36 M	*7.2*	3.75 M	*7.2*	11.8
SUV	Ford Explorer	4.58 M	*9.8*	5.72 M	*10.9*	25.0
Total		**46.51 M**	***100.0***	**52.38 M**	***100.0***	**12.5**

1998 Market Segmentation According to Units and Value

1998 Value (measured in units)		Segment	Models	1998 Value (measured in dollars)	
21.3%	*5.7%*	A	Ford Ka	2.2%	11.3%
	15.6%	B	Nissan Micra	9.1%	
52.4%	*25.4%*	C	VW Golf	21.2%	49.0%
	20.9%	D	Ford Mondeo	21.3%	
	6.1%	E	VW Passat	6.5%	
2.4%	*1.5%*	F	MB S-Class	5.5%	8.8%
	0.9%	G	Jaguar XJS	3.3%	
6.9%	*2.0%*	LCV	VW Caravan	3.1%	9.2%
	4.9%	MPV	Chrysler Minivan	6.1%	
17.0%	*7.2%*	Pick-Up	Ford F150	8.2%	21.7%
	9.8%	SUV	Ford Explorer	13.5%	
	100.0%		**Total**	**100.0%**	

EXHIBIT 2 The Global Segments for Automobiles

Source: Economist Intelligence Unit (EIU) Motor Business International, 3rd Quarter 1999: 42, IMD Research.

The products offered and their positioning varied widely among the different manufacturers. Price, design and image were the main differentiators among the products (refer to Exhibit 4 for the positioning of competing cars). The growth of mini-cars came at the expense of the B-Segment. This segment comprised cars that did not exceed 3.75 meters in length (12.5 feet). Typical cars in this segment included Ford Fiesta and Nissan Micra. Together, the A- and B-Segments accounted for 30% of the European market (equivalent to 4 million units), but there were clear regional differences (refer to Exhibit 5 for penetration rates of the A&B-Segments across Europe).

"REDUCE TO THE MAX"

To succeed, the smart had to change existing ways of doing business. The car was designed as a two-seater for urban dwellers. But the innovations went far beyond the product itself. In fact, smart revolutionized the production method and sales/distribution approaches.

Manufacturer	Model	1992	1993	1994	1995	1996	1997	1998
Ford	Ka	0	0	0	0	25,194	202,337	266,137
Renault	Twingo	0	124,735	214,099	227,944	214,063	208,533	199,148
Lancia	Ypsilon	119,098	91,129	76,556	59,187	80,907	135,571	145,507
Fiat	Panda	237,115	138,985	76,703	66,750	63,901	126,861	130,943
Fiat	Seicento	0	0	0	0	0	0	82,166
Fiat	Cinquecento	64,765	145,781	130,032	146,535	145,408	154,265	77,316
Seat	Arosa	0	0	0	0	0	0	46,375
Daewoo	Matiz	0	0	0	0	0	0	23,186
MCC	smart	0	0	0	0	0	52	20,000
Suzuki	Alto	7,813	3,181	3,867	9,377	16,020	20,330	16,908
Daihatsu	Cuore	9,949	7,191	6,073	7,779	7,541	7,511	9,281
Rover	Mini	20,547	15,363	14,021	10,840	9,980	6,486	7,517
Seat	Marbella	67,117	39,330	34,022	25,973	22,426	18,021	5,204
Subaru	Vivio	5,267	5,218	2,969	2,462	2,684	2,993	1,752
Hyundai	Atos	0	0	0	0	0	0	n/a
Volkswagen	Lupo	0	0	0	0	0	0	0
Total		**531,671**	**570,913**	**558,342**	**556,847**	**588,124**	**883,007**	**1,031,440**

Note: Peugeot 106 is not included in this list due to its size of 3.67 meters. Nevertheless, its annual production rate of 350,000 units (1997) makes it one of the best sellers in Europe.

EXHIBIT 3 Western European Market: Mini-Car Segment Sales by Model (1992–1998)

Source: *EIU Motor Business Europe,* 2nd Quarter 1999: 41.

PRODUCING A CAR IN ONLY 4.5 HOURS

MCC located its production site in Hambach, France. Internally, the plant was referred to as "Smartville." The plant was owned by MCC with a minority (25%) stake held by a French government agency. This agency was started in order to industrialize the region around Hambach. However, MCC was solely responsible for operations. Smartville may well have set the standard for future automotive manufacturing. The plant was a prime example of modular manufacturing and maximum supplier involvement. Overall, the suppliers were responsible for 85% of the value-added up to the end of the assembly line, 70% of which was produced or assembled on site. The assembly process took just 4.5 hours. In order to achieve this high level of supplier integration, the final assembly was laid out in the shape of a "plus sign" (refer to Exhibit 6 for an overview of the production site). But how could such supplier integration be achieved? MCC started looking for suppliers who could produce modules *and* had the financial strength to set up a factory on site. In return, MCC offered the suppliers contracts for the lifetime of the car (seven years) and a guaranteed minimum production rate of 140,000 units per annum (although the plant had a production capacity of 200,000 units).

Eventually, seven manufacturers located in Smartville, investing over €550 million. Many suppliers were also involved in the R&D processes and, as a result, MCC had an R&D staff of only 250. Although Mr. Lucien Rayer, managing director of Krupp-Hoesch, claimed that "this philosophy of transferring the responsibility makes a lot of sense . . . several other manufacturers work on similar concepts," the first few months were everything but smooth. The IT infrastructure was supposed to link the order from dealers directly with the factory and the corresponding suppliers. However, the production schedules produced by the system were wrong, and parts could not be located.

SELLING "MOBILITY" VS. SELLING "SMART"

Based on feasibility studies, the initial rollout was in Austria, Benelux, France, Germany, Italy, Spain and Switzerland, with an exclusive distribution channel. A second phase would include Greece, Portugal, Scandinavia as well as right-hand drive versions for the

Manufacturer	Model	Mfg. Start	Seats (#)	Price (incl. VAT) in Swiss Francs (June 2000) Low/Hi	Unloaded Weight /Loaded Weight (in kg)	Positioning	Additional Comments
Ford	Ka	1996	4	13,900–22,000	965/1,265	Targeted at the younger segment, more fashion-conscious than mainstream Fiesta buyers.	Based on the Fiesta platform; many components are shared. Cost of development has been estimated at around $250 million. Ka's success in the market affected sales of the Fiesta, which fell from 540,000 units in 1996 to 384,000 units in 1998.
Renault	Twingo	1993	4	13,940–17,450	820/1,230	Targeted at individualists, its revolutionary "bubble design" made it look like a micro minivan and gave it a modern image.	Designed to be simple and inexpensive to produce. Relaunch in 1998—Renault lowered the price and added new features in the base package. Price reduction equivalent to 14%.
Lancia	Ypsilon	na	4	14,900–22,000	935/1,330	Elegant, classy car that is comfortable, even chic. Price premium.	Lancia is owned by Fiat and has been plagued by declining sales. Out of 170,000 units sold in 1998, the Ypsilon accounted for 80%.
Fiat	Seicento	1998	4	11,200–17,500	730/1,200	2/3 of these cars are sold in Italy, where mini-cars are extremely popular.	Built in Poland. Available with automatic transmission and power steering.
Seat	Arosa	1997	4	13,770–21,590	950/1,335	Below Volkswagen Lupo.	Shares the same platform with the VW Lupo, and both were initially produced on the same line.
Daewoo	Matiz	1997	4	10,700–14,900	851/1,210	Italian Design is expected to attract new buyers to the Daewoo brand.	Developed in the UK as a world car. Development cost: $180 m. Initially imported from Korea, with production moving to India, Poland, and Romania.
Daihatsu	Cuore	na	4	12,300–12,990	715/1,040	Students, young executives, and the second car market.	One of the most fuel-efficient cars in the world (4.2 liters/100 km), imported from Japan and suffering from unfavorable exchange rates.
Rover	Mini	1959	4	16,100–18,500	700/1,050	"The Mini is marketed like a fashion accessory."	It was rumored that BMW, the owner of Rover, was going to distribute the new model of the Mini in its BMW outlets. Annual production volume was going to increase from 20,000 units to 100,000 units.
Hyundai	Atoz	1997	4	12,990–14,990	948/1,220	Small Minivan.	First mini-car produced by Hyundai, well-received in the European market, but strong demand in Korea restricted the number of units exported.
Suzuki	Alto	1995	4	12,790	740/1,170	Compact, quick, maneuverable.	Built in India.
Volkswagen	Lupo	1998	4	15,990–22,600	971/1,350	Safety, quality, fuel economy.	First mass-produced 3-liter car.

Note: 1 Swiss Franc = $0.61 or €0.64.

EXHIBIT 4 Western European Market: Positioning of Various Brands

Source: EIU Motor Business Europe, 2nd Quarter 1999: 40, IMD Research.

UK. Smart was considering entering the Japanese and Taiwanese markets as well.

Dealers were encouraged to build smart towers. These glass towers were, on average, seven stories high and could store up to 27 vehicles. The dealers were carefully selected and included entrepreneurs from different businesses, including fast food and furniture retailing. Each dealer was required to invest between €1 and €4 million (the banks would normally finance up to 80% of this) in return for exclusive territory rights, and dealers were expected to sell up to 1,500 cars per franchise (refer to Exhibit 7 for the break-even calculations for potential dealers). Out of 102 smart center owners, 55 were also MB dealers, 27 were dealers for other brands, and another 20 had no car experience whatsoever. In addition, dealers operated another 19 smaller stores, which they referred to as satellites (refer to Exhibit 8 for the distribution of dealers).

The marketing concept for smart, designed by Swatch executives, claimed to revolutionize car retailing. The smart was supposed to change the industry by changing the value proposition to the customers. The target market was defined:

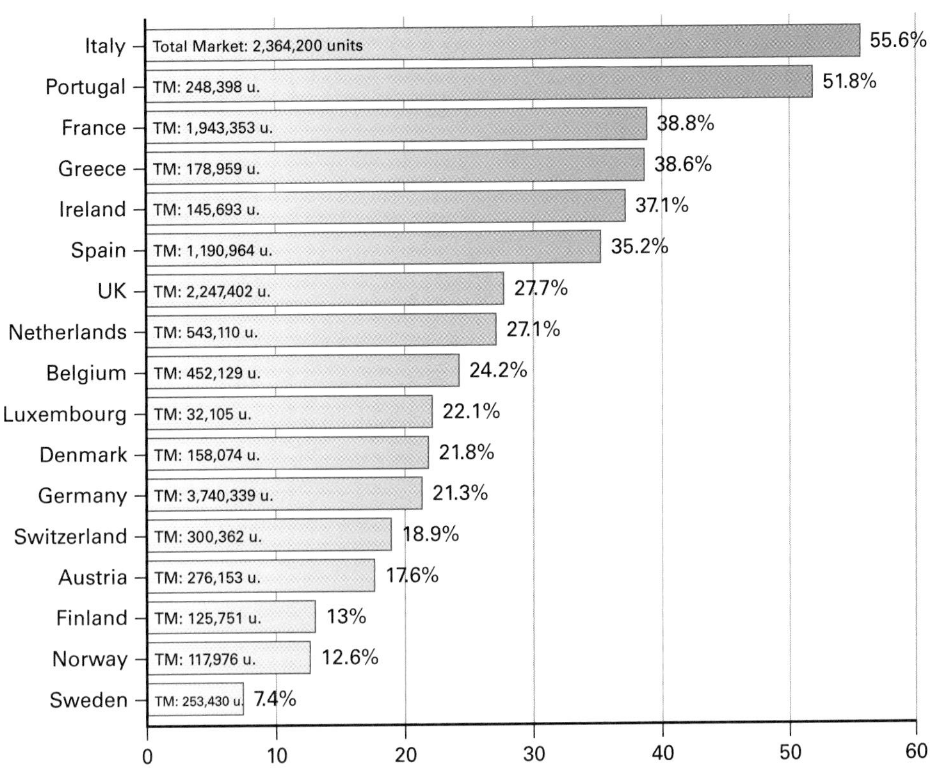

EXHIBIT 5 Penetration Rates of the A&B Segment in Europe

Source: EIU Motor Business International, 2nd quarter 1999: 39.

> The smart is starting a new market segment and attracts a wide variety of buyers. Singles and couples with double income, no kids [so-called dinks] represent the core market. The car will also be considered as a second or third car for families, while being attractive to "young at heart" senior citizens and corporate buyers.
>
> (MCC smart, July 1998)

Besides offering a car, smart would also offer a mobility concept. Acknowledging the space limitations of the vehicle, owners of a smart could switch to other modes of transportation when needed. The company organized a complete package of services including preferred rates for rental cars and train tickets. In addition, smart also negotiated special rates for parking garages, ferries and other public transportation (refer to Exhibit 9 for all services of the mobility concept). Based on this mobility concept, the smart was made the "environmental car of 1998" by a German environmental organization. However, the company was soon facing the realities of organizing a mobility system. The company had ten employees negotiating with the owners of parking garages and local authorities for special parking arrangements for the smart. Reinhard Hoßfeld, the manager of the system could not hide his frustrations: "It [the negotiation process] all took a bit longer."

The dealers were ready for a planned start in April 1998. However, top executives of DC were worried about their reputation after experiencing problems with a new model, the A-Class. The A-Class tipped in extreme cornering tests, and the production been stopped until the problem could be fixed. In the meantime, car journalists reported similar problems with the smart. The top management of MB did not want to take any further risks with the smart and postponed the launch to October 1998.

Smart reached its goal of 20,000 units for 1998, but the first snow of 1999 put smart back in the news. It proved unstable on snow-covered roads and pictures of smarts flipped on their backs were shown around the world. This caused sales to fall drastically. In February 1999, Avis Rent-A-Car stopped renting the car due to a

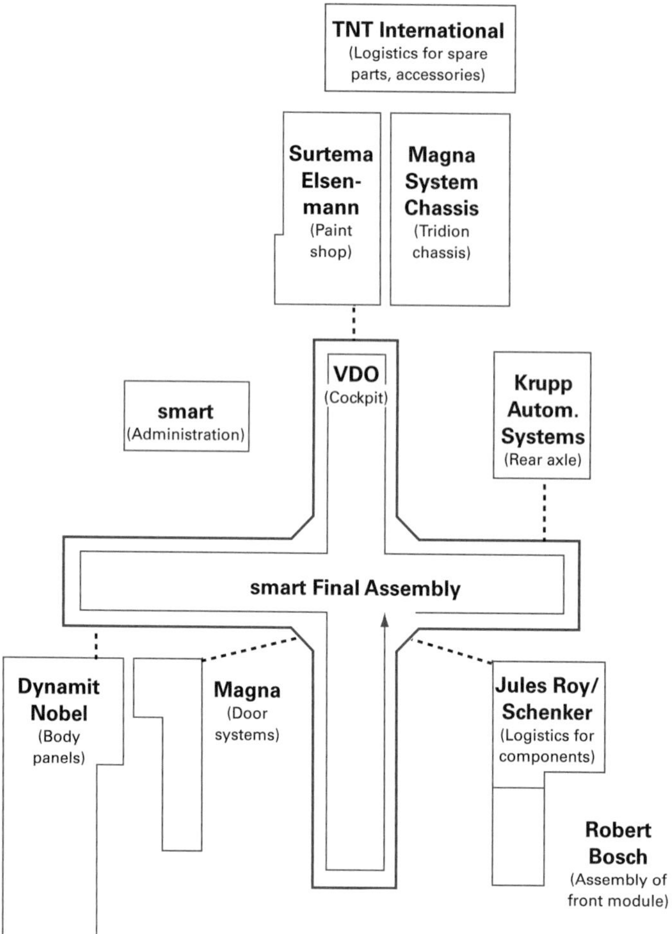

EXHIBIT 6 Smartville in Hambach, France

Source: MCC smart

poor safety record, and all advertising stopped completely. Dr. Dieter Zetsche, board member for sales and distribution at DaimlerChrysler recalled: "There was too much negative publicity about our production difficulties and later about the suspension."

Re-launch After Six Months: Operation Take-Off

In the spring of 1999, Mr. Jürgen E. Schrempp, the CEO of DC, made a public announcement that sales had to reach 80,000 units per annum, otherwise, he would stop the production of the smart car. As a first step, the price of the car was reduced by €250 to €8,000, and options formerly valued at €350 became standard. This was the beginning of "Operation Take-Off" (the name referred to the state of smart sales). Mr. Harald Bölstler, vice president of production and an early member of the smart team, remembered: "Initially we talked too much about the mobility system, rather than explaining the advantages of the car." The new advertising started in April 1999 and stressed the features of the smart, appealing to customers with the emotional aspects of the car. The headlines read: "Safety Cage with a Turbo" or "The First Formula 1 Gearbox Without a High Cost." Mr. Jürgen Hubbert stated that the communication would stress the "unique technology rather than the abstract mobility concept."

The partial withdrawal from the mobility concept met some criticism. Ferdinand Dudenhöffer, an automotive consultant to several car manufacturers, explained:

> The mobility concept was a real innovation, which clearly differentiated the smart from other mini-cars. With the new positioning, the

Break-Even Calculations for Potential Dealers

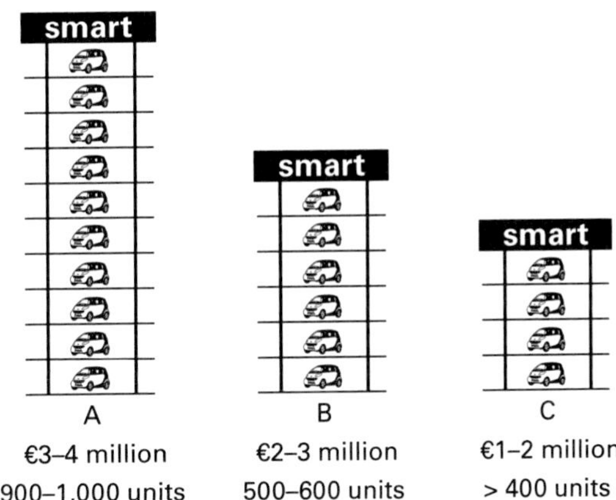

Center type	A	B	C
Required investment	€3–4 million	€2–3 million	€1–2 million
Annual sales target in order to break-even (in units)	900–1,000 units	500–600 units	> 400 units

Number of Cars Sold per Dealer in Germany (1997)

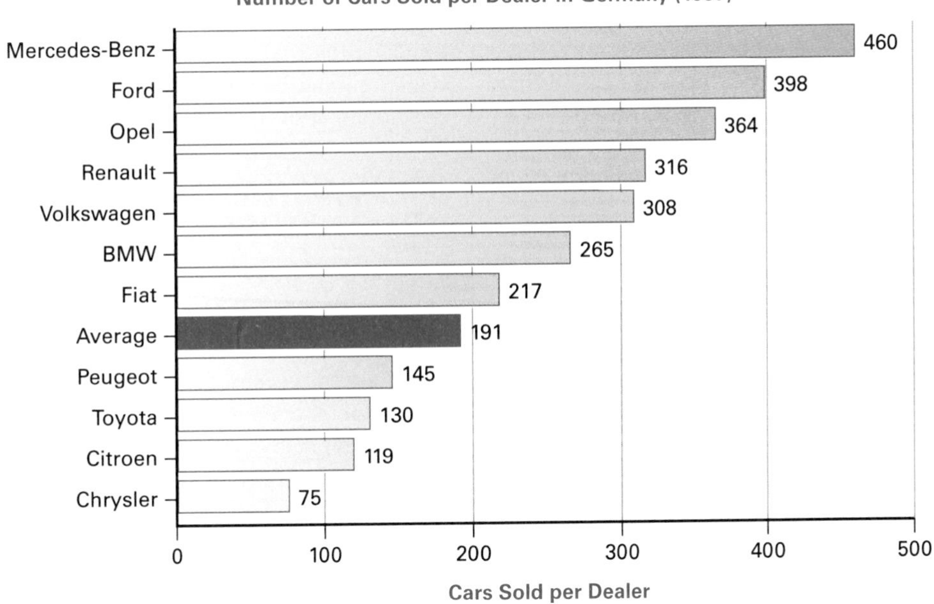

EXHIBIT 7 Break-Even Calculations for Potential Dealers; Number of Cars Sold per Dealer in Germany

Source: Viehöver, Ulrich. "Turmhohes Risiko." *Focus,* Vol. 52, 1998.

smart is just becoming like all other mini-cars and has to face the direct competition of the well-established mini-cars like the Renault Twingo, Ford Ka and VW Lupo. All of these cars have four seats, a larger trunk and a large distribution network. The smart cannot even compete on price.

With Operation Take-Off, the smart also obtained a new VP for marketing/sales. Mr. Klaus Fricke, a former BMW executive, considered his job to be "the last marketing adventure in the automotive industry." He was given an additional €50 million for repositioning the smart. This was spent on print media, TV advertising and a total of 1,600 smarts offering test drives in Europe.

At this time, leading managers of DC were increasingly concerned about the difficulties at smart and partly transferred the responsibility for sales to DC. The overall responsibility remained with MCC,

Germany:	41
Italy	29
France:	17
Switzerland:	10
Spain:	8
Austria:	7
Belgium:	5
Netherlands:	4
Luxembourg:	1

EXHIBIT 8 Smart Centers and Satellites in Europe (December 1999)

Source: MCC smart

but the local responsibility in each country was moved to the MB representatives.

Sales of smart improved, but Zetsche confessed: "The challenges were bigger than expected." Although sales climbed (refer to Exhibit 10 for the 1999 sales levels when Renschler entered), the profitability of dealers was still a major issue. Out of 102 dealers, only half were profitable, another 40% either at breakeven or close to it, and another 10% were having serious financial difficulties. By September 1999, the franchise in Berlin had to file for bankruptcy, and MCC took over three dealers in the Parisian market. Dealers complained about too little traffic in their showrooms.

GROW OR ABANDON?

Executives at DaimlerChrysler were becoming increasingly worried about the smart. Although Schrempp referred to it as an investment for the future, he added: "The smart polarizes very much. Some people love it while others question how we can allow ourselves to put a smart on the road." Shareholders had always been very critical of the smart, and the board of management used every opportunity to raise awareness for the voluntary self-restriction of European car companies for the year 2008 (see Appendix C).

As part of this voluntary self-restriction, car companies had to reduce the fuel consumption of their fleets to an average of 6.6 liters/100 km. In 1999, the fuel consumption of DC's fleet was a lot higher.

Although the perception of the smart in the marketplace was vastly improved (refer to Exhibit 11 for the brand images of mini-cars), skeptics questioned whether you could run a company with only one product. The arrival of the diesel engine and convertible models would certainly increase sales in 2000, but was it enough? Other alternatives included building a sporty, two-seat roadster, a four-seater passenger car and a family van.

Walking away from the smart was also an option many considered. Although DC had invested over €1 billion in the project, it would have cost at least another €1 billion to get out of it. This option would have raised the question of what to do with suppliers. They had long-term contracts, and DC had business relations with them in other areas. Many observers were also concerned about negative effects on the brand image of DC. In addition, the proposed sales goal of 80,000 units for the first year was in line with the beginnings of Saturn and Lexus (refer to Exhibit 12 for the sales development of both Saturn and Lexus).

IF YOU CAN'T BEAT YOUR COMPETITORS, JOIN THEM

In the fall of 1999, speculation started that smart could purchase platforms from competitors. These platforms consisted of the engines, gearboxes and axles. The advantage of this strategy was clearly to speed up development of other models. On the other hand, should smart and DaimlerChrysler really start closer relationships with other manufacturers?

PREPARING THE ORGANIZATION FOR 2001

As Mr. Renschler was reflecting on his first days, he clearly saw the challenges ahead. He had a strong team (refer to Exhibit 13 for the old and new management team), but what was the order for attacking these problems? Renschler was awaiting a phone call from his impatient boss, who would be asking for his view on what to do with the smart. As these questions were racing through his mind, he remembered the sentence of Mr. Jürgen Hubbert:

> The smart was and is a small revolution in the automobile industry. We really questioned every convention or, to put it another way, did everything differently.

But for Renschler the question was how to do it right.

Smartmove Parking

Reserved parking lots for compact cars at special rates.

Smartmove Assistance

Roadside Assistance Program.

Smartmove Ferry

Special rates on some ferries (owners of smart pay only for the equivalent of a motorbike, passengers travel for free).

Smartmove & More

Special rates for renting a vehicle at Avis Rent-A-Car.

Smartmove Train

Germany:

- smart owners pay half price for motorail trains.
- Travelers on special high-speed trains (Berlin-Frankfurt, Frankfurt-Munich) can make a reservation for a smart as a rental car at a discounted rate. The smart can be booked while purchasing the ticket or on the train.

Switzerland:

- smart owners get a 50% reduction on trains.
- smart owners are part of CarSharing Switzerland, Europe's largest car sharing agency. The agency rents cars at favorable rates.

Smartmove City

Reduced rates for public transport in selected cities (e.g., Zürich, Hamburg, Karlsruhe, Stuttgart), offerings depend on the city (e.g., in Zürich, second person travels for free).

Smartmove Plane

Partnership Swissair/Sabena:

Travelers in First Class, Business Class or holders of "e-tickets" in Economy Class can obtain a smart at the airports in Geneva, Zürich, Brussels, or Frankfurt. Travelers will obtain a smart for 24 hours free of charge (including insurance and fuel) except for Frankfurt, where a fee of €30 is charged for 24 hours. Other cities are likely to follow.

Smartmove Car Sharing

The purchase price of a smart includes access to "Carsharing BCS" in Germany (1,500 cars) and "Mobility" in Switzerland (1,200 cars).

EXHIBIT 9 Smartmove: The Mobility Concept

Source: MCC smart

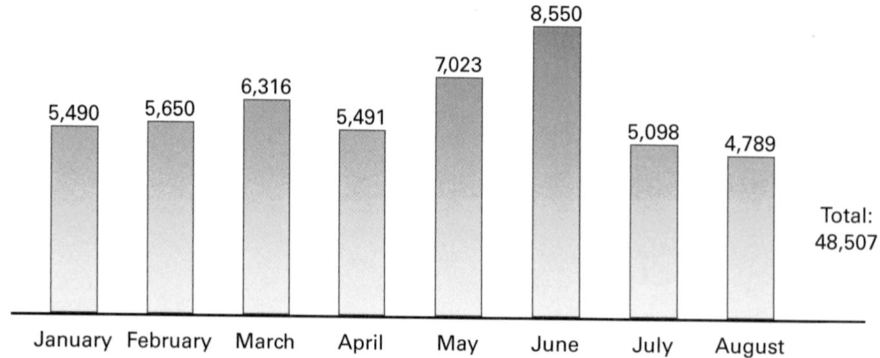

EXHIBIT 10 Sales Development January–August 1999

Source: Bilan, November 1999: 37.

Make	Model	Germany %	Germany Rank	Switzerland %	Switzerland Rank	Italy %	Italy Rank	France %	France Rank	Spain %	Spain Rank	Sweden %	Sweden Rank
VW	Lupo	54.0	1	34.4	1	17.0	3	12.2	2	19.7	2	45.8	1
Ford	Ka	14.4	2	9.0	5	9.2	5	7.4	3	12.6	4	20.3	2
MCC	**smart**	**11.9**	**3**	**16.4**	**2**	**10.6**	**4**	**6.7**	**4**	**21.7**	**1**	**5.8**	**4**
Renault	Twingo	7.8	4	13.2	3	6.9	6	64.7	1	5.0	7	5.0	5
Rover	Mini	6.1	5	9.7	4	3.4	7	2.1	5	7.1	6	14.0	3
Seat	Arosa	2.3	6	3.6	8	1.3	10	1.3	7	17.1	3	2.4	7
Fiat	Seicento	0.9	7	4.1	6	20.2	2	1.1	8	5.0	7	1.0	8
Daewoo	Matiz	0.8	8	4.1	6	23.3	1	1.9	6	8.3	5	0.2	10

Note: All other makes in this category (Suzuki Wagon R, Daihatsu Move, Hyundai Atos, Daihatsu Cuore, Subaru Vivio, Kia Pride, Suzuki Alto) received average scores less than 3.7%.

EXHIBIT 11 Brand Images of Mini-Cars in 1999: "Which is the best mini-car?"

Source: "The Best Cars 1999." *Motor Presse International* (Stuttgart): 4.

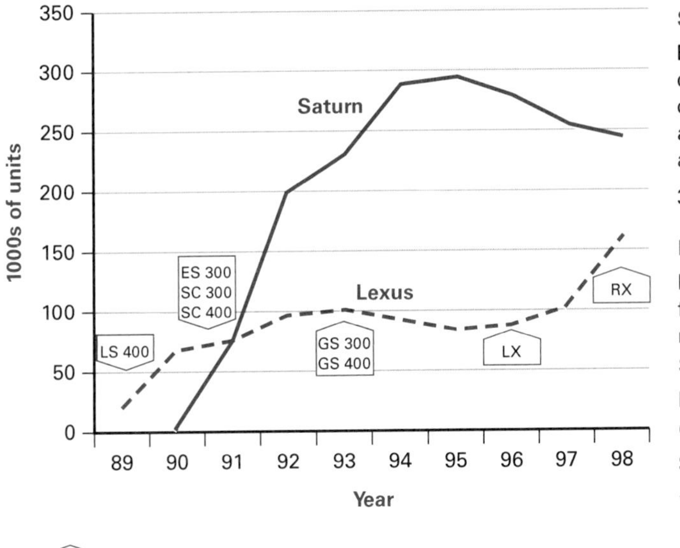

Saturn:

Entered the market with one car S-Series (sedan, wagon, coupe). The first new model after launch was expected to arrive in 1999.

335 dealers (1996)

Lexus:

Highly successful launch, followed by a large model variety:

Sedans:

LS 400, ES 300, GS 300/400

Coupe:

SC 300/400

Sport Utility Vehicle (SUV):

LX, RX

174 dealers (1999)

Note: Saturn and Lexus continued to advertise heavily even after launching the brand.

Lexus spent $154 million on advertising in 1997.

Saturn spent $223 million on advertising in 1998.

EXHIBIT 12 Sales Development of Saturn & Lexus in the U.S.

Source: Aaker, David A. *Building Strong Brands.* New York: The Free Press, 1996: 38; Lexus USA, IMD Research.

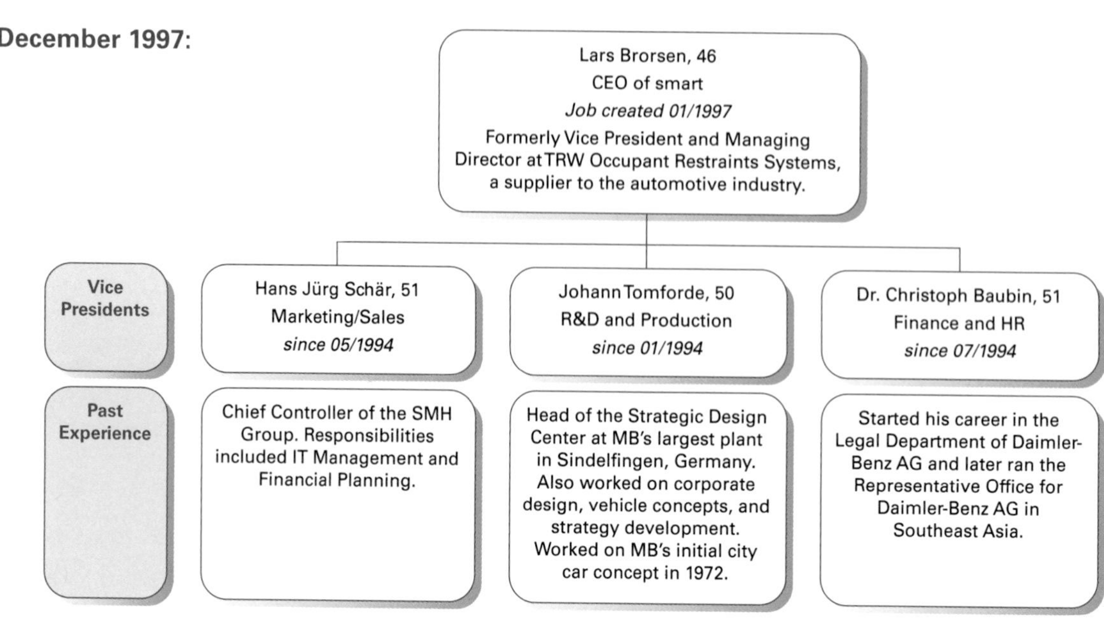

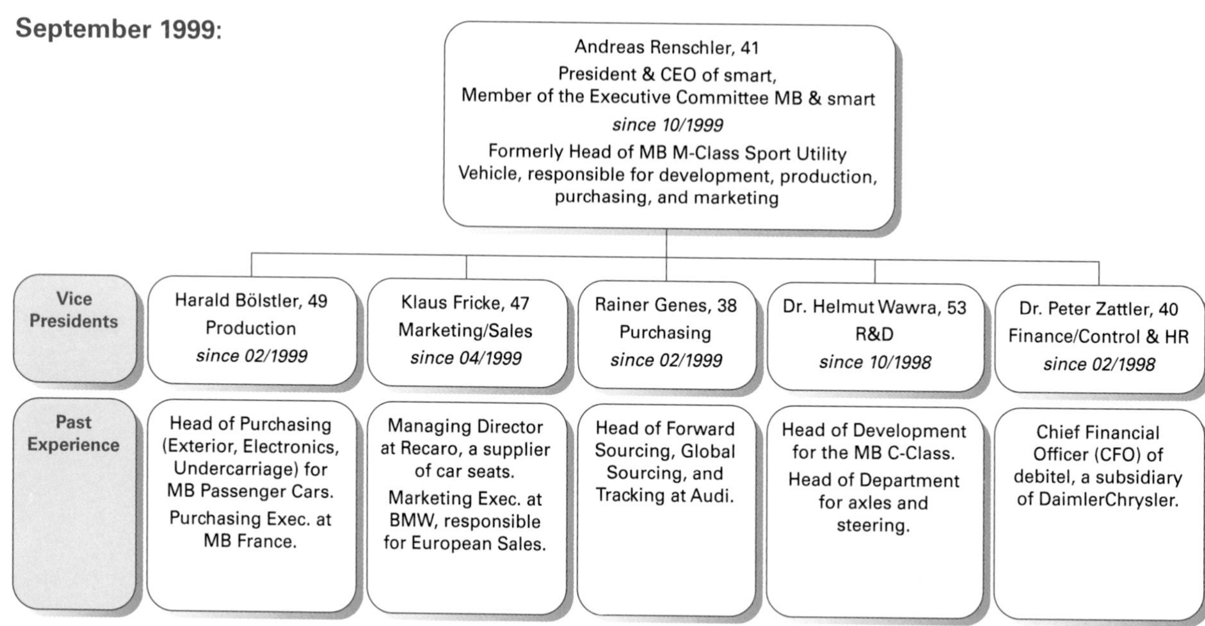

EXHIBIT 13 The Smart Board in 1997 and 1999

Source: MCC smart

APPENDIX A BACKGROUND ON MERCEDES-BENZ/DAIMLER-BENZ

Mercedes-Benz (MB) is the passenger car and truck brand of the former Daimler-Benz Group. MB is known for its high quality luxury cars; it is among the most highly valued brands in the world. In the late 1980s the company was attacked by strong competition from new Japanese entrants into the luxury segment. Moreover, MB's small size by global standards and high profitability could have made it a target for a takeover in the consolidating industry.

MB initially decided on a "go alone" strategy by stretching the Mercedes brand for passenger cars from 600,000 units annually in 1995 to 955,000 units by the year 2000. Mr. Jürgen Hubbert explained this strategy: "Of the 38 million cars sold around the world [in 1995], fewer than 6% were in the same class as classic Mercedes models." What followed was rapid model explosion at MB. Between 1984 and 1993, the company only launched seven new cars; in the four years up to 1998, it managed to introduce eleven cars. Output rose accordingly.

The move into lower segments was challenging and at the same time very successful. The A-Class, plagued by initial stability problems, was expected to reach its production capacity of 200,000 units by 1999. Moreover, the A-Class was highly successful in attracting new customers—75% of A-Class customers were new to the brand.

Although Mercedes-Benz continued to prosper, some other divisions of the Daimler-Benz Group had record losses. In 1995, the Group recorded an operating loss of DM 5.7 billion. Under the stewardship of the new CEO, the company sold many of its unprofitable businesses. As a general rule, subsidiaries were required to earn a minimum rate of return of 12%. In 1998, the Daimler-Benz Group announced a merger with the Chrysler Corporation and renamed into DaimlerChrysler AG.

	Model	1995 Output (in units)	Output (in units). This plan was published in 1995	1998 Actual Output (in units)
Family	C	314,000	300,000	330,000
Midsize	E	200,000	240,000	259,000
Flagship/Roadster	S/SL	81,000	80,000	58,000
Off-Road	G	5,000	5,000	4,000
Roadster	SLK	None	35,000	54,000
Minivan	V	None	25,000	25,000
Small Car	A	None	200,000	136,000
Sport Utility Vehicle	M	None	70,000	64,000
Total		**600,000**	**955,000**	**930,000**

Source: Mercedes-Benz

APPENDIX A-1

Financial Results

	1990	1991	1992	1993	1994	1995	1996	1997	1998
Net Sales (in billion $)	57.0	62.5	60.8	50.4	67.1	71.9	69.0	68.9	154.6
Net Income (in million $)	830.7	1,599.0	809.3	(1,408.0)	564.0	(1,179.0)	1,793.0	1,764.0	5,600.0

Note: 1998 numbers include Chrysler

APPENDIX A-2

Source: Value Line/DaimlerChrysler

APPENDIX B BACKGROUND ON SWATCH GROUP (FORMERLY SMH)

> Strong efforts have been made to reinforce the communication concepts for our key products. The objective is not to put the Swatch Group as a company in the foreground but to bring our products to the consumer's attention.
>
> Nicolas Hayek, CEO of Swatch group

In 1983, two of Switzerland's largest watchmakers faced liquidation, as they could not compete with the Japanese watch industry. Hayek, then CEO of Hayek Engineering, was called in to assess the chances of survival and to develop a strategy for both companies. In his report, Hayek recommended the merger of the two companies and the introduction of the Swatch line. He then took over the majority of shares and became CEO. Hayek, a charismatic leader, has often been described as a lifestyle and marketing guru.

The Swatch Group is the world's biggest producer of watches. In 1998 the company produced more than 118 million watches, movements, and stepping motors. The company operated fifty production sites located mainly in Switzerland. The Swatch Group recorded sales of SFr 3.185 billion and a net income of SFr 357 million.

	1990	1991	1992	1993	1994	1995	1996	1997	1998
Net Sales (in million SFr)	2,058	2,304	2,762	2,770	2,588	2,562	2,715	2,970	3,185
Net Income (in million SFr)	191	252	413	441	315	273	282	332	357

APPENDIX B-1

Source: Swatch Group

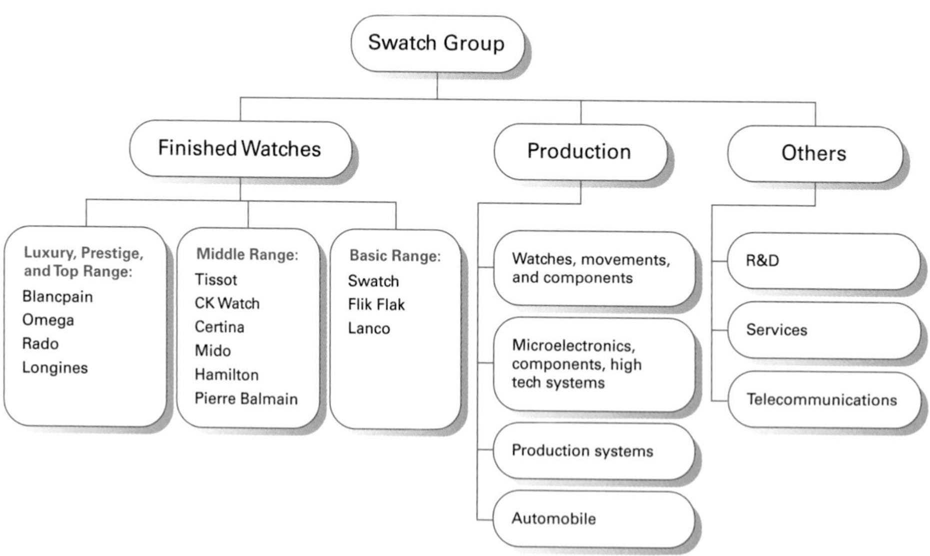

APPENDIX B-2

Source: Swatch Group

APPENDIX C EUROPEAN AGREEMENT FOR 25% CUT IN CARBON-DIOXIDE EMISSIONS

As part of an effort to curb global warming, the European Automobile Manufacturers Association committed its eleven members to reduce by 25% the amount of carbon dioxide that their vehicles emit between the 1995 level and 2008. That will require improving cars' fuel economy, because carbon dioxide is produced when fuel burns. And for DaimlerChrysler, whose Mercedes-Benz luxury cars are as thirsty as they are profitable, that will mean diversifying its product mix by adding smaller, more fuel-efficient cars.

The carbon dioxide agreement in Europe, technically a voluntary agreement, is friendlier to the auto industry than the U.S. fuel-economy law. The U.S. mandate forces every manufacturer to meet the same miles-per-gallon number for its car and truck fleets. That rankles Detroit's Big Three, which build lots of big pickups and sport-utility vehicles. The law forces them to heavily discount their smaller trucks so they'll sell enough of them to be able to keep pumping out the higher-profit large ones while still adhering to the fuel economy mandate.

In theory, the U.S. law presents the same problem for European makers, whose luxury cars have big, thirsty engines. But in practice, those European makers have dealt with the problem by essentially ignoring it, missing the fuel-economy targets and paying the resulting federal fines as a cost of doing business in the U.S.

Source: Ball, Jeffrey. "Mitsubishi Merger would help DaimlerChrysler on Fuel Pact." *Wall Street Journal Europe,* March 27, 2000.

INDEX

Note: Numbers in italics refer to figures or tables.